HUNGRY WORDS

First published in 2006 by
IRISH ACADEMIC PRESS
44, Northumberland Road, Dublin 4, Ireland

and in the United States of America by
IRISH ACADEMIC PRESS
c/o ISBS, Suite 300, 920 NE 58th Avenue
Portland, Oregon 97213–3644

WEBSITE: www.iap.ie

British Library Cataloguing in Publication Data
A catalogue entry is available on request

ISBN 0–7165–3386–3 (cloth)
0–7165–3387–1 (paper)

Library of Congress Cataloging-in-Publication Data
A catalog entry is available on request

Typeset by Carrigboy Typesetting Services, County Cork
Printed by MPG Books Ltd., Bodmin, Cornwall

HUNGRY WORDS

Images of Famine
in the Irish Canon

EDITED BY

GEORGE CUSACK

Auburn University, Montgomery

SARAH GOSS

University of San Francisco

IRISH ACADEMIC PRESS
DUBLIN • PORTLAND, OR

For Mark and Jennifer

CONTENTS

ABOUT THE AUTHORS

George Cusack is Assistant Professor of English at Auburn University Montgomery in Montgomery, Alabama. His publications include 'A cold eye cast inward: the retreat into narcissism in Seamus Heaney's *Field Work*', in *New Hibernia Review* and '"In the gripe of the ditch": Nationalism, famine, and *The Playboy of the Western World*', in *Modern Drama*. He is currently working on his first scholarly monograph, *Restaging Ireland: The Politics of Identity in the Early Drama of W.B. Yeats, Augusta Gregory and J.M. Synge*.

The **Reverend Jerome Joseph Day, OSB** is a member of the Benedictine monastic community at Saint Anselm College in Manchester, New Hampshire, where he is an Assistant Professor of English and Communications. He is also pastor of Saint Raphael the Archangel Parish, Manchester. Father Jerome's publications include 'Performing the famine: a look at contemporary Irish dramatists', in *Ireland's Great Hunger: Silence, Memory and Commemoration*, edited by David Valone and Christine Kinealy. He holds a Ph.D. degree in communications from McGill University, Montreal (2001).

Robert C. Evans has written or edited nearly 200 scholarly articles or notes, perhaps one-fifth written in collaboration with students. He has written two books on Frank O'Connor, one book on short fiction, one book on literary theory, one book on Kate Chopin, one book on Brian Friel and one book on Ambrose Bierce. His forthcoming work includes books on Kate Chopin, Anne Vaughan Lock, Matthew Hale, Jane Barker and poetry by Restoration Women.

Sarah Goss is a Lecturer in the Program in Rhetoric and Composition at the University of San Francisco. She recently completed her doctoral dissertation, 'The Agony of Consciousness: History and Memory in Nineteenth-Century Irish Gothic Novels', at the University of Oregon.

Nicholas Grene is a Professor of English Literature at Trinity College, Dublin. His publications include *The Politics of Irish Drama: Plays in Context from Boucicault to Friel, Shakespeare's Tragic Imagination* and *Bernard Shaw: a Critical View*.

Margaret Kelleher is a Senior Lecturer in the English Department of the National University of Ireland, Maynooth, and the co-editor of the forthcoming *Cambridge History of Irish Literature*. Her publications also include *The Feminization of Famine: Expressions of the Inexpressible?* and *Gender Perspectives in Nineteenth-Century Ireland* (with James H. Murphy).

Christine Kinealy is a Professor of History at the University of Central Lancashire. Her publications include *The Great Irish Famine: Impact, Ideology, and Rebellion; A Death-Dealing Famine: The Great Hunger in Ireland;* and *The Hidden Famine: Hunger, Poverty and Sectarianism in Belfast* (with Gerard MacAtasney).

Karen Hill McNamara is an Adjunct Assistant Professor at Drew University in Madison, New Jersey. Her publications include 'From Fairies to Famine: How cultural identity is constructed through Irish and Irish American children's literature', in *Children's Folklore Review* and the annotated bibliography 'Children's Literature of the Great Irish Famine', in *Foilsiu: An Interdisciplinary Journal of Irish Studies*.

Christopher Morash is Director of Media Studies, National University of Ireland Maynooth. His publications include *The Hungry Voice: Poetry of the Irish Famine* (editor), *Writing the Irish Famine, Fearful Realities: New Perspectives on the Famine* (editor) and *Irish Theatre: A History, 1601–2000*.

Katherine Parr is a Lecturer at University of Illinois-Chicago where she teaches composition and British Literature. Her dissertation, written at Northern Illinois University, explores the poetry of Eva Kelly and Mary Downing. She has presented papers at conferences for the Society for the Study of Nineteenth-Century Ireland and the American Conference for Irish Studies.

Nieves Pascual is an Associate Professor of English at Universidad de Jaén, Jaén, Spain. Her published articles include 'Depathologizing Anorexia: The Risks of Life Narratives', in *Style* and 'Hunger as a Prosthetic Skin in Tsitsi Dangarembga's *Nervous Conditions*', in *Atlantic Literary Review* (October–December, 2003).

Bonnie Roos is an Assistant Professor of English at West Texas A&M University. Her publications include 'Rehistoricizing the Conflicted Figure of Woman in Ngugi's *Petals of Blood*, in *Research in African Literatures* and 'James Joyce's "The Dead" and Bret Harte's *Gabriel Conroy*: The Nature of the Feast' in *Yale Journal of Criticism*.

Margaret Scanlan is a Professor of English at the University of Indiana, South Bend, Indiana. Her publications include *Traces of Another Time: History and Politics in Postwar British Fiction* and *Plotting Terror: Novelists and Terrorists in Contemporary Fiction*.

Julieann Ulin is a Ph.D. candidate at the University of Notre Dame's Keough Institute of Irish Studies, South Bend, Indiana. She received her BA from Washington and Lee University in Lexington, Virginia, and her MA in English from Fordham University in New York. Her primary areas of interest include the Irish Famine and Irish and American Modernism. She recently delivered a paper dealing with the role of Famine memory in *Ulysses* at the Bloomsday 100 Symposium in Dublin and has an article, 'Fluid Boarders and Naughty Girls: Music, Domesticity and Nation in James Joyce's "The Boarding House"', forthcoming in *James Joyce Quarterly*..

ACKNOWLEDGEMENTS

George Cusack would like to thank his wife, Jennifer Shaiman, and his parents, Michael and Dorothy, for their unfailing moral and emotional support. I am also indebted to my advisors, Paul Peppis and Ian Duncan, without whose advice this project would almost certainly never have taken shape. As I completed the research for my article, I relied heavily on the staff at the University of Oregon Library, the National Library of Ireland and the Trinity College Libraries, and I would like to express my gratitude to them. I am also grateful to the faculty and staff of the University of Notre Dame Irish Seminar, particularly Kevin Whelan, for their assistance with the research. As I revised the article into its current form, I also benefited tremendously from the editorial advice of Linda Kintz and Ann Weekes. My thanks also to the editors of Modern Drama, who published an earlier version of my article, for their permission to reprint the article here.

Sarah Goss would like to thank her husband, Mark Meritt, and her parents, Gary and Susan, for their support and encouragement. I am very grateful to Professors Ian Duncan, Richard Stevenson and Richard Stein for their help with my work and their willingness to continue assisting me even after I had moved away from the University of Oregon. I would especially like to thank Ian Duncan, whose suggestion to me of a possible connection between Dracula and the Great Famine was the first inspiration for my essay.

The editors would like to collectively thank our contributors, whose interest and brilliant scholarship made this anthology possible. Our thanks also to Lisa Hyde, our supervising editor at Irish Academic Press, and Jenny Oates, our IAP copy editor, for their efforts on behalf of this anthology. Thanks also to the staff of the University of Oregon English department, especially Mike Stamm, and to Karen Ford for her invaluable assistance during her tenure as Director of Graduate Studies. Finally, we would Like to express our gratitude to Linda Tredennick, Bianca Tredennick, Mita Mahato, Kellie Bond and Paul Johnson, for their camaraderie and good humour over the years.

INTRODUCTION

'The canon' is, to put the matter mildly, a loaded term in literary studies generally and Irish literary studies in particular. While the explosive debate that stemmed from the publication of *The Field Day Anthology of Irish Studies* in the 1990s is the most recent and dramatic illustration of this statement, I think it can safely be asserted that no attempt to select a finite set of authors or texts to represent Ireland has ever failed to meet with controversy. Indeed, it is likely that anyone reading this introduction has already perused the Table of Contents and mentally formed an opinion of 'our canon'. Moreover, it is extremely unlikely that that opinion is entirely favourable. As each reader passes his or her eyes over the authors, subjects and perhaps even contributors in this volume, at least one inclusion or omission almost certainly provokes surprise, if not active disapproval. This is not to mention those readers whose disapproval began when they read the word 'canon' on the title page.

Yet it would be hard to argue that the canon does not exist. Even those critics (among whom I would count myself) who insist that the canon is a fundamentally flawed concept, and that no definitive list of canonical Irish authors can or should be compiled, must concede that our understanding of Irish literature has always included the understanding that certain authors and texts are generally perceived as more important than others. For evidence of this, one need only compare the number of plaques in Dublin that refer to some triviality in *Ulysses* to the number that refer to, say, Flann O'Brien's *At Swim Two Birds*. The persistent lionization of certain authors and obfuscation of others give the canon a nebulous existence similar to that held by concepts like race and gender: it seems self-evident that certain Irish authors enjoy a canonical status, and yet no two people are likely to agree on exactly what qualities separate a canonical author from any other kind, let alone agree on exactly which authors belong 'in the canon'. Thus, the canon has identifiable members, but no clearly definable boundaries. It is real, but it is not.

The word 'Famine' presents a similar epistemic challenge. To mention 'the Famine' in any context related to Ireland is to evoke an instantly recognizable concept, and yet the boundaries of that thing signified as 'the Famine' are remarkably hard to locate. Is the Famine a historical period,

like the Victorian Age, or a series of interrelated events, like the First
World War? Does it begin in 1845 with the failure of the potato crop or in
1846 with the first deaths by starvation? Does it end in 1848, as the British
government insisted, or does it continue as long as its direct effects were
felt in Ireland? By the latter logic, did it end at all? And what exactly do
we call it? Is 'the Famine' sufficient, or must we describe it more precisely?
If we must, should we identify it by its magnitude ('the Great Famine'), its
historical location ('the Famine of the 1840s'), its geographical setting ('the
Irish Famine'), or by one of the many, many more evocative names that
have been applied to it over the years ('The Great Calamity')? Of course,
these questions do not even address the revisionist contention that the
Famine, in the sense that most of us understand it, did not happen at all.

Even the most radical revisionist, however, must concede that every Irish
generation since the 1840s has had to deal with the idea of the Famine and
its effects on Irish history and Irish identity. Consequently, this thing called
'the Famine' is quite real. If anything, the indeterminacy of the Famine
makes it more real. In the introduction to his 1995 book *Writing the Irish
Famine*, Christopher Morash observes that 'it may be precisely this unimagin-
able, indeterminate element – the absence of a stable, empirical reality –
which makes us constantly aware of the Famine dead whose defining
characteristic is their absence' (p.4). Morash, however, suggests that this sense
of absence, and the corresponding awareness that all concrete representations of the Famine fall short of reality, give the Famine something of a
stable, communal existence 'that transcends the running debate over the
numbers of the dead' (p.4). I would amend this notion slightly and argue that
the obsessive need to identify the Famine metonomized by Morash's 'running
debate over the numbers' is, and always has been, an inherent part of the
concept itself. To look at the body of writing about the Famine is to see
attempt after attempt to find the proper historical, political, mathematical,
social or literary lens through which the thing itself will finally come into
focus. Nor has time made this need less acute; in the ten years since Morash
wrote the statements quoted above, more books have been published about
the Famine than in the 150 years prior. The seemingly endless appetite for
new material on the Famine points to a paradox similar to the one created by
the canon: we of the scholarly and literary public clearly want the Famine
defined for us, and yet we seem to accept that no depiction of the Famine will
ever fully satisfy this desire.

The purpose of *Hungry Words* is not to define either the Famine or the
canon conclusively, but rather to trace the shared cultural dilemma behind

these terms. As this book reveals, all definitions of the Irish Famine and the Irish canon inevitably rest on ideology, because they require the definer to determine who is best qualified to speak for Ireland and how those people should speak. Consequently, to define either the Irish Famine or the Irish canon is, in effect, to answer the same question: 'What is Irish?' By examining these two phenomena in their mutual contexts, then, this anthology explores the very framework through which Ireland has sought to represent itself as a nation and a culture for the past 160 years.

Thematically, *Hungry Words* is divided into three Parts, each focusing on a different time period. Part 1 explores literary reactions to the Famine in the latter half of the nineteenth century, opening with Christine Kinealy's overview of the Famine's immediate cultural impact and the literary responses that it provoked. The chapters which follow, by Katharine Parr, Margaret Kelleher and Margaret Scanlan, examine the specific attempts of Maria Edgeworth, *Nation* poets Eva Kelly and Mary Dowling, and Anthony Trollope to bring context and meaning to their personal experience of the Famine. Part 1 concludes with Sarah Goss's essay on Stoker's *Dracula*, which demonstrates that the first generation of post-Famine Irish authors was already struggling with the challenges of understanding Irish history and Irish identity in the Famine's wake.

Part 2 focuses on the first half of the twentieth century. As the chapters in this section demonstrate, the divisive cultural politics of this period further complicated the problems of representation felt by Stoker and his generation, as the various factions of the Revival sought to reinterpret Irish history through a variety of political and artistic agendas. The first three chapters in Part 2 examine the ways three of the Revival's most influential authors attempted, with varying levels of success, to negotiate this nexus of political ideology and cultural memory and adapt Famine imagery to their own purposes. In Chapter 6, Jerome Day examines Yeats's failed attempt to de-historicize Irish famine in *The Countess Cathleen*; Chapter 7 reveals how Synge used allusions to the Famine in *The Playboy of the Western World* to manipulate his nationalist audience; and in Chapter 8 Bonnie Roos traces Joyce's more subtle use of Famine imagery to criticize British consumption of Irish culture in *Ulysses*. The section closes with Julieann Ulin's examination of Beckett's *Endgame*, which illustrates how the literary and political aftermath of the Revival affected the relationship between history and literature in Ireland and thus altered the way the next generation of Irish authors could represent the Famine in their work.

Part 3 closes the anthology by examining representations of the Famine by Irish authors in the latter half of the twentieth century. In many ways, the chapters here suggest that the Famine has become a presence that lurks beneath all formulations of Irish history and culture. At the same time, though, the Famine seems now to embody an essential aspect of Ireland's communal memory, and this has allowed contemporary authors to use Famine imagery to productively explore some of the most troubled aspects of Irish identity. In Chapter 10 Robert C. Evans examines Frank O'Connor's personal and literary engagement with the Famine. This is followed by Nicholas Grene's reading of Tom Murphy's *Famine*, Nieves Pascual's analysis of Eavan Boland's anorexia poems and Karen Hill McNamara's overview of Famine representations in contemporary Irish children's literature. Rounding out both this Part and the anthology as a whole is Christopher Morash's 'Afterword', which examines the problem of canonicity in the larger context of Famine studies over the last ten years.

Taken as a whole, these essays demonstrate that the Great Famine has left its deepest mark on that most complex, conflicted and protean of Irish qualities, the memory. Again and again in these pages we see authors (and scholars) confronting the Famine as something that both cannot be remembered and must be remembered, and it is on this front that the legacy of the Famine and the ideology of canon-building most assuredly intersect. For what is a canon but a structure through which we, as readers, scholars and inheritors of generations past, determine what and how we will remember? For this reason, 'the Irish Famine' and 'the Irish canon' will always remain contested terms, since any definition of them depends on a relationship between the present and the past that, by its very nature, is always in motion. Whatever meaning we derive from these concepts must therefore come from the constant, unfulfilled act of trying to define them, and it is by tracing this act over the last 160 years that the essays in *Hungry Words* derive their meaning.

George Cusack
January 2005

References

Morash, Christopher. *Writing the Irish Famine*. Oxford: Clarendon Press, 1995.

PART ONE:

THE BURDEN OF WITNESS

CHAPTER 1

The stricken land:[1]
the Great Hunger in Ireland

Christine Kinealy

Background

The 1840s formed a pivotal decade in the development of modern Ireland. Socially, politically, culturally and psychologically, this decade left an imprint that remained visible into the late twentieth century. Inevitably, however, the 1840s are overshadowed by the tragedy of the Great Famine, which was triggered by the failure of the potato crop in varying degrees between 1845 and 1851. While the devastation that ensued from the Famine is easy to measure in demographic terms – over 1 million people died and a further 1.5 million emigrated in the space of six years – its impact on other aspects of Irish life is more difficult to quantify or articulate. Moreover, its long term legacy, especially in literature and culture, remains little explored.

The Famine took place in a highly charged political atmosphere, which tested the legislative union between Britain and Ireland. On 1 January 1801, the Act of Union had come into existence, creating a new political entity, the United Kingdom of Great Britain and Ireland. As a consequence of the Union, Ireland lost its parliament in Dublin and instead sent 100 representatives (MPs), a number that was later raised to 105, to the imperial parliament in London. Continuity was maintained, as only Protestants could sit in the enlarged Westminster parliament. Furthermore, the Act of Union confirmed the minority Anglican Church as the state church of Ireland, regardless of the fact that over 80 per cent of Ireland's population was Catholic (Kinealy, 2004, p.146). Consequently, after 1800 the political and economic control of Ireland remained in the hands of a small Protestant elite. It was not until 1829, as the result of a campaign masterminded by the Catholic lawyer Daniel O'Connell, that Catholic MPs could be elected to the British parliament, where they remained in a minority. As a consequence of the Act of Union, at the time of the Famine all policies concerning relief were made in London rather than in Ireland.

The Union not only changed the political configuration of Ireland; a further outcome was that 'Ireland's identity as a separate cultural and political entity was to be submerged within the new United Kingdom' (Williams, 2003, p.26). But Catholic Ireland did not fit into the prevailing view of 'Britishness'. A key element of British identity was Protestantism – a religion that united England, Scotland and Wales but from which the majority of Irish people were excluded (Colley, 1992, p.23). Although anti-Catholicism had its roots in the Reformation of the sixteenth century, it was re-energized in the early nineteenth century as Britain's economic and political power spread, and part of the imperial imperative was to spread the Protestant faith worldwide. In Ireland, this desire culminated in the 'Second Reformation' of the 1820s, during which evangelical Protestants renewed their efforts to convert poor Catholics to Protestantism. One unlooked-for consequence of this renewed Protestant crusade was that it brought the Catholic people closer to the Church hierarchy, significant at a time when O'Connell was mobilizing the people in the demand for emancipation (Whelan, 1995, pp.136–7).

During the Famine, the desire to proselytize was revived. Some evangelical Protestants viewed the Famine through providentialist eyes, seeing it as a judgement of God on a backward and superstitious people. This view was shared by some of the leading relief administrators, including Charles Trevelyan, the Chief Secretary at the British Treasury, and Sir Charles Wood, the Chancellor of the Exchequer. At the local level, providentialism resulted in the hunger and desperation of the people being exploited for the purposes of religious conversion (Kinealy, 2002, Chapter 3). Although only a minority of relief agencies used these tactics, and moderate Protestants deplored these activities, the memory of 'souperism' left a bitter legacy in Ireland that remained influential at the end of the twentieth century (Whelan, 1995, p.135). Moreover, Leslie Williams has argued, 'It is hardly irrelevant, then, that Protestant Britain had to administer famine relief for a largely Roman Catholic Ireland' (Williams, 2003, p.18).

Despite the growth of evangelical Protestantism, in the 1830s a number of attempts were made by liberal members of the British government to conciliate Catholic opinion in Ireland. This was attempted through a series of reforms and concessions, including abolition of tithes (taxes for the upkeep of the Anglican Church) and the introduction of a Poor Law in 1838. For many Catholics, however, the reforms were too little and too late, while for conservative Protestants, who were determined to maintain a Protestant ascendancy in Ireland, both Catholic emancipation and the concessions were a worrying development. The limited success of the Catholic population, therefore, exacerbated the growth of a variety of militant Protestantism that believed that union with Britain was its only safeguard. One outcome of their disquiet was an increase in attacks on Catholics by the Orange Order, especially during their annual parades on 12 July (Haddick-Flynn, 1999, pp.242–56).

Education was an important vehicle in the battle for religious and political hegemony. A number of Protestant religious societies had established schools in the wake of the Union, and they used the Protestant Bible as the main tool of instruction. This development angered Catholics and resulted in some attempts to found separate Catholic schools. In an effort to soothe tensions concerning education, in 1831 the British government established a Board of Education in Ireland. This intervention made Ireland the first country in the United Kingdom to receive statutory funding for education, although little sensitivity was shown to Irish culture, with neither the Irish language nor Irish history being taught, although British poetry was on the curriculum. Also, all teaching was done through the medium of English, which contributed to a decline in the use of the Irish language. The Famine, with its enormous death toll among the poor, many of whom were Irish speakers, also expedited this decline. In the aftermath of the Famine, mass emigration to English-speaking countries further weakened the use of Irish as a living language. By the late nineteenth century, therefore, the English language was the first language of both the educated and the poorer classes.

The passage of the Act of Union did not have popular support in Ireland, but in the early decades of the nineteenth century, desire for political independence was overshadowed by the demand for Catholic emancipation – that is, for Catholics to be allowed to sit in the British parliament. The campaign was led by a Catholic lawyer, Daniel O'Connell, who throughout his lifetime rejected the use of physical force. The winning of Catholic emancipation in 1829, using only peaceful tactics, made O'Connell the undisputed leader of Catholic opinion in Ireland, earning for him the title 'the Liberator'. At the same time, he was applauded by radicals and nationalists throughout the rest of Europe. Inevitably, O'Connell was feared and disliked by many members of the

British establishment and the conservative press, including the influential London *Times* (Macintyre, 1965, pp.155–6). Nonetheless, O'Connell believed that it was possible to win justice for Ireland by supporting the British political system. Therefore, he used his election to the British parliament to bring about social reforms rather than a reversal of the Act of Union. This arrangement was formalized by the Lichfield House Compact in 1835, by which O'Connell pledged his allegiance to the Whig Party. However, the modest reforms achieved as a result of this alliance were too little to satisfy the expectations of either the emergent Irish Catholic middle classes or O'Connell's mass base of popular support.

In April 1840, Daniel O'Connell established the Loyal National Repeal Association, by which he hoped to revitalize his political career and Irish politics in general. The aim of the organization was to bring about a repeal of the Act of Union, although O'Connell stressed his loyalty to the Queen and the Empire. As with the emancipation movement, O'Connell pledged only to use constitutional tactics, the primary method being that of mass meetings. In 1841, O'Connell's arch political enemy, Sir Robert Peel, led the Tory Party to a massive electoral victory. In contrast, support for O'Connell declined, making it unlikely that he would be able to recreate the success of his emancipation movement. The faltering repeal movement, however, was revived in the following year by the emergence of a number of young intellectuals who established their own weekly newspaper, the *Nation*. The *Nation* was inspired by nationalist movements in Europe, but particularly in Italy. From the outset, it fused political with cultural nationalism, endeavouring to bring the history, culture and traditions of Ireland to a wide audience. This new approach to politics not only filled a vacuum in the Irish educational system; it was also a precursor of the cultural nationalism more generally associated with the late nineteenth century.

Within a few years, the *Nation* was the most widely read newspaper in Ireland, with a readership of 250,000 when it was suppressed in 1848. It brought together a glittering and diverse collection of intellectuals, who became collectively known as 'Young Ireland'. This eclectic group of writers included poets and romantics (Thomas Davis and James Clarence Mangan), conservative radicals (John Mitchel, 'Mary' and James Fintan Lalor), radical conservatives (Thomas Francis Meagher), women writers (Jane Francesca Elgee, Mary Kelly), Protestant intellectuals and landlords (Samuel Ferguson, William Smith O'Brien), outspoken Catholic priests (Father Kenyon, Bishop Magee) and disgruntled Catholics (Charles Gavan Duffy), although a number fitted into more than one category. Even

Daniel O'Connell (anonymously) and his son John were regular contributors during the early years of the newspaper's existence, although as the agenda of the paper became more radical, they distanced themselves. The *Nation's* strength lay in the fact that it brought together discontented people from the Protestant middle classes and the upwardly mobile Catholic middle classes who were united by their love of Ireland, even if they disagreed on what to do about Britain. Like Theobald Wolfe Tone, Young Ireland supported a non-sectarian approach to politics, and the *Nation* regularly printed letters from Protestant sympathizers who tried to induce their co-religionists to support repeal. Their justification was that they needed Protestant help to make Ireland free (*Nation*, 17 December 1842). This inclusive approach contrasted with the ambivalent relationship that both Daniel and John O'Connell had with Irish Protestants, which resulted in their decision in 1842 not to include the population of Ulster in the Repeal movement (Mitchel, 1917). The failure of some Irish nationalists to engage with Ulster Protestants was also one of the weaknesses of the Home Rule movement later in the century.

The success of the *Nation* energized the repeal movement and enhanced O'Connell's political and personal status. Increasingly, though, Daniel and his lacklustre son, John, resented the attention that the group was attracting. Moreover, the approaches of O'Connell and the Young Irelanders were becoming ever more diverse, with differences emerging over the question of non-denominational education, the use of physical versus moral force, and the continuing support for the Whig Party. The differences climaxed in 1846 during a public discussion about whether or not physical force was ever justified. The debate was used as a pretext to force the Young Ireland group, led by William Smith O'Brien, to resign from the repeal movement. At the beginning of 1847, Young Ireland formed the Irish Confederation, which attracted support from Irish nationalists not only in Ireland but also in Britain and the United States. The death of Daniel O'Connell in May 1847 and his replacement by his son John further contributed to a decline in the Repeal Association. The onset of famine, therefore, coincided with a period of intense political activity within Ireland, with divisions not only between nationalists and unionists, but also within the repeal movement.

The hunger

A new form of potato blight was noticed on the potato crop in Belgium early in 1845. From there it spread to other parts of Europe, reaching Ireland by late summer, where it destroyed approximately 50 per cent of the crop. The implications of the failure in Ireland were serious, as about half of the population depended on potatoes for a subsistence diet, while the vegetable was also used for feeding pigs and cattle. Yet, while potatoes were a crucial part of the Irish diet, the Irish economy was diverse, with large amounts of high-quality corn and cattle exported annually (Kinealy, 2002, Chapter 6). The British government, under the leadership of Sir Robert Peel, responded swiftly to news of the failure, introducing relief measures that had been used in earlier periods of food shortage. The relief measures included importing Indian corn (a low-grade grain) from the United States in order to both increase the food supply and stabilize the price of provisions. The relief measures were successful and nobody died during the first year of blight. Peel, however, had linked the subsistence crisis with his personal political agenda of repealing the Corn Laws, thus ending protection for corn production in the United Kingdom. The long-term consequence of this legislation was to change Ireland's commercial agricultural sector from grain production to pasture (Ó Gráda, 1993, pp.151–3). The most significant immediate consequence of the repeal of the Corn Laws was the fall of the Tory Party and the ending of Peel's premiership. Thus, in July 1846, coinciding with reports of a reappearance of the potato blight, the Whig Party, led by Lord John Russell, took control of the government.

In 1846 the potato disease was far more extensive than in the previous year, with the crop being almost totally destroyed. Moreover, the corn harvest was smaller than usual. Consequently, the impact of the food shortages was almost immediate and far more severe than the year before. Despite evidence of widespread shortages, the new Whig government decided to reduce its role in the import and sale of food, preferring to leave food supply to market forces. Public works were designated as the main mechanism for providing relief. The change was disastrous. The public works system was subject to so many bureaucratic checks that it failed as a means of providing emergency relief. Employment conditions were harsh, with those employed (including women and children) expected to work for twelve hours a day in physically gruelling labour, often on work that had little enduring value, summed up in the phrase 'roads that led nowhere and walls that surrounded nothing'. Wages were kept deliberately low and paid at piece-meal rates, with a ceiling placed on the maximum that could be earned. Unusually cold weather, including four months of snow in parts of the west, high food prices and low wages, all further limited the effectiveness of the public works (Kinealy, 1997, pp.66–77). Consequently, many poor people were forced to seek relief in the much-hated workhouses. By the end of 1846, over half of the 130 workhouses were full, but under the terms of the 1838 legislation, they were forbidden from providing additional relief (Thirteenth Annual Report of Poor Law Commissioners, 1847, Appendix). In the winter of 1846–47, high levels of disease, death, eviction and emigration were a grim attestation to the fact that the latest relief policies of the British government had failed.

The public works were not only ineffective as a mechanism for saving lives; they were also costly, with much of the expenditure absorbed in administrative charges (BPP, 1849, Vol.48). At the beginning of 1847, in what amounted to an admission of failure, the British government changed its relief policies. The public works were replaced by a network of soup kitchens extending over the country at which the destitute could obtain free rations of soup and bread. This change of policy was significant because for the first time since the blight had appeared, the government provided 'gratuitous relief', that is, they gave free food to people who remained in their own homes. Although the rations were small and sometimes had low nutritional value, their provision meant that the Irish poor were getting relief directly in the form of food. By July 1847, when the system was at its height, over 3 million people (almost 40 per cent of the population) were receiving free daily rations of food. The soup kitchen system was economical to operate, and during the summer of 1847 mortality decreased. Nonetheless, the soup kitchens were closed in August. This was because the government feared creating a culture of dependency more than it feared the consequences of hunger. Overall, the soup kitchens demonstrated that the British government did possess the administrative and logistical ability to feed the poor of Ireland, but ideo-logical and political constraints meant that regardless of its success, it was never meant to be other than a stop-gap measure.

Although there was little evidence of blight on the potato crop in 1847, the harvest was small. However, the government used the relative freedom from blight to announce that the Famine was over and to warn that if any further relief was required, it was to be paid for by Irish taxation and not by taxpayers in the rest of the United Kingdom. To facilitate the shift in fiscal responsibility, all temporary relief measures were ended and the Poor Law was made responsible for both temporary and emergency relief. Thirty-three new workhouses were quickly built and, for the first time, outdoor relief was permitted (*Act . . . for Relief of Destitute Poor*, 1847). For the government, the main advantage in this change was that Irish land-lords would now be forced to be responsible for providing relief in their localities, both through the administration of the local workhouse and by the payment of poor rates. The new system was intended to be harsh and to deter all but the most destitute from applying for assistance. The 'Gregory' or 'Quarter Acre Clause', which was part of the amended Poor Law, decreed that no person who occupied more than a quarter of an acre of land was entitled to receive relief (ibid., section 10). This provision forced many small tenants, who had survived two years of hardship, to choose between obtaining relief and holding on to their land.

Despite the government's proclamation, the Famine was not over in 1847, and in 1848 over 1 million people (out of a population of less than 8 million) were dependent on relief provided by the Poor Law (*First Report*, 1848, Appendix). Moreover, the blight had not disappeared. The potato harvest of 1848 was stricken by blight, and it was as virulent as it had been in 1846. Although the government felt compelled to permit a small number of emergency subventions to some of the most destitute unions in order to allow them to remain operative, the major part of relief continued to be provided through the mechanism of local taxation. The Whig government, however, was concerned that further financial interventions would lose it the support of British taxpayers. At the same time, they were determined to use the opportunity provided by the Famine to bring about substantial changes in the structure of landholding in Ireland (Senior, 1868, Vol.1, p.209).

The sharp increase in evictions after 1847 exacerbated the problems facing the poor while increasing the prevalence of lethal diseases. At this stage, even some high-ranking members of the government were privately expressing disquiet about the consequences of the government's refusal to intervene, despite evidence of extensive suffering. At the beginning of 1849, Lord Clarendon, the Lord Lieutenant of Ireland, secretly pleaded with the Prime Minister to provide more relief, arguing:

> Surely this is a state of things to justify you asking the House of Commons for an advance, for I don't think there is another legislature in Europe that would disregard such suffering as now exists in the west of Ireland, or coldly persist in a policy of extermination.
>
> (Clarendon to Russell, Clarendon Letter Books, 28 April 1849)

The government, however, chose not to interfere, and between 1849 (when recording commenced) and 1854, over a quarter of a million people were legally evicted from their homes. The figure would have been even higher if illegal evictions and voluntary surrenders had been included (Donnolly, 1995, pp.155–6). Emigration also increased after 1847, not for the poorest people, but as an outlet for those who had the energy and the resources to leave the country. Before 1845 emigration from Ireland had been high, but after 1846, the volume and profile of emigrants changed. Whereas previous emigration had primarily been carried out in spring and summer, throughout the Famine people were willing to risk the danger of a winter crossing in order to get out of the country, regardless of the dangers associated with the notorious 'coffin ships'. Most of the emigrants chose the United States as their final destination, often travelling via Liverpool or Canada in order to get the cheapest fares. The end of the blight did not mark an end to leaving Ireland, and emigration rates continued to rise, peaking in 1854, when almost 1 million people left the country. Much of the emigration in the later years of the Famine and in the post-Famine decades was financed by remittances – that is, money sent home by the original emigrants. The high level of emigration was generally viewed in a positive way by the British government, who regarded it as a means of clearing Ireland of what was believed to be its surplus population. This viewpoint was articulated by Charles Trevelyan, Secretary at the Treasury and unofficial head of relief administration in London, who asserted:

> I do not know how farms are to be consolidated if small farmers do not emigrate, and by acting for the purpose of keeping them at home, we should be defaulting at their own object. We must not complain of what we really want to obtain. If small farmers go, and their landlords are reduced to sell portions of their estates to persons who will invest capital, we shall at last arrive at something like a satisfactory settlement of the country.
>
> (Trevelyan to Twistleton, Home Office Papers, 14 September 1848)

In 1849, as demand for relief showed no signs of abating in the south and west of the country, a new relief measure was introduced as a means of providing financial assistance to some of the poorest unions without imposing a financial burden on the British Treasury. The so-called Rate-in-Aid imposed a new tax that was to be levied on Irish taxpayers only, with the Treasury then redistributing the money so raised. Some politicians and relief officials were opposed to the measure on the grounds that it contravened the spirit of the Act of Union. Clarendon, for example, viewed the tax as contrary to the idea of a *United* Kingdom and feared that it would exacerbate discontent in Ireland (Clarendon to Duke of Bedford, Clarendon Letter Books, 29 March 1849). The most intense criticism of the new tax came from Edward Twistleton, an Englishman who was in charge of the Irish Poor Law. He viewed the Rate-in-Aid as the final straw in a series of measures that amounted to an abandonment of Ireland and the desertion of imperial responsibility. Twistleton resigned, on the grounds that he could not implement the new legislation 'with honour' (Evidence of Edward Twistleton, BPP, 1849, Vol.16, pp.699–714). At the same time, he informed a parliamentary committee in London that 'it is quite possible for this country to prevent the death there [Ireland] of any death from starvation by the advance of a few hundred pounds' (Ibid., p.718). Charles Trevelyan, however, was unimpressed by such arguments, pointing out that the new tax was necessary in order to protect British taxpayers from 'the great injustice of the burden which belongs to the rate-payers of each [Irish] union being unnecessarily transferred to the taxpayers of the United Kingdom' (Treasury Minute, 16 January 1849, BPP, 1849, Vol.48, pp.3–4).

After 1852, the potato blight receded and good harvests returned to Ireland. Within the short space of six years, though, the country had changed irrevocably. Since 1845, the population had fallen by 25 per cent through a combination of death and emigration, which provided a stark measure of the human cost of inflexible and inappropriate relief policies. This demographic collapse made the Irish Famine one of the most lethal in modern history (Ó Gráda, 1995, pp.248–58). Mortality was particularly high among children under five and men over forty (Ó Gráda, 1993, pp.106–8). But apart from the short-term impact on population, the Famine precipitated a long-term demographic decline, and by 1901, the Irish population was only 4 million – approximately half of its pre-Famine size. Moreover, the impact of the Famine was not confined to Ireland; the memory of suffering was taken overseas by thousands of emigrants, many of whom viewed their flight as exile, and in the decades that followed the Famine, its remembrance was a painful reminder to nationalists of British misrule.

Political context

Between 1845 and 1848, the Famine dominated debate in the British parliament, while responses to it polarized political opinion in both Britain and Ireland. The fall of Peel's government in the summer of 1846 left the Tory Party in disarray as they split into Peelites (supporters of Peel) and Protectionists (led by Lord George Bentinck and Benjamin Disraeli).

Although the incoming Whig government only had minority support within the parliament, the divisions in the Tory party meant that there was no effective opposition to the government during the Famine years. Nor was there any united opposition in Ireland, where the majority of the 105 Irish MPs continued to support the main British political parties rather than unite to form a coherent Irish policy.

The new Whig administration had the support of O'Connell's party, but the repeal movement was weakened by internal divisions between 'Young' and 'Old' Ireland. The death of O'Connell in May 1847 temporarily increased support for repeal, but in the general election a few months later, only 37 repeal candidates were returned, one Young Ireland member (William Smith O'Brien), and 42 Tory and 35 Whig candidates. Despite the disastrous consequences of the Whigs' relief policies, the majority of Irish MPs, including John O'Connell, continued to support the Famine policies of the Whigs. Despite having only one parliamentary representative, the Irish Confederation remained the main voice of opposition to government relief policies in Ireland. In April 1848, due to a combination of disgust and frustration, Smith O'Brien withdrew from parliament on the grounds that he was wasting his time trying to obtain justice for Ireland in London (Kinealy, 2002, Chapter 1).

In 1847, a year that earned the sobriquet 'Black '47' due to the high levels of disease and death, nationalist politics in Ireland were riven by bitter and sometimes violent divisions. Not only did Young and Old Ireland remain antagonistic, but there were also internal disputes within the Irish Confederation, often concerning the role that landlords would play in winning independence. Smith O'Brien, who was a Protestant landlord and a political moderate, continued to hope that the Confederation could win both landlords and Protestants to their cause (Mitchel, 1917). Two implacable critics of government policy, and increasingly of Smith O'Brien's moderation, were John Mitchel, a Unitarian from County Derry, and James Fintan Lalor, a Catholic hunchback from County Laois. Both men were angered by the indifference of the British government and Irish landlords to the suffering caused by the Famine. Lalor's response was to propose that a social revolution should accompany the political revolution, believing that without a reform of the land system, political changes would be meaningless (Daly, 1989, pp.112–13). In the columns of the *Nation* Lalor urged all tenants to mount a campaign of civil disobedience, which included withholding rents. Lalor's proposals were not supported by the leaders of the Irish Confederation (ibid.). Even John Mitchel continued to hope that Irish landlords would lead the struggle for independence, and his conversion to anti-landlordism was not complete until the end of 1847. Despite Lalor's lack of influence on the main body of the Irish Confederation, his ideas for social change, based on a reform of the land system, re-emerged during the turbulent decade of the 1870s, providing a blueprint for the tactics employed by the Land League.

At the beginning of 1848, Mitchel broke from the Irish Confederation and established his own newspaper, the *United Irishman*. From the outset, the tone of the paper was more militant than either the O'Connellite *Freeman's Journal* or the *Nation*. Its prospectus claimed that the paper would provide a 'bolder voice' than those 'obsolete and superannuated' voices of both Young and Old Ireland (Prospectus, Mitchel, 1917, 12 February 1848). More controversially, it also claimed that Irish people who wanted to be free 'ought to have ARMS, and to practice the use of them' (ibid.). Although the newspaper's name paid tribute to the insurgents of 1798, Mitchel was keen to explain that 'we differ from the illustrious conspirators of ninety-eight, not in principle, no, not an iota, but as I shall presently show you, materially as to the mode of action. Theirs was a secret conspiracy – ours is a public one' (*United Irishman*, 12 February 1848). Following his arrest in May, Mitchel claimed that one of the paper's aims was 'in stimulating the just dissatisfaction of the people to the point of insurrection' (Mitchel, 1982, [1854], p.lii). Mitchel's former comrades in Young Ireland were critical of this confrontational tone. Nevertheless, they defended Mitchel's right to free speech when the government arrested him for sedition. The cost of the paper was initially 5d a copy, but demand was so great that subsequent editions were sold for up to four times that much (*United Irishman*, 4 March 1848). Within a few weeks, sales of the *United Irishman* in Dublin had risen to 12,000, with additional sales in Ireland and England (*New York Freeman*, 6 May 1848). The success of the paper may have been helped by the fact that within two weeks of its being established, a revolution in France was to have a dramatic impact on political developments in Ireland.

The French Revolution in February 1848, which resulted in the overthrow of Louis Philippe and the establishment of a republic, created a wave of revolutionary fervour in Ireland, where the revolution was applauded because it had been achieved with little violence or bloodshed. Throughout Ireland, bonfires were lit and meetings were convened to send messages of congratulation to the provisional government in Paris (Constabulary Reports, Home Office, March 1848). The French Revolution raised hopes among moderates in both Young and Old Ireland that repeal could be achieved in a similarly bloodless revolution. This unity worried the British authorities, who wanted to isolate the Irish nationalist groups. At the beginning of April, a delegation of Young Irelanders visited France to congratulate the new government. Even before they reached Paris, Lamartine, a leading member of the provisional government, responding to pressure from the British Ambassador, had decided that France would not help Ireland with armed intervention. The British government was delighted by this response, and they had copies of the French reply printed and displayed around Ireland (Clarendon to Grey, Clarendon Letter Books, 6 April 1848). French intervention in Irish affairs, therefore, appeared to have been neutralized.

The continuation of famine conditions and increasingly draconian measures by the British government, including the transportation of John Mitchel to Bermuda, made an insurrection appear inevitable. At the beginning of June, the Irish Confederation issued an address stating that in the approaching period, 'armed resistance to the oppressors will become a sacred obligation'. This address was printed in newspapers in Britain, as it was hoped that there would be diversionary outbreaks there (*Liverpool Mercury*, 6 June 1848). Two agents had also been sent to America with a letter signed by four Young Irelanders – the document was smeared in gun-powder and carried in a loaded pistol so that it could be destroyed if they were arrested (Duffy, 1883, pp.609–10). The timing of the uprising, however, remained unclear: radicals such as James Fintan Lalor argued that it should happen immediately, to take the authorities by surprise, while the majority opinion, led by the moderate Smith O'Brien, was that a rising should not take place until harvest, to allow the poor people to obtain food.

The government had even more draconian measures planned. On 22 July, the British Prime Minister announced the introduction of a bill to suspend the Habeas Corpus Act in Ireland, thus allowing the Irish Constabulary to apprehend and arrest any person suspected of treasonable designs (*Manchester Guardian*, 22 July 1848). The bill was a trigger for action as, in the words of one English newspaper, 'the leaders of the rebel movement in Ireland are now fairly driven to the wall. They must either fight or conceal themselves, or submit to be apprehended and lodged in prison until the government shall feel satisfied that their power of doing mischief is at an end' (*Liverpool Mercury*, 22 July 1848). Within Ireland, the suspension of habeas corpus intensified the general feeling that an uprising would have to take place immediately and that it would probably commence in the south of Ireland, as the troop presence in Dublin was so high.

On 28 July, a small uprising led by William Smith O'Brien took place in Ballingarry in County Tipperary. It was easily defeated with only two of the insurgents being killed. Charles Gavan Duffy, a moderate member of the Irish Confederation, believed that the uprising had taken place three months too late, allowing the government rather than the rebels to seize the initiative. Also significant was the fact that the Catholic Church had vociferously opposed the uprising, their resolve hardened by events in France in the previous few weeks, notably the murder of Bishop Affré in Paris during the June Days (Duffy, 1883, p.693). The leaders of the uprising, including Smith O'Brien and Francis Meagher, were arrested and tried in December on a charge of high treason by an Act dating back to 1799. They were sentenced to death, although in 1849, the sentence was commuted to transportation to Van Dieman's Land (Tasmania). A number of other participants fled from Ireland, many of them settling in New York, where they inspired the next generation of Irish nationalism, associated with the Fenian movement.

Throughout the Famine, the role of the British press in shaping attitudes toward relief policies was crucial. *The Times* and *Punch*, in particular, constantly reinforced negative stereotypes of Irish people and suggested that providing further relief would be a waste of British taxpayers' money (*The Times*, 9 August 1849). Moreover, following the rising in 1848, there were suggestions in the press that the suffering of the people was due to their indolence and their political activities (*Illustrated London News*, 8 September 1848). Leslie Williams has argued that many of the Famine deaths had 'resulted from imposing a set of policies based, not upon understanding and compassion, but upon preconceived assumptions, attitudes, stereotypes, and ideologies as expressed in the leading articles and cartoons in Britain's leading newspapers and journals' (Williams, 2003, p.4). In Ireland, press opinion was more divided, and the radical press, led by the *Nation* and joined briefly in 1848 by John Mitchel's *United Irishman*, the *Felon*, and the *Tribune*, offered sustained attacks on the British government. However, the radical press was silenced in the summer of 1848 with its editors being arrested, three of whom (John Mitchel, John Martin and Kevin O'Doherty) were transported.

Some of the most blistering attacks on Famine policy appeared in the columns of the *Nation* in the form of both prose and poetry. One of the most powerful poems was written by Jane Elgee, a young woman from a conservative, unionist, Protestant background, who wrote under the pen-name 'Speranza'. Her poem 'The Famine Year' combined poignancy about the suffering of the poor with a searing attack on the British government (*Nation*, 21 January 1847). Her contention that 'Golden corn' was being taken from the starving people in Ireland by 'the Stranger' was a theme developed by John Mitchel. When Charles Gavan Duffy was arrested in July 1848, she helped to edit the *Nation* and wrote an unsigned, inflammatory article entitled *Jacta Alea Est* ('The Die is Cast'), which was a call to arms of the men of Ireland (*Nation*, 29 July 1848). It was judged to be treasonable by the government, which seized the issue and suppressed the *Nation* for sedition (Melville, 1999, p.47). In 1851, Jane Elgee married the Dublin oculist William Wilde, and together they had two sons, William and Oscar.

While the *Nation* was at the forefront of printed attacks on government relief policies, other contemporary journals, including the *Dublin University Magazine* and *Cork Magazine*, also published poetry concerned with the Famine. Inevitably, most of the verse was written from a nationalist perspective, although a small amount was written from a unionist perspective (Morash, 1989, pp.244–53). Poetry, however, could not feed the people, and the romantic nationalism associated with the *Nation* became more politicized as a result of the Famine. Collectively, these writings added a fresh dimension to understanding of the Famine and an antidote to the negative stereotypes prevalent in the British press. In addition, by focusing on the impact of government policies, they gave a voice to people who would otherwise have been unheard. Among the overlooked legacies of the Famine years was the contribution to politics, literature and culture by the people around Young Ireland and the emergence of a new form of nationalism.

The achievement of Young Ireland was particularly impressive because until 1849, Ireland possessed one Anglican university (Trinity College), and Catholics, who accounted for approximately 85 per cent of the population, had never represented more than 10 per cent of the student body. The Irish intelligentsia was also small, probably totalling no more than 1 per cent of the population (Hill, 1980). Moreover, over 50 per cent of the Irish population was illiterate, and the majority of this group were Irish speakers. The form of cultural nationalism favoured by Young Ireland (and many nationalist intellectuals in Europe at the time) was essentially conservative, paternalistic, backward-looking and sometimes apolitical (Eagleton, 1999, p.61). A further remarkable achievement of Young Ireland, therefore, was that it transformed a group of what were essentially romantic nationalists into radicals and revolutionaries. And even if the rising in 1848 was an abject failure, its legacy was considerable.

Aftermath and legacy

Between 1840 and 1850, but particularly after 1845, events in Ireland constituted a social revolution that was to have a long-reaching impact not only on the development of Ireland and Britain, but also on the countries where Famine emigrants settled. At the same time, significant and far-reaching changes took place in the political sphere, while the death, disease, eviction and emigration associated with the Famine years informed much of the literature written at the time.

The most visible and easily quantifiable transformation occurred in the area of population, with a population loss of 25 per cent in only six years. Moreover, the population continued to fall even after good harvests had returned to Ireland. The demographic collapse not only had consequences for Ireland, but also changed the demographic configuration of the United Kingdom. At the time of the Act of Union, England accounted for 54 per cent of the population of the UK, Ireland for 33 per cent, Scotland for 10 per cent, and Wales for 3 per cent. After the Great Famine, Ireland's share of the population had fallen to less than 20 per cent and its share continued to decline (Kinealy, 2004, p.146). It was not until the 1970s that Ireland's demographic decline was to reverse. Much of the population loss was due to high levels of emigration, especially to the United States. Many saw themselves as reluctant emigrants, but few returned to Ireland. As a consequence, the popular view of emigration as exile was reinforced, strengthened by songs and poetry that lamented the leaving of Ireland. More importantly, emigration reinforced existing support for Irish nationalism in the United States, and many of the exiles from the 1848 uprising were sowing the seeds for the emergence of Fenianism twenty years later.

Death, dislocation and emigration were not the only consequences, as the Famine left its imprint on Irish society in many other ways. Within Ireland, the trauma of the Famine had a lasting impact on the lives and pastimes of the survivors. For those who had survived and remained in Ireland, life had changed in ways that were difficult to quantify or articulate. A poignant insight into the legacy of the Famine was provided by a female survivor from the Rosses in County Donegal who wrote:

The years of the Famine, of the bad life and the hunger, arrived and broke the spirit and strength of the community. People simply wanted to survive . . . Recreation and leisure ceased. Poetry, music and dancing died. These things were lost and completely forgotten. When life improved in other ways, these pursuits never returned as they had been.

The Famine killed everything.
(Ní Grianna quoted in Deane, 1991, pp.203–4)

The Famine years were also pivotal in the political development of Ireland. Despite being easily defeated, the 1848 uprising provided an important link between the republican uprisings in 1798 and 1916, while the intellectuals who led Young Ireland were inspired by, and contributed to, the wave of nationalist and revolutionary fervour that swept through Europe in the 1840s. At the same time, the inclusive approach of the Young Ireland leadership to religion kept alive the tradition of non-sectarian politics in Ireland. Moreover, women nationalists were given a voice in the columns of the *Nation*, even if their identities were disguised by pseudonyms. In 1901, the nationalist and feminist Maud Gonne offered her own assessment of the legacy of 1848, writing,

When one realises the condition of the country at that time, there is little wonder the Young Irelanders failed. It is a fallacy to think that the poorer and more miserable a people are the better they will fight; there is a degree of misery and poverty which saps all energy, moral and physical . . . Though John Mitchel failed in his manly and fearless teaching, he prepared the way for the Fenian movement. He cleared the air of the miasma of the decadent doctrine of peaceful agitation. Mitchel rendered James Stephens' organisation possible.
(Gonne, 28 September 1901)

The contribution of Young Ireland was not confined to politics; the group left an intellectual legacy in literature both within Ireland and among the Irish diaspora. The leaders of Young Ireland contributed to the emergence of cultural nationalism in Ireland, which sowed the seeds for the later Gaelic revival. W.B. Yeats, who was a great admirer of the power and energy of Mitchel's rhetoric, called him 'the only Young Ireland prose writer who had a style at all' (1965, p.136). When Queen Victoria visited Ireland in 1900, Yeats read some of Mitchel's words in which he condemned the Act of Union of 100 years earlier (Kelly, 1986, p.503). One of the most talented poets associated with the *Nation* was the eccentric but tragic James Clarence Mangan. One of his best-known

poems was 'My Dark Rosaleen', in which he pictured Ireland as a
sorrowful woman, a theme later explored by W.B. Yeats and Lady
Gregory in the play *Cathleen ni Houlihan*. Unlike many of the other writers,
he was not from the middle class but was born in penury and died in
poverty in 1849, due to a combination of cholera and malnutrition
(Morash, 1989, pp.22 and 282). James Joyce wrote of Mangan that despite
his short and tragic life, he 'sums up in himself the soul of a country and
an era' (quoted in Melville, 1999, p.33). Some of the poetry of Young
Ireland survived in a disguised form. The rousing ballad 'A Nation Once
Again', which captured Young Ireland's brand of cultural nationalism,
was written by Thomas Davis, one of the founders of the *Nation*, who had
died prematurely in 1845. This song was subsequently adopted as an
anthem by republican nationalists. In 2002 it was voted the world's most
popular song in a poll carried out by the BBC World Service, suggesting
that its message still has resonance today (http://news.bbc.co.uk/1/
entertainment, 20 December 2002).

The contribution of women to the *Nation* was significant; and even if
many of them were less visible than their male counterparts, their writings
demonstrated that they were no less educated or fervent. After 1848, both
Mary Kelly ('Eva') and Jane Elgee ('Speranza') continued to write and
publish, although neither was again directly involved in nationalist politics.
Moreover, all of their post-1848 writing was done with the knowledge that
attempts at a nationalist revolution had failed. They both also witnessed
the less genteel Fenian uprisings in 1867, which were even more spectacular, and violent, failures. Eva eventually married Kevin O'Doherty,
who had been transported for his activities in 1848, and they lived most of
their married life in Australia. The friendships that she had made during
the turbulent period when she wrote for the *Nation* and through her years
of separation from O'Doherty remained influential throughout her life.
When the first edition of her poetry, *Poems by Eva of the Nation*, was
published in the United States in 1877, the introduction read, 'To the
memory of John Mitchel and John Martin, "felons" of 1848. These
poems (associated with the cause for which they suffered) are dedicated by
their friend and compatriot, Eva' (1877). The dedication in the extended
edition, however, which was published in Ireland in 1909, simply read 'To
the Memory of the Dead' (MacManus, 'Introduction', in Eva, 1909).

Speranza published prolifically following her marriage, no longer as
'Speranza' but as Lady Wilde, although she maintained a link with the
past by usually signing herself as Francesca Speranza Wilde. Her earlier

writings included translations from Latin, French and German, but in her later years she wrote more on Irish history and folklore (Wilde, 1887, 1890). Yeats, who greatly admired her work, pondered before he met her, 'I wonder if I will find her as delightful as her book – as delightful as she is certainly unconventional' (quoted in Melville, 1999, p.217). Her contribution to the literary and Gaelic revival may have been overlooked due to her son Oscar's spectacular and public fall from grace. As Lady Wilde, however, she also achieved notoriety by hosting literary salons in Dublin and London, leading the *Irish Times* to describe her home in Merrion Square as 'the house where a guest met all the Dublin celebrities in literature, art and the drama, as well as any stray literary waif who might be either sojourning or passing through the city' *(Irish Times,* 11 March 1848). For many Irish people, though, it was her early writings that made the most lasting impression. When Oscar Wilde toured the United States in the 1880s, he was referred to by Irish-Americans as 'Speranza's Son' (Melville, 1999, p.13). In 1892, when Maud Gonne gave a series of nationalist lectures in France, Holland and Belgium, she was hailed as 'The New Speranza' (Gonne in White and Jeffares, 1992, pp.8–9).

Other writers for the *Nation* and the outlawed radical press also continued to be remembered long after they had faded from public view. James Fintan Lalor, who died prematurely in 1849, his poor health having been exacerbated by a period in prison in 1848, paved the way for the Tenant Rights movement in the 1850s and his writings inspired the New Departure and Land League in the 1870s. In the early twentieth century, the socialist James Connolly adopted some of Lalor's words as the motto for his Irish Citizen Army. Moreover, Lalor was identified by Patrick Pearse, one of the leaders of the 1916 Rising, as one of the four creators of Irish nationalism (Daly, 1989, p.111).

While the late 1840s are remembered for the tragedy of the Famine and the failure of the 1848 uprising, these years were also remarkable for giving rise to an extraordinary group of men and women who used their literary and scholarly talents to the benefit of Ireland's nationalist struggle. In the words of Terry Eagleton, 'Few groups of intellectuals have had such a spectacular impact on politics as Young Ireland . . . and not many pieces of newsprint have created such historical turmoil as the *Nation*' (1999, p.141). Perhaps even more importantly, the writers associated with the *Nation* and other radical journals helped to keep alive a memory of the Famine, albeit a nationalist one, which provides a direct link to the tragedy and a counterbalance to the sanitized, imperial representations found in so many British press reports. The 1840s left an intellectual legacy that is all the more remarkable considering the tragic context in which it emerged.

References

An Act to Make Further Provision for the Relief of the Destitute Poor in Ireland (10 Vic. cap.31, 8 June 1847).

BPP. *Select Committee on the Irish Poor Law* (1849, Vol.16).

BPP. *Papers relating to the aid afforded to the Distressed Unions in the west of Ireland* (1849, Vol.48).

BPP (British Parliamentary Papers). *Return of all sums of money either granted or advanced from the Exchequer of the United Kingdom, on account of the distress and famine, or in aid of the administration of the Poor Law in Ireland, during the famine years 1846, 1847 and 1848, with the amount of repayments* (1849, Vol.352).

Clarendon Letter Books. Bodleian Library, Oxford.

Colley, Linda. *Britons: Forging the Nation 1707–1837.* New Haven, CT: Yale University Press, 1992.

Constabulary Reports (Abstract), Home Office Papers, National Archives, London.

Daly, Mary E. 'James Fintan Lalor and rural revolution', in Ciaran Brady (ed.), *Worsted in the Game: Losers in Irish History.* Dublin: Liliput Press, 1989, pp.111–19.

Deane, Seamus (ed.). *The Field Day Anthology of Irish Writing.* Derry: Field Day, 1991.

Donnolly Jr, James S. 'Mass eviction and the Great Famine', in Cathal Póirtéir (ed.). *The Great Irish Famine.* Cork and Dublin: Mercier Press in association with Radio Telefís Éireann, 1995, pp.155–73.

Duffy, Charles Gavan. *Four Years of Irish History, 1845–1849.* London: Cassell, Petter, Galpin, 1883.

Eagleton, Terry. *Scholars and Rebels in Nineteenth-Century Ireland.* Oxford: Blackwell, 1999.

Eva. *Poems by Eva of the Nation.* First pub. San Francisco, CA, 1877; reprinted with Introduction by Seamus MacManus. Dublin: M. Gill, 1909.

First Report of Irish Poor Law Commissioners. Dublin: Thoms, 1848.

Gonne, Maud. 'Ireland today', *United Irishman*, 28 September 1901, reprinted in Karen Steele (ed.), *Maud Gonne's Irish Nationalist Writings 1895–1946.* Dublin: Irish Academic Press, 2004.

Gonne, Maud and W.B. Yeats. *The Gonne–Yeats Letters*. Anne MacBride White and A. Norman Jeffares (eds). London: Hutchinson, 1992.

Haddick-Flynn, Kevin. *Orangeism: The Making of a Tradition*. Dublin: Wolfhound Press, 1999.

Hill, Jacqueline. 'The intelligentsia and Irish nationalism in the 1840s', *Studia Hibernia*, No. 20, 1980, pp.104–5.

Home Office Papers, National Archives, London, T.64. 370. B/1, 1848.

Kelly, John. *Collected Letters of Yeats*. Oxford: Oxford University Press, 1986.

Kinealy, Christine. *A Death Dealing Famine: The Great Hunger in Ireland*. London: Pluto Press, 1997.

Kinealy, Christine. *The Great Irish Famine: Impact, Ideology and Rebellion*. Hampshire: Palgrave, 2002.

Kinealy, Christine. *A New History of Ireland*. Gloucestershire: Sutton, 2004.

Macintyre, Angus. *The Liberator: Daniel O'Connell and the Irish Party 1830–1847*. New York: Macmillan, 1965.

Melville, Joy. *Mother of Oscar: The Life of Jane Francesca Wilde*. London: John Murray, 1999 (first pub. 1994).

Mitchel, John. *An Ulsterman for Ireland, being letters to the Protestant farmers, labourers and artisans of the North of Ireland* (with a foreword by Eoin MacNeill). Dublin: Candle Press, 1917.

Mitchel, John. *Jail Journal* (1854). Dublin: University Press of Ireland, 1982. [The *Journal* was originally published in 1854 in Mitchel's paper *The Citizen*; this is a facsimile version of the 1913 edition, with a critical introduction by Thomas Flanagan.]

Morash, Christopher (ed.). *The Hungry Voice*. Dublin: Irish Academic Press, 1989.

Ó Gráda, Cormac. *Ireland before and after the Famine: Explorations in Economic History, 1800–1925*. Manchester: Manchester University Press, 1993.

Ó Gráda, Cormac. 'The Great Famine and today's famines', in Cathal Póirtéir (ed.), *The Great Irish Famine*. Cork and Dublin: Mercier Press in association with Radio Telefis Éireann, 1995, pp.248–58.

Póirtéir, Cathal (ed.). *The Great Irish Famine*. Cork and Dublin: Mercier Press in association with Radio Telefis Éireann, 1995.

Senior, Nassau W. *Ireland: Journals, Conversations and Essays*. London: John Murray, 1868, Vol.1.

Thirteenth Annual Report of Poor Law Commissioners. Dublin: Thoms, 1847.

Whelan, Irene. 'The stigma of souperism', in Cathal Póirtéir (ed.), *The Great Irish Famine*. Cork and Dublin: Mercier Press in association with Radio Telefis Éireann, 1995, pp.135–54.

Lady Wilde [Speranza]. *Ancient Legends, Mystic Charms and Superstitions of Ireland*. Dublin: Ward & Downey, 1887.

Lady Wilde [Speranza]. *Ancient Cures, Charms and Superstitions of Ireland*. Dublin: Ward & Downey, Dublin, 1890.

Williams, Leslie A. *Daniel O'Connell, The British Press and the Irish Famine: Killing Remarks*. Aldershot: Ashgate. 2003.

Yeats, W.B. *Autobiography of W. B. Yeats*. New York: Collier, 1965.

CHAPTER 2

The *caoineadh* in Famine poetry:
a communal expression of defiance

Katherine Parr

In mid-nineteenth-century Ireland, two young women poets captured the hearts and minds of Irish readers. Ellen Mary Downing and Mary Anne Kelly were only in their teens when they began to write for Thomas Davis's political and literary journal the *Nation*, yet their contributions during the Famine became especially poignant expressions of despair, reflecting the consciousness of both those who observed Famine events and those who experienced them directly. Recognized today primarily for political and inflammatory rhetoric, Downing and Kelly served the readers of the *Nation* in several important aspects and established themselves as important social and poetic voices in the emerging republic. Certainly, their voices were important in the call to action against colonial rule, but they also wrote romantic verses delineating Ireland's landscape and memorializing its mythical heroes. Furthermore, they served the cause of women's rights in Ireland, writing both poems and articles that demanded equality for women. At times, they served as confidantes to their readers, reassuring their admirers in affairs of the heart. Yet during the Famine, they became spokespersons for the underclass, the peasants and tenant farmers on whom the worst of famine horrors descended.

Downing and Kelly wrote the Famine *caoineadh*, the legendary lament for the dead and were among only a few poets who applied this ancient Celtic lament to the Famine.[1] These lament poems did more than mourn the dead or vilify the agents of disease and starvation; through their speakers, the poets' voices undertook the role of the keening woman who rents the air with her cries, draws others into a protective circle around the dead, and performs a death ritual as old as time. These speakers represent the *bean chaointe* or tragic actress of the *caoineadh* as described by Angela Bourke (2002, p.1365). The women who performed the keening ritual, according to Bourke, would 'experience disturbing emotions to the full

[providing] a catharsis for everyone who witnessed her performance. [. . .]
In her self–presentation she acts out the disorder brought about by death'
(1993, p.165).

In presenting the following discussion of the *caoineadh* as written by
Downing and Kelly, I hope to raise awareness of the loss of these women
as major nineteenth-century Irish poets and to argue that not only did
they serve their readers as interpretive voices during the Famine, but that
they also indirectly hold influence for today's women poets. In *Object
Lessons*, Eavan Boland expressed her longing for the voice of a woman
who had also faced the blank page after attending to the day's chores,
women's chores (1995, p.xvi). In addition, Nuala Ni Dhomhnaill decries
the suggestion that Irish women poets have 'a long and healthy chain of
foremothers' upon whom modern poets can rely (1996, pp.8–9). Hence,
today's poets note that the poetic history of Irish women is flawed and that
what is needed is a topography in which they and other Irish women can
find their identities, as poets and as participants in the body politic.

The erasure of Downing and Kelly from the canon over which they
held sway for half a century has led to a discernable gap in the history of
Irish women's poetry, yet we know that their presence was keenly felt
on Ireland's literary scene throughout the second half of the nineteenth
century and into the twentieth. Two turn-of-the-century Irish literary
anthologies illustrate the importance of their work: M'Carthy's *Irish
Literature* and O'Connor's *Cabinet of Irish Literature*. Yet despite efforts
to examine the poetry by Maria Luddy, Spurgeon Thompson, Jan
Cannavan, Maria Pilar Pulido and Marjorie Howes, the *Nation's* women
poets remain marginalized in Irish studies.[2] The danger of such mar-
ginalization has been considered by Margaret Kelleher who recognizes
that the recovery effort of Irish women's writing, which gained momen-
tum in the late twentieth century, is in peril. In 'Writing Irish Women's
Literary History', she states, 'One especially worrying trend is the
reluctance by institutions, most notably universities, to resource a
consolidation of current research . . . As argued earlier, discontinuities lead
all too often to erasure' (p.11).

To the detriment of Irish studies, scholarly investment in both the
personal histories and the work of Downing and Kelly has been limited by
a process that once devalued, and perhaps still does devalue, women's
writing, mistaking it as overly emotive and worthless. Hence, silence
surrounding these nineteenth-century women poets should come as no
surprise. Talented women also disappeared from English and American

Literature, and in twentieth-century Ireland, the emerging Irish canon also dismissed the voices of women poets.

When Downing and Kelly included in their Famine poetry the *caoineadh*, however, they undertook one chore designated to women, the legendary lament for the dead. Close to their native roots, Downing in Cork and Kelly in Galway, these women responded to the failure of the potato crop and the resulting disease and emigration that marked four years of Irish history. As avid readers of, and contributors to, nationalist newspapers, the young poets took to heart the accounts of the Famine and its ravaging effects, which became regular reading in both the Irish and the English presses. In 1847, the *Nation* had begun a special section devoted to Famine accounts, 'State of the Country'. From a reporter in Cork, the following, horrific depiction appeared:

> In one day eight dead bodies were removed from the workhouse to their last tenement, and of each preceding day of this week, a similar, if not a greater number, have left that abode dead . . . Yesterday evening, about five o'clock, a woman with six of the most miserable and ragged children I ever saw, all crying at the same time, came and beseeched me, for the Mother of Mercy, for something to appease their hunger. Since the Wednesday morning previous those six children and herself had divided between them one penny-worth of bread . . . She is since, I am informed, numbered among the dead. (Ibid., p.262)

In the same column a report from Galway described the number of deaths from starvation, 'the dead buried without ceremony of a funeral, and frequently without the covering of a coffin'. Yet another report in the *Dublin Medical Press*, by Dr Daniel Donovan, described an abominable scene: 'I have seen mothers snatch food from the hands of their starving children; known a son to engage in a fatal struggle with his father for a potato; and have seen parents look upon the putrid bodies of their starving offspring without evincing a symptom of sorrow' (quoted in Kelleher, 1997, p.24).

Having established themselves as major poets for the *Nation*, both Downing and Kelly responded to scenes of suffering and death with the *caoineadh*, which Angela Bourke identifies as an early 'feminist utterance' dating to the time of ancient Greece, an 'art in which women collaborated with other women . . . remembering and quoting each other's laments, often over many generations' (Bourke, 1993, p.163). Likewise, the lament poems written by Downing and Kelly engaged the women poets in a ritualized practice that tied them to those women who most acutely experienced the Famine and protested the instruments of famine, which they believed to have issued from England. This is not to say that the lament poems penned by Downing and Kelly duplicate exactly the traditional Irish form; the *caoineadh* recorded and preserved in the oral tradition, such as 'The Lament for Art O'Leary', are much longer than those written by our poets.[3] The familiarity of these young poets with the tradition most probably came secondhand, through lore and descriptions of the ritual, so theirs should be regarded as attempts to revive an oral tradition that by the 1840s was nearly extinct in Ireland. Bourke explains that as early as 1670, the Catholic clergy threatened practitioners with excommunication, and priests were forbidden 'to take part in funerals where the "heathenish" and "savage" custom was practiced' (1993, p.161). By the time of the Famine, the *caoineadh* was scarcely performed.

Nevertheless, as poets of the lament, Downing and Kelly were, according to Bourke, 'grief therapists, as well as inciters of public outrage' (2002, p.1366). As national poets, they spoke to the victims of famine and against the forces that perpetuated its effects. Their famine poems reflect Bourke's description of 'a traditional "theater of death", the ritual of the wake and funeral, over which certain skilled women presided and through which the entire community adjusted to death and loss' (Bourke, 1993, p.163).

Ellen Mary Downing: 'Mary of the *Nation*'

Ellen Mary Patrick Downing was born in Cork to a family devoted to the care of the suffering. Her father was the resident medical officer at the Cork Fever Hospital and her mother served as its matron. The Downings were Roman Catholic, and they saw to the care and education of their daughter, both religious and intellectual. At the tender age of sixteen, Downing contributed her first of 40 poems, written between 1845 and 1848, to the *Nation*. 'Song' appeared on 10 May 1845, signed with the pseudonym 'Kate' (Markham, n.d. p.5; O'Sullivan, 1944, p.117). Her second poem, 'Verses for My Own Nannie', about childhood dreams of fairies and mermaids, illustrated the importance of Ireland's folk tales as inspiration for the young poet. Downing continued to rely on myth and legend in her years as a national poet until the failure of the Young Ireland rebellion in 1848. Then, she suffered a breakdown, abandoned writing nationalist songs, and entered the convent where she began writing children's and religious verse. In 1869, she died of a congenital affliction, little understood today, yet she is remembered by the good sisters of Cork's North Presentation Convent who remind us that her verses appear today in mass hymnals.[4]

Downing's 'A Lament' appeared in early December of 1846 and bears a prescience that anticipated later reports of Famine deaths at Skibbereen. Although the poem does not allude to early mortality associated with the Famine, its timing coincides with its eruption and must be read as an early Famine poem. Downing chose as her speaker for the poem a mourner who has witnessed the death of a spouse, suggesting aspects of the ritual *caoine*. It opens with the traditional address to the deceased, then follows with passages that praise the deceased in life, punctuated at regular intervals with 'the wailing cries' of the *caoineadh* (O'Tuama, 1995, p.82):

Good bye, good bye at last – I thought it was not true –
I never till this moment felt what 'twas to part from you;
Your love so strong and patient, which clasped me round and round,
Till a shelter and a home in your true heart I found;
Your care so fond and watchful, you life's first bloom
Your youth and your beauty – are they all in the tomb?

Good bye, good bye at last – why do I live,
The last look to take, the last kiss to give!
Weak, sad and lonely; I live all in vain –
Oh! take the breath from out me and raise him up again.
Where shall I go now? What shall I do?
Sense is not in me since parted from you –
You bore with me, and strengthened me, and were my all below,
My life was bound up in you. Why did you go?

Why did you go on Heaven's blessed shore,
You who loved me so much, will you never miss me more?
You who loved me so well, will you never wish to be
Back on the dark earth to comfort me?
Wild are my words, and selfish my prayer;
I don't wish you back if you're happier there;
But sure you won't forget, in that country of delight,
To think upon the lonely heart that breaks for you tonight?

Why did you die, then – why did you die?
There was strength in your soul, light in your eye.
The pride of life was in you: I thought you could not go,
And never loved you half enough while you were here below.

Oh! would you but rise up again, I'd pay you back the debt –
You'd be adored and cherished as man was never yet.
Look on me – speak to me – worlds I would resign
For the least breath from out those dear lips of thine.

Stern to my prayer – cold to my touch –
What is this death that has changed you so much?
Wake, wake, my darling, 'tis bitter to go down
Into the damp ground alone – alone.
No friend is before you a welcome to give –
I was your only one. Why do I live?
How long, oh! how long, will the dark night be
Till the grave where they lay you is opened for me?

The very form denotes the ebb and flow of uncontained emotion, and as a woman's lament, it reflects what Isobel Armstrong has observed about other women's lament poetry: It 'presents itself as *flow*, as unmediated secretion of feeling naturalized as effusion' (Armstrong, 1999, p.16). Visually, the poem flows over its boundaries while linguistically the lines read like prose, ending with rhymes. The emotive lines of the lament remain unchecked by meter and rhyme. Instead, they swell with grief and are restrained only by questions of desperation.

One linguistic trait suggesting the flow of emotions appears in Downing's use of pronouns that move the perspective of the reader from narrator to the object of her lament, back and forth again. The movement marks the turbulence of emotional outburst, its resistance to death followed by resignation. Imagery also supports the ebb and flow of emotion incited by desire and loss. The poet juxtaposes images of desire, marital bliss, with those of loss, the burial: the shelter of a home contrasts with the tomb in the first stanza while the stability of life is disrupted by death. In the second stanza, the darkness of the world contrasts with 'Heaven . . . that country of delight'. Ultimately, the fourth stanza attests to the lamenter's realization that not having loved enough in life generates guilt in death: 'And never loved you half enough while you were here below'. The movement represented in the language of the lament underscores the mourner's confusion; desire is 'here' but the object of that desire is 'below'. Moreover, the mourner stands above the corpse while both stand metaphysically below heaven and the Almighty's judgement. The result is the experience of death rocked by disorientation.

In Downing's lament, repeated questions underscore confusion in the mourner. The parallelism of the third stanza emphasizes her inability to comprehend the death of her beloved: 'You who loved me so much, will you never miss me more?/You who loved me so well, will you never wish to be/ Back on the dark earth to comfort me?' She prays for the restoration of the desired object, yet the answer to the prayer makes it more hopeless and the speaker more helpless. Furthermore, the speaker attempts to bargain with death, 'Wake, wake, my darling, /'tis bitter to go down/ Into the damp ground alone – alone./ No friend is before you a welcome to give –/I was your only one.' Death, whether sudden or prolonged, is always traumatic and violently disruptive, and grieving becomes a dynamic process. As Bourke remarks about the *caoineadh*, the poem represents what modern psychologists identify as stages of grief, including denial and bargaining for the return of the beloved (Bourke, 2002, p.1366).

Thus, Downing's poem provides the modern reader with insight into the Famine experience within a population that was at the time being decimated by famine and emigration. Familiar themes of loss and isolation describe the unbearably difficult survival of those who escaped famine death and those who were left in Ireland after family members emigrated. In February of 1847, Downing reintroduced the keen with 'Erin Aroon' (Ireland Together). The song mourns Ireland's losses and signifies that it is a *caoineadh* for the nation. Its speaker voices what so many God-fearing Irish must have wondered: Was the Famine apocalyptic, God's punishment for unrepented sins? 'May be our secret sins, Erin Aroon,/ Prolong your sufferings, Erin Aroon' (ll.11–12). This religious perspective reflected nineteenth-century Protestant millenarianism which Morash recognizes as influential on Young Ireland poets in anticipating a utopian state for Ireland. Images of apocalypse also factored in the role of religious institutions in Famine Ireland as used by both Protestant and Catholic clergy in their attempts to shepherd the souls of the Irish peasantry into their churches (Bowen, 1978, pp.185–9).

Among the last of Downing's poems for 1847 is 'Night Watching', which foreshadowed her break with the *Nation's* editor, Charles Gavan Duffy, and the failure of the Young Ireland rebellion, which resulted in the deportation of many republican activists. As winter gripped Ireland, bringing deeper starvation and more disease, it also forshadowed Downing's own psychological breakdown, and thus the poet fulfills the role of the *bean choainte* in her 'willingness to experience disturbing emotions to the full' (Bourke, 1993, p.165):

Good night, good night, acushla machree,
Dark is the night which is setting for me,
And my tears that are falling so quietly
          Will gush in a torrent soon.
There is no one beside me to cheer to-night,
No one to tell me God's will is right –
But I know 'tis a deadly sin to fright
          The soul which is going to Him.
So I hold my peace, and in murmurs low,
Till none could guess I am grieving so,
To Him and his angels I tell my woe –
          And pray for the soul departing.
He was my all in the world below
No other friend did I seek or know,
But I will not grudge him to heaven now
          Since 'tis God's high will to take him.
Long, long, the dark night seems to stay,
Yet more I dread the morning gray,
For the weakening breath will have chid away
          Ere its full rays brighten round him.
He will not bid me cease my moan;
My sorrow now must be all my own,
My darkest grief I must bear alone,
          Astor machree, you're going.
I will watch no more with longing ear
The fall of your proud light foot to hear,
When our quiet home you are drawing near,
          Oh! – dark 'twill be without you.
I will thrill no more to your words so fond,
Nor proudly think how a fairy's wand
Could never bring me a joy beyond
          The bliss of being near you.
I will hold my head less lofty now,
When you are laid in the churchyard low –
Too much I gloried long ago
          In the happy lot God gave me.
Nor more for me is the laugh and sun:
But still as the darkening night comes on,
The neighbours will see me creep along

> To the cold ground where you're lying.
> And they'll tell the young how my heart beat high,
> And the flashing joy was in mine eye,
> And small thought of care or death had I
> When first we two were plighted.

The resignation voiced in the poem is absolute. As life slips away, the speaker prepares for the inevitable, yet the poem's restraint of emotion suggests the force of what will follow, the release of such restraint in the keening wail. Whereas the verses recount the death of a beloved, an experience enacted daily in Ireland's countryside where women buried their spouses, their parents and their children, the lines also suggest the 'rocking or swaying of the lamenter's body . . . as a way of altering her consciousness: of tuning in to particular areas of emotion, memory and experience' (Bourke, 2002, p.1366).

At the time of the poem's publication, John Mitchel, Duffy's co-editor, was about to leave the *Nation*, fed up with Duffy's and Young Ireland's reluctance to confront the atrocity. He believed that the Famine was intentionally orchestrated and intended as genocide, a colonial programme of depopulating the country and regaining land for the Crown. Downing followed Mitchel to the *United Irishman*. Her biographer later explained her reasoning: 'Duffy was cautious and compromising, and the *Nation* reflected his temperament . . . The severance with her "old friend and teacher", as she styled Gavan Duffy, acutely pained her. But her aid went to where her conscience directed' (Markham, n.d., p.10).

'Night Watching' reflects dark times for Downing, Young Ireland and the country. More deeply, it reveals the poet's unwavering belief in the nationalist cause and the emotional burden she carried as the *bean choainte* for a nation in Famine.

Mary Kelly: 'Eva of the *Nation*'

In 1908, Mary Kelly O'Doherty was asked to compose her memoirs of Young Ireland. Kelly began her notes with the following description:

> It is called memory town, a quaint but interesting old ruin. But which they aver is still rich in relics of a treasured past. Gold and jewels they say lie hidden in these crumbling walls. Who so treads these sad and silent streets will find indeed, nought but ruin and wreck.
>
> (O'Doherty Notebook)

Living in Australia, far from her nurturing family and with her daughter, her only surviving child, the poet known as 'Eva of the *Nation*' struggled with the memories of pre-Famine Dublin. She wrote, 'A number of antiquarian friends [are] still strangely interested in the past of that ruined city. I believe I am the only survivor. You want me to go back there to view the ruin of the city in which I once dwelt when it was the city beautiful' (O'Doherty Notebook). Thus, Kelly painted her own portrait as the emblematic *bean choainte*, the remaining witness left to keen the past. She had lived through the Famine, endured separation from her deported fiancé, Kevin O'Doherty, and when they were reunited, she emigrated with him to Australia, leaving a close and supportive family in Galway. Half way around the world from her childhood home, she continued to experience loss; she had buried her husband and her three sons.

Kelly first submitted poems to the *Nation* under the pseudonym 'Fionnuala'. The first was 'The Leprechuan', which appeared on 26 December 1844. A child's poem, it describes the legendary Irish creature who hides his gold so coveted by humans. That poem was followed in April 1845 by 'The Irish Mother. A Story of '98', commemorating the 1798 uprising, and it has recently resurfaced in two efforts to revive the work of this important poet. Maria Luddy reproduces a revised version of the poem taken from the 1909 collection of Kelly's poems. Additionally, Spurgeon Thompson offers an analysis of the same poem, citing its importance as 'anti-colonial propaganda' and as a subversive text demonstrating Kelly's deliberate choice 'to write in an implicitly anti-sexist fashion' (Thompson, 1997, p.103). This observation that Kelly wrote subversive texts fits with Bourke's description of the *bean choainte*. Bourke writes that the *caoineadh* often contained subversive, coded or subdued messages that were unintelligible to the audience outside the keening circle of women. Whereas most verses would have been flattering and reassuring, detailing personal relationships of the deceased, others were scathing and vindictive, addressing wrongs done either to or by the deceased. These 'subversive messages' were muffled by sounds of wailing and clapping that accompanied the performance (Bourke, 1993, p.167).

Published in 1848, Kelly's poem 'No More' reflects many of the characteristics of the keen that appear in Downing's laments, yet Kelly's poem addresses a different kind of loss – not death but exile. A second by-product of the Famine was emigration, sometimes forced. Those who escaped, either voluntarily or involuntarily, left behind loved ones to mourn. While 1 million are estimated to have perished from famine and its disease, another million left Ireland. Some received passage from their landlords who found sea fares cheaper that maintaining a hungry family (Laxton, 1996, pp.74–5n). Others were deported for insurrection and treasonous activities. In 'No More', the speaker has no object, no corpse to regard. Utilizing nature's imagery, Kelly's lament applies contrastive images of loss and hope that establish the tension of the lament. The sensory images of sight served Kelly as vehicles to juxtapose life and loss. The form of the poem suggests the *caoineadh*, although it does not carry the traditional address to the deceased. Instead, the poem represents the repeated cry or wail that accompanies the lament:

> I watch the dead leaf fluttering, and I watch the sunset sky;
> But, if I watch'd from morn till eve, I never see you nigh;
> Oh, no! oh, no! – if I look'd for aye,
> I'll never see you in the night or day.
>
> I'll see the river winding by, and I'll see the mountains tall,
> And the lonely glen where the trees are dim and the
> wavering shadows fall;
> But while rivers run and while green leaves grow,
> I'll never see you again, I know.
>
> I'll look o'er heath, and hill, and moor, on the still
> skies and streams,
> Wav'ring before my longing eyes like a silent dance of dreams;
> But long and weary my watch will be
> Before a glimpse of your face I'll see.
>
> Years on years are gliding on – and there thro' the livelong day,
> With dimming sight I muse alone till my gold locks turn to gray;
> But no! oh no! look while I will,
> In no place but my heart will I find you still!

Each verse ends with the characteristic wail. Further, Kelly's use of a consistent point of view, the first person, emphasizes the isolation of the lamenter, she has no visible object to keen. Whereas staggered lines create a visual sense of emotional turbulence, end rhymes mark the scansion, and the final lines of each stanza punctuate the emotional outburst in a series of elongated vowels. Thus, both form and language emphasize the disorientation of the mourner.

Points of vision add to panic brought on by the speaker's grief. As the poem's perspective moves from leaf to sunset, from winding river to tall mountains, then back to a lonely glen, the reader senses disorientation within the constancy of nature. Hope tantalizes desire, and nature seems to tease the narrator with serene images while the emotional strain sends her into a dizzying recognition that psychic space will never again find equilibrium. Isobel Armstrong notes similar effects in her study of Victorian lament poetry, '[I]t aspires to a psychological language bordered on the one hand by somatic and on the other by psychic experience, oscillating between the body and the ethereal, both dematerialized and literal' (Armstrong, 1999, p.17). The poem subverts the certainty of perception, undermining and exaggerating the psychological imbalance that accompanies immeasurable loss and borders on madness. Whereas the mourner in Downing's 'A Lament' has the gravesite for a point of reference, providing some degree of stability, Kelly's mourner cannot even imagine that which she desires. She is left with no context for her loss. Thus Kelly's speaker enacts the role of the *bean choainte*. She leads the community of her readers in an 'oral performance' demonstrating the 'emotional experience of loss'. Thus the poet, like the actress of the keen, 'provided a catharsis for everyone who witnessed her performance', according to Bourke (1993, p.165).

Additionally, Kelly's lament becomes subversive in that it rejects romantic imagery adopted by Young Ireland poets. The poem refuses poetic figures of speech. The dead leaf flutters literally; no comparison to the heart nor to sight occurs. Neither do the objects of nature serve metonymically; they are real boundaries, not symbolic images. Because they lack the impetus of symbology, nature's objects exaggerate the emptiness of the landscape. If Nature were to gaze at this poet-narrator, she would do so dumbly, impassively. The poem becomes more disturbing because Nature, so often portrayed as an active force, does not act – she provides no comfort, no reassurance. Neither does Nature shake the subject from her reverie; she is ultimately indifferent.

A second lament poem by Kelly indicates her deliberate intent to write the *caoineadh*; she chose as its title 'A Caoine':

Gone, gone from me, and from the earth and from the Summer sky;
And all the bright, wild hope and love that swelled so proud and high;
And all this heart had stored for thee within its endless deep –
With me – with me, o! nevermore thoul't smile or joy or weep!

There are gold nails on your coffin; there are snowy plumes bove;
They pour their pomp and honours there, but I this woe and love –
The hopeless woe, the longing love, that turn from earth away,
And pray for refuge and a home within the silent clay!
Come, wild deer of the mountain side! Come, sweet bird of the plain!
To cheer the cold and trembling heart that beats for you in vain!
Oh! Come, from woe, and cold, and gloom, to her that's warm and true,
And has no hope or throb for aught within this world but you!
To the sad winds I have scattered the treasures of my soul –
The sorrow that no tongue could speak, or mortal power control –
And wept the weary night and day, until my heart was sore,
And every germ of peace and joy was withered at its core.
In vain, in vain, this yearning cry – this dark and deep despair!
I droop alone and trembling here, and thou art lying there.
But though thy smile upon the earth I never more may see,
And thou will never come to me – yet I may fly to thee!
I never stood within your home – I do not bear your name –
Life parted us for many a day, but Death now seals my claim,
In darkness, silence, and decay, and here at last alone,
You're but more truly bound to me – my darling and my own!

Central to this poem is the image of the fallen hero whose coffin is adorned with gold nails and processional plumes. Hence, an interpretation must hinge on the relationship between the woman who speaks the lament and the deceased. In such a reading, the fallen hero might represent the Young Ireland rebellion of 1848 that scattered the leaders of that political organization, sending them into exile. It was a bloodless rebellion, yet by crushing it, the colonial government sealed the hope of Irish republicans. Thus, the land becomes the female speaker who keens for her lost hero. Margaret Kelleher's observation that famine and the feminine image are inextricably linked in Famine literature suggests this interpretation. In *The Feminisation of Famine*, Kelleher explains,

> Feminist critics such as Alice Jardine and Jacqueline Rose have drawn attention to the frequency with which 'the unspeakable' is characterized as female; again and again, images of women are used to figure moments of breakdown or crisis – in social body, in political authority, or in representation itself.
>
> (1997, p.6)

Yet this may be too simple an interpretation. Kelly as the poet of the keen iterates her participation in protest. Since her first contribution to the *Nation*, Kelly had voiced opposition to the political and social abuses of colonization. Her poetry and her prose contributions to anti-establishment presses bore common themes. She spoke for the cause of a free state and in defence of those most miserably affected by colonial rule, the dependent farmers.

In the aftermath of the Famine, Kelly reintroduced rebellious themes. In January of 1850, her poem 'Implora Pace' details the disruptive force of the previous four years and implores heaven to bring stability back to the land. She followed that with 'Edom' adding to its title the biblical verse, 'And Edom shall be desolate; every one that shall pass by it, shall be astonished and shall hiss at its plagues'.[5] The allusion points us to the devastation of the Famine and indicts the colonizer that maintained its grip on Ireland. 'Progress' ran in May and urged revival of the Irish cause for nationhood. Since 'A Caoine' appeared in July, its purpose becomes more clear within the context of the poet's other works. The object of the lament is not simply Young Ireland, its members having been scattered after the 1848 rebellion. The deceased becomes the embodiment of the republican cause. While the speaker retains her image as Eire, she mourns the dream that dissipated with half the inhabitants of the land. She laments, 'And all the bright, wild hope and love that swelled so proud and high/And all this heart had stored for thee within its endless deep – /With me – with me, o! nevermore thoul't smile or joy or weep!' The hope for freedom and self-rule lies on the catafalque. Further evidence of the poet's intent lies in the line, 'To the sad winds I have scattered the treasures of my soul'. These treasures suggest those who fled from famine death and disease, as well as those convicted of the insurrection of 1848. The 'sorrow that no tongue could speak' invokes the unspeakable horrors of the preceding years when, like the blighted potato, 'every germ of peace and joy was withered at its core'. Finally, the speaker laments that she never stood within the 'home' – a metaphor for Home Rule; hence, she does not 'bear' the 'name' of republic. Her 'claim' to freedom is instead sealed by the instrument of colonialism, 'Death'.

In this interpretation, Kelly would have intended to represent the land as the victimized woman, an allegory typical in Famine literature, but to read it as reflecting a moment of weakness misjudges the poet. Instead, the reading presented here corresponds with themes of rebellion and defiance, written by Downing and Kelly, and places Kelly's 'A Caoine' within the bounds of Angela Bourke's examination of the *caoineadh* as a feminist expression. In grief, the poet speaks against authority; she undermines the simplified reading of her lament with allusions to a larger tragedy, coding her message to make a political point (Bourke, 2002, p.1367).

In this reading of the poem, one recognizes a final characteristic of the *caoineadh*, sublimated anger, and its subversive quality, the coded challenge to authority (Bourke, 1993, p.161). By recalling Ireland's loss, Kelly reasserts her call for rebellion. The ending of the poem suggests this ironically, 'and here at last alone,/You're but more truly bound to me – my darling and my own!' The line becomes a statement of resolve for the nation to hold dearly to the ideals represented by the Young Ireland rebellion.

Conclusion

Recent discussions of Young Ireland have nullified its poetry and most of its poets. Whereas Seamus Deane calls the poets 'occasional', and Sean Ryder sees them as *bourgeois*, such sweeping judgements deter scholarship that looks at Kelly and Downing individually and at their poems collectively (Deane, 1991, p.2; Ryder, 1996, p.161). We have only bits of the poetry penned by Downing and Kelly, yet what has been written about their work by Luddy, Thompson and others indicates that these women poets are worthwhile subjects for Irish studies. In terms of their lament poems, the poets demonstrate 'an assertion of personal freedom' that Bourke finds expressed by the artist of the *caoineadh* poetry:

> But the *caoineadh* was always at least potentially an assertion of personal freedom. The texts that survive howl in protest and anger at death and at injustice in the world of the living, and they frequently challenge prestigious persons and institutions. Although *caoineadh* was a communal, public activity, all our examples represent the voices of individual women. None of them can be construed as passively accepting of the inevitable – such an interpretation can only have been gathered from the uncomprehending descriptions of unsympathetic colonists who witnessed the Irish *caoineadh* in performance but could not understand the words being spoken.
>
> (1997, pp.144–5)

Hence, in the tradition of the *caoineadh*, Kelly and Downing rejected the passive images of the Famine feminized and instead presented for their readers another image, one of angry defiance. When Marjorie Howes reads Kelly's 'A Scene for Ireland' as belonging to 'a literature of Irish misery [that] still equated weeping with helplessness' (quoted in Morash, 1989, p.61), her interpretation lacks the context of Kelly's work (Howes, 1998, p.157). In that poem, a famished woman with her starving baby 'has no food to give it now/Save those hot tears outgushing' (quoted in ibid., p.157). The scene in the poem, however, is juxtaposed with that of an image of Queen Victoria, 'Far, far away, with pearls and gold/ My lady's hair is gleaming;/ For every gem our eyes behold/ A crimson drop in streaming!' (quoted in Morash, 1989, p.61). This is most certainly a challenge to the British Crown. Whereas, the 'hot tears' can be read at one level as feverish, Kelly might also have intended another usage: hot tears of anger that fed the survivors of the Famine, fuelling further the rebellion against colonial rule. It is that image that most characterizes Kelly's writing, inflammatory by intent. As for Downing, who had taken the veil and renounced her fiery expressions against the Crown, she nevertheless wrote a poem that she titled 'England', in which the speaker prays for the repose of her enemy's soul, yet admonishes its policy makers:

> The wail of *our* orphans may plaintively rise,
> There's a Mother that hears it far up in the skies, –
> But where shall *thy* nurse and thy comfortress be,
> If the kind hands of Mary be tied up by thee?
>
> (Downing, 1881, pp.194–5)

Prior to her convent life, Downing had written to a friend, 'If I get toothaches here, it is through means of those English, clenching my teeth when I think of them, and look at the country they have darkened' (Leahy, 1881, p.xiii). Even if she had forgiven, she would never 'Forget old wrongs', the opening line of her first submission to the *Nation* ('Song').

References

Armstrong, Isobel. 'Misrepresentations: codes of affect and politics in nineteenth-century women's poetry', in Isobel Armstrong and Virginia Blain (eds), *Women's Poetry, Late Romantic to Late Victorian: Gender and Genre, 1830–1900*. New York: St Martin's Press, 1999.

Boland, Eavan. *Object Lessons: The Life of the Woman and the Poet in Our Time*. New York: W.W. Norton, 1995.

Bourke, Angela. 'More in anger than in sorrow: Irish women's lament poetry', in Joan Newlon Radner (ed.), *Feminist Messages*. Urbana, IL: University of Illinois Press, 1993, pp.160–82.

Bourke, Angela. 'Performing, not writing: the reception of an Irish woman's lament', in Yopie Prins and Maeera Shreiber (eds), *Dwelling in Possibility: Women Poets and Critics on Poetry*. Ithaca, NY: Cornell University Press, 1997, pp.132–46.

Bourke, Angela. 'Lamenting the Dead', *Field Day Anthology of Irish Writing*, Vol.4. *Irish Women's Writing and Traditions*. Angela Bourke *et al.* (eds). New York: New York University Press, 2002, pp.1365–7.

Bowen, Desmond. *The Protestant Crusade in Ireland, 1800–70: A Study of Protestant–Catholic Relations Between the Act of Union and Disestablishment.* Dublin: Gill & Macmillan, 1978.

Cannavan, Jan. 'Romantic Revolutionary Irish Women: Women, Young Ireland and 1848', in Margaret Kelleher and James H. Murphy (eds), *Gender and Perspectives in Nineteenth-Century Ireland: Public and Private Spheres.* Dublin: Irish Academic Press, 1997.

Deane, Seamus. 'Poetry and Song 1800–1890', in Seamus Deane (ed.), *Field Day Anthology of Irish Writing*. Vol.2. Derry: Field Day, 1991.

Downing, Ellen Mary. 'Song', *Nation*. 10 May 1845, p.504.

Downing, Ellen Mary. 'A Lament', *Nation*, 5 December 1846, p.14.

Downing, Ellen Mary. 'Erin Aroon', *Nation*. 27 February 1847, p.31.

Downing, Ellen Mary. 'Night Watching', *Nation*, 20 November 1847, p.939.

Downing, Ellen Mary. 'England', *Voices from the Heart*. Dublin: M.H. Gill, 1881.

Howes, Marjorie. 'Tears and blood: Lady Wilde and the emergence of Irish cultural nationalism', in Tadhg Foley and Sean Ryder (eds), *Ideology and Ireland in the Nineteenth Century*. Dublin: Four Courts Press, 1998.

Kelleher, Margaret. *The Feminisation of Famine: Expressions of the Inexpressible?* Cork and Durham, NC: Cork University Press and Duke University Press, 1997.

Kelleher, Margaret. 'Writing Irish women's literary history', *Irish Sudies Review*, Vol.9, No.1 (2001), pp.5–14.

Kelly, Eva. 'The Leprechaun', *Nation*, 26 December 1844, p.203.

Kelly, Eva. 'The Irish Mother. A Story of '98', *Nation*, 12 April 1845, p.440.

Kelly, Eva. 'No More', *Nation*, 1 January 1848, p.11.

Kelly, Eva. 'Implora Pace', *Nation*, 5 January 1850, p.298.

Kelly, Eva. 'Edom', *Nation*, 19 January 1850, p.331.

Kelly, Eva. 'Progress', *Nation*, 11 May 1850, p.587.

Kelly, Eva. 'A Caoine', *Nation*, 13 July 1850, p.730.

Laxton, Edward. *The Famine Ships: The Irish Exodus to America*. London: Bloomsbury, 1996.

Leahy, Patrick. 'Preface', *Voices from the Heart*. Dublin: M.H. Gill & Son, 1881, pp.vii–xxi.

Luddy, Maria. 'An agenda for women's history in Ireland, 1500–1900, Part II', *Irish Historical Studies*, Vol.28, No.109 (1992), pp.19–37.

Markham, Thomas. *Ellen Mary Downing, 'Mary of the Nation'*, Dublin: Catholic Truth Society of Ireland, n.d.

M'Carthy, Justin. *Irish Literature*, Vol.10. Chicago, IL: DeBower-Elliott, 1904.

Morash, Christopher (ed.). *The Hungry Voice: The Poetry of the Irish Famine*. Dublin: Irish Academic Press, 1989.

Ni Dhomhnaill, Nuala. 'What foremothers?', in Theresa O'Connor (ed.), *The Comic Tradition in Irish Women Writers*. Gainesville, FL: University Press of Florida, 1996.

O'Connell, Eileen. 'The Lament for Art O'Leary', *Field Day Anthology of Irish Writing*. Vol.4. *Irish Women's Writing and Traditions*. Angela Bourke *et al.* (eds). New York: New York University Press, 2002.

O'Connor, T.P. (ed.). *The Cabinet of Irish Literature: Selections from the Works of the Chief Poets, Orators, and Prose Writers of Ireland*. Vol.IV. London: Blackie & Son, n.d.

O'Doherty, Eva. Notebook. OM 71–6, envelope 5. John Oxley Library, South Brisbane.

O'Sullivan, T.F. *The Young Irelanders*. Tralee: Kerryman, 1944.

O'Tuama, Sean. 'The Lament for Art O'Leary', in *Repossessions: Selected Essays on the Irish Literary Heritage*. Cork: Cork University Press, 1995, pp.78–100.

Pulido, Maria Pilar. 'The ballad history of Ireland: the poetic legacy of the Young Ireland Movement', in Susana Onega (ed.), *Telling Histories: Narrativizing History, Historicizing Literature*. Atlanta, GA: Rodopi, 1995, p.49.

Ryder, Sean. 'Reading lessons: famine and the *Nation*, 1845–1849', in Christopher Morash and Richard Hayes (eds), *Fearful Realities: New Perspectives on the Famine*. Dublin: Irish Academic Press, 1996.

'State of the Country', *Nation*, 30 January 1847, p.262.

Thompson, Spurgeon. 'Feminist recovery work and women's poetry in Ireland', *Irish Journal of Feminist Studies*, Vol.2, No.2 (1997) pp.94–105.

CHAPTER 3

'Philosophick views'?
Maria Edgeworth and the Great Famine[1]

Margaret Kelleher

Maria Edgeworth's writings have become the object of particular scrutiny in recent years. Yet Edgeworth remains a figure curiously difficult to categorize; enlightenment thinker *and* post-revolutionary novelist, she belongs both to eighteenth-and nineteenth-century literary culture, and her work may be read within regional, national and international contexts.[2] Recent critical studies have renewed interest in her Irish narratives, not alone in her most famous text, *Castle Rackrent*, where the 'sly civility'[3] of Thady Quirk continues to fascinate, but also in less well-known tales such as *Ennui* and *The Absentee*. The republication by Pandora Press of *Belinda*, *Patronage* and *Helen* provided access to other examples of Edgeworth's work, chiefly her English society tales; and the recently completed Pickering twelve-volume edition consolidates this extension of Edgeworth's *œuvre*.[4]

Accounts of Maria Edgeworth's writing life frequently mention one particular quotation, taken from a February 1834 letter written to her brother Michael Pakenham Edgeworth. These famous sentences, known as the looking-glass passage, warn her brother 'beforehand' that her recently completed novel *Helen* will not contain humour or Irish character. Edgeworth writes that

> [i]t is impossible to draw Ireland as she now is in a book of fiction – realities are too strong, party passions too violent to bear to see, or care to look at their faces in the looking-glass. The people would only break the glass, and curse the fool who held the mirror up to nature – distorted nature, in a fever.[5]

The popularity, and perceived relevance, of this extract for readers and critics in the late twentieth century seems easily explained; the passage is reproduced, for example, not only in studies of Edgeworth's work but also in general, and influential, cultural studies such as David Lloyd's *Anomalous*

States and Terry Eagleton's *Heathcliff and the Great Hunger*. For Lloyd the letter testifies to 'the remarkable consensus among writers of the 1830s as to the intractable difficulties presented by Irish social realities to novelistic representation'. Eagleton views the excerpt as the author's 'mournful' acknowledgment that 'the inherently contradictory unity known as Ireland' had 'finally passed beyond the frame of her representing'.[6]

The letter to Michael Pakenham, commenting on the state of Ireland, continues, however, with lines that are very rarely cited, but which look forward, beyond the historical moment, in suggestive ways:

> We are in too perilous a case to laugh, humour would be out of season, worse than bad taste. Whenever the danger is past, as the man in the sonnet says, 'We may look back on the hardest part and laugh.' Then I shall be ready to join in the laugh. Sir Walter Scott once said to me 'Do explain to the public why Pat, who gets forward so well in other countries, is so miserable in his own.' A very difficult question: I fear above my power. But I shall think of it continually, and listen, and look, and read.[7]

The exclusion of these lines is in turn symptomatic of a much more significant omission – that is, the scant attention paid to the last 15 years of Maria Edgeworth's life. It is still a surprise to many readers, students and teachers that Edgeworth did indeed live until May 1849. A review of Edgeworth criticism shows that late nineteenth-century biographies such as Grace Oliver's study (1882) pay significantly more attention to those years than many twentieth-century studies.[8] One reason for such critical neglect is obvious: with the exception – an interesting exception – of *Orlandino*, which appeared in 1848, Edgeworth did not publish any new fictional works after *Helen*. Thus commentators speak of the author's 'lapsing into silence' in the 1830s. Yet this description risks obscuring the many ways in which Edgeworth listened, looked, read and wrote in the years after 1834, evidenced most powerfully by her many letters to family members and friends, and also attested to by the many visitors to Edgeworthstown during the 1830s and 1840s.[9]

Edgeworth's extensive correspondence includes many letters written during the years of the Great Famine, from her home in Edgeworthstown in County Longford. As a famine source, the letters cast important light on the perspective of a member of the landholding class, resident in Ireland, whose opinions combined conservatism and enlightened reform,[10] revealing the deep challenges the famine posed to Edgeworth's philosophical views. The interactive nature of this correspondence, particularly where it involved friends and acquaintances resident outside Ireland, gives it an additional dimension lacking in other famine testimonies such as newspaper accounts or diaries.[11] While Edgeworth's comments on the famine share the concerns expressed by many fellow landowners – recognition of the need for relief to the poor, given this most 'perilous' and 'miserable' case, tempered by fears of the dangers of giving such relief – her meditations on charity and its operations have a special interest. As the correspondence documents, Edgeworth's status as an author of international renown gave her a unique position in lobbying for aid, a status which she fully exploited.

Edgeworth's many correspondents during the famine years ranged through family and friends.[12] As early as 1833 she was involved in written 'conversations' with Richard Jones, a prominent political economist and Malthus's successor as chair of political economy at the East India College in Haileybury.[13] Some of Edgeworth's most private, but most significant, meditations on the famine are to be found in her letters to Jones, whom she called 'the Voltaire of political economists'. Friends with whom Edgeworth corresponded at length on the subject of the famine also included Mrs Louisa Moore of Moore Hall, County Mayo,[14] and Harriet Cruger (born Harriet Douglas), an American woman who visited Edgeworthstown in 1827 and with whom Edgeworth continued to communicate.[15] Other correspondence was of a more official and immediate nature, such as that directed to the Society of Friends' Central Relief Committee in Dublin, specifically to members such as Dr Joshua Harvey, and Messrs Bewley and Pim.[16] Selections from some of these letters, together with extracts from letters addressed to family members such as Edgeworth's sisters, have appeared in print previously.[17] To date, many others, available in the manuscript collections of the Bodleian Library, Oxford, and the National Library, Dublin, remain uncirculated and undiscussed.

Edgeworth's Famine correspondence

The precise extent of distress in Edgeworthstown during the famine years is difficult to judge; yet the evidence from Maria Edgeworth's correspondence (and elsewhere) suggests that, although the area did not endure the worst extremities of famine experienced elsewhere, distress and suffering were considerable.[18] Edgeworth's own frustration at the difficulties of estimating general famine suffering is vividly expressed in a letter dated 8 May 1847 to her sister Honora Beaufort, who lived in London.[19]

I cannot answer your Admiral's question as to the amount of the deaths in
Ireland during the past bad days – and caused by the famine – I believe that
no one can make a just estimate – there are no means of forming a calculation
. . . the estimates and assertions made are so widely different, in such vast
extremes and in reality so incalculable that the men of the North cannot
believe the men of the South – the Leinster man cannot believe the
Connaught man's statement of the numbers that have perished or that have
been fed and saved in their different experience ... But two hundred and fifty
thousand deaths in the report made by the Police up to April.[20]

One estimate, provided by the Edgeworths' friend and Longford neighbour
Mr Tuite, suggested a 'third more deaths since the famine commenced in
his neighbourhood than the average number in ordinary times'; yet in
Maria's reckoning, using information from family and neighbours, average
deaths 'above the ordinary' in Edgeworthstown were 'not so much as a
third'.[21]

A questionnaire completed by Maria Edgeworth for the Society of
Friends' Dublin Central Relief Committee on 30 January 1847 provides
more detailed indications of the destitution present in Edgeworthstown.[22]
Of approximately 5,000 inhabitants, she notes, about 3,000 are in need of
public relief; 100 labourers find employment in the ordinary manner with
wages from eight to ten pence a day; and 400 labourers are employed in
the public works. Widows, children and old persons incapable of labour
she estimates as exceeding 500 persons. An application to the subcom-
mittee for clothing, returned by Edgeworth on 13 February 1847, attests
to the presence of 750 poor people wanting clothing in the district of
Edgeworthstown; in her words: 'about 500 *desperately* shiveringly cold in
this weather – Frost – Snow – Thermometer 20 at Edgeworthstown'.[23]

Maria Edgeworth gathered the above information for the Society of
Friends in Dublin mostly from family and neighbours – chiefly her stepmother Frances Edgeworth, from whom much of her daughter's understanding of the plight of tenants came – as well as from Edgeworthstown's
vicar John Powell and Powell's mother and sister. Edgeworth's answers to
the questions asked by the Central Relief Committee are strikingly brief,
even terse. One query concerned whether the earnings of the able-bodied
labourers 'in public works or otherwise' were 'sufficient to preserve
themselves and their families from want'. Edgeworth's reply has a ringing
tone: 'Certainly not in the present price of food.' To the lengthy question,
'In what Poor Law Union does the place lie? How far distant is the Poor
House and what spare accommodation does it at present afford?' the

answer reads: 'Longford – 7 miles – it is full.' Given the option of 'additional observation', Edgeworth states, '[t]he want of shoes is great and affects health and the power of labour, especially in draining work'.[24]

In subsequent letters to the Central Relief Committee, Edgeworth elaborates on the measures that have been taken to alleviate famine, including the sale of food at a reasonable rate to the poor, and indicates what she considers the best actions for the future.[25] What was to prove the central tenet of her famine philosophy – that the poor should work to help themselves as far as possible – is clearly expressed. More striking, and more rare, however, is her related argument that this doctrine be equally applied to poor women and girls. Writing to Dr Joshua Harvey, member of the Dublin Relief Committee, on 1 February, in a letter which accompanied the January questionnaire, she expands on this theme:

> We are particularly anxious to enable the poor to work for themselves, wherever health and strength permit, that they may preserve some sense of self respect, and some spirit of independence and industry. We find among the poorest women and children, even in their present distressed condition, sparks of this same principle of independence. A poor woman the other day in thanking our vicar for the assistance he gave in employing men and boys, according to the government arrangements, regretted that when so much was done for men, nothing has been thought of for women and children, who are, as she said, also willing to work, if they could be employed and paid, they would work to their utmost. If we could be aided by a small sum to buy materials and to pay for women's work, we would set them to such needle work, knitting &c as would be in some degree profitable in a pecuniary point of view, and in a much greater degree useful both now and hereafter in preventing them from losing the proper sense of shame, or becoming mere beggars and paupers, and sinking into idleness and consequent vice.[26]

The committee responded speedily to the information and request with a £30 grant toward increased distribution of soup and a grant of £10 for the 'especial project of promoting female employment'.[27]

Edgeworth's early letters to the committee in 1847 are humble, even subservient in tone; as the year progresses, and as she is strengthened by the arrival of subscriptions and support from abroad, the letters become much more insistent. In May she firmly reminds Messrs Bewley and Pim that she has been notified by her friend, Mr Everett, 'head of Cambridge university, Boston' (Harvard University), that 'great American subscriptions' have been remitted and that fresh supplies lie in Dublin.[28] Five months later, in October 1847, the Dublin committee received the following instruction from the Cincinnati Irish relief committee:

> We have had an intimation from a friend of Miss Edgeworth that she would be grateful to receive and distribute some portion of the charity of this country and we have concluded to send the small balance in our hands 180 dollars to her in cornmeal. If we conclude to consign this to your care, be [*sic*] beg to bespeak your kind offices in the matter. We feel this to be a compliment due to Miss Edgeworth, and which we have much pleasure in paying.[29]

In December, Edgeworth communicated to Bewley and Pim detailed instructions for the delivery of the cornmeal to her, 'without any trouble or expense on my part'.[30] By now her letters had come to earn, unsurprisingly, 'speedy' and, in her own words, 'most satisfactory' replies.[31]

Correspondence with the Society of Friends, as well as observations made more privately in letters to her family, show that Maria Edgeworth was a formidable lobbyist. Writing in April 1847 to her sister Harriet Butler in Trim, County Offaly, Edgeworth explains the strategy she has adopted on hearing that Australian funds have been directed to Dr Murray, as Archbishop of Dublin, and not, as it first appeared, to his Church of Ireland counterpart:

> I wrote to our Archbishop Whately, playing upon this graceless proceeding towards him, and to the best of my capacity without flattery, which is twice cursed in my opinion giving or receiving. I did what I could to make my letter honestly pleasing to His Grace, and I received the most prompt, polite, and to the point, reply, assuring me that the Australians were not so *graceless* in their doings as in their words, that they had made a remittance of a considerable sum to him (he did not say how much) and that if I apply to the Central Relief Committee, in whose hands he placed it, he has no doubt my application will be attended to.[32]

As the Ohio communication shows, Edgeworth's name alone had sufficient power to generate funds; and many other subscriptions, especially from the United States, were sent personally to her in Edgeworthstown. In letters written in July and December 1847 to her sister Emmeline King in England, she refers to 'the generosity of my American friends to me': 'the Ticknors, Everett and others who have sent me for our poor of Edgeworthstown at my own disposal such quantities of barrels of meal etc. as will turn into £150'.[33] Further American donations came from 'about thirty young people and children of Boston for me from their pocket money, some of the children so very young that they could only scribble their names, up and down crookedly'.[34]

Two less well-known episodes, relating to Edgeworth's lobbying for American aid, reveal some of its more complex, and occasionally bizarre, operations. In April 1847, news of the arrival of the Jamestown, an American sloop of war, to Cork, bringing foodstuffs and other goods to the value of over $40,000, prompted Edgeworth to write to its captain Robert Bennett Forbes with a specific request – one, she explained, which was 'encouraged in my mind by your being an American gentleman':

> I have many good friends in America who flatter me that though I am personally a stranger, yet my family name is known and popular with your young people still – and perhaps it was known to you of the present generation in your childhood?[35]

Edgeworth's request was the granting of free or low-cost passage to ten poor men and their families, or twenty or thirty single men – not a compulsory emigration but certainly an encouraged and aided one. On her discovery, having written the letter, that Forbes's stated policy was that 'the ship will not take back any emigrants', she continued in the letter's postscript to urge the captain to make 'a judicious exception'. The letter was received by Forbes only after his return, yet, curiously, in the published account of his voyage, the letter from Edgeworth is published as a type of foreword. The citing of Edgeworth's name alone, in association with the published narrative, seems the intended point rather than the content of the letter, which is, at the very least, irrelevant to the volume, if not contradictory to its project. In his accompanying note, Forbes explains that Edgeworth's letter has been included against his original intention and delivers the justification that 280 dollars and 100 barrels of supplies have since been sent from Boston to Edgeworthstown.[36]

A further episode concerning Edgeworth's role and status in raising famine funds may be traced in her correspondence with her friend Harriet Cruger of New York. On 8 February 1847, Cruger wrote to Edgeworth suggesting, on behalf of Jacob Harvey, a central figure in the New York Society of Friends, that she write a letter 'in her terse and offhand manner to the Ladies of America', since this, in his opinion, 'would do more good than anything else'.[37] By March, Edgeworth had replied, and her letter was circulated among certain 'ladies of America' and published in a

Boston newspaper. In addition, Edgeworth delivered a private reply to
Cruger, requesting a specific grant to the parish of Edgeworthstown from
the ladies' committee, thus, quite characteristically, availing herself of the
general opportunity to make a specific request for Edgeworthstown. To
her annoyance, however, this note did not receive a reply and was in turn
the subject of an angry letter to Cruger in May of 1847.[38] According to
Cruger, the May 1847 letter was received by her only in January 1849 due
to her travels abroad and also because of her 'over careful brother'.[39] Her
letter explaining this delay and including a subscription was not received
before Edgeworth's death.

A strange epilogue to this correspondence emerges with the printing of
a circular after Edgeworth's death for distribution in the United States.
The circular includes Cruger's February 1847 letter, Edgeworth's angry
letter of May, a note referring to the novelist's death, and a suggestion that
friends join Harriet Cruger in subscribing one dollar annually to a
permanent fund for 'the poor of her [ME's] beloved town'.[40] Thus placed
in general circulation were not only letters written for a public fund-raising
function but also letters of an obviously personal nature; this unabashed
marketing of Edgeworth's name, initiated partly by the author herself, was
not to be interrupted even by her death. From these episodes, together
with other Edgeworth correspondence, thus emerge some suggestive
indications as to how the business of private philanthropy operated,
especially in its international dimensions – a topic which, in historical
studies of the Great Famine, is only beginning to be explored.[41]

Orlandino: A Famine story for young people

The writing of a text whose consumption would in turn alleviate the
distress of the poor is the well-known origin of Edgeworth's short tale
Orlandino. Writing in January 1848 to express her gratitude to Miss Ryan
in Cincinnati for the latter's role in lobbying the Ohio relief committee for
aid, Edgeworth offered as thanks a copy of her recently published 'little
book'.

> It was written at the invitation of Mssrs. Chambers who are publishing a new
> series of tales for young people and offered me in short anything I pleased to
> ask for a new story – if I would write one for them and the temptation they
> held out to me of paying immediately what I might give to the poor then in
> great distress, made me contrary to my previous resolve to write no more
> stories for children comply with their request.

And most handsomely and promptly even before publication they paid me 50 good pounds for this Orlandino.[42]

From January 1847 onward, references to *Orlandino* occur throughout Edgeworth's letters to her sisters, Harriet and Fanny, whose approval and advice she sought while composing the tale. In letters to Fanny in late January and early February,[43] a more personal motivation for the story's inception appears in Maria's acknowledged discomfort with her current writing of 'begging letters':

I believe that I am the more disposed to try to *earn* something for our poor because I have so little to give and that I have been prevailed upon by Mr Powell much against the grain at least to write two begging letters for him or for the poor – one to Dr Harvey the Quaker and Quaker Association and another to the Ladies Association – I have been all day except when at Church concocting a *morceau d'eloquence* for the Quakers that should contain no falsehood and be palatable and not to *demean* myself . . . [44]

Story-writing, and specifically the story of children's philanthropic endeavours – 'what children can or should do in charity' – becomes a means through which the author herself can 'do something',[45] thus distancing herself from 'begging', which is in the Edgeworth lexicon the worst charge of all.

Orlandino is a temperance story, telling, as the last line summarizes, how 'a youth of superior talents' was 'redeemed from disgrace, misery, and vice'.[46] The topic of temperance is treated at length; included in the narrative is a long eulogy to the work of temperance-advocate Fr Mathew and a facsimile of the Fr Mathew medal. Given the preoccupations of the day, it is not surprising that Edgeworth's story would concern the temperance movement – although the topic's appearance in a narrative dedicated to famine relief produces more troubling conjunctions. Thus the story warns its readers that the excesses practiced by Orlandino are at least partly responsible for his family's destitution and hunger. The wider, political contexts of the famine are not directly present in the story, although contemporary events shadow the narrative in a number of ways. One such instance is the story's emphasis on the importance of emigrants' remittances, what it describes as money sent 'home from their banishment' by Irish emigrants, totalling some £400,000 'from our own in America'.[47] The American dimension makes a further appearance in the narrative through an American letter which, as Edgeworth explains in a footnote, has been 'literally copied' from an Irish emigrant's letter, received by his mother in April 1847, urging her to leave this 'much-beloved but miserable country'.[48]

A feature of this tale, as in many other children's stories, is its insistence on the value of children's actions, in particular those actions adults consider insignificant. In Edgeworth's tale, the children whose agency is responsible for Orlandino's reform acquire the opportunity to prove to sceptical adults that their philanthropic efforts are of real effect, since their earlier famine works, such as knitting and sewing, were dismissed as 'much ado about nothing' works. Early in 1847, in the course of writing the story, Maria had indicated to her sister Fanny her plans to refer 'playfully' to the wider issues of political philosophy and economy relating to the famine in her children's story.[49] The final story, however, is much narrower in its scope and constitutes a striking retreat from the more vexed political and economic questions; instead, as the story of one character's reform becomes central, moral economy replaces the considerations of political economy. By the narrative's conclusion, we are placed firmly in a post-famine setting, as 'medical men and well-informed gentlemen of the country'[50] debate means to 'restore industry and order, after the panic and confusion incident on a state of extraordinary distress', but an 'extraordinary distress' whose causes remain markedly outside the parameters of this narrative.

The famine and 'philosophical reasoning'

Rarely in her correspondence does Edgeworth allude to the famine in specific, individualized terms. One such occasion is in the course of the letter of 8 May 1847, addressed to her sister, Honora Beaufort, prompted by Honora's husband's query as to the number of famine-related deaths in Ireland.[51]

> Some of the individual assertion of facts to one's own knowledge are almost too dreadful to repeat to you. Mr Tuite told us that in coming here yesterday on the road near Edgeworthstown he saw a woman tottering along who did not beg from him and who seemed too much stupefied by hunger or despair or disease to notice him at all – he saw hanging at her back, the head bobbing around from side to side without her minding or seeming to feel it a dead child!
>
> This sort of *insensibility* to the feelings of nature has been seen by him in many cases – even where he knew that strong domestic and parental affections had existed before famine and disease came – Physicians give the same

testimony. Alas! *You* may judge my dear Honora how difficult it is to keep any judgment or powers of calculation and belief cool and sane while such facts are brought daily and hourly before the senses.

This passage echoes many of the testimonies published in newspapers and in pamphlets in late 1846 and 1847, a frequently employed index of famine's horror being the breakdown of parental relationships and, specifically, of maternal protection. Reading between the lines of her letters, however, one sees that Edgeworth's direct experience of the conditions endured by the poorest victims was limited; 'anecdotes' and more specific details are drawn from information supplied by her stepmother's conversations with tenants, by Vicar Powell from his visits to the poor, and by neighbours such as Tuite.[52]

Instead, and in spite of the difficulties mentioned above, the bulk of Edgeworth's famine correspondence is dedicated to 'cool judgement' and to a continual inspection of political belief, her own and others, in the face of the challenges now present. Her efforts to reconcile belief with practice are most evident in her letters to Richard Jones. Throughout the correspondence, Edgeworth appears extremely well-informed in matters of political economy and highly engaged by contemporary arguments concerning the administration of relief. In the spring of 1847, the passing of the Temporary Relief Act saw a sharp change in government policy; in a reversal of previous opposition to gratuitous relief, free food was now to be provided in government soup kitchens throughout the country.[53] To Edgeworth, however, this 'granting outdoor relief to the poor of Ireland' was the greatest 'blunder' possibly committed 'by any legislator in the present circumstances'.[54] Her recurring anxiety that gratuitous relief would 'increase national defects and dangers'[55] and damage spirits of 'independence and industry'[56] is most graphically expressed in a letter to Jones dated 14 June 1847:

How shall we get the people who have been fed gratis to believe that the government and their landlords are not bound to feed them always? They evidently have formed this idea. It was impolitic in the past circumstances to adhere strictly to the wholesome maxim: 'They who do not work shall not eat.' There were such numbers who had no *work* – who could not work from extenuation, disease, etc. Humanity could not leave these to perish from hunger – or if humanity had been out of the question Fear could not have ventured it. The character of Paddy knows well how to take advantage of his own misfortunes and of all fears and blunders.[57]

This passage is disturbing, no less so when viewed in its historical moment. By July 1847, more than 3 million individuals (well over one-third of the population) were receiving free and, for the most part, urgently needed soup rations. Recent work on the Great Famine has shown that the shift in policy from public works was not welcomed unanimously in Ireland and generated some protest, even from labourers themselves, over the demeaning nature of outdoor relief.[58] In this context, Edgeworth's opposition is less startling; as the public discourse of our own time continues to demonstrate, debates over the feared 'pauperization' of the poor and the perceived threat of their continuing 'dependence' are hardly unique. Underlying Edgeworth's comments, however, is a particularly problematic construction of 'the character of Paddy'. In her sketch, Paddy is more a colonial 'other' than a fellow creature, in relation to whom negotiations of what is 'politic' and what is humane are tempered, strikingly, by 'fear'.

Yet, as the letter concludes, a tone of uncertainty emerges: 'Am I foolish in saying or thinking this? Please to tell me what I ought to think and why.'[59] Furthermore, when earlier letters between author and economist are placed alongside other 1847 correspondence, Edgeworth's views on relief for the poor emerge as significantly more complex. Ten years previously, in a letter to Jones partly prompted by George Nicholls's poor-law report,[60] Edgeworth delivered a passionate denunciation of Harriet Martineau's poor-law views as 'impossible and hard-hearted'. Martineau's writings largely supported the 1834 Poor Law Amendment Act and its principle of 'less eligibility', whereby all relief would be provided through workhouses – and only as a last, desperate resort. Martineau's doctrines, in particular her opposition to individual charitable actions and to private philanthropy, remained loathsome to Edgeworth.[61]

> I mentioned Miss Martineau's system – I mean her anti-charity principles. Her reasoning appears unanswerable – but if we attempt to *carry it out* – to *carry it through* – into practice it must appear either impossible or it must create more evil to society than it could produce good . . . to refuse any relief by charity to those who are perishing and perhaps before the eyes of the anti-charitableist in the death struggle, would require a heart of iron – a nature in which the natural instinct of sympathy or pity ha[s] been expelled or destroyed . . .
>
> Take away horror of seeing human creatures perish – without offering aid – by famine even without supposing the sight of blood. You diminish you destroy the horror of murder the dread of being *the cause of death* proximate or remote – you raise you educate a race of political philosophical Thugs – There

are whole bands of the *selfish* well prepared for this education and quite ready
to seize philosophical reasoning as a pretext – a mask – a safeguard from
public execration.[62]

The actual occurrence of famine was to generate very different fears, as
the later letter to Jones testifies; yet even then, the moral and political
dangers of refusing charity to the poor, what Edgeworth sarcastically termed
the 'Martineau principle', continued to trouble her. In a letter written to
Fanny on 5 February 1847 – one which echoes strongly the 1837 Jones letter
– she reiterated her view that 'the reasonable and large-minded political
economist would', and should, 'allow that exigencies *require* exceptions'.[63]

> Here would be not false principle or mawkish sentiment, but sound moral and
> I will say political philosophy and economy. Push to the extreme the Martineau
> principle, say that you must not relieve misery to gratify your own feelings of
> compassion and that you must weigh the merits and comparative merits etc.
> But while doing so the sufferer perhaps starves – Now if this rigid justice were
> to be really adhered to – it would in the first place be an excuse to selfishness
> to indolence for giving nothing and doing nothing for charity . . . The next step
> which must follow after becoming hardened to the sight of death and to the
> preservation of life is the lessening the feeling of horror at the deprivation of
> life in any human creature – Thence from passive murder to active – and the
> bonds of society are dissolved – This would be a greater evil than any that
> could be committed by poor weak mistaken compassion or charity giving away
> a few blankets foolishly for the gratification even of her own foolish dislike to
> the sight of shivering wretchedness.

Read from such a historical distance, Edgeworth's comments seem difficult
to reconcile fully; yet from their contradictions and conflicts emerges some
of her most significant famine testimony. Similarly, moments in the diary
of Elizabeth Smith, Co. Wicklow landowner, reveal, as late as 1849, the
attempt to adhere to 'philosophick views', and its failure:

> If I could manage to give a bit of bread daily to each pauper child, but we
> have no money, much more than we can afford is spent on labour, the best
> kind of charity, leaving little for ought else, people not being quixotic enough
> to deny themselves the decencies they have been accustomed to for the support
> of those who have no claim upon them, who little deserve help and who would
> not be really benefited by it, only a temporary assistance it would be resulting
> in no good. These philosophick views are right doubtless, yet when I see
> hungry children I long to give them food.[64]

What Smith records at an individual and more simplistic level, Edgeworth examines in terms of a political and economic system: the fault-lines of charity and relief, of exigencies and exceptions.

Edgeworth's views about the larger significance of the famine, and its consequences for Irish–British relations, are given at length in letters to her friend Louisa Moore. Optimism pervades one letter written on 30 July 1847.[65]

> The conduct of Irish proprietors during these distresses must convince England as it has convinced the Irish of their good will by their good deeds . . . I see also that the feeling excited in England by Irish distress still more than the munificent contributions they have made towards the relief of our poor has created gratitude and has counteracted that mischievous spirit of national hatred which O'Connell (Peace to his too clever undisciplined soul!) raised between the Irish and the Sarsenach. I am persuaded that the Union between the two countries will be more strongly cemented now than it has yet ever been. The edges have been washed clean and the asperities cleared away and simply by the cohesion and happy contiguity they will fit and stick together – solidly – permanently.

The belief that union between the two countries 'will be more strongly cemented now than it has yet ever been' makes strange reading over 150 years later – especially in light of successive generations of famine historiography. It also contrasts strikingly with the views of Elizabeth Smith who, by the late 1840s, writes of her growing, though reluctant, belief in the need for some limited form of Repeal.[66] However, political developments quickly challenged Edgeworth's optimism; a year later, castigating the government's indecision regarding the Young Irelanders, she writes, 'Heaven help us. There is no help upon earth or in the wisdom of men – or even of women.' By now, political upheaval, chiefly the Young Ireland rebellion, coupled with personal loss (the death of her sister Fanny), constitute a 'darkness' not easily seen through.[67] Yet six months later, her resilient energy for political and economic questions is once again evident: on 20 March 1849, in a formidable list of literary projects 'which I might have written if I had time or capacity so to do', and compiled only weeks before her death, the 'consequences for Ireland if potatoes ceased to be the national food' is first on the list.[68]

Maria Edgeworth's famine correspondence, in its multiple forms, is an important reminder that contemporary views of the Great Famine are far from being the unidimensional, monolithic construct sometimes presented. The attitudes of even one individual are complex and variable; when expressed at such length and in so many different contexts – personal and public, to family members and friends outside Ireland and to philanthropic organizations within – by an author still, despite years of public silence, extremely well-known, their significance is considerable. Written on some occasions with an avowed public purpose, on others as private meditations, Edgeworth's correspondence both deliberated on famine relief and constituted part of relief operations. The political and economic issues it raises, whether directly or indirectly, continue as subjects for debate.

Afterword (January 2005)

The years 1994–2004, including the period marking the sesquicentenary of the Irish Famine, have seen the welcome republication of a number of eye-witness accounts; these include contemporary accounts by Alexander Somerville,[69] edited by K.D.M. Snell (1994); Asenath Nicholson's *Annals of the Famine in Ireland* (1851), edited by Maureen Murphy (1998); and the memoir of a Donegal teacher and writing-clerk, Hugh Dorian, published for the first time in 2001, edited by Breandán Mac Suibhne and David Dickson. The republication in 1996 of *Transactions of the Central Relief Committee of the Society of Friends during the Famine in Ireland in 1846 and 1847* (1852) restored to attention other haunting and influential contemporary testimonies, along with a body of documentation regarding the Quaker relief effort, which continues to instruct. A notable example is the response of the Society, conveyed by Jonathan Pim, to a government enquiry issued by Charles Trevelyan in June 1848 as to the future plans of their Relief Committee (and to the offer of £100 by Lord John Russell towards such relief); its forceful charge, underlying an ostensibly polite rejoinder, and written in the face of 'great and increasing distress', resonates powerfully in the present:

> Seeing that the difficulty was so far beyond the reach of private exertion, and that the only machinery which it was practicable to employ was that under the control of the public authorities; and believing that the Government alone could raise the funds, or carry out the measures necessary in many districts to save the lives of the people, we feared that if we ventured to undertake a work for which our resources were so inadequate, we might, through our incompetency, injure the cause of those whom we desired to serve.
>
> Under these circumstances, we are not now in a position to undertake the distribution of charitable relief; and we are truly sorry that it is therefore out

of our power to offer ourselves as the distributors of Lord John Russell's
bounty to our suffering fellow-countrymen.[70]

More recently, historians and literary scholars have begun the necessary
task of interrogating the function, accuracy and efficacy of such testimony,
an endeavour in which the skills of both rigorous contextual study and
close textual analysis are required.[71] In this regard, David Fitzpatrick's
caution as to the limits of many such accounts convinces to a point:

> From Black '47 to the present, the personal experience of suffering has eluded
> interpreters of the Irish Famine, largely dependent upon the attempts of
> contemporary analysts to generalize and simplify the chaotic reality. The
> reports of outsiders such as travel writers, journalists, philanthropists and
> government officials provide moving but often conventional evocations of
> suffering, which typically reveal more about the assumptions of the observer
> than the experience of those observed.[72]

And yet an over-fatalism as to the limits of these sources is also to be avoided.
What is needed is a more discriminating mode of analysis that can distinguish between the various sources of witness – between local schoolteacher,
famine emigrant, Irish landlord, relief official, journalist or philanthropic
visitor – but crucially also within these categories, where the differences, for
example, between the contemporary responses of government officials or
among the reactions and interpretations of privileged upper-class observers
are also notable and significant. In addition, what precisely constitutes a
'moving' evocation (be it in the view of contemporary readers or of today's
observers), what may be deemed 'conventional' (whether at the time or from
a later perspective), and which and whose words go beyond convention to
articulate horror and possibly to effect change, are questions worth much
more detailed attention.

To return to Maria Edgeworth, the limits of her direct encounters with
famine and hunger may certainly be traced between the lines of her writings.
Yet in its public manifestation, her famine correspondence was an important
part of a local relief operation, and her 'private' letters (the distinction
between public and private to be blurred over time) offer an extended insight
into one individual's negotiations with 'philosophical reasoning', or, to put it
more baldly, into the encounter of privilege with hunger. The pretexts,
contradictions and internal prevarications, thus laid bare, simultaneous with
the manifest challenge to preserve the 'feeling of horror at the deprivation of
life in any human creature', are themselves a crucial famine source.

References

Manuscript Sources

Ballitore Papers, National Library Dublin: Maria Edgeworth correspondence, 1847. Edgeworth Papers, National Library Dublin:
> Ms. 495: Maria Edgeworth – Louisa Moore correspondence, 1845–1848.
> Ms. 989: Maria Edgeworth – Dublin Central Relief Committee, Society of Friends, 1847–1848.
> Ms. 8, 145: Maria Edgeworth miscellaneous correspondence, 1813–1849.
> Ms. 18, 754: Maria Edgeworth letter diary, 1846.
> Ms. 18, 995: Maria Edgeworth – Harriet (Douglas) Cruger, 1827–1847.
> Ms. 22, 822: Maria Edgeworth – Richard Jones correspondence, 1833–1849.

Women, Education and Literature: The Papers of Maria Edgeworth, 1768–1849. 45 reels. 2 parts. Reading: Adam Matthew, 1995. [Microfilm version of Edgeworth papers from the Bodleian Library, Oxford, and the National Library, Dublin.]

Society of Friends Relief of Distress Papers, National Archives, Dublin.

Secondary Sources

Butler, Marilyn. *Maria Edgeworth: A Literary Biography*. Oxford: Oxford University Press, 1972.

Clarke, Isabel. *Maria Edgeworth: Her Family and Friends*. London: Hutchinson, 1950.

Dorian, Hugh. *The Outer Edge of Ulster: A Memoir of Social Life in Nineteenth-Century Donegal*. Breandán Mac Suibhne and David Dickson (eds). South Bend, IN and Dublin: University of Notre Dame Press and Lilliput, 2001.

Dunne, Tom. *Maria Edgeworth and the Colonial Mind*. Dublin: National University of Ireland, 1985.

Eagleton, Terry. *Heathcliff and the Great Hunger: Studies in Irish Culture*. London: Verso, 1995.

Edgeworth, Frances (Beaufort). *A Memoir of Maria Edgeworth*, 3 vols. n.p., 1867.

Edgeworth, Maria. *Letters for Literary Ladies*, 1795; Claire Connolly (ed.) London: Everyman, 1993.

Edgeworth, Maria. *Orlandino*. Chambers' Library for Young People. Edinburgh: Chambers, 1848.

Fitzpatrick, David. 'The failure: representations of the Irish Famine in letters to Australia', in E. Margaret Crawford (ed.), *The Hungry Stream: Essays on Famine and Emigration*. Belfast: Institute of Irish Studies, 1997.

Forbes, R.B. *The Voyage of the Jamestown on her Errand of Mercy*. Boston, MA: Eastburn, 1847.

Gray, Peter. *The Irish Famine*. London: New Horizons, 1995.

Hall, Anna Maria (Mrs. S.C.). 'Edgeworthstown: memories of Maria Edgeworth', *Art Journal*, Vol.1 (1849), pp.225–9, and Vol.18 (1866), pp.345–9.

Hare, Augustus J.C. (ed.). *The Life and Letters of Maria Edgeworth*, 2 vols. London: Arnold, 1894.

Hone, Joseph. *The Moores of Moore Hall*. London: Cape, 1939.

Hurst, Michael. *Maria Edgeworth and the Public Scene: Intellect, Fine Feeling and Landlordism in the Age of Reform*. London: Macmillan, 1969.

Kelleher, Margaret. *The Feminisation of Famine: Expressions of the Inexpressible?* Cork and Durham, NC: Cork University Press and Duke University Press, 1997.

Kelleher, Margaret and James H. Murphy (eds). *Gender Perspectives in Nineteenth-Century Ireland: Public and Private Spheres*. Dublin: Irish Academic Press, 1997.

Kinealy, Christine. *This Great Calamity: The Irish Famine, 1845–1852*. Dublin: Gill & Macmillan, 1994.

Kinealy, Christine. *A Death-Dealing Famine: The Great Hunger in Ireland*. London and Chicago, IL: Pluto, 1997.

Lee, J.J. 'The Irish diaspora', in Laurence M. Geary and Margaret Kelleher (eds), *Nineteenth-Century Ireland: A Guide to Recent Research*. Dublin: University College Dublin Press, 2005.

Lloyd, David. *Anomalous States: Irish Writing and the Post-Colonial Moment*. Dublin: Lilliput, 1993.

McCormack, W.J. *Ascendancy and Tradition in Anglo-Irish Literary History from 1789 to 1939*. Oxford: Clarendon, 1985.

Murphy, Sharon. *Edgeworth and Romance*. Dublin: Four Courts, 2004.

Nicholson, Asenath. *Annals of the Famine in Ireland*. Maureen Murphy (ed.). 1851; Dublin: Lilliput, 1998.

Oliver, Grace A. *A Study of Maria Edgeworth, with Notices of her Father and Friends*. Boston, MA: Williams, 1882.

Pelly, Patricia and Andrew Tod (eds). *The Highland Lady in Ireland: Elizabeth Grant of Rothiemurchus*. Edinburgh: Canongate, 1991.

Somerville, Alexander. *Letters from Ireland during the Famine of 1847*, K.D.M. Snell (ed.) 1852; Dublin: Irish Academic Press, 1994.

Thomson, David and Moyra McGusty (eds). *The Irish Journals of Elizabeth Smith: 1840–1850*. Oxford: Clarendon, 1980.

Transactions of the Central Relief Committee of the Society of Friends during the Famine in Ireland. Dublin: Hodges & Smith,1852; facsimile edition printed Dublin: Éamonn de Búrca, 1996.

Zimmern, Helen. *Maria Edgeworth*, Eminent Women Series. London: Allen, 1883.

CHAPTER 4

The limits of empathy:
Trollope's *Castle Richmond*

Margaret Scanlan

In 1996, for the first time in history, the Irish economy 'produced more wealth per head of population than Britain did' (Eagleton, 1999, p.37). A development that would have seemed almost as improbable in 1970 as it did in 1847, Irish prosperity inevitably reconfigures the psychic relationship between the two nations. Fifty years ago, an Irish person could look back to the Famine's victims with something like unproblematic identification: relative poverty and economic dependence on the English were still familiar experiences; immigration to England with the prospect of facing anti-Irish bigotry still loomed like a fate for many of the young. Irishness still connoted innocence, a certain untested confidence that a country that had sent a higher proportion of emigrants to the new world than any other in Europe would always empathize with the displaced and oppressed. In the last decade, that innocence has been lost, as an Ireland besieged by refugees and asylum-seekers has faced up to its own propensity for racism and exclusion. To take one example, an overwhelming majority voted in June 2004 to repeal the Republic's longstanding practice of granting citizenship to every child born within its borders. Children with at least one Irish parent will now be granted citizenship, no matter where they are born; children born in Ireland will not be counted as citizens if their parents are non-nationals who have lived there fewer than three years. One might wonder if the Irish majority has forgotten the Famine.

It seems more likely, however, that the contemporary Irish, like contemporary Americans, occupy the position that middle-class English people occupied in the 1840s. They are not victims of the dominant economic system, but its beneficiaries, an uneasy moral position for anyone contemplating its human costs. Such people may wish to empathize with the starving, yet the leap is such that empathy risks seeming sentimental or presumptuous. As Kathleen Lundeen notes, today 'writers or readers who appear to empathize with another's life experiences are often accused of arrogating a cultural authority to which they have no natural claim' (2001, p.83). If today's Irish people lack the 'natural claim' to identify with the Famine's victims, then they are uncomfortably close to identifying with those middle-class Victorians who read many accounts, both sympathetic and unsympathetic, of the victims' sufferings and donated sporadically to charities designed to relieve them. Yet the British lacked the imagination or political will to make the radical choices that alone might have relieved the Famine, deficiencies that from the victims' point of view made them the cold-hearted and ruthless oppressors of nationalist memory. How the world looked to such people, what the distractions were that kept them from the heroic sacrifices that a massive catastrophe seems to demand, is an issue with new implications for Irish readers. There is no better time to re-read Anthony Trollope's disturbing and imperfect *Castle Richmond*, the only Famine novel by a major Victorian writer.

It was an extraordinary topic for Trollope, usually a novelist of English manners, and he addressed his subject without the appeals to empathy for lower-class victims with which readers of Charles Dickens and George Eliot had grown familiar. The narrative never enters the minds of the mostly nameless Catholic Irish; the starving have no psychological conflicts, no history, no culture; although they live in rural Cork, they do not even speak Irish.[1] Appearing in 1860, a decade too late to satisfy our desire to see a great writer summoning his nation to action, *Castle Richmond* seems never to have satisfied anyone. Looking back in his *Autobiography*, Trollope complained that his heroine was a girl of 'no character' and his hero 'a prig'; the heroine's mother, passionately in love with her daughter's first suitor, struck him as 'almost revolting'. Recent historians are more often revolted by the apologies Trollope's narrator makes for the 'prompt, wise, and beneficent' measures the British government took to relieve the Famine (*Castle Richmond*, p.127). At home with the alternately Christian providential and Malthusian rhetoric that Christopher Morash finds in so many Victorian accounts, this narrator prattles on about God's mercy and mass starvation as a 'violent remedy' for over-population and rack-renting (ibid., p.126). Surely few readers would dispute an early reviewer's complaint that the novel's melodramatic plots – a heroine's vacillation between her suitors, the blackmail of an

Anglo-Irish gentleman by his wife's first husband – clash with its grimly historical background.

To be unpleasant and unsettling is not, however, the worst of flaws in a Famine narrative, and actually reading *Castle Richmond* proves a more complex and interesting experience than this dismissive summary suggests. If Trollope fails by the standards of empathic realism, he also avoids its appropriating and colonizing – 'I am you' – pitfalls. If the English and Anglo-Irish melodramas of the novel's foreground seem incongruous against its catastrophic background, they illuminate the author's struggle to make sense of a disorienting world. Like the Manchester industrialist who could not reconcile the mass graves of Limerick with the knowledge that he was not in 'some far-off primitive land', but only a 'twenty-four hours' ride' from home, Trollope registers the 'spatial and temporal implosion' the Famine caused (Morash, 1995, p.16). If the conventions of Victorian realism seem absurd when pressured by disaster, so too did conventional morality, economics and the 'idea of progress' (ibid., p.16). As the strategies with which Trollope's narrator attempts to rationalize the ways of God and the British government fail, the novel gives us a remarkably unsentimental vision of how the Famine looked to outsiders of goodwill and limited imagination. Because it does so, the book deserves to be brought into contemporary discussions about the difficulties of representing historical trauma.

Had Trollope simply been the mouthpiece of his culture's bigotry, it is unlikely that he would have begun his novel by antagonizing his implicitly English readers. Even in 1860, being castigated for a 'strong feeling against all things Irish' (*Castle Richmond*, p.1) in the second sentence must have disconcerted some readers. Asking us whether we will be offended by an Irish story, Trollope presses us to identify with 'a novel-reading world' to which 'no Irish need apply' (ibid., p.1). Distinguishing himself from us, the narrator presents himself as a Famine witness who 'travelled all over Ireland . . . as few other men can have done' (ibid., p.2). This fractious beginning simultaneously reminds us that the story is a fiction and that its author is the historical Trollope, the officer of Her Majesty's post, whose letters to *The Times* he will occasionally cite without attribution. The text's strategies for yoking history to fiction reflect the same stresses, if not antagonisms: the conventionality and artifices of the plot contrast with, rather than assimilate themselves to, the facts.

The major story lines, as we have said, belong to the Anglo-Irish and the English. Insipid Clara, penniless daughter of a widowed Countess, has two lovers. Owen, the rake, proposes to her in the third chapter; but the Countess, who wants Owen for herself and a richer husband for her daughter, enforces a separation. Enter Herbert Fitzgerald, the prig, heir to a landed estate; when he proposes, Clara, who had been too shy to answer her first suitor, says yes. But there's a problem: Herbert's father, Sir Thomas, is going bankrupt paying huge sums to an Englishman named Mollett, once thought dead, who is still legally married to Herbert's mother. In the eyes of the law, the rightful heir is Herbert's cousin and rival, Owen. The Countess, not fancying an illegitimate and bankrupt Herbert for her daughter, tries to break the second engagement, but this time Clara stands by her man. Fortunately, Sir Thomas's lawyer tracks down the blackmailer and obtains a marriage license proving that Mollett was already married when he proposed to the future lady Fitzgerald. True, Sir Thomas has in the meantime died a broken man but, as his heir, Sir Herbert is free to marry Clara. Owen, one of nature's noblemen, pretends not to hear an eleventh-hour proposition from Clara's formidable mamma and goes off to try the hunting in Africa (ibid., p.873). A cruel fate, doubtless, yet better, the Countess tells him, than marriage to her daughter, who is 'cold as ice' and would have 'turned [his] heart to stone' within a year (ibid., p.891).

As this summary suggests, *Castle Richmond* seems downright lurid for Trollope. One reason for the blackmail and suggestions of incest may be the impulse to match the psychological suffering of the Anglo-Irish to the physical suffering of the native Irish, lest the novel break in two entirely, or seem only to satirize the folks in the Big House.[2] Sympathetic comparisons between the psychic suffering of the upper classes and the physical suffering of the poor are, after all, a commonplace of the period. Even Zola, far more politically radical than Trollope, takes seriously Hennebeau's wish that he, like the striking coal miners, 'were dying of starvation', because the pain of an 'empty belly . . . might deaden [his] relentless grief' over his wife's unfaithfulness (*Germinal*, p.338). Trollope suggests many such analogies; the 'horrible catastrophe' that causes Aunt Letty Fitzgerald to cling to her family more closely than ever is the loss of Castle Richmond. When he says 'the tragedy was do deep he could not believe in it', the narrator is describing Owen's reaction, not to the fact that so many of his tenants are dying, but to the quasi-Gothic revelation that Lady Fitzgerald's first husband is still living (*Castle Richmond*, p.509).[3] Herbert's self-pity, when faced with the loss of his father's property, includes the reflection that it would be easier to be poor from birth than to come down in the world (ibid., pp.524 and 526).

Yet no matter how Trollope piles on incidents, he never succeeds in assimilating his Anglo-Irish melodrama with the brutal historical facts; indeed, we may question how far he intended to do so. As a twenty-first century reader, I may be rather too quick to read an ironic intention into Trollope's description of the fun Clara and Herbert's sisters have making their plans for the new soup kitchen, which keep them 'busy, contented . . . though their work arose from the contiguity of such infinite misery' (ibid., p.146). Juxtaposing the complaints of a wretched road crew with Herbert's depressed inner monologue, Trollope allows the reader to hear Irishmen saying what any modern history would document, that a scanty diet of cornmeal leaves adults weak and is 'bad . . . intirely' for children (ibid., p.529). Readers know Herbert's fears for his family, his livelihood, and his engagement, know that 'he could not think of their sorrows; his own sorrow seemed to him to be so much the heavier' (ibid., p.530). But the narrator discourages us from sharing Herbert's judgement: 'Nothing is so powerful in making a man selfish as misfortune' (ibid., p.530).

Indeed, that unsentimental idea recurs in the novel. Its least attractive characters, Lady Desmond and the Molletts, are also the most indifferent to the Famine. Matthew Mollett works out his argument systematically: 'What were rags and starvation to him? He was worse off than they were. They were merely dying, as all men must do. But he was inhabiting a hell on earth . . . What right had they to torment with their misery one so much more wretched than themselves?' (ibid., p.427). Lady Desmond simply stays in her rundown house; when Herbert tries to tell her about a starving Irishwoman and her dead child, Lady Desmond 'soon quelled the expression of his feelings' and 'put a stop' to her own son's proposal to send help (ibid., p.695). Yet the narrator, who seldom appeals to us to feel for the starving Irish, instructs us to empathize with her. Does Lady Desmond lust after her daughter's suitor? 'Reader, good-natured, middle-aged reader, remember that she was only thirty-eight' (ibid., p.35). Eight hundred more pages pass, and the narrator is still urging readers to consider her perspective. If he feels superior to Lady Desmond, the narrator reminds himself that 'no horrible old earl with gloating eyes . . . robbed me of the pleasure of my youth' (ibid., p.880).

An ironic intention seems clearer when the narrator instructs us to consider 'the violent demands on a man's courage' that crime makes: 'Let any one think of the difference of attacking a thief, and being attacked as a thief' (ibid., p.430). We may have trouble understanding why Matthew Mollett ages ten years in the few weeks it takes Mr Prendergast to track him down, for 'it is hard for any tame domestic animal to know through what fire and water a poor fox is driven as it is hunted' (ibid., p.821). Indeed, the narrator goes so far as to say that 'his strongest feeling' is for the Molletts' wretchedness, since a human sympathy that limits itself to the 'good, or worse still . . . the graceful' is no 'better than terrestrial' (ibid., p.474). Fractious to the end, he defends his decision to let the Molletts escape British justice against his readers' anticipated protests.

Through the Molletts and Lady Desmond, Trollope illustrates the problems of a social ethic based on empathy – the ease with which appeals are made, the difficulty of responding helpfully to them. When Herbert stalks out of Lady Desmond's parlour, furious at her indifference, he asks himself, 'Was not his story one that would have melted the heart of a stranger?'; yet the narrator points out that in his self-preoccupation, 'he almost forgot his father and his mother' (ibid., p.557). This moral bears in on him when he wakes at the fireside where he collapsed on his return home and finds the angel of the house, his mother, tending 'him as she had done when he was a child', although she has just 'heard of her great ruin' (ibid., p.565).

Yet although the narrator alludes conventionally to Lady Fitzgerald's charity to the poor, he never confronts her with Famine victims. Indeed, though the Molletts and others occasionally note Famine sights, our priggish Herbert is the only character present at every scene in which the victims tell their stories. By twenty-first century standards, he almost always comes off badly, taking the official line on centralization and character building – soup kitchens, subsidized shops, workhouses and road works – instead of a promiscuous private charity or the almost unspeakable option of violence.[4] Victorians might have been more upset by his tendency to capitulate with the odd shilling or sixpence, especially the time he does so because Brigid Sheehy tells him that Owen, his rival, would not refuse a sick child milk (ibid., p.355). His reluctance is also a narrative device that allows the starving to tell their stories and present many realistic details that cast doubt on official policies. Much as in a nationalist history, we hear that wages are so depressed that a man's children may starve, even if he has work; subsidizing the cost of cornmeal to bring its price within the reach of the poor is useless to those who have no work or money at all. Centralized soup kitchens and shops force the poor to walk long distances for scant meals; make-work road projects force starving and ragged men to do hard labour in freezing weather and leave the landscape an 'artificial quagmire of slush' (ibid., p.527). Herbert's preoccupation with his own problems and his defensiveness about the time and money he devotes to Famine relief do not prevent us from hearing these voices.

Herbert is the only witness of the novel's best-known Famine scene, which several histories of the Famine and its literature analyze.[5] What particularly interests me is how much the scene hinges on an oddly Lacanian equation between law and language. As Herbert rides glumly to Desmond Court to see Clara for the last time before setting off to read the law in London, a rain sets in and Herbert walks his horse into a peasant cottage. Anticipating our disapproval, Trollope's narrator hastens to explain that in England 'no one would think of' doing so, but in Ireland 'people . . . take greater liberties': 'It is no uncommon thing on a wet hunting-day to see a cabin packed with horses, and the children moving about among them, almost as unconcernedly as though the animals were pigs' (ibid., p.682). The cabin is 'empty of everything', without furniture or fire, but on the floor a skeletal woman in rags crouches with a baby girl covered with 'dirt and sores'. In a corner, under a pile of straw, is the naked body of an older daughter. Herbert at first 'hardly thought that the object before him was a human being', and to the end is 'stricken with horror' by the scene (ibid., p.691). He asks the woman a few questions, whether the child is her own, whether the baby is cold, but for once does not lecture the victim on seeking public charity. The narrator has no such reluctance, explaining that she and her husband ought to have gone to the poorhouse, since his rheumatism prevents road work. But Mike insists on taking a less demanding job, even though it pays only enough 'food . . . to keep himself alive' (ibid., p.688). So why does she not take the children to the poorhouse? Official policy turns away a woman and her children if her husband has a job. This rule, the narrator explains, was 'salutary' because it prevented welfare abuse, though its effects in the worst cases 'pressed very cruelly' (ibid., p.689).

At one of those junctures where he seems closest to the author, the narrator remarks on the logic of British policy: the 'wisdom of its action and the wisdom of its abstinence from action were very good' (ibid., p.643). British law and order must be defended, it seems, because Trollope cannot imagine a better alternative; to feed 4 million people, he says, requires organization, discipline and strict rules against cheating. Yet what this scene shows is the cruelty that law, abetted by a father's bad decision, permits: that the victims in this case are all female further underscores the gulf between those who formulate regulations and those who suffer their consequences. Nor are the rural Irish the only victims of English justice.

As Aby puts it twice to Sir Thomas, his father 'could take [Lady Fitzgerald] away with him tomorrow if he chose, according to the law of the land . . .' (ibid., p.471).

While Herbert searches for words with which to describe the Famine scene he has just witnessed to the Countess, the narrator asks us why he should describe it at all. 'That is what we should all say', he comments, noting that Herbert should keep the dying woman's memory in his heart, but 'not embarrass himself with any mention of her for the present' (ibid., p.694). Pressed again into the collective novel-reading world, 'we' are assumed to share an English reticence, whereas the emotionally expressive Irish take leave of emigrating friends with 'loud wailings, and clapping of hands, and tearings of hair' (ibid., p.672). Though the narrator professes to admire this emotional fluency, even on one occasion allowing Herbert to sob 'like a woman' (ibid., p.717), he hardly imagines that he will be any more able than Herbert to find words to tell the Famine story fully and effectively.

This ambivalence about telling the Famine story perhaps accounts for the awkward lurches from the melodramatic Anglo-Irish plot to the actual disaster, and for the otherwise inadequate explanation – a dislike of double titles – for his refusal to subtitle the novel 'A Tale of the Famine Year in Ireland' (ibid., p.894). Buried in the final celebrations of God's mercy and the recovery of Irish rents is the acknowledgement that 'if one did in truth write a tale of the Famine, after that it would behove the author to write a tale of the pestilence; and then another, a tale of the exodus' (ibid., p.896). But those novels remain unwritten, as Patrick Desmond and Owen Fitzgerald stand momentarily speechless when they have too much to express: 'It is so easy to speak when one has little or nothing to say; but often so difficult when there is much that must be said: and the same paradox is equally true of writing' (ibid., p.741). Thus Trollope's affirmation of Tory policy is haunted by the gap it imagines between the policy and the real experience, just as Clara's marriage to Herbert will be haunted by the possibility that her unspoken assent to his rival's proposal expressed her deepest wishes.

The narrator does not comment on Herbert's silence before the dying woman, though he notes censoriously that all of Herbert's gestures – pressing money on a woman too weak to walk, covering her dead child with his silk handkerchief – are useless. He interjects his own story of a relief worker who pronounced a boy as good as dead without troubling to get out of earshot, presumably to evoke the hard-headed charity Herbert normally favours.[6] But Herbert's inclination to self-dramatization has received a fatal shock: 'Whatever might be the extent of his own calamity, how could he think himself unhappy after what he had seen? How could he repine . . . having now witnessed to how low a state of misery a fellow human being might be brought?' (ibid., p.692). When Lady Desmond murmurs tremulously, 'My poor unfortunate child', he can only think of the other woman (ibid., p.701). Even in London, when Mr Prendergast expresses sympathy for the loss of Castle Richmond, Herbert recalls 'the woman whom he had seen in the cabin, and reflected that . . . he had no right to be unhappy' (ibid., p.731).

Herbert has only a few brief scenes left. He's not the stuff of which dramatic transformations of character are made, and the narrator does not tell us whether the 'true good conscientious . . . energy' he devotes to the poor after he inherits the estate is marked by greater compassion than his previous famine work (ibid., p.896). He has simply understood that his own misery and that of the starving Irish cannot be weighed on the same scale: absolute deprivation takes absolute priority because it is incommensurable with middle-class experience. Trollope's failure to reconcile the two worlds of his novel is an aesthetic failure, but not an oversight.

We should add that as a masterful novelist of manners Trollope is able to see the daily politics of famine with unusual clarity. 'If they cannot manage for themselves they must fall into our way of managing for them', remarks a Protestant gentleman, urging that all the indigent be herded into workhouses (ibid., p.385). Yet humorous as Trollope always is when he puts into play the settled prejudices and interests of a group of self-satisfied functionaries, we are chilled in a moment when the local priest, hardly nobler, says that there are not enough 'houses in county Cork . . . to hold them' (ibid., p.388). His satirist's eye notes the religious estrangement of Irish Protestants from their English brethren. Letty's fears that her nephew will fall under the influences of the Puseyites at Oxford, Mrs Townsend's notion of England as a 'land . . . in which the light of the gospel no longer shone in its purity' (ibid., p.667), and the suspicion with which an English clergyman visits his Irish counterpart, sure that he is using relief donations to coerce Catholics to convert (ibid., p.766), are only its most obvious manifestations.

Castle Richmond measures the estrangement of the English from the Anglo-Irish in other matters as well, and in doing so comes close to discrediting the nation with which it asks the reader to identify. Like Aby's obtrusive Cockney accent, Mr Prendergast's prejudices underscore his foreignness; he finds even Herbert and his Aunt Letty 'Wild Irish' 'whom it would be insane to trust, and of whom it was absurd to make inquiries' (ibid., p.396). Though Prendergast is the very model of British probity, the narrator cannot pronounce a man with such 'thin lips . . . genially human at all points', and the reader must flinch at the metaphors of 'ruthless surgeon' and 'iron-wristed dentist' which Trollope uses to describe him (ibid., p.393 and 394). Though he will eventually track down Mr Mollett and the damning marriage certificate, Mr Prendergast almost regrets his success, so thoroughly has he been convinced of Mollett's claims and so little does he 'like to find that he is ever in the wrong' (ibid., p.834). Perhaps, as the narrator claims, Mr Prendergast's affection for Mollett is like that of the hunter for the wiliest fox. But it is hard to avoid the observation that they are fellow countrymen, the only native English seen at any length in the novel.

If Trollope's overt commitments to a famine policy that a British official who resigned in protest characterized as 'one of extermination' signify his distance from the twenty-first century reader, their ambivalence and contradictions bring us closer. The question of why English novelists apparently found it so hard to empathize with Irish victims is, of course, finally unanswerable. Yet if we attend to the circumstances in which human beings resist identification with others, we may become more conscious of ourselves as readers of Trollope and as readers of past catastrophes. Some of us are Irish, or at least have Irish names, and we want to read the famine through the eyes of the victims. To think of ourselves as the censorious English, forever worrying that free cornmeal might weaken the Irish character, is almost as bad as imagining ourselves training Alsatians for the SS. Yet of course most of us, even graduate students, know poverty only in the relative sense that the Countess Desmond does. Famine and pestilence continue, but most of us will never be more than onlookers, watching the spectacle on television, sending the occasional cheque to Oxfam or the Catholic Charities. We will not have the burning evangelical fervour of an Asenath Nicholson, who left her family in New York to live in a Dublin tenement and feed the people who surrounded her, and we may even distrust such passion when we see it in others. Yet from the point of view of history's worst victims, anything less is idleness and indifference, Letty and Mrs Townsend chatting before the fire about the 'perilous state of the country . . . for many a pleasant hour' (ibid., p.662). If we want an ethical problem, perhaps we should stop asking why respectable Victorians found it so hard to empathize with the

Irish, and wonder instead why we are so reluctant to empathize with them.

References

Eagleton, Terry. *The Truth about the Irish*. Dublin: New Island, 1999.

Lundeen, Kathleen. 'Who has the right to feel? The ethics of literary empathy', in Todd F. Davis and Kenneth Womack (eds), *Mapping the Ethical Turn: A Reader in Ethics, Culture, and Literary Theory*. Charlottesville, VA, and London: University Press of Virginia, 2001.

Morash, Christopher. *Writing the Irish Famine*. Oxford: Clarendon Press, 1995.

Nicholson, Asenath. *Annals of the Famine in Ireland*. 1851, Maureen Murphy (ed.). Dublin: Lilliput, 1998.

Trollope, Anthony. *The MacDermots of Ballycloran*. [1847] London: Penguin, 1993.

Trollope, Anthony. *The Kellys and the O'Kellys*. [1848] London: Penguin, 1993.

Trollope, Anthony. *Castle Richmond*. [1860] London: Penguin, 1993.

Zola, Emile. *Germinal*. Leonard Tancock (trans.). [1954] Harmondsworth: Penguin, 1977.

CHAPTER 5

Dracula and the spectre of Famine

Sarah Goss

He come again, and again, and again. Look at his persistence and his endurance. With the child-brain that was to him he have long since conceive the idea of coming to a great city. What does he do? He find out the place of all the world most of promise for him. Then he deliberately set himself down to prepare for the task . . . He study new tongues. He learn new social life; new environment of old ways, the politic, the law, the science, the habit of a new land and a new people . . . He have done this all alone; all alone! from a ruin tomb in a forgotten land. What more may he not do when the greater world of thought is open to him? He that can smile at death, as we know him; who can flourish in the midst of diseases that kill off whole peoples. Oh! if such an one was to come from God, and not the Devil, what a force for good might he not be in this old world of ours!

(Bram Stoker, Dracula, 1998, p.321)

In having crawled 'from a ruin tomb in a forgotten land' and survived 'diseases that kill off whole peoples', Dracula is reminiscent of a survivor of Ireland's Great Hunger. In his refusal to die and stay buried, in his 'persistence' and 'endurance' and his manner of appearing on the scene 'again, and again, and again', he can be seen as an image of the Famine's dead, forcing a reluctant memory from the Old pre-industrialized world on the modern New.

In a novel dominated by a heavy sense of evil, it is easy to forget that in the few places where Dracula actually appears in the novel named for him, his speech is often more pensive and nostalgic than sinister or threatening. 'I seek not gaiety nor mirth', he tells Jonathan.

I am no longer young. And my heart, through weary years of mourning over the dead, is not attuned to mirth. Moreover, the walls of my castle are broken; the shadows are many, and the wind breathes cold through the broken battlements and casements. I love the shade and the shadow, and would be alone with my thoughts when I may.

(Dracula, p.24)

His loneliness and mourning align Dracula with survivors of the Famine; the broken walls of his castle suggest the neglected status of the parliament at College Green (or of Dublin Castle) after the Act of Union 'killed' Ireland and made official Ireland's colonial relationship to Britain (the relationship that radical Irish voices would later blame for the severity of the Famine). The world that Dracula knew is gone and he speaks as one shell-shocked, inexplicably left alive after a catastrophe of immense magnitude. His isolation is reminiscent of the phenomena of broken community and cultural loss experienced by survivors of the Famine who did not emigrate; death and emigration left depopulated villages of the elderly and the sick, particularly in the west of Ireland. Famine recollections often focus on the desolate silence over the landscape, the melancholy sight of deserted villages that were once well-populated, and the loss of native Irish speakers.[1]

Of course, Dracula has more in common with a feudal lord than an Irish peasant, and he is not only grief-stricken but also angry. In the spirit of vengeance and for the propagation of his vanquished race, he immigrates to London, bringing with him a curse that replicates the dissolution of bonds the Famine caused in Ireland. He comes to break all ties and relations, to sever the strength and spirit of the culture, so that the protagonists have to fight him, not only through superior technology and the amassing of information, but also through the power of unity they demonstrate in the reconstituted bonds of their broken community.

In view of the recent spate of criticism on the 'Irish' *Dracula*, it is fair to wonder why we need another such reading. While critics have focused on historical parallels – for instance, there is Michael Moses's persuasive reading of *Dracula* as Parnell – there has yet to be a substantive reading of Dracula as a Famine text. Such readings may have been discouraged by what Joseph Valente characterizes as an over-readiness on the part of critics to see Bram Stoker as a solidly bourgeois member of the Anglo-Protestant Dublin elite. As Valente points out, Stoker was Anglo-Celtic, 'not a standard middle-class Anglo-Irish Protestant closely identified with Ascendancy rule, as has been almost universally imagined' (Valente, 2000, p.633). In fact, Stoker's father was the only member of the family who 'could claim strictly Anglo-Saxon or even British descent' (ibid.). Stoker's mother grew up in the rural west of Ireland and related to the young Bram gruesome stories of the 1832 cholera epidemic in Sligo. Her descriptions of the spread of disease across the countryside influenced his short story 'The Invisible Giant' (Belford, 1996, p.19) and later find their

way into *Dracula*. As a result of Stoker's being 'a stealth version of the sort
of racial mixing that made . . . [the Anglo Irish] uneasy', at once a
member 'of a conquering and a vanquished race, a ruling and a subject
people, an imperial and an occupied nation' (Valente, 2000, p.633),
Valente argues that it is inaccurate to read his work as simply reflective of
an entrenched Protestant Anglo-Irishman's anxiety over the rising strength
of the Catholic community. Thinking of Stoker as a 'philosophical' sup-
porter of Home Rule (Belford, 1996, p.230), and, as Valente puts it, as 'an
inter-ethnic half-caste' (2000, p.633), complicates the picture of the author
of *Dracula* drawn by critics who have assumed Stoker's Anglo-Irishness
(Victor Sage, Cannon Schmitt, Michael Moses and Kellie Donovan
Wixson all discuss *Dracula* at least partly in terms of Stoker's assumed
Anglo-Irishness). These kinds of tensions find expression in the gothic
forms with which Stoker works in his novel.

The gothic novel can be read as a 'fragmented fable of identity' (Kilgour,
1995, p.5) as well as 'a confused and self-contradictory form, ambivalent
or unsure about its own aims and implications' (ibid.). Fred Botting writes,
'Gothic subjects were alienated, divided from themselves, no longer in
control' (1996, p.12), and reminds us that gothic is, by definition, a 'hybrid
form' (ibid., p.14). It is fitting, then, that Stoker would represent Ireland's
conflicted history, and his own relationship to it, through the conventions
of the gothic. Born in the year the Famine was at its worst – 'Black '47' –
Stoker grew up in the immediate aftermath of Ireland's shattering trauma.
He could not have failed to be influenced by it, even had he not been an
avid audience for his mother's stories of poverty and disease in western
Ireland. Stoker's biographer, Barbara Belford, describes his early years in
Clontarf as haunted by signs of the Famine, even while his own middle-
class family was protected from its very worst effects. In the distance from
his house 'was the North Wall docking slip, from which thousands sailed,
fleeing the Irish famine of the 1840s' (1996, p.13). She asks about the
undefined illness Stoker suffered as a child, which prevented him from
walking till he was seven, 'Was his malady one of the mysterious fevers
that swept through Ireland after the famine?' (ibid., p.14).

But what kind of Famine representation can we expect to find in
Dracula, a novel set primarily in late nineteenth-century England? And if
the Famine does creep in, in what ways does it do so? As Margaret
Kelleher writes, 'One of the first questions raised by a study of famine
literature is that of the very possibility of representation: is it possible to
depict the horror and scale of an event such as famine; are literature and

language adequate to the task?' (1997, p.2). In *Heathcliff and the Great Hunger*, Terry Eagleton argues that a 'repression or evasion' operating in Irish culture has prevented the Famine from finding adequate expression in the arts: 'There is a handful of novels and a body of poems, but few truly distinguished works. Where is the Famine in the literature of the Revival? Where is it in Joyce?' (Eagleton, 1995, p.13). Christopher Morash argues that attempts to write the Famine must come at the subject indirectly, that all such texts 'inscribe the dead in discourses other than that of famine *per se*. The literature of the Famine thus exists as a series of tangents to the elusive event itself. We encounter only the ghosts of the dead who are, as ever, absent' (Morash, 1995, p.187). This seems a fitting way of encountering the figure of Dracula himself – an abyss, more an absence in the text than a presence, a site where meanings internally contradict and collapse. For David Lloyd, post-Famine Ireland possesses a culture 'constituted around and marked by an unworked-through loss' (1997, p.45). The Irish gothic novel is one place we can look for this not-fully-processed material, for the 'inevitable recurrence' of trauma so great as to be beyond the full power of articulation and where material not representable within the bounds of realism can take shape.

With such observations in mind, this essay will consider *Dracula* as a specifically Irish gothic novel. In the aftermath of mid-century attempts by, for example, Anthony Trollope and Annie Keary to write realist novels addressing the Famine, I will argue that toward the end of the century the Famine found expression (obliquely) in Stoker's *fin-de-siècle* Irish gothic. Stoker's *Dracula*, although not immediately classifiable as a 'Famine novel', is a good place to look for the evaded, but nonetheless inescapable, legacy of the Famine; the Famine haunts *Dracula*.

Stoker's version of the vampire is comparable to two different figures in Irish culture and folklore, the banshee and the keener. The representations of Lucy and Dracula arguably draw on these sources. It is Lucy who most clearly embodies the Famine's devastating physical effects, written graphically on her deteriorating body. As Kelleher argues, 'The spectacle of famine, as early as the 1840s, is frequently constructed through female figures, its traces inscribed on hunger-ravaged, unclothed bodies' (1997, p.29). Lucy embodies the horrors of the Famine, as well as the threat of Irish retribution, but then she is brutally killed in a way that seems to suggest the past ought to stay dead and buried. Her death seems meant to be final, cleansing and cathartic, and yet the stability of her 'real death' (Stoker, 1998, p.229), as Mina calls it, is contingent upon the killing of a much more elusive and ambiguous figure, the vampire leader – Dracula himself. Furthermore, in the wake of Lucy's narrative follows the more fragmented and unstable one of Renfield, the 'religious and homicidal maniac'. With his ferocious, unnatural appetites and willingness to do anything to please his leader, Renfield conjures up a much more threatening image of the return of the Famine's victims to British consciousness.

Dracula himself encompasses similar contradictions as the legendary-historical Irish keener – awful and awe-inspiring, mysterious, uncanny and gender-ambiguous. He possesses a signifying power less easily named or categorized (and thus less easily contained) than Lucy's. He is never staked or dismembered like Lucy and the three vampire women, and he never undergoes the terrible physical torment they do. Instead, he elusively disintegrates into dust. In *Dracula*, then, different representations of the Famine allow Stoker to say seemingly contradictory things about Famine memory. Through a brutal scene of bodily suffering he dispatches Lucy and the threat she represents (that the wronged dead will come back, resurface into memory), but he allows Dracula a more fluid identity that resists staking. As both blood-sucker and keener, he is allowed to function in opposing ways: he depletes the living, but he also revives the dead. He remembers, reminisces and grieves for his proud, 'conquering race' (Stoker, 1998, p.29). In numerous passages he is associated with the relentless howling of the 'children of the night' (ibid., p.18) whose 'music' resembles the uncanny sounds which obsessively recur in depictions of post-Famine Ireland. The radical Young Irelander John Mitchel argued that any attempt on the part of the Irish to interrupt Britain in 'her way of telling *our* story' would only be heard by the dominant nation as an inarticulate, unmannerly '*Irish howl*' (quoted in Morash, 1995, p.70) and dismissed, as the stories of the 'defeated' always are in a post-Enlightenment age. The howls that follow Dracula, and for which Dracula acts as a musical conductor or director, may stand for just such an attempt to interrupt and tell a different history that as yet had not been told.

The Famine Embodied

The *fin-de-siècle* gothic resurgence allowed Stoker to bring back to life a gothic discourse of the Famine that had roots in the poetry and editorials published by the *Nation* in the 1840s. To offer just a brief example, a *United Irishman* newspaper report of 1848 declared of the Famine's effects, 'The streets of every town in the country are overrun with stalking skeletons' (quoted in Morash, 1995, p.5). English writing about Ireland had long been characterized 'by the establishment of Ireland as the demonic, barbaric Other of a pious, civilized England' (Morash, 1995, p.114), and nationalist writers, Morash argues, laid claim 'to the same bestial and demonic images which were so much a part of the imperial discourse of Ireland' (ibid., p.114) and turned them to different effect as a powerful rhetorical strategy in their critiques of the British government's misman-agement of the Famine. Here is an excerpt from the anonymous Famine poem 'Thanatos', published in 1849:

> A mother's heart was marble-clad, her eye was fierce and wild –
> A hungry Demon lurked therein, while gazing on her child.
> The mother-love was warm and true; the Want was long withstood –
> Strength failed at last; she gorged the flesh – the offspring of her blood.
>
> (quoted in Morash, 1995, p.114)

The strategy of this poem is to embrace a version of anti-Irish rhetoric and turn it to cross-purposes. As a piece in the *Nation* of 5 February 1848 stated, 'Mrs. Anne Radcliffe being dead . . . it is now our part to furnish England with monsters, thugs, and "devils great and devils small"' (ibid. p.116). Young Ireland, with its revolutionary vision, used the association of Ireland with the monstrous to argue its own political points. If ordinarily pious, law-abiding mothers were now capable of eating the bodies of their babies, this proved the point that nothing short of apocalyptic revolution would suffice. Nothing but the rooting out and scourging of the very source of the evil (Ireland's colonial relationship to England) could reverse the trend and release Ireland from the devil's grip. Similarly, Irish nationalists co-opted Malthusian and providential discourses used by their political opponents to rationalize the Famine as an act of nature or God to balance the population or punish the sinful. A piece possibly by Mitchel, appearing in the *Nation* on 6 February 1847, angrily concurred that the Famine was a divine judgement and a punishment for national sins, but a judgement on the Anglo-Irish ascendancy rather than the native Irish; the Protestant nation had sold out their own country in exchange for seats in Westminster and abdicated their responsibility to the Irish. The piece concludes that until the Anglo-Irish, and England by extension, repent of this sin, 'the hand of God shall be heavy on their land; the famine shall waste them, and the Pestilence that walketh in darkness shall wear and wither them' (quoted in Morash, 1995, pp.103–4). This curse could be the starting point for my reading of *Dracula*, in which the Great Famine's dead are imagined as returning to punish and deplete England.

Though it makes no direct references to Ireland or the Famine, *Dracula* nevertheless draws on prevalent gothic tropes used to paint the horrors of the Famine in the 1840s and 1850s. In 'Thanatos', in the image of a once-loving mother driven mad by desperate circumstances, we perhaps see the prototype of Lucy Westenra, who also, in her transformed state, feeds on the bodies of children. Stoker certainly does not deploy gothic imagery in a pointedly political way, as did Young Ireland as part of their anti-British polemics. Yet by turning to the popular gothic novel form, Stoker is afforded a vehicle for critique arguably more powerful than the strategies available to other Irish writers who were more closely associated with the contemporary Irish literary and cultural revival (though, of course, Yeats and Joyce do incorporate elements of the gothic into their more 'serious' work). *Dracula*'s painful lingering on scenes of Lucy's slow deterioration – which, I will argue, echo depictions of the suffering of Famine victims earlier in the century – followed by her death and reincarnation as a demon, unleash some of the gothic's power to work as social critique. Lucy's vamping instigates a power reversal that puts the starved victim in a position to drain the life out of the institutions that allowed or even caused her death. Once infected, she nearly bleeds the life out of four men representing a cross-section of institutional power and is still famished; and as the Bloofer Lady, she becomes a would-be devourer of English children.[2]

Dracula comes to England aboard a ship named for the Greek goddess of harvest, the *Demeter*, which he transforms into a ship of death. It meanders aimlessly into the harbour with its captain dead, tied to the mast and clutching a crucifix (the rest of the crew having already died) in a scene reminiscent of the ship of death that brings Moncada to the shores of Ireland in *Melmoth the Wanderer*, an Irish gothic novel written by one of Stoker's important literary predecessors, Charles Maturin. Seamus Deane has identified the similarity between this ship that brings Dracula and 'that resonant image from Famine times', the coffin-ship, of which the *Demeter* is 'a literal version' (1997, p.89). Such similarities remind us that Dracula is the offspring not only of foundational English gothic novels by Walpole, Radcliffe and Lewis, but also of earlier Irish novelists such as Maturin and Sheridan Le Fanu.

Stoker's allusion to Demeter recalls Ovid's version of the myth of Ceres's encounter with Famine, recounted by Kelleher in *The Feminisation of Famine*. As Kelleher relates, Famine, personified by a decrepit old woman, agrees to afflict Erysichthon as an act of revenge for Ceres, who is angered when Erysichthon cuts down a sacred oak. Erysichthon wastes away, feeding himself by 'consuming his own body' (Kelleher, 1997, p.1). In *Dracula*, the villain sails into the harbour on a ship named for nourishment and plenty, but ironically, he is bringing with him hunger, disease and death. While his presence was physical, palpable, in the first section of the novel (set in his home country, safe in his castle), in this next part of the novel (set in England) he all but vanishes. Now, his peculiar evil – depletion, deprivation, starvation – becomes manifest through signs on the body of a young Englishwoman, Lucy Westenra. Reversing the gender roles in Ovid's parable, Demeter brings a *male* figure of Famine to enact a vengeance that takes place upon a *woman's* body. Lucy withers, her body consuming itself like Erysichthon's under Famine's curse. She is transformed into a recognizable icon of the Famine, bearing on her body all of its symptomatic horrors, its painful and divisive ambivalences.

Lucy, like Dracula's vampire wives, in her affliction with symptoms of the Famine, comes to resemble the 'Dearg-due' (red bloodsucker), the female vampire imagined to lure men in and then suck their blood (Belford, 1996, p.64). Lucy's vampirism also has connections with the Irish banshee legends. As Robert Tracy explains, Sheridan Le Fanu drew his portrait of the vampire Carmilla from stories of the *ban sidh*, 'a woman who dwells in one of the ancient burial mounds so common in the Irish countryside, a woman of the dead' (Tracy, 1999, p.xxii). Similarly, the Irish fairy can easily be seen as a source for Carmilla and for Stoker's Lucy. Irish fairies (*si* or *sidhe*),

> are more sinister than Shakespeare's Mustardseeds and Peaseblossoms. They crave human beings, especially children, but also young men and women, luring them away to live a kind of half-life under the earth. In some way they live on – or through – these captives, as vampires live on blood . . . Like vampires, they are undead and hungry.
>
> (Ibid., p.xxii)

The main effect of the Count's bite is to cause his victims to feel the same illicit appetites, to crave that to which, in William Carleton's words, only a 'famished maniac' (1991, p.129) would resort. First Lucy and later Mina begin to crave the blood of those around them, even though to consume it means to bring sickness and death on themselves. The vampire's consumption of blood for sustenance recalls Charlotte Stoker's memories of the 1832 Sligo cholera epidemic, which Stoker asked her to put down in writing for him. (Cholera returned during the Famine, an epidemic occurring in 1848–49.) Charlotte reported that during the epidemic some people, in desperation, drank blood from the veins of cattle (Belford, 1996, p.18), which, as Van Helsing points out in *Dracula*, is the behaviour of the vampire bat: 'there are bats that come at night and open the veins of cattle and horses and suck dry their veins' (Stoker, 1998, p.192). Charlotte's description of the effects of the cholera plague in her 1875 letter to Stoker could easily be mistaken for a description of Dracula himself: 'Its bitter, strange kiss, and man's want of experience or knowledge of its nature, or how best to resist its attacks, added, if anything could, to its horrors' (Stoker, 1993, pp.498–9).

Once Dracula's invisible predations begin, the Westenra house rapidly becomes a house of death. The symptoms of his attack include deterioration of the body – pallor, weakness, a skeletal appearance, lethargy, apathy and the inability to eat. These are all symptoms repeatedly described in accounts of the famine, even the last, when after months of starvation, the sudden introduction of food to the stomach often made people sick; some families even resorted to eating the blighted potatoes, which made them nauseated, or were made sick by incorrectly prepared Indian corn that was shipped to Ireland as famine relief. The Westenra family's increasing isolation, the symptoms of contagion (the daughter's death quickly succeeding the mother's), and the garlic on the window-sill all echo recurring images from the Famine. The vampire bite and its symptoms link together the multiple threats of starvation, malnutrition and disease that characterized the Famine and its representations.

As Christine Kinealy explains in her history of the Famine, 'Malnutrition and disease, rather than starvation, became the main enemy of the Irish poor after 1846' (1997, p.93), particularly during 'Black '47'. Fever, dysentery and smallpox, extremely contagious diseases, were the most common, while other illnesses such as bronchitis, influenza, measles and tuberculosis also contributed to the mounting death toll (ibid.). One of the particular horrors of the fever was that one never knew who would catch it next, and family, friends and neighbours were shunned. Those suspected of having the disease often became outcasts. Carleton writes in *The Black Prophet* (1847) (one of the most famous works about famine in Ireland, published the year Stoker was born),

The moment fever was ascertained, or even supposed, to visit a family, at that moment the infected persons were avoided by their neighbours and friends as if they carried death, as they often did, about them, so that its presence occasioned all the usual interchanges of civility and good-neighbourhood to be discontinued.

(1991, p.127)[3]

Richard Delaney of Wexford recalled,

When a person in any house got fever the people of the house would hide it from the neighbours. If the neighbours suspected there was any fever in the house, they used to steal up to the house at night time and put an onion on the window sill. They would split the onion in two. If the onion turned green they would know that there was fever in that particular house and they would avoid it.

(Quoted in Kinealy, 1997, p.93)

The placing of the onion in the window at night-time is echoed in *Dracula* by the garlic placed in Lucy's window when she is a suspected victim of a vampire bite. For cholera, plates of salt with vitriol, or sulfuric acid, poured on it were placed outside all the windows and doors, as this was thought to prevent the disease from getting into the house (Stoker, 1993, p.501). The five protagonists of the novel are faced with the necessity of a double betrayal – shunning Lucy's touch when she is ill, and killing her when she is 'dead' so that her disease will not spread to others. Lucy's vampirism, like Famine-related disease, is clearly dangerously contagious. Seward recalls that when Arthur bends over Lucy to kiss her, Van Helsing 'swooped upon him, and catching him by the neck with both hands, dragged him back with a fury of strength which I never thought he could have possessed, and actually hurled him almost across the room' (Stoker, 1998, p.161). In the later case of Mina, the vampire's baptism of blood necessitates not only that she be avoided physically but also kept out of the confidences and social exchanges of the others. It is a horror even greater than the vamping of 'loose' Lucy that the seemingly impervious Mina Harker could be infected. The vulnerability to attack and unpredictability of the vampire disease make it not unlike the cholera epidemic, about which Charlotte Stoker wrote, 'There was no telling who would go next, and when one said goodbye to a friend he said it as if for ever' (Stoker, 1993, p.499).

But perhaps the single symptom that most strongly connects Lucy's illness, her deterioration and wasting away, with the sufferings of Famine victims is the recurring emphasis placed on the *mouth*. Dr Seward reports, in the early stages of Lucy's illness, 'She was ghastly, chalkily pale; the red seemed to have gone even from her lips and gums, and the bones of her face stood out prominently; her breathing was painful to see or hear' (Stoker, 1998, p.120). Lucy's appearance arouses sympathy rather than fear and loathing in Seward (as occurs later) because at this point she still displays the signs of a person passively perishing. She is pale, weak, lethargic and seems to be fading away quietly. Later in the development of her affliction, however, Seward adds to his description of pale gums with drawn-back lips the image of sharp, aggressive canine teeth: 'her face was at its worst, for the open mouth showed the pale gums. Her teeth, in the dim, uncertain light, seemed longer and sharper than they had been in the morning. In particular, by some trick of the light, the canine teeth looked longer and sharper than the rest' (ibid., p.159). Just before Lucy dies, Seward observes, 'the mouth opened, and the pale gums, drawn back, made the teeth look longer and sharper than ever' (ibid., p.161).[4]

This focus on the mouth and particularly on the pronounced appearance of teeth was common in representations of the suffering of Famine victims. For example, in *Castle Richmond* the narrator describes a young child dying by the roadside during the Famine: 'its cheeks were wan, and yellow and sunken, and the two teeth which it had already cut were seen with terrible plainness through its emaciated lips' (Trollope, 1993 [1860], p.354). Later the narrator claims that one could read the doom of the famine sufferer specifically in the appearance of the mouth. It 'would fall and seem to hang, the lips at the two ends of the mouth would be dragged down, and the lower parts of the cheeks would fall as though they had been dragged and pulled'. When such signs around the mouth became 'easily legible, the poor doomed wretch was known with certainty' (ibid., pp.684–5).

More specifically, a sense of ambivalence about the afflicted person – wavering between sympathy for the waning humanity and a sort of disgust at what are seen as animalistic, savage traits – runs through contemporary accounts of the famine. Peadar O Laoghaire's autobiography focuses on the mouth and teeth of the Famine victims, evincing both sympathy and disgust. A woman he had known before the potato blight, now sadly changed, comes across sympathetically, 'walking very slowly and panting, as if she had been running. She was blowing so much, her mouth was wide open, so that I had a sight of her teeth' (O Laoghaire, 1991, p.130). But a subsequent description of a starving boy is more mixed. His 'mouth was wide open and his lips, upper and lower both, were drawn back, so that his teeth – the amount he had of them – were exposed. I saw the two, big, long, yellow eye-teeth in his mouth, the terror in his eyes and the confusion in his face.' The terror humanizes the boy, but he also appears animalistic. When offered food, 'He snatched the bread and turned his back to us and his face to the wall and he started right into eating it so ravenously that you would think he would choke himself' (ibid., p.130). A similar duality in Lucy's symptoms – a shifting back and forth between passively fading victim and animalistic aggressor – comes across in descriptions of her mouth that alternate between a focus on the pale gums and on the sharp canine teeth.

Kelleher observes this duality in *The Black Prophet*. In addition to ridiculing Prime Minister Russell's defence of a free market in the face of such a catastrophe, Carleton blames the 'the hard-hearted and well-known misers' (Carleton, 1991, p.126) and the 'vast number of strong farmers' who had 'bursting granaries' but hoarded their food and kept it from others. Advocating for the Irish people, Carleton writes that under circumstances like these, 'it is not surprising that the starving multitudes should, in the ravening madness of famine, follow up its outrageous impulses, and forget those legal restraints, or moral principles, that protect property under ordinary or different circumstances' (ibid.). However, he goes on to characterize the behaviour of a mob of hungry people in a way that could only have aroused fear in his readers. His description draws upon similar themes used by Stoker in his depiction of the vampire threat: violence, insanity and contagion. Like a vampire bite, the affliction of Famine changes ordinarily law-abiding and moral citizens into their own barbaric others. Carleton graphically describes the degeneration into savagery of a group of starving people, while at the same time somewhat mitigating the terror of his description by giving exculpating explanations of the cause; if the people had not been driven to the brink of destruction, their 'strong intellect and reason' would probably not have given way.

Such contradictions and ambivalences also surface in Stoker's text. Before her death, Lucy's behaviour shifts between an appropriately Victorian feminine passivity and a kind of submission that seems, contradictorily, to signify both resignation and anger. For example, shifting into vampire mode before she dies, Lucy speaks 'in a sort of sleep-waking, vague, unconscious way', with eyes 'now dull and hard at once' (Stoker, 1998, p.161). Before she dies, Lucy wavers back and forth between two conflicting states. The good Lucy moves toward accepting death in a peaceful attitude of Christian resignation, but this is not so easily distinguished from the symptoms of the vampire infection itself, which are fatigue, listlessness and long periods of silence. When Mina becomes infected later in the novel, Van Helsing's observations show the same duality: 'Her teeth are some sharper, and at times her eyes are more hard. But these are not all, there is to her the silence now so often; as so it was with Miss Lucy' (ibid., p.323). In the case of Lucy, however, this ambivalent portrayal soon gives way to a full-fledged image of horror following her death. The imagery of the effects of Famine, which till now had been characterized by a tension between sympathy and fear, is simplified as Lucy is turned into a figure of animal appetites, wrath and the desire to wreak retribution, on whom it is permissible (and even fun, in the case of Dr Seward) to hate, brutalize and dismember. Lucy as the Undead is represented in the most negative terms which Carleton and other writers of the Famine employed to describe the behaviour of the starving. In this way the novel seems to resolve the moral ambiguities it otherwise so provocatively raises.

The dehumanization of Lucy accomplishes two things. First, it presents a counter to the commonplace that those who died in the Famine did so with resignation, even apathy. There may be a tension in Carleton's work between representation of the pain and anger (on the one hand) and the dullness and fatuity (on the other) of Famine sufferers, but the mid-century Famine novels of Trollope, Brew and Walshe give much more credence to the latter interpretation. It had become the norm for writers to stress the passivity with which the starving received their deaths. As the narrator of Trollope's *Castle Richmond* explains, for example, 'There were no signs of acute agony', when the affliction reached its worst stage; 'none of the horrid symptoms of gnawing hunger by which one generally supposes that famine is accompanied. The look is one of apathy, desolation, and death' (Trollope, 1993 [1860], pp.684–5). Such descriptions in part function to strip the scenes of the dying of some of their horror, but one should note, in fairness to Trollope, that they also puncture another damaging stereotype – that of the wild, savage, animalistic Irish. As is typical of the novel as a whole, Trollope's narrator is eager to rectify English misunder-standings of the Irish character. However, this particular act of rectification concludes by assigning a different stigma: 'One would think that starving men would become violent, taking food by open theft . . . But such was by no means the case . . . The fault of the people was apathy' (ibid., pp.640–1). Stoker's depiction of Lucy after her death returns the pain and anger to the Famine sufferer, giving back the stripped-away emotion of the mid-century realist novels and restoring the sense of outrage to which the people had so much right. Lucy as the Undead is anything but passive and hardly accepts her own death with apathy or resignation. In death, she preys on the figures of patriarchal institutional power, which many Irish believed responsible for the severity of the crisis, and so she can be read as avenging the Famine dead. At the same time, however, Stoker's vilifying portrait of her allows for, even demands, her brutal punishment.

One of the most obvious ways in which the novel tries to make it permissible for the reader to enjoy the violent suppression of Lucy is that it makes her promiscuous and anti-maternal. Two recurring images found markedly in representations of the Famine are the semi-clad, sexualized, shameless woman who provokes discomfort in onlookers and the monstrous mother. As Kelleher argues, when the Great Hunger is individuated – when its effects are made visible through the depiction of an individual body – that figure is usually female and often a mother: 'One of the most frequent figures in famine texts is that of a hunger-stricken mother, holding a child at her breast' (Kelleher, 1997, p.22). In addition, it is often rendered in the language and imagery of *horror*; some Famine scenes show a mother competing with her child for scraps of food or even willing to cannibalize her own offspring. In his *Jail Journal* (1854), John Mitchel reports that during the Famine, 'maniac mothers stowed away their dead children to be devoured at midnight' (quoted in Morash, 1995, p.74). The horror Lucy generates in her former admirers stems from the chilling ambiguity of her gesture: she holds a child to her breast as if to feed it, but they gather she means to feed *on* it. Of course, the gesture horrifies because it makes a mockery of the cherished image of the Victorian angel of the house, but it also would have recalled an image terribly common in contemporary writing of the Famine.

Lucy's transformation also renders her a sexual temptress. It is worth noting that the inappropriate sexual exposure of women is another pervasive theme of Famine literature. As Kelleher points out, 'Observers highlight the woman's nakedness or quasi-nakedness, often with references to their own, resulting, discomfort' (1997, p.24). In *The Black Prophet*, Carleton lingers on the horror of seeing women and girls lose their natural modesty and self-control.[5] For William Bennett, the 'miserably clad female forms we met along the public road were disgraceful, – disgusting' (quoted in Kelleher, 1997, p.25). Perhaps Dracula's most horrifying power, like-wise, is his ability to rob girls and mothers of their timidity and modesty, their sense of shame and decency. In vamped Lucy, Carleton's description of Famine-stricken women is perfectly realized: 'all sense of modesty was cast to the winds', 'all the lingering traces of self-respect' vanish, and 'everything like shame was forgotten' (Carleton, 1991, p.126). Dracula transforms chaste young women into wanton temptresses, and he inverts maternal instincts into the desire to maim children. Seward's description of Lucy seeking to gratify her 'wild and tyrannical cravings' stresses the same themes as Carleton's account of the transformed women: 'savagery', animal behaviour, and loss of restraint, modesty and decency – which Carleton says he can only attribute to 'the insanity of desolation'. When the band of vampire-hunters interrupts Lucy's meal in the graveyard, 'she drew back with an angry snarl, such as a cat gives when taken unawares' (Stoker, 1998, p.211). Prevented by Van Helsing's crucifix from feasting on Arthur, 'She recoiled from it, and, with a suddenly distorted face, full of rage, dashed past him' (ibid., p.212). Seward solemnly reports, 'Never did I see such baffled malice on a face . . . . If a face ever meant death – if looks could kill – we saw it at that moment' (ibid.).

Lucy, who in life had wandered the graveyard clad only in her night clothes (a behaviour which causes Mina to fear as much 'for her reputation' as for her health and safety), now haunts the night clad in a burial shroud, which (as Penelope Shuttle and Peter Redgrove note), is much less hampering than a corset (Ellmann, 1998, pp.xxvi–xxvii). Seward describes her eyes as 'unclean and full of hell-fire, instead of the pure, gentle orbs we knew' (Stoker, 1998, p.211). The dark stains on Lucy's mouth and robe recall other recurring Famine images mentioned by Kelleher, which include 'the walking dead' and descriptions of people, usually children, 'with mouths stained green from eating grass' (Kelleher, 1997, p.8). Van Helsing 'raised his lantern and drew the slide; by the concentrated light that fell on Lucy's face we could see that the lips were crimson with fresh blood, and that the stream had trickled over her chin and stained the purity of her lawn death-robe' (Stoker, 1998, p.211).

Noticeably missing from the ensuing scene of Lucy's staking and decapitation is any sense of sorrow or regret. Even when Van Helsing first suggests the plan to Seward – before Seward has had a chance to digest the notion or see Van Helsing's 'proof' – he is not wholly opposed: 'It made me shudder to think of so mutilating the body of the woman whom I had loved. And yet the feeling was not so strong as I had expected' (ibid., p.201). Ten pages later, Seward's inner struggle has been completely resolved: 'At that moment the remnant of my love passed into hate and loathing; had she then to be killed, I could have done it with savage delight' (ibid, p.211). Even Lucy's betrothed begins to share in the feeling. Seward says, 'I could see even Arthur's face grow hard as he looked' (ibid., p.214). As Van Helsing begins to unload from his bag the tools he will use in Lucy's murder – soldering iron, various knives, a wooden stake, a hammer – Dr Seward feels an almost eager anticipation. 'To me, a doctor's preparations for work of any kind are stimulating and bracing' (ibid.), he reports with no apparent irony. After Arthur drives the stake through Lucy's heart, she returns to her original form, yet Seward and Van Helsing have no difficulty in chopping off the head that now bears the beloved woman's face of 'unequalled sweetness and purity' (ibid., p.217). Seward briskly reports that after Arthur kisses Lucy goodbye, 'we cut off the head and filled the mouth with garlic . . . Outside, the air was sweet, the sun shone, and the birds sang, and it seemed as if all nature were tuned to a different pitch. There was gladness and mirth and peace everywhere' (ibid.).

As has been argued, this scene would seem to resolve the moral ambiguities raised earlier in the novel. Lucy, who so often fluctuated between the proper and the improper, the passive and the aggressive, the human and the animal, is finally presented as utterly inhuman in order to justify the destruction wreaked upon her by the 'heroes'. However, Seward's declaration that gladness, mirth and peace reign everywhere after Lucy's death rings hollow. Although the novel tries to provide closure by means of Lucy's 'real' death, it is not convincing in a novel which also asserts, 'Truly there is no such thing as finality' (ibid., p.189) and which is plotted on the basis of a recurring, transhistorical evil. Arguably the most memorable part of the novel, the narrative of Lucy's suffering, death and attempt at vengeance does more to resurrect the memory of the Famine dead than to bury it. And as Lucy's narrative recedes, the character of Renfield enters the foreground to offer a masculinized, violent and more threatening representation of the suffering of the native Irish in the Famine.

Dying of institutions

Stoker appears to have drawn upon the character of Stanton (the imprisoned prey of the novel's antihero in *Melmoth the Wanderer*) for his creation of Renfield, just as the Wanderer is likely one of the progenitors of Dracula.[6] In imagery familiar to readers of *Dracula*, Melmoth taunts Stanton with his cell-mates, 'the spider and the rat' (Maturin, 1998, p.55):

> I have known prisoners in the Bastile to feed them for companions – why don't you begin your task? I have known a spider to descend at the tap of a finger,

and a rat to come forth when the daily meal was brought, to share it with his fellow-prisoner! – How delightful to have vermin for your guests!

(Ibid.)

The threat Melmoth makes to Stanton (that he will eventually feel himself being eaten alive by the vermin that collect in his cell) is reversed in *Dracula*: Renfield makes first the flies, then the spiders, the companions of his daily meal, and then he begins to consume them.

It is this focus on deviant forms of consumption that most distinguishes Renfield from earlier Irish gothic madhouse victims like Stanton and Sheridan Le Fanu's Maud Vernon. Dr Seward claims, for his part, to have identified in him a new kind of madman:

> I shall have to invent a new classification for him, and call him a zoophagous (life-eating) maniac; what he desires is to absorb as many lives as he can, and he has laid himself out to achieve it in a cumulative way. He gave many flies to one spider and many spiders to one bird, and then wanted a cat to eat the many birds. What would have been his later steps?
>
> (Stoker, 1998, pp.70–1)

Seward hints here at cannibalism and bestiality, 'unnatural' appetites associated with the desperation and 'madness' of victims of the Great Hunger. I read Renfield as another kind of Famine sufferer: afflicted by the madness Carleton described as taking hold of ordinarily sane, reasonable people when starving, making them susceptible to strange appetites.

The symptoms of Renfield's madness, in a novel published just on the verge of the twentieth century, can be read as reflective of the incipient stirrings of a militarized Irish Catholic nationalism. The contradictory poles of Renfield's nature resemble Victorian ethnographic stereotypes of the native Irish temperament: naturally weak and servile, but impressionable and undisciplined enough to be incited to violence and savagery by opportunistic leaders. Like the puritan weaver in *Melmoth*'s madhouse, Renfield has a split personality, which ranges from 'naturally' passive and subservient (when left to his own devices) to enraged and homicidal (when under the influence of his charismatic leader, the Count). Seward's diary records, 'His moods change so rapidly that I find it difficult to keep touch with them' (Stoker, 1998, p.268). He goes from being 'perpetually violent' (ibid., p.106) to behaving 'in a very humble, cringing way' (ibid., p.116). When Dracula is not around, Renfield tends to be obsequious, but under the power of the Count's leadership he becomes both haughty and violent (lending support to Michael Moses's reading of Dracula as an undead Parnell).

As is the case for the puritan weaver and the loyalist tailor in the mad-house scene in *Melmoth*, Renfield's madness superficially resembles religious fanaticism. Seward opines, 'a strong man with homicidal and religious mania at once might be dangerous. The combination is a dreadful one' (ibid., p.100). Renfield's religious fervour (which has been developing ever since Dracula's appearance in England) can be interpreted as a parody of Catholicism: his 'Master' is the Old-World Count, who comes from a land of peasants, crucifixes, wildness and superstition. Renfield's combination of 'homicidal and religious mania' raises connotations of a new, late-nineteenth-century, strongly Catholicized Irish nationalism. The Catholic Church had been playing a larger role in nationalist politics, and, as the historian Brian Walker points out (Walker, 2000), violent sectarian conflicts from distant history (such as the rebellion – or the Protestant massacre – of 1641 and the 1688–89 siege of Derry) were being more actively revived and commemorated in Protestant unionist circles as Home Rule became an increasingly vexed issue.[7] In other words, fears of mass Catholic violence were not far from many Irish Protestant minds.

Renfield's threatening behaviour crystallizes a number of recurring concerns of late nineteenth-century Ireland. When he escapes from his cell, he runs to Carfax, Dracula's property, and presses himself against the door of the musty old chapel, repeating, 'I am here to do Your bidding, Master. I am Your slave, and You will reward me, for I shall be faithful' (Stoker, 1998, p.102). This caricatured pledge and the ominously zealous obedience and loyalty it implies suggest several analogues in late nineteenth-century Irish politics: ghoulishly imagined pledges of the Irish Republican Brotherhood, founded in 1858; the strategies of the 'agrarian Fenians' (Valente, 2000, p. 639) of the National Land League, founded in 1879, and pictured as an Irish vampire in a *Punch* cartoon of October 1885 (Riquelme, 2002, p.376); and the 'Fenian cult of the dead leader' (Fitzpatrick, 1991, p.225) Parnell, created soon after Parnell's death in 1891.[8] Of course, one of Dracula's most threatening qualities is that he creates minions in his own image; he is gathering an army that he plans will eventually colonize England. The danger Dracula poses in his returns from the past – and his ability to postpone his vengeance for centuries – is like that which the native Irish were supposed to represent: oppressed for centuries, possessing a long historical memory of failed but glorious rebellions, and always threatening to rise up again to repeat, in nightmare logic, the events of 1641 and 1798. As Van Helsing says of Dracula, if events do not go his way this particular time, 'he may choose to sleep him for a century' (Stoker, 1998, p.355) and then return when the opportunity for his vengeance seems more propitious. Similarly, the native Irish were feared to be awaiting their moment to rise up again, and even when they seemed harmless this could be deceptive, as proven by their recalcitrance over centuries, their obstinate retention of their religion and culture in spite of many waves of British colonization and attempted anglicization and conversion.

Reading Renfield as one of the first members of Dracula's army, we can see Seward's asylum (and his attempts to contain Renfield with the techniques of medical science and psychology) as one of the many fields of battle on which the novel's 'heroes' face the enemy. Valente argues that *Dracula* contains direct allusions to the 'Plan of Campaign', organized by the nationalist leaders William O'Brien and John Dillon in response to the insufficiencies of government land reforms in the 1880s (Valente, 2000, p.639). Indeed, the protagonists deploy the rhetoric of military campaign and battle strategy in their pursuit of Dracula.[9] Reading the coalition this way, Van Helsing is not unlike a recruiter for an underground organization who uses techniques of terror to induce loyalty. His now-faithful men would not have joined his side had they not been hardened to their murderous task by the 'most harrowing' event of witnessing (at his instigation) Lucy's torture and demise. When they emerge from the graveyard afterward, Van Helsing seizes the moment to make his pitch:

it is a long task, and a difficult, and there is danger in it, and pain. Shall you not all help me? We have learned to believe, all of us – is it not so? . . . And since so, do we not see our duty? Yes! And do we not promise to go on to the bitter end?

(Stoker, 1998, pp.217–18)

The promise is sealed with an oath shortly thereafter: 'Then without a word we all knelt down together, and, all holding hands, swore to be true to each other. We men pledged ourselves to raise the veil of sorrow' (ibid., p.297). Their mission, however often they try to justify it to themselves, is to commit a murder, a fact that they acknowledge in numerous places in the novel. In this sense, their actions resemble those of a secret society.

Their rationale has to be repeated often, precisely because it seems not entirely convincing, even to them. They frequently demonstrate awareness of the illegality and possible immorality of their actions, preparing in advance plans to cover up the murder if necessary.[10] Their course of action is given justification by the representation of Dracula's (and Renfield's) brutality. Renfield possesses stereotypical ethnographic traits of the native Irish, seen as angry, vengeful and susceptible to the leadership of dangerous demagogues. His unnatural appetites make him resemble a Famine victim – one who is determined not only to survive but to live the span of many natural lives, and not to allow the history of the Famine to be repressed or put to rest.

Yet Renfield is not simply an emanation of reactionary Protestant fears of Catholic-nationalist mobilization and violence. His identity is not stable enough to admit of such a simple interpretation. After all, he was once a gentleman, and he still retains vestiges of 'civilization'. At times, Seward admits, he seems 'as sane as anyone I ever saw' (ibid., p.225). Stoker not only undermines the grounds on which Renfield's 'mad' diagnosis is based; he also destabilizes the foundations of the heroes' claim to sanity. Dracula forces the protagonists to become like him in the process of combating him, adopting his beliefs and means, fighting with his weapons, even becoming as 'mad' as Renfield.[11] It is not much of a stretch to read Dr Seward as a sinister figure, especially given that he is the descendant of a slew of mad or evil doctors in nineteenth-century gothic fiction. Hawthorne created doctor-scientist villains in short stories like 'The Birthmark' and 'Rappaccini's Daughter' earlier in the century, and of course Mary Shelley had made famous the morally ambiguous Dr Frankenstein in 1818. In the mid-century, sensation novelists popularized the figure of the villainous doctor, akin to Dr Antomarchi and Dr Malkin in Le Fanu's *The Rose and the Key*. Perhaps most relevant to *Dracula*, however, the gothic revival at the end of the century produced the notorious Dr Jekyll and Dr Moreau. Dr Seward and, certainly, Dr Van Helsing, inherit this rich history of villainous doctors. In fact, Dr Van Helsing is connected to the novel's villain by more than the trope of his foreignness. Van Helsing's techniques (hypnotizing Mina, for example) closely resemble Dracula's own. Seward refers to Van Helsing's ideas as 'monstrous' and at one point even considers that Van Helsing himself could be responsible for Lucy's death.[12] Seward himself, as Van Helsing's protégé, is implicated in his own accusation.

Renfield's resistance to Seward's medical techniques can be interpreted as a critique of the mechanisms of coercion underlying ostensibly benevolent institutional relief. Maturin used religious divisions in a madhouse as a trope to represent Irish politics, and Stoker does so too, but to different ends. When Dr Seward repeatedly tries to focus Renfield's attention on his 'religious mania' (Stoker, 1998, p.100), which he believes is the key to Renfield's madness and thus to his 'cure', Renfield persistently brings the subject back to his bottom line: eating, consuming and pro-longing his *earthly* life. Despite the trappings of religious mania, Renfield's problem has materialist origins. When Seward attempts to get Renfield to talk in abstractions about the spiritual dimension of his obsession, Renfield obstinately brings him back down to the level of the physical, the bodily. When Seward tries to focus him on his aspirations to a godlike status, Renfield retorts, 'I am not even concerned in His especially spiritual doings' (ibid., p.268). Rather, he has more concern in things 'purely terrestrial' (ibid., p.269). He rebuffs Seward, who accuses him of 'being after' souls, 'Oh no, oh no! I want no souls. Life is all I want' (ibid., p.268). Most tellingly, Renfield adds, 'I don't want any souls, indeed, indeed! I don't. I couldn't use them if I had them! they would be no manner of use to me. I couldn't eat them or –' (ibid., p.269). (In one of Stoker's charac-teristically heavy-handed touches, Renfield cannot bring himself to say 'drink them'.) Later, Renfield again insists to Seward that he does not want flies or spiders: 'What's the use of spiders? There isn't anything in them to eat or –' (ibid., p.271). This desublimating (and amusing) pragmatism undercuts the effect of the more high-flown religious metaphors Renfield uses in other places in the novel.

Dr Seward's strategic doling out and withholding of sustenance to Renfield for his own purposes reflects policies of the British government satirized in nationalist polemics like those of Mitchel, who argued that the Famine was a product of British policy – not simply mismanagement but a desire to see Ireland finally and completely weakened and subjugated.[13] In *The Last Conquest of Ireland (Perhaps)* (1861), Mitchel focused on the symbol of the poor-house, which he compared to a 'fortress of Giant Despair' (quoted in Morash, 1995, p.64). According to Morash, 'In Mitchel's text, the Poor-house becomes the single object capable of standing as a symbol of Famine Ireland . . . In Mitchel's writing of the Famine, true horror lies not in cholera, typhus, or starvation, but in the increased amount of government control which they occasioned', always in the name of 'relieving' or 'ameliorating' (ibid., p.65). Mitchel wrote in *The Last Conquest*, 'we are sickening and dying of these institutions, fast; they are consuming us like a plague, degrading us to paupers' (ibid., p.66). Though

Mitchel was describing the poor-house, not the madhouse, the same may be argued of Seward's techniques of amelioration and relief, especially as they apply to Renfield's hunger. Both strategies link the receiving of sustenance and the relief from hunger to an institution's moral or ethical judgements about the subjects in question. In the case of Ireland, food was not simply to be given out but worked for, even when the work itself was not useful (there are famous jokes about roads to nowhere constructed during the Famine) or when the people were too weak to do it.

Dr Seward wields his power unethically when he decides to use Renfield's 'cravings', as he calls them, as leverage with which to bargain and deal with him, as well as test him in order to gather information about him for his research. Seward is pleased with himself for having discovered a new kind of mental patient – a zoophagous madman – and, accordingly, is willing to manipulate his bizarre cravings to further his own ends. Sometimes he encourages Renfield's eating habits, and at other times he denies them. In both cases, his motive is a desire to increase his own knowledge, rather than a genuine concern for Renfield's well-being; Renfield is no more than Seward's 'pet lunatic' (Stoker, 1998, p.233). For instance, Seward leads Renfield to believe he may permit him to have a cat in the future when he really has no such intention, thinking, 'I shall test him with his present craving and see how it will work out; then I shall know more' (ibid., p.70). Seward firmly establishes that he holds total control over life and death, a god-like figure to rival Dracula's own powers. He can determine what Renfield will and will not consume; he can withhold Renfield's nourishment in order to 'test' him.

Renfield is aware of Dr Seward's self-centred use of him. He comments with dripping sarcasm on the doctor's attempts to manipulate him through the selective granting and withholding of his peculiar forms of sustenance. As long as "'I have friends – good friends – like you, Doctor Seward", he said with a leer of inexpressible cunning; "I know that I shall never lack the means of life!"' (ibid., p.269). This statement becomes grossly literal parody when Renfield tries to attack and eat Dr Seward himself (as if to imply, if you won't let me eat what I need to survive, I'll eat *you*). Seward is in his study when Renfield runs in with a dinner-knife in hand, slices into Seward's left wrist, and begins to lick up the blood (ibid., p.141). The doctor feels sick as he watches Renfield 'lying on his belly on the floor licking up, like a dog, the blood which had fallen from my wounded wrist' (ibid.).

In the asylum, Renfield undergoes a reversion to animalism resonant with nineteenth-century accounts of famine victims, such as Carleton's account, in which he uses phrases such as 'the insanity of desolation', 'the insane spirit of violence' (Carleton, 1991, p.128) and 'famished maniacs' (ibid., p.129). Carleton compares a hungry mob to 'savage animals', 'wild, savage, and ferocious', akin to beasts 'in the deepest jungle of Africa itself' (ibid., p.128). Renfield's servile and violent moods correspond figuratively to descriptions of him as a domesticated and a wild animal, respectively. One evening Seward sees him sniffing along the floor of his cell 'as a dog does when setting' (Stoker, 1998, p.100). Later he escapes from his cell and '[w]hen we closed in on him he fought like a tiger' and 'was more like a wild beast than a man' (ibid., p.102). Renfield's mad behaviour resembles that in representations of hungry Famine mobs. He brutally attacks two men carrying carts to Carfax. The incident is violent enough that Renfield has to be put into a strait-jacket and removed to a padded room, and one of the men calls him a 'wild beast' (ibid., p.156). Similarly, Carleton describes a hungry mob attacking provision vehicles on their way to market, beating those who resist, and going on to attack and pillage mills. They even consume raw flour or oatmeal, the more fortunate 'devouring bread, with a fury, to which only the unnatural appetites of so many famished maniacs could be compared' (ibid., p.129). This is followed by sickness: 'giddiness, retchings, fainting-fits, convulsions, and, in some cases, death itself, were induced by this wolfish and frightful gluttony on the part of the starving people' (ibid., p.129). The consumption of inappropriate or 'unnatural' nutriment is a dominant theme in Renfield's characterization, of course, as are 'retchings' and 'convulsions' that follow such consumption. In one such incident, Renfield devours all the birds he has been collecting, leaving behind just a drop of blood on his pillow and a few feathers. Later, he grows nauseated and regurgitates: 'Renfield has been very sick and has disgorged a whole lot of feathers.' The attendant speculates in horror, 'My belief is . . . that he just took and ate them raw!' (ibid., p.70).

Renfield's eventual death is shameful for the asylum. The doctors decide to make up a false account of his death for the official record.[14] They find Renfield lying on the floor in a pool of blood, his head crushed, his back broken. The attendant speculates that he could have beaten his own head on the ground, and broken his back, by falling out of bed. But, as he himself admits, it would have been impossible for him to beat his own head after breaking his back (ibid., p.275). Seward (the *steward* of the asylum, its authority in charge of caring for and protecting the inmates) gives his assent to the cover-up, which brings back to mind old Mr Swales's assertion to Mina that 'gravestones lie'. The true stories of the deaths of the disenfranchised will perhaps never be known because there is no history that records them.[15] Renfield dies asking Seward to remove the *strait-waistcoat*: his paralysis – though, as we know, it was caused by Dracula's attack on him – feels to Renfield like the remedies (or punishments) and constraints of Seward's own supposedly beneficent asylum.

A wolf-haunted nation

The comparison of Renfield to a wild beast and a tiger connects him to the tropes of wildness and keening, the final element of *Dracula* as a gothic Famine novel that I want to explore. Renfield is one of Dracula's subjects, as are the wolves, which Dracula has the power to direct and control. I would argue that the wolves who populate the otherwise 'barren land' (Stoker, 1998, p.319) – barren of thriving humanity – of Dracula's home country may represent a grieving, decimated, but also potentially dangerous native Irish population.[16] When the protagonists visit Dracula's land at the end of the novel, they are all struck by the howling of the wolves. Mina writes in her journal of the Carpathians, 'There was something wild and uncanny about the place. We could hear the distant howling of wolves. They were far off, but the sound, even though coming muffled through the deadening snowfall, was full of terror' (ibid., p.372). As the search for Dracula goes on the wolves get nearer, and their howling draws 'louder and closer' (ibid., p.374). This association with wolves and howling connects with the issue, frequently visited by critics, of Dracula's power (or lack thereof) to tell his own story.

One of the main symptoms of the vampire bite is the loss of the power of articulation and increasing silence. When Renfield is under Dracula's influence, he is less articulate and more given to both wild cries (keens) and ominous silences. For example, while he is strait-jacketed and chained to a wall in the padded room, 'His cries are at times awful, but the silences that follow are more deadly still' (ibid., p.102). Observing the changes in Mina, Van Helsing notes, '[T]here is to her the silence now often; as so it was with Miss Lucy' (ibid., p.323). Lucy as her original self writes down notes in a journal to record her experience, but shifting into her vampire state, she rips them up. Dracula himself, the most powerful of the vampire kind, seems capable only of the destruction of others' records, rather than the creation of his own. When he comes into the asylum to prey on Mina, he visits the study and burns all the manuscripts he can find, along with the cylinders of the phonograph. This scene closely resembles the one in

Melmoth in which the Wanderer destroys the manuscripts of the collector and then murders him in what is ultimately a gesture of futility (Maturin, 1998, pp.395–8 and 439). Similarly, falling silent as the novel goes on, Dracula seems to lack the authority to create his own narrative.

Dracula's diminishing presence and loss of articulation are of course connected to the increasing effectiveness of the heroes in combating him with their body of amassed 'knowledge' and their greater access to the tools of 'progress' and technology (as in Thomas Richards's argument that the British administered their empire through the deployment of an 'imperial archive' during the Victorian era). But Dracula's loss of speech takes on another meaning when viewed in an Irish gothic context. Rather than narrating his own history, Dracula replaces narrative with an 'almost musical', arguably Irish, howl. He challenges the narrative bounds established by the other characters, continuing to elude their capture by changing shape, sliding into the gaps in their laboriously assembled text, and manipulating the conditions by which they can know him (and hence kill him). In a specifically Irish context, Dracula may be read as a gothic figure whose associations and function in the novel connect him with an Irish articulator of the inarticulate: the keener.

David Lloyd describes the recurrence in prose accounts of Ireland during and after the Famine of the representation of a deadly silent land, counterpointed by an uncanny, human/animal howl or wail.[17] According to Lloyd, the wail noted in these accounts adapts a motif frequently found in representations of pre-Famine Ireland: keening, an expression of grief for the dead that puzzled and unsettled tourists. A sense of instability, of even 'sinister connotations' (Lloyd, 1997, p.37), arose from a series of contradictions associated with the keener and the keen. Once the sound traditionally associated with mourning for the dead, the keen undergoes a historical shift to become the uncanny wail described in accounts of the post-Famine landscape. Rather than simply being a cry of mourning for the dead, Lloyd argues, the wail becomes a way of marking the very silence it counterpoints, an expression of the inexpressible: 'It is, rather, the representation of a vanishing population regarded as inhabiting the borderlines of nature and culture, as giving vent to an inarticulate and animal cry against a catastrophe' (ibid., p.45). It marks the boundary of the articulable, uncannily straddling the line between human and animal.[18] Whereas the keen was seen as dangerous – potentially seditious, a mark of inassimilable Irish cultural difference – the wail is fatalistic, representing what is seen as Ireland's hopelessness and passivity in the face of the calamity.

Dracula presides over just such a land of the dead as the one Lloyd describes. As Jonathan says of Dracula's estate, 'I fear I am myself the only living soul within the place' (Stoker, 1998, p.25). Van Helsing tells Mina that Dracula is here to feed off Londoners because his own country has been depopulated: 'the measure of leaving his own barren land – barren of people – and coming to a new land where life of men teems till they are like the multitude of standing corn, was the work of centuries' (ibid., p.319). The barren land inhabited by Dracula is a land of howling; in fact, howling is one of the first features of Transylvania mentioned by Jonathan before he even meets Dracula (ibid., p.2). Like the keeners described by Mrs S.C. Hall, Thomas Crofton Croker and others, Dracula is uncannily both human and animal. His ability to control the wolves unsettles Jonathan: 'This was all so strange and uncanny that a dreadful fear came upon me' (ibid., p.14). Like the quasi-supernatural, 'decrepit and powerful' keener (Lloyd, 1997, p.38), Dracula is an 'old man' (Stoker, 1998, p.15) but with ruddy lips that show an 'astonishing vitality in a man of his years' (ibid., p.17) and 'prodigious strength' (ibid., p.14). Like the keener, he can be both old and young (as Jonathan realizes when he sees a youthful version of him in a London park).

The Count at first speaks to Jonathan as a mourner of the dead who is seemingly passive and defeated. He assures Jonathan of his resignation in what could pass for a speech by a failed Young Ireland rebel or retired Fenian: 'The warlike days are over. Blood is too precious a thing in these days of dishonourable peace; and the glories of the great races are as a tale that is told' (ibid., p.30). However, this posture of defeat is only one of the Count's many disguises. The wailing and howling that occur throughout *Dracula*, following the Count wherever he goes, are not passive, fatalistic sounds. Rather, they are linked to the wildness and violence of a 'wild beast' like Renfield.

Stoker's depiction of a land of wild howling puts a twist on a theme that had become common in the wake of the Famine, here expressed by George Petrie: 'The "land of song" is no longer tuneful; or, if a human sound met the traveller's ear, it was only that of the feeble and despairing wail for the dead' (quoted in Lloyd, 1997, p.33). In *Dracula*, however, the wailing and howling is anything but feeble, and it is itself *musical*. Reading the Count along the same lines as does Michael Moses (Dracula as Parnell, or as a nationalist leader), musical howling aligns with notions of Irish music as a vehicle of Irish national identity, an idea born during the Romantic period and given new life in the 1890s cultural revival. As the sun rises after Jonathan's first night in the castle, 'There seemed a strange stillness over everything; but as I listened I heard, as if from down below in the valley, the howling of many wolves. The Count's eyes gleamed, and he said: "Listen to them – the children of the night. What music they make!"' (Stoker, 1998, p.18). Dracula is not the only one who finds tunefulness in the uncanny howling. Here is Jonathan's own description: 'Close at hand came the howling of many wolves. It was almost as if the sound sprang up at the raising of his hand, just as the music of a great orchestra seems to leap under the baton of the conductor' (ibid., p.49). Rather than an aimless, resigned or despairing sound (or simply wild and savage), this howling is directed by a powerful figure, and it comes about strategically and meaningfully.

In his home country, Dracula functions as a keener: the conductor of an orchestra of mourners whose sound is organized and purposeful and whose message, though 'inarticulate', is nonetheless meaningful. In a key scene, he leads what seems to be a spontaneous yet disciplined concert of howling that begins with nearby domesticated animals and spreads to the wild, marginalized fringes, till the whole country seems united:

> Then a dog began to howl somewhere in a farmhouse far down the road – a long, agonized wailing, as if from fear. The sound was taken up by another dog, then another and another, till, borne on the wind which now sighed softly through the Pass, a wild howling began, which seemed to come from all over the country, as far as the imagination could grasp it through the gloom of the night. At the first howl the horses began to strain and rear, but the driver spoke to them soothingly, and they quieted down, but shivered and sweated as though after a runaway from sudden fright. Then, far off in the distance, from the mountains on each side of us began a louder and sharper howling – that of wolves – which affected both the horses and myself in the same way – for I was minded to jump from the caleche and run . . . In a few minutes, however, my own ears got accustomed to the sound, and the horses so far became quiet that the driver was able to descend and to stand before them.
>
> (Stoker, 1998, pp.11–12)

The depiction of howling seems alternately musical and menacing. Although the howling at first elicits fear from Jonathan, his ears become 'accustomed to the sound' and Dracula is able to soothe the horses. Clearly, the howling is most dangerous when the wild animals, the wolves, are dominant in the chorus: 'The keen wind still carried the howling of the dogs, though this grew fainter as we went on our way. The baying of the wolves sounded nearer and nearer, as though they were closing round us from every side' (ibid., p.12). The wild animals on the fringes of the scene recall the frequent characterization of the native Irish as uncivilized or wolfish, a manner of representation that intensified during the Famine.

Again, it has been frequently argued about *Dracula* that the protagonists' ability to compile disparate fragments of information to form one coherent, linear narrative, written in an increasingly homogenized voice that absorbs or negates foreign or 'deviant' voices, is a mark of their victory over their opponent. In a reading of *Dracula* as a gothic Famine novel, however, the vampire leader embodies a history that has not yet been written and therefore cannot simply be 'killed'. As he approaches his ostensible death – the protagonists closing in on him in the Transylvanian snow – the motif of howling grows more pervasive, as if to suggest that Dracula's death will not be able to silence the inarticulate protest of his loyal followers. Dracula's not 'being in possession of the floor'[19] at the end of the novel – his having been narrated out of existence by the Western characters' indefatigable writing, typing and collating – does not necessarily close off the possibility of future Dracula narratives (as has been amply proven in popular culture since the novel's publication in 1897) or of other attempts to tell an Irish history he might represent. There is certainly a Famine history yet to be told in 1897, one that seemed to have been overwritten by the accommodating progress narratives of novels like Trollope's *Castle Richmond* and Annie Keary's *Castle Daly*. As the novel goes on, Dracula may speak less frequently, but he also becomes increasingly associated with motifs of inarticulate or non-verbal communication: mists that change shape and briefly materialize and a variety of wild animals, most memorably wolves. He may not be remembered at the end of the novel as a narrator, but rather as the leader of a purposeful, organized concert of Irish howls.

If the killing of Lucy seems a strong indication that the Famine dead ought to stay dead, by contrast, the pursuit and capture of Dracula is hardly as conclusive. The heroes fail to kill him according to the proper procedures outlined by Van Helsing (a strange oversight, if that, in a novel obsessed with establishing rules and verifying facts) and in the end he crumbles away into dust, ambiguous and interpretable as one of his many different shapes. Like Melmoth before him, Dracula vanishes rather than being graphically killed like Lucy and the vampire women, an ending that suggests the staying power of the alterity he represents. Dracula, finally, is a much harder figure to stake than Lucy, whose death at least appears to signify the putting to rest of the alternate history she represented. Dracula stands for the ambivalent and often contradictory versions of his country's history; he stands for the Famine dead who will not stay buried; and he stands for the potential to speak of the past in a new way. He represents a challenge to dominant narratives of the Famine, his shape-shifting, mutability and experiments with time a threat to progressive, linear tellings of history. Dracula represents the potential that the horrors of the Famine will not remain buried in the past, safely incorporated as an episode of Providence (or of the law of population growth) intervening to clear the way for progress.

As Dracula has already taught Seward, when his reappearance on the scene compelled the doctor to reopen the narrative he thought he had ended, 'Truly there is no such thing as finality' (Stoker, 1998, p.189). Although his powers never allow him control of the narrative, his resistance to the protagonists' efforts to trap him within their textual web remains one of the novel's most memorable gothic uncertainties. As a figure who continually undermines the authority of narrative itself, he can perhaps be most eloquent when he is not speaking at all. Finally, and despite the dubious triumph of the heroes, it is not easy to dismiss the image of Jonathan, an English middle-class Everyman, cowering within Dracula's coach while a vengeful, howling country seems to close in, united and organized against a common enemy.

References

Belford, Barbara. *Bram Stoker: A Biography of the Author of Dracula*. New York: Alfred A. Knopf, 1996.

Botting, Fred. *Gothic*. New York: Routledge, 1996.

Brew, Margaret. *The Chronicles of Castle Cloyne: Or, Pictures of the Munster People*. New York: Garland, 1979. First published 1885.

Carleton, William. *The Works of William Carleton*, Vol.3. New York: P.F. Collier, 1881.

Carleton, William. 'Extract from *The Black Prophet*', in Seamus Deane (ed.), *The Field Day Anthology of Irish Writing*, Vol.2. Derry: Field Day Publications, 1991.

Crofton Croker, T. *Researches in the South of Ireland, Illustrative of the Scenery, Architectural Remains, and the Manners and Superstitions of the Peasantry*. London: John Murray, 1824.

Deane, Seamus (ed.). *The Field Day Anthology of Irish Writing*, Vol.2. Derry: Field Day Publications, 1991.

Deane, Seamus. *Strange Country: Modernity and Nationhood in Irish Writing since 1790*. Oxford: Clarendon Press, 1997.

Eagleton, Terry. *Heathcliff and the Great Hunger: Studies in Irish Culture*. London: Verso, 1995.

Ellmann, Maud. 'Introduction', in Bram Stoker, *Dracula*. New York: Oxford University Press, 1998.

Fitzpatrick, David. 'Ireland since 1870', in R.F. Foster (ed.), *The Oxford Illustrated History of Ireland*. Oxford: Oxford University Press, 1991.

Foster, R.F. (ed.). *The Oxford Illustrated History of Ireland*. Oxford: Oxford University Press, 1991.

Hall, Mr and Mrs S.C. *Ireland: Its Scenery, Character, and History*, Vol.1. Boston, MA: Nicholls & Co., 1911. First published 1841.

Hawthorne, Nathaniel. *Nathaniel Hawthorne's Tales: Authoritative Texts, Background, Criticism*. Selected and edited by James McIntosh. New York and London: W.W. Norton, 1987.

Hayden, Tom (ed.). *Irish Hunger: Personal Reflections on the Legacy of the Famine*. Boulder, CO: Roberts Rinehart Publishers, 1997.

'The Irish Vampire' (artist unknown). Cartoon in 'Contextual illustrations and documents', in Bram Stoker, *Dracula*, Paul Riquelme (ed.). Boston, MA: Bedford/St Martin's, 2002.

Keary, Annie. *Castle Daly: The Story of an Irish Home Thirty Years Ago*. New York: Garland Publishing, 1979. First published 1875.

Kelleher, Margaret. *The Feminisation of Famine: Expressions of the Inexpressible*. Cork and Durham, NC: Cork University Press and Duke University Press, 1997.

Kilgour, Maggie. *The Rise of the Gothic Novel*. London and New York: Routledge, 1995.

Kinealy, Christine. *A Death-Dealing Famine: The Great Hunger in Ireland*. Chicago, IL: Pluto Press, 1997.

Le Fanu, Sheridan. *The Rose and the Key*. Dover, NH: Alan Sutton 1994. First published 1871.

Lloyd, David. 'The memory of hunger', in Tom Hayden (ed.), *Irish Hunger: Personal Reflections on the Legacy of the Famine*. Boulder, CO: Roberts Rinehart Publishers, 1997.

Maturin, Charles Robert. *Melmoth the Wanderer*. Chris Baldick (ed.). New York: Oxford University Press, 1998. First published 1820.

Mitchel, John. *Jail Journal* (1854). Dublin: University Press of Ireland, 1982. [The *Journal* was originally published in 1854 in Mitchel's paper *The Citizen*; this is a facsimile version of the 1913 edition, with a critical introduction by Thomas Flanagan.]

Mitchel, John. *The Last Conquest of Ireland (Perhaps)*. London, n.d. (1861).

Morash, Christopher. *Writing the Irish Famine*. Oxford: Clarendon Press, 1995.

Moses, Michael Valdez. 'The Irish vampire: *Dracula*, Parnell, and the troubled dreams of nationhood'. *Journal x: A Journal in Culture and Criticism*, Vol.2, No.1 (1997), pp.67–111.

O Laoghaire, Peadar. 'Extract from *Mo Sgeal Fein (My Own Story)*', in Seamus Deane (ed.), *The Field Day Anthology of Irish Writing*, Vol.2. Derry: Field Day Publications, 1991.

Petrie, George. *The Ancient Music of Ireland*, (1855), in Seamus Deane (ed.). *A Short History of Irish Literature* (Notre Dame, IN: University of Notre Dame Press, 1994).

Richards, Thomas. *The Imperial Archive: Knowledge and the Fantasy of Empire*. London: Verso, 1993.

Riquelme, John Paul. 'Contextual illustrations and documents', in Bram Stoker, *Dracula*, John Paul Riquelme (ed.). Boston, MA: Bedford/St Martin's, 2002.

Shelley, Mary. *Frankenstein*. New York: Bantam Books, 1991. First published 1818.

Shuttle, Penelope and Peter Redgrove. *The Wise Wound: Menstruation and Everywoman*. London: Gollancz, 1978.

Stoker, Bram. *Dracula*, Maud Ellmann (ed.). New York: Oxford University Press, 1998.

Stoker, Charlotte. 'Letter to Bram Stoker', (1875), in Bram Stoker, *Dracula*, Maurice Hindle (ed.). New York: Viking Penguin, 1993.

Tracy, Robert. 'Introduction', in Sheridan Le Fanu, *Through a Glass Darkly*. Oxford: Oxford University Press, 1999.

Trollope, Anthony. *Castle Richmond*. London and New York: Penguin Books, 1993.

Valente, Joseph. '"Double born": Bram Stoker and the metrocolonial gothic', *Modern Fiction Studies*, Vol.46, No.3 (2000), pp.632–645.

Walker, Brian. *Past and Present: History, Identity and Politics in Ireland*. Belfast: The Institute of Irish Studies, Queen's University of Belfast, 2000.

Walshe, Elizabeth Hely. *Golden Hills: A Tale of the Irish Famine*. London: n.d. 1865.

PART TWO:

THE POLITICS OF MEMORY

CHAPTER 6

Feeding on gossamer, caught in the web: Famine tensions in Yeats's *The Countess Cathleen*

Jerome Joseph Day

For Ireland's cultural revival, the poet and dramatist William Butler Yeats believed passionately that a new spiritual and heroic elite must emerge to educate and lead the population into an authentic Celtic ethos suited to the dawning twentieth century. To help stimulate this ethos, Yeats provided his first play, *The Countess Cathleen*, written in 1892 and constantly reworked, to help inaugurate the new Irish Literary Theatre (ILT). When *The Countess* premiered on 8 May 1899 in the Antient Concert Rooms, across from Trinity College Dublin, his play sparked a controversy that engaged politicians, journalists, theatre professionals, educators, students, clergymen and even a cardinal archbishop. To anyone familiar with Yeats's own background, his circle of friends and his proximity to the Great Irish Famine, it is ironic in the extreme that he could so structure his play that the explosive implications of the text eluded him. Yeats wanted to present a drama connecting the real world to the spiritual aspirations he set for Ireland by gossamer and fairy dust. Unwittingly, however, he ensnared his play in the web of competing discourses originating in the Famine era and continuing to polarize Ireland. That Yeats's body of work would never return to the Famine in any substantive way suggests the degree to which the intrusion of historical reality and contemporary politics disrupted his sense of order and possibility.

Once controversy erupted, Yeats publicly de-emphasized the Famine's connection with *The Countess Cathleen*. Examination of the play, however, shows that the script forecloses such a cavalier dismissal. Likewise, Yeats's first audiences recognized the connections and the implications. This essay will explore how the drama's elements, rooted in the 'selling of a soul', impale themselves on history, politics and audience reaction. The play's setting, characterization, narrative frame, dramatic structure and theme all conspire to connect it to the historical Famine, which was only a generation removed from those who saw the performances and those who read the contending letters in the Dublin press. Many in those first audiences would have had first-hand experience of *an Gorta Mór*. They certainly would know, and participate in, the discourses of agency, religion and nationality.

The action of the plot is relatively simple and straightforward. A beautiful noblewoman, the Countess Cathleen, sacrifices her wealth and, ultimately, her life to save her people first from hunger and then from demons seducing them into bartering their souls for food. To spare her peasants, she bargains away her own soul, but wins entry to heaven because of her pure motives. The countess is an exemplary landowner, concerned and sacrificial. The landscape, meanwhile, is mystical and allegorized, set 'in Ireland and in old times' amid 'the trees of a wood' under a 'gold or diapered sky' such that the 'scene should have the effect of a missal painting' (*The Collected Plays*, p.2).[1] The play's mystical, expressionistic style distances it from the Famine, without abandoning it. It becomes a kind of medieval Book of Hours, almost a *tableau vivant*. The play is set 'not in history . . . but in one's own heart', Yeats wrote in the Irish arts magazine *Bealtaine* in May 1899 (quoted in Flanagan, 1976, p.124). Maybe so, but the Famine's echo is strong; indeed, the play relies on iconic references to Irish hunger.

The origins of Yeats's play can be traced to a story published in *The Shamrock*, a Dublin paper, on Saturday, 5 October 1867. The story is a translation of Léo Léspès' 'Les Marchands d'âmes', published in *Les Matinées de Timothée Trim* (Paris: Librairie du Petit Journal, 1865). Yeats found the story of the Countess Kathleen O'Shea as he was researching material for his *Fairy and Folk Tales of the Irish Peasantry* (1888) and eventually determined the French provenance of this Irish story (Sidnell and Chapman, 1999, p.xxxvii).

Among the characters in *The Countess Cathleen* are Shemus Rua (James the Red) and Teigue, his son. The father's Gaelic name and sobriquet mark him as a stereotypical Irish Catholic, and indeed his son's name was a derogatory synonym accorded papists by the Ascendancy and colonial occupation. Mary, Shemus's wife and Teigue's mother, bears the name of the Mother of God, of course, who will be invoked for deliverance and exoneration by the play's end. In the face of famine, the family's desperation has led them to consider eating grass and weeds – one of the characteristic descriptions contemporary observers recorded to suggest the severity of the Famine. 'The land is famine-struck / The graves are walking', Teigue observes, while Shemus asks, 'When the hen's gone / What can we do but live on sorrel and dock, / And dandelion, till our mouths are green?' (*The Collected Plays*, p.2). Subsequent Famine literature frequently employs the green-stained, gaping mouth of the starving, as well as the processions of half-dead spectres. Unfortunately for the image of Irish Catholic peasants, however, both Shemus Rua and Teigue emerge as brutal toward Mary and unfaithful to their creed – indeed to any creed. When demons, disguised as merchants, offer them food for their souls, they readily agree. So do virtually all the villagers on the countess's estate. Mary is the only peasant character who resists their deal – but she dies of hunger for her trouble.

Yeats's contempt for the growing mercantile middle class, heavily Catholic but also Protestant, is well-documented, so the disguises of his demons are a bit thin. Even more ironic, however, is his dismissal of a long, controversial discourse in Irish Famine literature and politics over the role of Evangelical Protestants who sought to convert Irish Catholics from the folly of their papism. Those who 'took the soup', though their conversion was sometimes no more sincere than the demons' offer to help, were regarded by most Famine survivors and their descendants as traitors to their ancestral faith. One sympathetic priest in Newmarket, County Cork, wrote of such soupers, 'This is an awful state of things but what can be done – their children are starving about them and they would go to hell, they say, to relieve them' (quoted in O'Dwyer, 1995, p.229). Scorn for those who administered this system was particularly intense. For Yeats's 1899 audience, then, the victims, peasants who remained overwhelmingly faithful to Roman Catholicism, have been made into the villains, churls who will sell their souls for a bowl of soup – and yet the poet-playwright does capture something of their desperation. Susan Cannon Harris, citing Cathal Póirtéir's *Famine Echoes* (1995), observes,

> By . . . [the time of the 1899 controversy over the play] that sinister Protestant with his bowl of soup had become a metaphor for the network of economic and bureaucratic institutions that turned a natural disaster into an opportunity to consolidate imperial power. Stories collected after the Famine depict public works administrators, landlords, and educators . . . collaborating with proselytizing Protestants in their efforts to lure Catholics away from the fold. *The Countess Cathleen* participates in this tradition.
>
> (Harris, 2002, p.36)

Just as offensive to the original audience was the rescue of the peasants by the countess. Yeats traverses at least three danger zones in his depiction of Cathleen. First, her name and concern for the people invest her with a strong resemblance to Kathleen ni Houlihan, Ireland's folkloric alter ego – but the play positions her as a titled landowner. While a number of landowning aristocrats undertook significant efforts to assist their tenants, the majority failed to address their responsibilities. Indeed, the entire land tenure system in early nineteenth-century Ireland contributed directly to the causes of the Famine. Kerby Miller, for example, argues that the growing trend of 'progressive' landlords to raise rents, limit leases and enter the market economy left tenants increasingly vulnerable (1988, p.45). Roy Foster's contention that the landlord system's fault in the Famine is 'arguable', given the 'fragile equilibrium' caused by a soaring population on '[t]iny, subdivided holdings', skirts the origins and consequences of such holdings (1992, p.166). Cormac Ó Gráda argues that the land tenure system and the Famine are linked through a failure to prevent mush-rooming population and subdivision, through the precarious financial condition of most landlords and through landlord absenteeism (1999, pp.26–7). Finally, Christine Kinealy observes that the social engineering undertaken by government policy during and after the Famine rectified many of the problems associated with the land tenure system and its social consequences (1995, p.357; 2002, pp.18–19). The company the Countess Cathleen keeps as a landlord renders her suspect. Her title, contrary to Yeats's claim of an 'olden times' setting, marks her as part of the British imperial system – which propped up the land tenure system, denied Catholics political rights and treated the 'third kingdom' as a poor stepsister.

A second major problem for the original audience lies in the fact that Cathleen's rescue of the peasants comes through her own Faustian bargain with the demons – if they free the souls of her tenants, she will surrender her own eternal happiness. Even if one acknowledges her motives, as does her vindication at the climax of the play, Yeats's implication is clear: the souls of Irish peasants are not of the same order as that of the countess. That the first audiences identified such a glaringly condescending implication, despite the play's charms, should surprise no one.

A third difficulty lies in the fact that Countess Cathleen's range of action is as limited as her tenants' – yet *her* motivation saves her, while the peasants are doomed for *theirs*, which is portrayed as a naive and misguided effort to survive. While the countess certainly is high-minded, her own wealth and status depend upon the continued functioning of her estate. Massive depopulation can only deprive her of workers and impoverish her; she is not part of the 'improving landlord' class which wanted to rid estates of excess population in the mid-nineteenth century. Consequently, an implicit economic motivation underlies her efforts to save the starving peasants, as was the case for many landlords during the Famine itself. Unlike improving landlords, who saw economic potential in mass clearings, the Countess Cathleen is trapped in an older economic order as surely as her tenants. Just as Yeats ignores the countess's relatively pedestrian but implicit motive, so too does he overlook the peasants' utter desperation. 'What Yeats had done', writes Adrian Frazier, 'was to trans-value the greatest experience of the Irish, turning a Protestant moral catastrophe into a miracle of benevolence, and one of the world's remarkable cases of a people's devotion to a faith into wholesale infidelity' (1990, p.14).

For Yeats to have bypassed the hard edge of Famine discourse is likewise no surprise. His aesthetic interests in a heroic and spiritual elite leading a national cultural revival demanded a common myth, which he found in the Celtic heroes of the ancient past. His attempt to recruit a medieval figure from a distant famine, however, comes too close to the realities of the Great Famine of the 1840s to permit the excuse that either its significance or implications could be ignored. Yeats's personal connections to the Famine are considerable. He spent his early years in Sligo in the west of Ireland, where his grandfather and great-grandfather on the Yeats side had been rectors of Church of Ireland parishes, Tullylish in County Down and Drumcliffe in County Sligo. During Yeats's life, the growth of an industrial and mercantile class on both sides of the religious divide tended to isolate the genteel landlord class, even at its lower levels, with which Yeats identified, from co-religionists. Ironically, however, Yeats's mother's family, the Polloxfens, contributed substantially to the industrial and mercantile class in Sligo – and it was from his mother, Susan Polloxfen Yeats, that the poet was grounded in story-telling and mythic imagination (Brown, 1999, p.17).

No myths need be found to underline the impact of the Famine on the Sligo district. In terms of mortality during the Famine, the west of Ireland was the part of the country worst hit. Economic historian Joel Mokyr has estimated between 1.1 million and 1.5 million Famine-related Irish deaths during the years 1846 to 1850 (quoted Kennedy *et al.*, 1999, p.36). Sligo, along with Mayo, Roscommon and Galway, had excess death rates at

40:1,000 or more, in many areas at 60:1,000 or higher (ibid., p.37). Only
Mayo, with a death rate of 60 per 1,000 population, exceeded Sligo's,
which hovered around 50 per 1,000 (ibid., p.38). The reasons for the
region's stress have been well-documented in Famine studies:

> The western counties were characterized by tiny landholdings, low levels of
> income, low levels of urbanization and industrialization, and heavy depen-
> dence on the potato crop. The result was vulnerability to famine, under the
> stress of repeated crop failures. The role of landlords, as a bulwark against
> disaster, also seems to have varied regionally, being at its most efficacious in
> Ulster and at its most malign in parts of the West. Mass evictions which were
> put into effect on some estates, added to the sum of human suffering and
> further exposed families to the ravages of disease.
>
> (Ibid., p.38)

Emigration, the other great calamity accelerated by the Famine, was
likewise high in the west, at least among those with the means to flee;
Galway and Sligo saw their share of departures. The point here is that
through much of his life, Yeats lived cheek by jowl with the social consequences of the Famine. In his defence, however, the evidence is strong that
Yeats spent his early years wrapped in a protective mantle of family love
and separation from suffering. According to Roy Foster, his

> [a]utobiographies stressed the respectability and rootedness of his family
> background in Sligo: possessive love of the landscape conferred a claim on the
> land, free of politics and suffused with a sense of belonging . . . The sense of a
> lost Eden remained. 'No one will ever see Sligo as we saw it', he told his sister
> shortly before his death. This vanished dream stood for more than the lost
> domain of childhood; it was the world of the Protestant Irish bourgeoisie,
> integrated into the life of their native place, still (in the 1870s) calmly conscious
> of a social and economic ascendancy which appeared theirs by right.
>
> (Foster, 1997, p.24)

Perhaps the greatest Famine tensions in Yeats's biography lie with his
friendship and collaboration with two women of immense importance
in his life: Lady Augusta Gregory of Coole Park, County Galway, and
Maude Gonne, the firebrand actress and revolutionary.

Lady Gregory's husband, Sir William Gregory, who died in 1892 before
she met Yeats, was the author of the much-hated Gregory clause (Foster,
1997, p.169). Gregory, who held a parliamentary seat for County Dublin,

was a landowner, and he wanted as much of the poor relief burden shifted off his shoulders as possible. He secured passage of legislation that prohibited anyone in Ireland who owned more than a quarter of an acre from being classified as destitute. Many landowners saw the Poor Law Extension Act of 1847, popularly called the Gregory clause, as an immediate escape from rising relief rates for the poor, as it was the landlord who was required to pay such levies on land valued under £4. Evictions rapidly increased after the law was enacted (Kinealy, 1995, pp.218–19).

Many of the names associated with Yeats's life are in the west of Ireland. To be interested in folklore and yet miss the Famine's legacy seems hard to imagine. Stories after reports after chronicles of Famine misery abound. One report, dated 2 March 1847, from a Captain O'Brien to a Colonel Jones is illustrative:

> Having proceeded to Sligo . . . I became aware that great destitution existed . . . especially in the barony of Carbury. I therefore acceded to the desire of Sir Robert Gore Booth, that I should personally satisfy myself by inspection of the exact state of affairs there. The first place I visited was a wretched hamlet of three cottages containing three families, numbering in all 32 persons, belonging to three brothers, the whole having lived on 12 acres of land . . . Last year they thought themselves so well off, they refused to take £60 to give up the lease and depart. Now they are starving. One of the brothers and three others of the families had died during the previous week. The widow was lying on the ground in fever, and unable to move. The children were bloated in their faces and bodies, their limbs were withered to bones and sinews, with rags on them which scarcely preserved decency, and assuredly afforded no protection from the weather. They had been found that day, gnawing the flesh from the bones of a pig which had died in an out-house . . . Sir Robert Booth's estate is large, and the supplies he has procured would keep those of his own well enough, were he not pressed also to feed his neighbours' tenants. At his own place, Lissadell, he has established two soup boilers . . . He gives gratuitously 280 gallons of this soup per day, every day, including Sundays. He sells, six days in the week, 150 loaves per day . . . and 30 tons of Indian corn per week . . . In the baronies I have alluded to, the people are dying from starvation by dozens daily . . . Many cannot crawl to the public works, much less do anything when there . . . In the neighbourhood of the poorhouse they come to die in order that they may receive a decent burial. Typhus fever and dysentery have added to their horrors . . . There were in Sligo poorhouse on 24 February, 208 cases of fever and 145 of dysentery. The master of the poorhouse and his four sons, the matron and her daughter, the schoolmaster and his assistant were among them; eleven had died the previous night; the matron is since dead.
>
> (Swords, 1999, pp.147–9)

In due course, Yeats would be much involved with the Gore-Booths, visiting their family seat at Lissadel and befriending the daughters, Eva and Constance, who both became active Irish nationalists and feminists. Eva Gore-Booth advocated for the poor and for women, while Constance Gore-Booth Markiewicz, who married a Polish count, was the first woman elected to Parliament, though as an Irish nationalist, she refused to take her seat. Yeats wrote poems about both women (Macrae, 1995, p.115).

Famine and Catholic tensions in the play were readily apparent prior to its first performance. On the one hand, Yeats's ILT collaborator, Edward Martyn, had expressed fears that *The Countess Cathleen* included 'several passages of an uncatholic & heretical nature that would over here [in Ireland] create a scandal especially if the work was promoted & championed by a person like myself who everyone knows to be a Catholic' (Yeats, 1997, p.384).[2] Likewise, Thomas Patrick Gill had warned Yeats and George Moore, another of the ILT's founders, that popular Famine memories, particularly of souperism, might create problems for the play (ibid., p.381).[3] To help resolve the problem, several Roman Catholic priests were discussed as possible arbiters of the theological issues in the play. Their views, on the other hand, tended to confirm Yeats's opinion that the play crossed no lines.

The Reverend William Barry wrote to Yeats that the play was 'beautiful and touching; I hope you will not be kept back from giving it by foolish talk' (ibid., p.383).[4] Father Barry added,

> no one is free to sell his soul in order to buy bread even for the starving. But St. Paul says 'I wished to be anathema for my brethren,' [Rom. 9:3] – which is another way of expressing what you have put into a story. I would give the play first and explanations afterwards . . . [I]f people will not read or look at a play of this kind in the spirit which dictated it no change you might make would satisfy them. You have given us what is really an Auto, in the manner of Calderon.
>
> (Ibid., p.383)[5]

The Reverend Thomas Finlay, S.J., another of several clerical consultants, apparently approved the play with a few minor changes in a letter sent to Martyn, who regarded him as the best potential adjudicator. Yeats is thought to have received a copy, but the letter does not appear to have survived (ibid., p.386).[6] Still another clerical voice came, *after* the premiere of the play, from the Most Reverend John Healy, Bishop of Clonfert and later Archbishop of Tuam, who expressed his approval to Martyn.

Such clerical firepower was insufficient to derail the controversy that erupted when the play, first published in 1892, was ready to open. When Frank Hugh O'Donnell attacked *The Countess Cathleen* first in the *Freeman's Journal* on 1 April 1899 and then in a reprinted version in *Souls for Gold: A Pseudo-Celtic Drama in Dublin*, demons of a polemical sort were unleashed. O'Donnell writes:

> Out of all the mass of our national traditions it is precisely the baseness which is utterly alien to all our national traditions, the barter of Faith for Gold, which Mr. W.B. Yeats selects as the fundamental idea of his Celtic drama! I could understand such a theme being welcome at a souper meeting at Exeter Hall; but to propose it to the applause of an Irish Literary Association argues in appreciation of the Ireland of to-day as characteristic as the knowledge of Ireland in the past.
>
> (Ibid., p.675)

O'Donnell cites three specific objections to the play: the kicking of a shrine to the Blessed Virgin Mary by Shemus Rua; the 'blasphemous apostasy' of the countess, who sells her own soul to ransom those of her 'soul-selling and soup-buying' tenants, followed by her reward, a kiss from 'Mary of the seven times wounded heart'; and the approval of the countess's actions by the minor poet Aleel, 'getting more and more daft with love for the demented heroine' (ibid., p.675). O'Donnell sees nothing but ridicule of Catholic Ireland in Yeats's depiction of the shrine's destruction and the killing of Father John the Priest, reading his breviary, by a demon in the shape of a pig. The priest's soul is snatched away by the demon and thrust into a sack (ibid., p. 676).

One might argue with O'Donnell. Is Yeats not free to inquire dramatically into how many Irish Catholics, including their priests, lost their faith as they confronted the Famine's brutality? The two incidents, destroying the shrine and killing Father John, suggest the insidious social and spiritual erosion that stemmed from the Famine. Nonetheless, O'Donnell's questions are legitimate given Yeats's insistence on the setting of the play:

> We are told that the land is full of famine, and that it is the Ireland of old days. Where was the aid of friendly and generous chiefs and clansmen to the suffering district? Where was the charitable hospitality of a hundred monastic foundations, which were afterwards to be 'kicked to pieces', not by Catholic peasants, but by the reformed chivalry of England?
>
> (Ibid., p.677)

Readers could hear his high dudgeon as he excoriated Yeats for depicting
in ancient Ireland 'an unmanly, an impious and renegade people, crouched
in degraded awe before demons and goblins, and sprites, and sowlths, and
thivishes, – just like a sordid tribe of black devil-worshippers and fetish-
worshippers on the Congo or the Niger' (ibid., p.677). Leaving aside
O'Donnell's wholesale acceptance of Britain's imperial rhetoric of the
Other, it is easy to see in the discourse the invocation of old grievances
against Protestant England, complaints renewed and exacerbated by the
Famine: the destruction of the Gaelic clan system, the flight of the Gaelic
nobility and the suppression of the monasteries.

To add to the irony of Yeats's seeming ignorance of Famine discourse
in *The Countess Cathleen*, his letters show that shortly after the *Freeman's
Journal* ruckus with O'Donnell, Yeats and Maude Gonne planned a
meeting with Horace Plunkett about the problem of evicted tenants in a
County Mayo district contending with a local famine.

Yeats's comments in his *Bealtaine* article insist that although Lionel
Johnson's introduction to the printed text had situated *The Countess Cathleen*
in the sixteenth century, the play 'is not historic, but symbolic' (ibid.,
p.399).[7] However, Yeats himself employed the late medieval date for the
countess (ibid., p.399).[8] The early prose version of the play in Yeats's own
hand indicates '17 century' (Yeats, 1999, p.4).

Still another dimension of *The Countess Cathleen* controversy was the ILT
skirmish with authorities of the Roman Catholic Church; such fencing
between theatre and Church would continue through the decades. When
asked by a Dublin newspaper to weigh in on the suitability of the play
for the inaugural performance of the ILT, Michael, Cardinal Logue,
Archbishop of Armagh and Primate of All-Ireland, told the *Daily Nation*,
'I have no hesitation in saying that an Irish Catholic audience which could
patiently sit out such a play must have sadly degenerated, both in religion
and patriotism. As to the opinions said to have been given by Catholic
divines, no doubt the authors of these opinions will undertake to justify
them; but I should not like the task were mine' (Yeats, 1997, p.410).[9] The
cardinal, however, admitted that he had not read the script and had based
his views on O'Donnell's pamphlet. It would have been hard for Yeats to
have found a more visible opponent – and yet the poet-dramatist savaged
the cardinal's critique as 'singular naiveté' and 'reckless indignation' from
one who 'in no way represents the opinion of the younger and more
intellectual Catholics, who have read his letter with astonishment' (ibid.,
p.410).[10] Logue was a Donegal man born in 1840 and, therefore, a

youngster during the Famine's worst years. An Irish-speaker, he strongly supported the Gaelic League's call for cultural nationalism and revival. He had raised funds in Ireland and the United States for victims of subsequent regional famines. But he was a social conservative likely to be offended by Yeats's inattention to discursive boundaries. Yeats argued that the play

> is a spiritual drama, and the blind bigots of journalism, who have made no protest against the musical burlesques full of immoral suggestion which have of late possessed the Dublin theatres, have called it a blasphemy and a slander. These attacks are welcome, for there is no discussion so fruitful as the discussion of intellectual things, and no discussion so needed in Ireland. The applause of the theatre has already shown what party has the victory.
>
> (Ibid., p.411)[11]

'Victory' came at the cost of a discovery for Yeats and his ILT colleagues. Ireland's discursive web was so thick that some topics could not be invoked even by cultural nationalists in certain ways if their pedigree was tainted with the morally ambivalent record of the Ascendancy. Lionel Pilkington writes that the setting and thematics of Yeats's play, evoking souperism, put ILT claims to be above and beyond divisive politics 'under immense strain' (Pilkington, 2001, p.28). The play and the critique it engendered expose at least two important divergences from Yeats's theatre rhetoric. First, the play's treatment of the Famine is so dehistoricized that it ignores fundamental realities not only in the Irish past but also in the Irish psyche. Second, resistance to the play in pamphlet, letter and protest is not explained adequately by allegations of excessive nationalist zeal, hostility to the remains of the Ascendancy and Catholic cultural philistinism. Instead, Pilkington argues, the protests show the limits of theatre itself as a public sphere when a society lacks political independence. The problem lies in ILT assumptions that it could be national, autonomous and modern when the meaning and locus of those terms were contested within Irish society (ibid., p.27).

Majorie Howes recognizes this difficulty and situates it within the instability created by the appropriation of 'Celticism' by contending voices in late-nineteenth- and early twentieth-century Ireland. She writes, 'Celticism claimed to be a movement based on recovery rather than innovation; it naturalized the version of ancient Irish culture it offered, claiming that it merely revealed the true national being. Celticism was also based on enlisting the Irish peasantry, both symbolically and literally, in a shared national project while continuing to dominate them politically and economically. These Celticist ambivalences help to account for what most critics have seen as the play's poor construction, unresolved tensions, and contradictory themes' (Howes, 1996, p.45).

Before examining the opening of *The Countess Cathleen*, at least one other element should be considered: the potent mix in popular imagination of blood sacrifice, Irish nationalism and the Famine. In the autumn of 1897, Yeats and Maude Gonne were in the west of Ireland. Terence Brown observes:

> Famine was again threatening mass starvation, and the movement to commemorate the dead of 1798 became linked to the memory of the famine dead of the hungry forties. Gonne embarked on a policy of resistance and attempted to organize a relief scheme, but in highly politicized terms. She made Mayo, where the French had landed in 1798 and where hunger was gnawing intensely, the focus of her campaign.
>
> (Brown, 1999, p.100)

Gonne was certainly not alone in invoking the memory of 1798; crowds gathered at public events throughout the country. Brown adds:

> The statuary erected in many towns and villages at this time, though Yeats was to find it vulgar and unappealing, bore witness to the fact that the tradition of Irish armed rebellion still had an imaginative purchase on many Irish minds at a level beneath the apparent passivity of the population at large. The blend of this military symbolism with Catholic iconography of sacrifice and bloodshed, with processions that seemed at once ceremonial celebration and funeral cortege, gave to mass meetings the quasi-mystical appeal of some religious, even occult, gathering. In a culture where funerary traditions were potent ritual expressions of communal solidarity there was a sense that a people was at last defining sacred cultural spaces for itself in the modernized cityscape.
>
> (Ibid., p.101).

Is it any great surprise, then, that the first play of a theatrical group dedicated to Ireland's cultural revival, a play in which a beautiful, ethereal woman of strength and compassion sacrifices herself to save her starving people, should trigger conflicting feelings traceable to the Famine? Christopher Morash, speaking of various theatrical traditions and audiences, might well be considering discursive content when he observes, 'In a sense, the Irish Literary Theatre came into being by imagining an empty space where in fact there was a crowded room' (Morash, 2002, p.117). The national 'room' was crowded with discourse, the potential national stage was filled with the web of historical memory.

One dimension of this discursive push and shove was the politicized figure of the Irish body. One cannot discuss the Famine without a consideration of the ravages it inflicted on the human body and the legacy it left on any understanding of corporeal reality – particularly in its feminine representation. In contrast to Matthew Arnold's view of the weak, hysterical, femininized Celt, Irish nationalists imagined Hibernia as strong, resolute and self-sacrificing. In this regard, Yeats's countess provides a compelling but ambiguous figure. Harris writes,

> As a parable about the spirit's susceptibility of the sufferings of the body, *The Countess Cathleen* contradicts nationalist assertions of the absolute incorruptibility of the Irish character in the face of British economic and military oppression. Worse, as the story of a woman who saves her people by sacrificing her soul, it disables one of the main strategies nationalism used to back up those assertions – the idealization of the Irish woman.
>
> (Harris, 2002, p.35)

The Countess Cathleen, despite her sacrifice and noble motivations, fails to fulfill the conventional nationalist image of the idealized Irish woman due to her blasphemous bargain and her swooning weakness. Harris quips pointedly, 'Not all Cathleens are created equal', but makes the further point that Yeats accords the countess a martyr's death despite her lack of orthodoxy (ibid., pp.35 and 40). In the Irish tradition, the self-sacrificing victim, usually male, and the idealized national personification, usually female, become one in the Countess Cathleen – much to the disquiet of nationalist critics. No less than other nationalists, Yeats wanted to imagine a nation. Yeats's view of an aesthetically sensitive Ireland was one that would adopt the values he ascribed to an Anglo-Irish aristocracy – values that, to be charitable, history shows unevenly distributed among the elite. His *Countess Cathleen* was 'integrationist propaganda', according to Frazier, which called upon its audience to admire and imitate Cathleen's heroic generosity and self-sacrifice, as well as the play's artistic freedom and expression. The play's Famine frame, however, rendered such claims patently false. Frazier writes, 'The audience did not share his utopia: the world of *The Countess Cathleen* was neither what Ireland really was nor what they [the first audiences] wanted it to be. Yeats certainly produced propaganda, but the first production did not succeed completely because it was recognized to be propaganda' (Frazier, 1990, p.19).

Questions of competing politics (nationalism *versus* unionism) and religion (revived Catholicism *versus* still-entrenched Protestantism) could be

found underneath an exchange of letters, reviews and commentaries in
the Dublin press – papers such as the *Daily Nation*, the *Freeman's Journal*, the
Daily Express, the *United Irishman*, the *Irish Times* and *An Claidheamh Soluis*,
the weekly organ of the Gaelic League – before and after the play's opening. Indeed, on the very day *The Countess Cathleen* was to be performed, the
Daily Nation called upon theatre-goers 'to make emphatic judgment against
these anti-Irish, anti-Catholic monstrosities' (Kavanagh, 1950, p.15). When
the much-revised play, begun in 1888, finally made it to the stage of the
Antient Concert Rooms, it attracted some of the greatest literary lights in
the Irish cultural renaissance: George Russell (Æ), John Eglington, T.W.
Rolleston, Standish O'Grady, Douglas Hyde, and, of course, Lady Gregory
(Jeffares and Knowland, 1975, p.2; Murray, 1997, p.2; Yeats, 1999, p.xxxvii).
British critics such as Max Beerbohm and Arthur Symons came to Dublin to
see the play (Morash, 2002, p.118). Among student members of the
audience was James Joyce. Another theatre-goer was the ubiquitous Joseph
Holloway, whose diary records the dust-up on the opening night:

> About twenty brainless, beardless, idiotic-looking youths did all they knew to
> interfere with the progress of the play and frequently mentioned the name of
> [19th century Irish nationalist poet Thomas] Davis. The play, however, ended
> amidst thunders of applause and Yeats was called onto the stage to take a bow.
> When he came out on the stage he appeared embarrassed and did not know
> what to do until prompted by Trevor Lowe, he took Miss Whittey's [*sic*] hand
> and shook it heartily and then did the same with Miss Farr.
>
> (Quoted in Kavanagh, 1950, p.16)

Rowdiness by nationalist students from the Royal University was repaid
later by an uproar from unionist Trinity College students. Yeats had good
reason to request that a detail of Dublin police be on hand.

Yeats should have sensed the potent subtext in his play, according to
Brown, who writes:

> Many . . . would have reckoned its setting to be a direct enough reference to
> the tragic famine which had occurred in all-too-recent history. Furthermore, the
> Great Famine of the 1840s was increasingly being employed by the century's end
> by nationalist propagandists as a definitive example of the malign effects of
> British rule in Ireland which had, as it continued to have, the support of the
> Anglo-Irish Protestant caste with which Yeats and Lady Gregory were easily
> identified. That, in Yeats's imagining of famine conditions, it is an aristocrat
> who is noble and self-sacrificing, while the peasantry are venal and ripe for
> subornation by the devil's agents, would have seemed intolerable. To add

injury to insult, it seemed that Yeats was perversely rewriting known history in a mischievous way. In the 1840s it had been Protestants who offered soup to starving Catholics prepared to embrace the reformed faith.

(Brown, 1999, p.127)

Christopher Murray emphasizes this point, for Yeats offers

a play about famine; it confronts the greatest catastrophe in modern Irish history. Yet it coolly indicates that Catholics have a price in crisis time, and are willing to sell their souls to save their skins. Further, Yeats shows how the lady of the manor, the good Countess and Lady Bountiful herself, redeems the souls of all her tenants by selling her own (infinitely more valuable) soul and yet, . . . gets off scot-free.

(Murray, 1997, pp.18–19)

That *The Countess Cathleen* had an early *tableau vivant* performance in January of 1899 to boost public interest did not enhance the public perception of Yeats's identification with the common man. The performance was at the Chief Secretary's Lodge in Phoenix Park, where Elizabeth, Lady Fingall, performed the title role before an upper-crust Ascendancy audience.

Yeats disdained the bourgeoisie, Catholic and Protestant, of his day, a class whose ancestors, in the poet-dramatist's thinking, can be seen in Shemus Rua and his son Teigue (Foster, 1997, p.256). On every level, these peasants lose when contrasted with the countess. In terms of religious faith and the endurance of suffering, the peasants are degenerate and ripe for the picking by demons – a view not very different from the Evangelical assessment of Catholic Ireland during the Famine. Teigue declares, 'God and the Mother of God have dropped asleep, / What do they care, he says though the whole land / Squeal like a rabbit under a weasel's tooth' (*The Collected Plays*, p.3). Meanwhile, the countess, whom an audience of the 1890s would inevitably read as Ascendancy Protestant, remains prayerful and mystical. She is steadfast in faith and charity, the antithesis of the brutal, callous and faithless Shemus and Teigue. Yet for some in Yeats's audience, the countess represented the religion and class to whom those morally laden adjectives properly belonged. She manages to become lost on her own estate, thus suggesting her tenuous connection to the management of her own lands. She does not know her tenants, despite generations of family service. Perhaps unwittingly, Yeats approximates the mid-nineteenth-century landlord, often an absentee, more closely than he might have realized.

Still another dimension of the play is Yeats's complication of gender. Male figures are problematic. Shemus and Teigue are petty despots, their actions neither reflexive nor humane. Aleel the bard may have a poetic soul, but he cannot move beyond art to enter the real world, where sacrifice and gesture must be enacted. The demons are genderless spirits, but they assume avian, animal and human forms. As men, the demons are peddlers out to swindle helpless peasants – Yeats's view of the bourgeoisie. The countess, however, manifests ethereal beauty, spiritual essence and *noblesse oblige*. Loosely, Cathleen may be connected to the Irish tradition of the earth goddess, the sovereignty myth, the Saint Brigid cult and Irish nationalism in the folk figure of Kathleen ni Houlihan. The countess commands easily, makes decisions with care and displays courage and self-sacrifice. Less noticed is Mary, wife of Shemus, but she too is spiritually wise and sacrifices herself in adherence to her faith (*The Collected Plays*, pp.4–7 and 23).

The central point of the play is not who gets away with what – despite the legitimate annoyances Yeats inserts. *The Countess Cathleen* stands as an early and important expression of Yeats's understanding of agency: what constitutes meaningful action, who can undertake such action, and what are the well-springs of such action. For Yeats, style, dignity, purpose and motivation are constitutive of heroic action. The Countess Cathleen's sale of her soul, Cuchulain's battle against the waves, Airman Robert Gregory's sacrifice in the skies, and even the men of 'Easter 1916', in whose defeat at the GPO a 'terrible beauty is born', all share in this Yeatsian quality of heroic gesture (*The Collected Poems*, p.203). External success is peripheral in Yeats's understanding; what matters is internal disposition and external gesture. Michael's departure with Kathleen ni Houlihan in the play of the same name is important because of style and aspiration, not ultimate success. In this regard, the Countess Cathleen fulfills Yeats's image of the gallant act fully. It is worth remembering that the poet-dramatist entreated Maude Gonne, his ideal-in-the-flesh, to play the countess in the play dedicated to her. Although she turned Yeats down in favour of her political agitation, she provides a good prism through which to view the role of the countess (Brown, 1999, p.123).

The Countess Cathleen demonstrates her agency in ways that are inextricably related to her class – thus making Yeats's collision with competing discourses inevitable. She freely chooses to resist hunger and even the demons, but she is able to do so only because of her wealth, both financial and spiritual. When she meets Shemus and Teigue at their home, she empties her purse for the father and tells the son to 'take the purse, / The silver clasps on't may be worth a trifle / And if you'll come to-morrow to my house / You shall have twice the sum' (*The Collected Plays*, p.5). Later, when Cathleen learns that her manor has been robbed and some of the last food, 'a cart-load of green cabage', has been taken, she acknowledges the desperate dilemma of the hungry, 'to rob or starve' (*The Collected Plays*, p.13). Moreover, she understands the moral compass, recognizing that 'starving men may take what's necessary, / And yet be sinless' (*The Collected Plays*, pp.13–14). Ironically, given the critics of the play, much of the countess's moral theology is rooted in Saint Thomas Aquinas. In the *Summa Theologiae* 2a2ae, in Replies to Objections in Question 66, Article 7, Thomas considers theft and robbery as part of his treatment of the virtue of justice and the vice of injustice. Thomas writes:

> If, however, there is so urgent and blatant a necessity that the immediate needs must be met out of whatever is available, as when a person is in imminent danger and he cannot be helped in any other way, then a person may legitimately supply his own needs out of another's property, whether he do so secretly or flagrantly. And in such a case there is strictly speaking no theft or robbery . . . If one is to speak quite strictly, it is improper to say that using somebody else's property taken out of extreme necessity is theft. For such necessity renders what a person takes to support his life his own . . . A person is even entitled to take somebody else's property by stealth in order to help another where that other is also in extreme need.
>
> (pp.81–3)

Thomas, of course, does not envision the metaphysical conundrum of bartering souls for food, but at least his emphasis on motivation supports the countess.

Appalled by the trade in souls beneath her walls, the countess orders an inventory of her castles, pastures and forests, as well as requisitioning her 'hundred kegs of gold' (*The Collected Plays*, pp.14–15). All of it will go not only for relief but to buy back souls snatched by the demons. She cries, 'Give twice and thrice and twenty times their money, / And get your souls again. I will pay all' (*The Collected Plays*, p.14). The countess arranges with her steward that everything she possesses, excepting only her home, will go to save her tenants. The countess is aware of help beyond her own district, and orders her steward, 'Go barter where you please, but come again / With herds of cattle and with ships of meal' (*The Collected Plays*, p.15). Then, discovering that Aleel has been wounded by a demon, she resolves to 'have changed my house so such a refuge / That the old and ailing, and all weak of heart / May escape from beak and claw; all, all, shall come / Till the walls burst and the roof fall on us / From this day out I have nothing of my own' (*The Collected Plays*, p.15). Broadly speaking, this is precisely what did *not* happen during the Famine years, although Yeats engages in perhaps unintended irony by making a Big House into a workhouse. Indeed, on this level, Cathleen seems the very antithesis of Famine-era landowners in her sympathy and action on behalf of starving tenants. She is clear-headed in her analysis of the situation; she recognizes the price-gouging by the nascent Irish bourgeoisie. She declares, 'Thanks be to God there's money in the house / That can buy grain from those who have stored it up / To prosper on the hunger of the poor' (*The Collected Plays*, p.19).

Her most significant act, however, is a challenge not to the economic order but to the moral one. In this single act, the countess makes the gallant, self-sacrificing gesture. Oona the maid bursts in upon Cathleen to inform her that even the gold has been stolen (*The Collected Plays*, p.21). Unlike Famine-era landlords, the countess is acutely aware of the suffering around her. 'I have heard / A sound of wailing in unnumbered hovels, / And I must go down, down – I know not where – / Pray for all men and women mad from famine; / Pray, you good neighbours. Mary, Queen of angels, / And all you clouds on clouds of saints, farewell!' (*The Collected Plays*, p.22).

Already in her thinking, Cathleen has provided the moral excuse for the peasants. The famine has so maddened them that they are not responsible for the folly of their sale of souls. Cathleen, however, is clear-headed about her own proposition to the demon merchants. She knows her soul is of great value. She knows they want it. She thus has leverage to demand that her tenants be freed, their souls restored. Despite the pleas of the peasants, Cathleen offers her own soul – to the demons' delight. The first merchant declares, 'Five hundred thousand crowns; we give the price. / The gold is here; the souls even while you speak / Have slipped out of our bond, because your face / Has shed a light on them and filled their hearts' (*The Collected Plays*, p.27). Heartbroken by the nature of her deed, yet still insistent that it be completed, Cathleen's last words, apart from her farewell to Oona and Aleel, direct the distribution of her remaining funds to every one of her tenants 'according to their need' (*The Collected Plays*, p.30). Her agency is assured. Indeed, she challenges not only the demons but also the conventional moral order by seeing more deeply, more empathically than even the poets and the priests. Her choice embodies

Saint Paul's sentiments in Romans 9:3 in which he expresses willingness to endure damnation, separation from Christ, for the sake of his Jewish co-religionists (Yeats, 1997, p.383).[12] For the countess, the sentiment is deed, not rhetoric. Cathleen's gesture is precisely the way Yeats imagined the elite leadership of a renewed and reformed Ireland would behave. The warring angels and demons, seen by Aleel, suggest the significance of this challenge. Cathleen, of course, is vindicated and redeemed because 'The Light of Lights / Looks always on the motive, not the deed, / The Shadow of Shadows on the deed alone' (*The Collected Plays*, p.31). The countess, though not restored to life, seems assured of eternal bliss for 'the gates of pearl are wide; / And she is passing to the floor of peace, / And Mary of the seven times wounded heart / Has kissed her lips' (*The Collected Plays*, p.31). In many ways, the Countess Cathleen is the Anglo-Irish Ascendancy as it would like to have seen itself in the decades following the Famine. For the majority of the population, however, the realities of starvation, eviction, emigration and souperism refocused the lens of memory, and the image was starkly different.

The presence of the poet Aleel in the play provides perhaps Yeats's unwitting acknowledgment of the enormity of the Famine. Like the Shoah, and war in general, the Famine challenges art to capture, express and contain it. For Yeats, the relationship between Aleel and Cathleen mirrored his own frustrated wooing of Maude Gonne. Aleel's presence in the play is awkward in part because romantic love can insulate one from human pain and suffering for a time. In the end, romance is no match for sacrificial love. Aleel, and the poetry he represents, may make a mad grab at a passing angel, but he can neither redeem nor restore the countess. In Aleel, one easily sees Yeats's fears and frustrations over his unrequited love for Maude Gonne.

The encounter William Butler Yeats had with *an Gorta Mór* through the first production of *The Countess Cathleen* in 1899 was simultaneously sobering and stimulating. He discovered that just below the surface of the gauzy, gossamer world of fairy folklore and Celtic mysticism was the hard edge of reality: starving millions, gaping green mouths and years of emigration. Likewise, he discovered the communicational power of discourse. Frazier, citing J.G.A. Pocock's observations on the writer's 'act of power' in using words taken from a pre-existing 'polity of discourse', notes, 'From the first word that is written, then, the author enters upon a long conversation that continues until the last word is said, a conversation that is continuous with other acts of language and acts of power in the society' (Frazier, 1990, pp.22–3).[13] By invoking images and themes of hunger, however useful, Yeats came to realize in time that he was recruiting strands of discourse

more powerful and more extensive than even his own pen. These strands
formed webs of meaning that often conflicted, and occasionally coalesced,
particularly in areas of religion, nationalism, socio-economic status,
gender and agency. While Yeats's subsequent work continued to address
Celtic mythology, as well as ancient and medieval Irish history and
contemporary social and political controversies, he avoided the Famine.
Given its pervasive impact, its continued presence in living memory, and
its formative influence on contemporary political discourse, the Famine
might easily have sprung to mind as a likely topic – but Yeats, having been
gored in disputes surrounding the opening of the Irish Literary Theatre,
apparently found little utility in his nation's greatest catastrophe. Despite
the heroic gestures of many Famine survivors and rescuers, Yeats's own
social situation, especially in terms of class and religion, and particularly
in light of *The Countess Cathleen*, demonstrated to him the impossibility of
mentioning the topic without self-entrapment. In some respects, precisely
because the landowning class to which he was connected failed to
demonstrate something of the countess's own courage and compassion,
Yeats finds his voice muffled by the web of discourse surrounding him.

This web of discursive tension was dense when Yeats crafted his play,
and it has only grown since then. Among its elements, one finds consistent
efforts by political factions, the church and other elements of society to
silence perspectives at odds with the nationalist majority view. Disputes
over who is authorized to speak from an 'Irish' perspective and how that
speech must proceed bubbled up repeatedly in literature and drama.
Controversies over what constitutes 'Irishness' and the degrees of Irishness
that pertain to Catholics, Anglicans, other Protestants, non-Christians and
non-believers, as well as to the Anglo-Irish aristocracy and the Catholic/
Protestant bourgeoisie, invaded discussion of social, educational and
health policy, as well as national and international political questions.
Uncertainties over the Irish bourgeoisie's loyalty to nation, language,
culture, religion, political cause and identity were raised routinely. Finally,
debate erupted over the *locus* of Ireland's leadership: its spiritual, heroic,
artistic, political, business, or social centres of power, as well as its Celtic,
Catholic, Protestant, Gaelic, Anglo-Irish, Ulster Scots, nationalist, unionist
and European/internationalist traditions. What might have been the
shape and direction of the Irish literary canon had Yeats engaged the
Famine in a meaningful and sustained way, posterity can only conjecture.
Perhaps it is sufficient to recognize the tensions that emerged in *The
Countess Cathleen*; they have shaped Irish letters for more than a century.

References

Aquinas, Saint Thomas. *Summa Theologiae* 2a2ae. Vol. 38 on Injustice. Marcus Lefébure, O.P. (trans.). London: Blackfriars, 1975.

Brown, Terence. *The Life of W.B. Yeats: A Critical Biography*. Oxford: Blackwell, 1999.

Flanagan, James W. *W.B. Yeats and the Idea of a Theatre: The Early Abbey Theatre in Theory and Practice*. New Haven, CT: Yale University Press, 1976.

Foster, R.F. 'Ascendancy and Union', in R.F. Foster (ed.), *The Oxford History of Ireland*. Oxford: Oxford University Press, 1992.

Foster, R.F. *W.B. Yeats: A Life: I: The Apprentice Mage 1865–1914*. Oxford: Oxford University Press, 1997.

Frazier, Adrian. *Behind the Scenes: Yeats, Horniman, and the Struggle for the Abbey Theatre*. Berkeley, CA: University of California Press, 1990.

Harris, Susan Cannon. *Gender and Modern Irish Drama*. Bloomington and Indianapolis, IN: Indiana University Press, 2002.

Howes, Majorie. *Yeats's Nations: Gender, Class amd Irishness*. Cambridge: Cambridge University Press, 1996.

Jeffares, A. Norman and A.S. Knowland. *A Commentary on the Collected Plays of W.B. Yeats*. London: Macmillan, 1975.

Kavanagh, Peter. *The Story of the Abbey Theatre from Its Origins in 1899 to the Present*. New York: Devin-Adair, 1950.

Kennedy, Liam, Paul S. Ell, E.M. Crawford and L.A. Clarkson. *Mapping the Great Irish Famine: A Survey of the Famine Decades*. Dublin: Four Courts Press, 1999.

Kinealy, Christine. *This Great Calamity: The Irish Famine 1845–52*. Boulder, CO: Roberts Rinehart Publishers, 1995.

Kinealy, Christine. *The Great Irish Famine: Impact, Ideology and Rebellion*. Basingstoke: Palgrove, 2002.

Léspès, Léo. 'Les Marchandes d'âmes', in *Les Matinées de Timothée Trim*. Paris: Librairie du Petit Journal, 1865. Published in translation by W.B. Yeats, under the title 'Sellers of Souls', *The Shamrock*, 5 October 1867.

Macrae, Alisdair. *W.B. Yeats: A Literary Life*. New York: St Martin's Press, 1995.

Miller, Kerby A. *Emigrants and Exiles: Ireland and the Irish Exodus to North America*. Oxford: Oxford University Press, 1988.

Morash, Christopher. *A History of Irish Theatre: 1601–2000*. Cambridge: Cambridge University Press, 2002.

Murray, Christopher. *Twentieth Century Irish Drama: Mirror Up to Nation*. Manchester: Manchester University Press, 1997.

O'Donnell, F. Hugh. *Souls for Gold: Pseudo-Celtic Drama in Dublin*. London: Nassau Press, 1899.

O'Dwyer, O.Carm., Peter. *Towards a History of Irish Spirituality*. Dublin: Columba Press, 1995.

Ó Gráda, Cormac. *Black '47 and Beyond: The Great Irish Famine in History, Economy and Memory*. Princeton, NJ: Princeton University Press, 1999.

Pilkington, Lionel. *Theatre and State in Twentieth-Century Ireland: Cultivating the People*. London: Routledge, 2001.

Pocock, J.G.A. 'Verbalizing a political act: towards a politics of speech', in Michael J. Shapiro (ed.), *Language and Politics*. New York: New York University Press, 1984.

Póirtéir, Cathal, (ed.). *Famine Echoes*. Dublin: Gill & Macmillan, 1995.

Sidnell, Michael J. and Wayne K. Chapman (eds). *The Countess Cathleen: Manuscript Materials* [by W.B. Yeats]. Ithaca, NY: Cornell University Press, 1999.

Swords, Reverend Liam. *In Their Own Words: The Famine in North Connacht 1845–1849*. Dublin: Columba Press, 1999.

Yeats, W.B., (ed.). *Fairy and Folk Tales of the Irish Peasantry*. London: W. Scott, 1888.

Yeats, W.B. *The Collected Poems of W.B. Yeats*. 2nd edn. London: Macmillan 1950.

Yeats, W.B. *The Collected Plays of W.B. Yeats*. 2nd edn. New York: Macmillan, 1953.

Yeats, W.B. *The Collected Letters of W.B. Yeats. Vol.2: 1896–1900*. John Kelly (ed.). Oxford: Clarendon Press, Oxford University Press, 1997.

Yeats, W.B. *The Countess Cathleen: Manuscript Materials*. Michael J. Sidnell and Wayne K. Chapman (eds). Ithaca, NY: Cornell University Press, 1999.

CHAPTER 7

'In the gripe of the ditch': nationalism, famine and *The Playboy of the Western World*[1]

George Cusack

The first description audiences receive of Christy Mahon, the dubious hero of Synge's *The Playboy of the Western World*, is one well-suited to, but not often associated with, epic heroism. Entering his fiancée's house from the 'great darkness' of an Irish night, the cowardly Shawn Keogh describes a figure he passed on the road, 'a kind of fellow above in the furzy ditch, groaning like a maddening dog' (p.115). The image should be a familiar one to modern readers, and would be no less so to Synge's audience; a lone figure lying in a ditch in the Irish countryside, moaning to the point of being subhuman is one of the most commonly used symbols of the Great Famine. The connection between Synge's hero and the Famine, perhaps the most significant and signified period in Irish history, is no accident. Rather, it is the opening move in a carefully wrought satire of Irish nationalism as formulated by the Gaelic Revival. By using Famine imagery in a peasant comedy, Synge brings together two well-worn but mutually exclusive representations of Ireland: the bastion of a vital and heroic culture and the land stricken with eternal suffering. Throughout *Playboy*, Synge plays these two models of Ireland against each other to demonstrate that the perpetuation of both models in the rhetoric of the Gaelic Revival undermines the very premise of revolutionary nationalism. In their place, Synge proposes an alternative vision for Irish identity which focuses on the ability of individual storytellers to adapt the desires and imagination of their community to fit the needs of the present day. Although Synge's model has its own flaws, most of which stem from his questionable position as a member of the Ascendancy writing about the state and character of the rural poor, the tension *Playboy* creates between Synge's vision of Irish identity and the one favoured by the Revival reveals how Famine imagery became tangled in the cultural and political conflicts that preceded Irish independence.

Famine narratives and Revival rhetoric

Synge's evocation of the Famine in the opening scene of *Playboy* locates the play within a cultural discourse that was central to the project of Irish nationalism at the turn of the twentieth century. Margaret Kelleher has observed that there is a strong rhetorical tradition extending through the Revival that represents the Famine as a fundamental source of Irish identity: 'What is clear in the literature of the Irish revival, specifically in its attempts to stage the themes of hunger and starvation, is a concern with the symbolic significance of Famine deaths and the implications, occasionally even more fearful, of survival' (Kelleher, 1997, p.127).[2] By most turn-of-the-century accounts, the 'symbolic significance' of the Famine is palpable and far-reaching, extending not just to the people but to the very landscape of contemporary Ireland. For example, Kelleher cites an 1892 lecture Maude Gonne delivered at the Catholic University of Cercle du Luxembourg: addressing the subject of Irish history, Gonne insists that, 'If you come to my country, every stone will repeat with this tragic history. It was only fifty years ago. It lives in a thousand memories' (ibid., p.112). This infusion of the Famine into the very stones of Ireland served a specific purpose for activists such as Gonne, who was at this time touring France to raise support for Irish independence from England. Gonne saw constant recollection of Irish suffering as crucial to the claim that Ireland had been greatly abused by England's misrule, which was (and generally still is) blamed for the Famine's devastation. By perpetuating the image of Ireland as the 'poor old woman' who dwelt perpetually in the shadow of the Great Hunger, Gonne and her colleagues could more effectively raise support at home and abroad for Irish independence.

However, Gonne and her contemporaries did not invent this description of the Famine. In fact, English reporters and authorities created this rhetorical tradition during the Famine itself, a which fact imbues the image with an indelible and, for the Revivalists' purposes, rather unfortunate colonial association. Throughout the 1840s, reports emerged from the English press and officials of the British government which tried to make sense of the Famine for English audiences. These accounts create the narrative framework that portrays Ireland in terms of endless, atemporal suffering, a framework which Gonne and the other Revivalists would appropriate in their rhetoric. Several scholars, most notably Kelleher and Christopher Morash, have charted the way in which British observers constructed the Famine as an endorsement of British imperialism. In particular, both Kelleher and Morash identify the Malthusian rhetoric of 'natural law' that permeates these accounts.[3] Explaining the Famine in Malthusian terms served a convenient purpose for the English authorities: it laid blame for the devastation on providence and the Irish themselves rather than on England, and thereby justified Parliament's halfhearted attempts to provide aid. Under the Malthusian conviction that cataclysmic events are necessary reactions to the misuse of natural resources, the Famine became an equalizing force that would cleanse the Irish landscape of the overpopulation and excesses of the Irish people.

In a broader sense, though, Malthusian logic could be used to validate England's colonial project in Ireland. Portraying the Famine as a cataclysmic force that effectively ended Irish civilization, created a new justification for England's attempt to erase the last traces of Irish culture and identity and assimilate Ireland into the British state. The full extension of this reasoning can be seen in *The Times*' eulogy for Daniel O'Connell published on 27 May 1947. Connecting O'Connell's death to both the devastation of the Famine and the (erroneously) anticipated collapse of nationalism in Ireland, *The Times* declared:

> The man who just closed his career . . . found the Irish a nation of rebels and left them a nation of paupers. Of the two, there is more hope in a weak civility than in a fierce independence. Both are painful, both are disgraceful, and both are costly. But from time immemorial, among races as amongst individual men, humility has been the step to promotion; and they whose lot is cast lowest in the political scale, and who have either lagged or been thrust to the rear of civilization, must make up for lost centuries by accepting the help and guidance of their more fortunate neighbours.

Through this description, *The Times* identifies the Famine as an ultimately positive force in Ireland. By driving the Irish people to the brink of destitution, the Famine has accomplished what the English government could not; it has forced the Irish people to abandon their quest for national independence and supplicate themselves to English law. Hereafter, the same article goes on to predict, 'the peasantry will be the servants of the proprietors and of the British public, with whom it rests whether that service shall be the means of social regeneration'. By this reasoning, the Famine has finally realized the dream of English colonialism by bringing Irish resistance to an end. According to *The Times*'s prediction, Ireland can progress from this point only as an extension of England.

This understanding of the Famine and its utility for colonial purposes permanently altered the way the Irish peasantry were perceived, even after the Famine was over. According to the narrative of progress that infuses the Mathusian account of the Famine, the Irish as a people with a language, history and way of life independent from England cease to exist somewhere in the 1840s, after which Ireland and the Irish are merely subcategories of the British nation. Consequently, as Morash observes, the people of Ireland who survive and all aspects of pre-Famine Irishness that survive with them are perceived in 'the horror of an everlasting present' (Morash, 1995, p.96). If the only path from past to future passes through England, then an Irish people who maintain an existence apart from English rule can exist only as anachronisms from a previous civilization that linger on the present land-scape. The metonymic images that have come to represent the Famine ever since – the lone woman keening for her dead family, animal noises in an empty field, and, of course, the shadowy figure lying in a ditch – demon-strate this belief. The power of these images comes from their evocation of absence; by emphasizing the scattered traces of humanity in an otherwise empty terrain, each image suggests that the Irish people and the material culture they created survive only as remnants of the Famine.

Of course, it hardly needs to be said that Irish culture did not die out with the Famine. Nonetheless, by focusing on the western Irish peasantry, who were seen by both England and Ireland as the last bastion of Gaelic Ireland untouched by colonization, the English narrative of the Famine effectively cut off the unbroken, independent history of the Irish people which, by the end of the nineteenth century, was an essential component of national identity. As Edward Hirsch observes, this made the represen-tation of the peasantry a central concern for Irish nationalists at the time of the Revival: 'The country people were important to Irish cultural and political nationalists not for their own sake but because of what they signified as a concept and as a language. To speak about the 'peasant' was to speak about something beyond actual rural life' (Hirsch, 1991, p.1118). As a result, much of the Revivalists' work revolves around an attempt to reclaim the peasantry from colonial rhetoric, despite the fact that neither the colonial representation of rural Ireland nor its nationalist counterpart had much basis in reality.

Gonne's description of the Famine as a living presence in Ireland, then, does not correct the English rhetoric of the Famine so much as redirect it. Like *The Times* editorial which predicted the end of Irish culture, Gonne's speech depicts the Famine and its aftermath as permanent features of the Irish landscape and Irish identity. Gonne simply places the blame on different shoulders. In her rhetoric, the Famine represents not the inevitable consequence of Irish excess, but the inevitable result of English oppression and misrule. Nonetheless, her argument rests on the same conclusion as *The Times*'s: for the people and culture of rural Ireland, the Famine left a wound that can never be healed. The case for Irish independence represented by Gonne's speech, then, ultimately depends on English perceptions of the state of Ireland at the end of the nineteenth century. This paradox and the Revival's answer to it would provide the basis for Synge's criticism of Revival nationalism in *Playboy*.

As Synge seeks to demonstrate through Christy Mahon and his adventures in Mayo, the depiction of Ireland as a land perpetually suffering from the Famine cannot be divorced from its deeper implication that Irish history effectively ended in the 1840s. This posed a further problem for the cause of Irish nationalism, since a continual narrative of Irish history is necessary to meet the criteria of nationhood. As Seamus Deane has noted, the primary requirement for national consciousness among a colonized people is an unbroken indigenous history that can replace the one imposed by the colonizer and define the source of national difference: 'Insurgent nationalisms attempt to create a version of history for themselves in which their intrinsic essence has always manifested itself, thereby producing readings of the past that are as monolithic as those they are trying to supplant' (Deane, 1990, p.9). In Ireland, as noted above, the source of this history and difference lay in the peasantry, who held the strongest connections to pre-conquest Gaelic culture. Unfortunately, according to the rhetoric of both the British Empire and nationalist agitators such as Gonne, this same peasantry had been fossilized in the wake of the Famine.

Proponents of Irish nationalism, Deane observes, avoided these complications of history by 'rerouting the claim of cultural exceptionalism through legend' (Deane, 1997, p.51). The Revival turned its attention to the depictions of Ireland that existed in myth and folklore, projecting them onto the contemporary landscape and people of Ireland to create an alternative vision of Irish national identity. Hence, in his 1914 speech 'To the Boys of Ireland', Padraic Pearse declares:

Two occasions are spoken of in ancient Irish story upon which Irish boys
marched to the rescue of their country when it was sore beset – once when
Cuchulainn and the boy-troop of Ulster held the frontier until the Ulster
heroes rose, and again when the boys of Ireland kept the foreign invaders in
check . . . until Fionn had rallied the Fianna: it may be that a similar tale shall
be told of us.

(Pearse, 1916, Vol.2, p.111)

Pearse's insistence that the present boys of Ireland should model
themselves after the figures of mythology connects the present struggle
for independence to an idealized past, when the warriors of an uncon-
quered Ireland successfully fought and repelled foreign invaders. This
construction enables him to establish a continuity between the alternative
history of the Cuchulain and Fianna myths and the anticipated future of
Ireland, effectively eliding both the supposed obliteration of Irish culture
by the Famine and 600 years of foreign occupation. By claiming the
heroes of these stories as the *real* people of Ireland, then, nationalist
rhetoric could overlook the post-famine perception of the Irish as a
defeated people who had been left behind by history, replacing it with an
Irish nation that existed once in a mythologized past and might exist again
in an idealized future. The flaw in this narrative, as Synge saw it, is that it
effectively excludes the present from Irish history. While valorizing the
actions of past Irish heroes, it does not engage the colonial narrative of
the Irish people as they are, and thus it creates no framework for new
heroes or actions to emerge. Consequently, the national identity this
narrative seeks to create remains forever beyond the grasp of the people it
is meant to serve – the would-be Irish heroes who exist in the present.

Thus, revolutionary rhetoric at the turn of the twentieth century
projected two mutually exclusive images of Ireland in general, and the
Irish peasantry in particular. One image, represented by the Revival's
fixation on myth and folklore, held the peasantry up as the source of an
ancient and distinct culture that had thrived in the past and might thrive
again in the future. The second image, represented by the strategic use of
Famine imagery in nationalist rhetoric, imagined Ireland as a land whose
present was eternally blighted. These two constructions fundamentally
contradict each other, preventing the smooth connection of past to present
to future that is necessary for a national identity to exist and trapping the
real people of western Ireland in what Terry Eagleton calls, 'the sheer,
empty homogenous time of the body' (Eagleton, 1995, p.14).[4] While they

both imagine a vital Irish nation that existed in the past and might exist in the future, the discontinuity between the two images actually perpetuates the English vision of Ireland in the present.

Synge satirizes this discontinuity in *Playboy*. Christy's transformation from a symbolic Famine victim to a community hero makes him exactly the sort of Cuchulainoid revolutionary figure that Pearse's rhetoric valorizes. In keeping with this ideology, the Mayo villagers deliberately fashion Christy's heroism to suit the needs of their community, which would seem to support the nationalist contention that the culture of the past can revitalize the Irish people in their times of need. However, when Christy apparently re-enacts the crime that forms the basis of his heroic status before the eyes of the villagers, that heroism instantly shatters. Since it is based only on conceptions of the past and future, the myth of the Playboy cannot survive its translation into real action in the present.

This narrative forms a two-pronged attack on the nationalism of the Revival. First, by presenting a western Irish community that subscribes to both nationalist myths at the same time, Synge demonstrates the self-destructive effects that these competing myths have on the people they represent. The villagers in the play create a hero who can embody their own repressed desires, but they are so rooted in their own oppression that they reject their hero as soon as he truly gains potency. This suggests that the Irish people, unable to conform to the myths the Revival has created for them, are left behind by its narrative of Irish history. Moreover, as an allegory for Irish nationalism, the villagers also represent the Revivalists themselves, who, to Synge's mind, refused to abandon their contradictory models of Irish identity, and savagely defended their right to remain stuck in the paradox they create. As many critics have observed, the riots during the play's opening run demonstrated the poignancy of Synge's criticism. Like the villagers who form a lynch mob rather than face the reality of their Playboy's deeds, the most extreme factions of the Revival could not bear to see their own myths subjected to critical scrutiny, and so they, like the villagers, chose to violently expel the offending images from their midst.

The famine and its aftermath in Synge's Mayo

The description of Christy moaning in a ditch is one of the play's most obvious links to Famine narrative, but it is by no means the only one. The Mayo village in which the play opens shows many signs of trauma which echo accounts of the Famine. There is an emptiness to the landscape that strikes fear into the hearts of its inhabitants. Before Christy arrives, Pegeen Mike complains to her father that she fears to be left alone in the isolated shebeen overnight: 'its a queer father'd be leaving me lonesome these twelve hours of dark, and I piling the turf with the dogs barking and the calves mooing and my own teeth rattling with fear' (Synge, *Playboy*, p.116). Peg later goes on to point to specific, human, dangers that might come in the night: madmen, tinkers and the like, but her initial statement suggests that it is not so much the presence of predators that frightens her as the absence of humanity. The villagers' awareness of death infuses the land itself, and that awareness can be pushed back only tenuously through the presence of others.

This recalls the 'haunting projection' Morash identifies in Irish writing during and after the Famine, in which the absence of humanity evokes the presence of the dead (Morash, 1995, p.180). William Carleton's 1847 novel *The Black Prophet*, for example, presents the Irish landscape as a desolate reflection of its people's suffering:

> The evening . . . had impressed on it a character of such dark and hopeless desolation as weighed down the heart with a feeling of cold and chilling gloom that was communicated by the dreary aspect of every thing around . . . A brooding stillness, too, lay over all nature; cheerfulness had disappeared, even the groves and hedges were silent, for the very birds had ceased to sing, and the earth seemed as if it mourned for the approaching calamity, as well as for that which had already been felt.
>
> (Carleton [1847], 1996, pp.22–4)

Carleton is one of the few Irish authors in the nineteenth century who addressed the Famine at all, and thus his novel may be the first to depict the devastation it wrought as a negative impression that seems to turn nature itself malevolent. It was by no means the last such depiction, though; this evocation of death through a conspicuous emptiness appears in descriptions of the Famine to this day. Commenting on Sinead O'Connor's 1994 song 'Famine', which begins with the sound of a howling dog, David Lloyd observes that 'this animal lament accentuates the absence or the silence of what properly should be the sound of human mourning: it is as if the field of human society itself has been decimated to the extent that all that remains . . . is this anguish of the domestic animal on the verge of reverting to its wildness' (Lloyd, 1997, p.32). Thus, while O'Connor emphasizes the sound of animals rather than the lack of such sound, her imagery, like Carleton's, evokes dread through the absence of humanity. By evoking the same dread in *Playboy*, then, Synge locates the play within a cultural discourse that both he and his audience could immediately associate with the Famine.

This emptiness of the landscape, both in traditional Famine narratives and in Synge's play, is not merely a passive ambience; it actually limits the community's ability to function: Michael Flaherty plans to leave his daughter in order to attend a wake, and thus Peg's demand for her father to stay with her forces Michael to choose between the duty to protect his living daughter and his duty to properly mourn the dead (Synge, *Playboy*, p.114).[5] Kelleher observes that 'the importance of burial', and the corresponding 'threat posed by famine to custom and human decencies' is a common synecdoche for the supposedly 'inexpressible' effects of widespread suffering in nineteenth-century accounts of the Famine. By emphasizing that the population is so thinned and so stricken that the proper maintenance of Christian burial conditions has become difficult or impossible, the experience of witnessing the Famine itself could be articulated to non-Irish readers whose physical and financial security made them too removed to fully imagine it (Kelleher, 1997, p.142). Thus, Synge locates the play in an Ireland still suffering from the effects of the Famine, where the basic social institutions of mourning and familial responsibility cannot be maintained at the same time.

The elements of this opening scene already demonstrate Synge's blending of Famine rhetoric with the myth of a vital and cunning peasantry. The quick-witted dialogue in which Peg and her father square off over his responsibility reflects what Synge himself describes in his Preface to the play as 'a popular imagination that is fiery, and magnificent' (Synge, *Playboy*, p.112).[6] With the exception of Shawn Keogh, who serves as the perpetual straight man, the villagers are all masters of verbal repartee; none of them, least of all Peg, seems to have the slightest problem defending their interests, or the slightest fear of speaking their mind. Nonetheless, beneath the flashing wit, both Peg and her father are motivated by fears that stem directly from the emptiness outside: Peg demands protection because she fears to be alone in the desolate landscape, and Michael defends himself because he knows he cannot fulfill his duties as a father. From the beginning then, the villagers' vitality competes with the underlying emptiness of the land, which constantly threatens to disrupt the fragile cohesion of the village.

The specific combination of strength and vulnerability in Pegeen Mike, who is afraid to be alone at night but contentious enough to belittle her father for leaving her, points to larger breakdown in the social structure of the village: gender roles among the Mayonites, at least according to patriarchal definitions, are reversed. The men of the village are weak and feminized, an effect which is most noticeable in the character of Shawn. As Peg's fiancée, he should accept at least partial responsibility for her welfare, but Shawn refuses to stay with Peg while her father is away because he fears both the empty landscape and the watchful eyes of the Church: 'What at all would the Holy Father and the Cardinals of Rome be saying if they heard I did the like of that?' (Synge, *Playboy*, p.117). Indeed, Shawn seems to accept his entire identity passively from the authority figures around him: he enters his fiancée's home only after carefully considering if he has 'a right to pass on or walk in and see' her (ibid., p.114). This fear of, and deference to, authority makes Shawn unable to act without the approval of priest or peeler. His marriage to Peg is currently on hold until he can get a dispensation from the bishop and, when nearly forced by Michael and his friends to stay with Peg, he flees in terror lest he raise the censure of Father Reilly (ibid., p.117).

The women of Synge's play, by contrast, are famously strong and vital, which underscores the absence of male authority among the villagers. Peg is clearly too powerful for the men around her. 'The fright of seven townlands for [her] biting tongue', she dominates Shawn, her father, and, initially, Christy (ibid., p.156). In reaction to the paralysis of the men, she takes the active role throughout the play: when the villagers try to raise a mob to string up Christy in the final act, Peg alone has the courage to slip the rope over Christy's neck (ibid., p.163). This representation of female strength in the face of male weakness recalls yet another trope of Famine narratives, in which 'women frequently appear as the sole adult survivor, having outlived their male relatives and now lacking their support, suggesting at once a greater resilience and a particular vulnerability' (Kelleher, 1997, p.10). Occurring only after the loss of male assistance, this emphasis on female strength serves, like the absence of burial rituals, to accentuate the cataclysmic effect the Famine has on the social order, since the strength of Irish women emerges only because there are no strong men left to care for them. Synge's attribution of this quality to his heroine, despite the fact that her father and fiancée still live, demonstrates the villagers' failure to recover from the loss of their patriarchy. Although Peg has a father and a mate, they are both uniformly incapable of fulfilling their roles in her life, which indicates that the vacuum of male authority left by the Famine has never been filled.

In this context, the vitality of the Mayo women is antithetical to the vitality of the village. Patriarchal society depends on the presence of women as bearers and nurturers of children, but the absence of male authority figures forces the Mayonite women to vacate their nurturing roles and assume commanding ones. As a result, instances of female authority negatively affect the fertility of the village as a whole, as the Widow Quin's ostracism demonstrates. The Widow's murder of her husband mirrors the patricide that makes Christy a celebrity, a connection she makes immediately upon meeting Christy: 'you'll find we're great company, young fellow, when it's the like of you and me you'd hear the penny poets singing in an August Fair' (Synge, *Playboy*, p.128). Furthermore, the Widow clearly possesses the same qualities of intelligence and self-determination which the villagers ascribe to Christy upon hearing of his alleged crime, making her perfectly capable of taking on the self-sustaining duties necessary in her husband's absence: 'When you see me contriving in my little gardens', she assures Christy, 'you'll swear the Lord God formed me to be living alone, and that there isn't my match in Mayo for thatching, or mowing, or shearing a sheep' (ibid., p.129). However, since the Widow has outlived both her husband and her children, she cannot pass these qualities on to another generation. Consequently, the narrative of her deeds created by the villagers demonizes her rather than valorizing her: 'She hit [her husband] with a worn pick', Peg informs Christy, 'and the rusted poison did corrode his blood, the way he never overed it, and died after. That was a sneaky kind of murder did win small glory with the boys itself' (ibid., p.128). This version of events projects the flaws which the villagers' see in their community onto the Widow; she did not merely kill her husband, she corrupted his body, making him weak through her show of strength. In keeping with the tautological self-perception of the village, this interpretation transforms the Widow's symbolic infertility into practical fact. As a social outcast, her infamy ensures that she will never find another husband in the village, and thus never have any more children.

Similarly, the match between Peg and Shawn offers little promise of future generations. Peg shows only a passing interest in the marriage, declaring that she 'wouldn't give a thraneen for a lad hadn't a mighty spirit in him and a gamy heart' (ibid., p.140). For his part, Shawn shows little interest in fighting for Peg's affections. He can hardly bear to be in the same room with her, and as soon as Christy proves to be a threat Shawn decides, 'I'd leifer live a bachelor, simmering in passions until the end of time, than face a lepping savage the like of him' (ibid., p.159). Peg is too strong to submit to such a union, and Shawn is too weak to persuade her. Even if their marriage were to occur, their respective unfitness to serve as mother and father to each other's children makes the prospects for the next generation bleak. Michael even jokes about the potential offspring of Shawn and Peg: 'I'd leifer face the grave untimely', he assures his daughter, 'than go peopling my bedside with puny weeds the like of what you'd breed out of Shaneen Keogh' (ibid., p.159). The eugenic tone of such a statement demonstrates the Darwinian mentality which underlies the villagers' understanding of their own situation. In Michael's eyes, his daughter's only choice for a mate is too inferior to sire children worthy of his genes. By this logic, the village itself will soon die out if things do not change drastically.

The barrenness of the village does more than simply cast aspersions on the future, though. In the emerging discourse of nationalism in nineteenth- and twentieth-century Europe, the importance of reproduction symbolically represented through womanhood encapsulates the two essential elements of nationalism: the maintenance of a race over time and the progress of that race from generation to generation. Thus, if the subjectivity of the Mayonites is antithetical to human reproduction, the progression of history comes to a halt, and the village is essentially stuck in the present. It is not that the village has a bleak future; epistemically, it has no future. As in the English conception of Ireland after the Famine, the Mayonites are already a dead race, cut off from the discourse of history.

As I will demonstrate below, Synge clearly does not believe that this patriarchal subjectivity is either natural or native to the Irish peasantry. The villagers, however, seem to accept without question that the survival and progress of their society depends on male authority. Consequently, the villagers define themselves by narratives which reinforce the stasis of their existence. Lamenting the absence of strong men, Peg describes 'this place where you'll meet none but Red Linahan, has a squint in his eye, and Patcheen is lame in his heel, or the mad Mulrannies were driven from California and lost their wits' (ibid., p.114). Such a statement not only notes the lack of local heroes; it denies the possibility that any heroic (or even functional) individual could emerge from this setting. Instead, Mayo men are defined by their disfigurement and insanity – physical and mental reflections of the village's spiritual deformation.

As with the demonization of the Widow Quin, the villagers' self-conception incorporates any evidence of activity or agency in the village as proof of their sterility. While female acts of resistance like the Widow's lead to barrenness, male agency can only be remembered in contrast to its present absence. Continuing her lament for the lack of heroes, Peg asks, 'Where now will you meet the like of Daneen Sullivan knocked the eye from a peeler; or Marcus Quin, god rest him, got six months for maiming ewes, and he a great warrant to tell stories of holy Ireland till he'd have the old women shedding down tears about their feet' (ibid., p.114). This directly contradicts the Revival claim that heroes of the past can be used to overshadow the complications of the present. In Peg's eyes, the defining characteristic of Daneen Sullivan and Marcus Quin is that they do not exist in the present. Their actions cannot inspire the villagers to imitate them, but they can be used to illuminate the villagers' failure to do so. Removed from the dominant historical continuity, the villagers can only use the past to accentuate the flaws in the present, not to envision the future.

This stasis of the villagers satirizes Revival rhetoric on several fronts. First, it ridicules the myth of a vital Irish peasantry waiting to emerge as the dominant national culture. Peg and the girls of the village can only remember heroes that they assume are lost forever, and rather than serving as a model for future action these memories only serve to accentuate the fact that no one in the village at present can take the absent heroes' place. Synge's real assault, though, is on the Revival's contradictory attempts to use the peasantry for political capitol. Synge's villagers demonstrate what happens when a people try to embody at once the myths of a heroic past and an eternally suffering present. Faced with the breakdown of history these two narratives create, the villagers are incapable of the sort of revitalization promised by the Revival.

However, Synge does more than simply question the efficacy of the Revival's rhetoric. In his Mayo, the discontinuity between an ideally remembered past and grimly perceived future actually serves to cement the villagers' status as colonial subjects. Though the villagers' self-conception perpetuates their stasis, Synge indicates that that English authority is the real source of their detachment from history. It is no coincidence that both of the local heroes Peg recalls are criminals; in Peg's mind, heroism is synonymous with law breaking.[7] This perception provides a more concrete explanation for why no such heroes remain in the village, because the very acts that would allow them to emerge would also cause them to be imprisoned, executed or forced to emigrate.[8] The barrenness of the village, then, stems directly from colonial oppression; male agency, as Peg defines it, is illegal. Furthermore, in the case of Marcus Quin, Peg's recollection directly links his criminal activity with his ability to 'tell stories of holy Ireland' (ibid., pp.114–15). Thus, the absence of Marcus and anyone like him corresponds with the loss of narrative ability in the village. Heroes, storytelling and criminality are all aspects of the same identity, which colonial authority has robbed the village of its ability to sustain. Significantly, no agents of colonial authority (or indeed, of any authority) are ever shown in the play, and there is no indication that the British government plays a direct role in the villagers' lives. The conviction with which the villagers lament their impotence is self-maintaining; they have internalized their abject position in the colonial power hierarchy so thoroughly that the actual representatives of that hierarchy are no longer necessary.

This self-maintained colonial subjectivity is so complete that the villagers actively sabotage all opportunities to escape it. The appearance of Christy Mahon and the legend which the villagers create for him briefly offer a respite from the rhetoric of history in which they are mired. However, Christy's heroic identity never effectively challenges the power of colonial authority in the village; it merely circumvents it for a time. Thus, when the reoccurrence of Christy's 'crime' forces the villagers to confront the act and its consequences in their immediate presence, they revert to their status as colonial subjects and become active agents of English law. This reversal discredits the nationalist conception of Irish identity which sought a direct connection between the present nation and the heroes of legend but tried to avoid the complications of historical reality. Christy's rise and fall among the villagers is a grotesque allegory for the outcome of the national myth.

From this perspective, it's easy to see why Synge's nationalist audiences objected so violently to the play. Hirsch notes that 'In effect, the audience was being asked to give up the politically encoded figure of the peasant by laughing at it and to submit to Synge's aesthetic rewriting of the figure in literary language' (Hirsch, 1993, pp.95–6). Synge brought onstage the Irish peasantry, the symbolic core of the Irish nation, but he did so in a way that negated the peasantry's revolutionary potential. Revolutionary rhetoric requires both a vision of the future that is fundamentally different from the present and a plausible claim that the people as they are in the present can realize that vision. The Irish peasants depicted in *Playboy* have neither of these things. Discursively, they have no future, and their conviction of that fact is so complete that all of their actions perpetuate their present condition. Synge offers a vision of the peasantry so dehumanized by English authority that they cannot conceive of themselves as anything but objects of colonial rule, a vision hardly compatible with a budding national consciousness. Furthermore, Synge's staging of this condition for the Dublin audience of the self-proclaimed Irish National Theatre carries with it the inevitable contention that this problem exists not merely in the peasantry itself, but in the national identity they supposedly embody. By trying to subvert rather than negate the narrative of Irish history created by England, Synge argues, the nationalist rhetoric favoured by the Revival only reinforces Ireland's colonial subjectivity.

'The Playboy' and the collapse of heroism

Christy Mahon seems to emerge onto the scene from the land itself. Rising from his ditch to become the focal point of the village and the play, he embodies the villagers' desire for a hero. He is both a Christ figure and a Famine victim restored to life in their midst. His very presence should reverse the narrative of decay that ensnares the village. The villagers, however, are less interested in Christy's historical symbolism than in his lack of personal history. Coming from 'a windy corner of high, distant hills', he is immune to the blight of temporality from which they suffer (Synge, *Playboy*, p.122). Christy's narrative can be controlled, and as each detail of his 'patricide' is coaxed out of him, they integrate it seamlessly into a legend of his courage and heroism:

CHRISTY: [*twisting round on* (Peg) *with a sharp cry of horror*] Don't strike me. I killed my poor father, Tuesday a week, for doing the like of that.
PEGEEN: [*with blank amazement*] Is it killed your father?
CHRISTY: [*subsiding*] With the help of God I did, surely . . .
PHILLY: [*retreating with Jimmy*] There's a daring fellow.
JIMMY: Oh glory be to God!
MICHAEL: [*with great respect*] That was a hanging crime, mister honey. You should have had a good reason for doing the like of that.

(ibid., p.121)

Not only does the revelation that Christy is (apparently) a murderer win him instant respect, but the severity of his crime only increases that respect. The fact that he has committed a 'hanging crime' convinces

Michael that Christy must have had a legitimate reason.[9] The villagers offer an equally questionable interpretation when Christy gives the details of his escape:

MICHAEL: [*Making a sign to Peg to fill Christy's glass*] And what way weren't you hanged, mister? Did you bury him then?
CHRISTY: [*considering*] Aye. I buried him then. Wasn't I digging spuds in the field?
MICHAEL: And the peelers never followed after you the eleven days that you're out?
CHRISTY: [*shaking his head*] Never a one of them . . .
PHILLY: [*nodding wisely*] It's only with a common weekday murder them lads be trusting their carcass, and that man should be a great terror when his temper's roused.

(ibid., p.122)

According to his own story, Christy has not been hung because he took steps to hide his actions. But rather than interpreting this as a sign of cowardice, the villagers see it as a sign of strength: Christy's murder is actually *too* audacious for the peelers to investigate. The more criminal Christy appears, the more attractive he becomes.

Embellished or not, the nature of Christy's crime is particularly well-suited to the villagers' desires. He may not have attacked a peeler, like the legendary Daneen Sullivan, but he did overthrow a domineering authority figure, at least according to the version of the story that emerges. The interpretations of the crime the villagers derive from Christy's confession further tailor his legend to fit their needs: Philly's conclusion that 'that man should be a great terror' to the peelers 'when his temper's roused', equates Christy's resistance to patriarchal authority with the ability to disrupt colonial authority. By killing his father, Christy proves that even an apparently submissive man can still rise up and slay his master when pushed too far, a fact which ought to make the authorities take care. It is this aspect of Christy's image which convinces the villagers to keep Christy among them: Philly suggests to Michael that employing Christy as his pot boy will ward off the police, because 'if you'd that lad in the house there isn't one of them would come smelling around' (ibid., p.122). Peg reiterates this claim, assuring her father that, with Christy in the house, she 'wouldn't be fearing the loosed khaki cut-throats' (ibid.). Christy's role in the community, then, is practical as well as symbolic; his presence will protect them from the intrusion of the law.[10] By assimilating Christy, the villagers hope that their community will gain his perceived immunity to authority.

This equation by the villagers of patricide with resistance points to the contradiction that will cause Christy's downfall in the village. Patricide is a perversion of the patriarchal system: rather than inheriting the father's position when he matures, the son seizes it by force, thereby destroying the father's previously uncontested authority. Patriarchal ascendancy hinges on the father's right to determine when the son deserves to inherit his mantle, without which it crumbles into the nightmare of the Oedipus myth. To glorify patricide, then, is to glorify the breakdown of the patriarchal system. Furthermore, the immediate connection between patricide and resistance to colonialism made by the villagers indicates an awareness, if only a subconscious one, that the logic of patriarchy and the logic of empire are one and the same. England justified the domination of Ireland by alternately claiming that the Irish were too feminine (meaning irrational or emotional) or too primitive to govern themselves. Thus, to rise up against the colonizer means to seize the mantle of authority from a ruling body that believes you are unworthy of it or unready for it, which is essentially patricide.

But the Mayonites do not adopt Christy into their community in order to subvert patriarchal authority in the village; they adopt him to recreate that authority. By making Christy part of the village, they hope to circumvent the belief that no strong men can come from there, and thereby reestablish a continuity of history based on patriarchal relationships. To accompany their exaggerated interpretation of his deed, the villagers attribute heroic characteristics to Christy. As soon as his story's told, Philly credits him with 'the sense of Solomon', and Peg declares him 'a fine, handsome young fellow with a noble brow' (ibid., pp.122 and 124). As with the crime itself, this perception of nobility assimilates even the seemingly negative or innocuous details of Christy's character, such as Peg's conclusion that Christy's 'little, small feet' prove that he 'should have had great people in [his] family' (ibid., p.124). Such a conclusion not only portrays Christy as a hero the like of Daneen Sullivan and Marcus Quin, it also projects his nobility back over an imagined hereditary line, despite the obvious fact that Christy's immediate forebearer is the very person demonized by his story. This way, when Christy completes his assimilation by marrying and having children here, the village as a whole will inherit this lineage, which will finally liberate it from the stasis generated by the colonial Famine narrative. As noted above, though, the definition of social progress in patriarchal terms rationalizes colonialism; thus, the villagers are attempting to escape from one colonial narrative into another.

By pinning their hopes for rebirth on the fabricated heroism of Christy, then, villagers are re-entering the narrative of history without questioning its terms. As I will demonstrate below, this not only fails to liberate the villagers from colonial subjectivity, it actually causes them to involuntarily support that authority when Christy becomes a threat to it. This represents a direct attack by Synge on the Revival's model of Irish identity, which maintains the history of the Famine provided by England but nonetheless claims the subjects of that history as the foundation of Irish difference. In Synge's depiction, this model makes Ireland's identity a function of the very narrative used to justify its conquest. The history of Ireland provided by England ends with the defeat and erasure of the Irish as a distinctive people by the Famine, and therefore, by clinging to this history, the Revivalists cling to the identification of the Irish as a perpetually dying race.

Contradictory though it may be, this strategy initially works for the villagers, as the myth of heroism they create soon imbues Christy with the power to embody that heroism. The morning after he arrives in the village, Christy begins to see himself as the villagers see him: '[*He takes the looking glass from the wall and puts it on the back of a chair; then sits down in front of it and begins washing his face*] Didn't I know rightly, I was handsome, though it was the divil's own mirror we had beyond' (ibid., p.131). This alteration in Christy extends from attractiveness to physical prowess, allowing him to sweep the local games (ibid., p.154). He also gains eloquence: Peg accepts his proposal in Act 3 with the assurance that 'any girl would walk her heart out before she'd meet a young man was your like for eloquence, or talk at all' (ibid., p.155). The specific promise of Peg and Christys' marriage completes his transformation into the embodiment of the villagers' desire. Not only does he possess the eloquence and the ability to transgress the law missed in the like of Daneen Sullivan and Marcus Quin, but he will also use those qualities to cement a marriage in the village and sire a new generation.

That Christy should first perceive these changes in himself while looking in the mirror demonstrates the completeness with which external perception determines his subjectivity. In 'the divil's own mirror' of his home town, Christy admits he was no more attractive or capable than any of the Mayonite men. The obvious reason for this is that his father and the people of his home village explicitly told Christy that he was inferior. Before he sees his son in Mayo, Old Mahon describes Christy as 'an ugly young streeler with a murderous gob on him' (ibid., p.145). It is clear that Christy heard this description of himself often: when Peg asks him if any of the women at home had commented on his 'noble brow', Christy responds '*with venom*' that 'they're bloody liars in the naked parish where I grew a man' (ibid., p.125). Christy sees his own beauty in the mirror only after he has been assured by the Mayonites that it is there to be seen. The narrative of his abilities determines their reality to such an extent that, from his perspective, his very reflection has altered.

This immediate translation of perception into reality shows the power Synge located in narrative, and helps to explain why he was so bitter with the failure he perceived in the narratives offered by Irish nationalism in his time. Christy transforms from an anonymous Famine victim into a potential revolutionary simply because the villagers can construct a story which identifies him as such. If this can be achieved, then surely Ireland can overcome the entropy of English domination by producing a coherent narrative of Irish success. However, by Synge's reckoning, the competing narratives created by the Revival offer no such sustainable vision, and thus only serve to perpetuate the failure mandated by the English narrative of history.

The inevitability of this failure is demonstrated through the ruin of Christy's heroism in the village. The creation of Christy's legend mirrors the mythic alternative to history favoured by Irish nationalism in Synge's time. The distance of his actions from the village, both temporal and physical, relieves the Mayonites of responsibility for reconciling the past with the present; Christy is simply the heroic ideal come to life, with no messy details to get in the way. This embodiment, however, depends on the villagers' ability to remove Christy entirely from the context of his former life and recreate him with their own desires. His very title, 'the Playboy of the Western World', integrates him into the legends of noble criminals and corrupt authorities that power the legendary imagination of the people, as demonstrated by Sara's toast to Christy in Act 2: 'Drink a health to the wonders of the Western World: the pirates, preachers, poteen-makers, jobbing jockies; parching peelers, and the juries fill their stomachs selling judgements of the English law' (ibid., p.136). Such a configuration precludes the idea that the conflict between English law and Irish lawlessness is a historical one that may be brought to an end, instead declaring it the source of 'the western world's' distinctiveness, effectively making it an eternal peculiarity of Ireland.

Christy's title also strips him of the last vestige of his individual identity: by the middle of the second act, the villagers refer to him almost

exclusively as 'the Playboy'. With this title, Christy becomes more personification than person, a vessel through which the suppressed aggression of
the village can be emptied into myth. A champion such as this, however,
can only accentuate the desires he embodies; he can never satisfy them.
Christy's 'Playboy' persona may bring a living hero into the village, but it
does nothing to counter the narrative of stasis and impotence for which
the Playboy was the envisaged solution. The Playboy's legend depends on
the fact that his crime did not happen in the village, and thus, by
definition, it cannot disprove the villagers' conviction that no heroes can
emerge from among them. Furthermore, the positive actions attributed to
the Playboy after he arrives all hinge on his superiority to the village men:
he sweeps the local games because he is stronger and faster than any man
in the village, and Peg accepts his proposal because he is more eloquent
than any man in the village.

More importantly, the complete erasure of Christy's previous identity
wrought by his transformation into the Playboy leaves no room for any
non-heroic action or characteristic in his image. As Kaja Silverman has
noted, 'the subject who aspires to incarnate or embody the ideal . . . surrenders all negotiating distance with respect to ideality, and all agency in
the larger field of vision' (Silverman, 1996, p.40). As the projection of the
villagers' ideal object onto a human being, the Playboy can maintain his
existence only as long as he acts within the boundaries of that ideal. Once
Christy appears to be anything in addition to the Playboy, the Playboy will
be obliterated.

The arrival of Christy's father brings about this obliteration. In the
presence of Old Mahon, Christy reverts to the passive object of patriarchal authority his father made him: '[*getting up in shy terror*] What is it
drives you to torment me here, when I'd asked the thunders of the might
of God to blast me if I ever did hurt to anything saving only that one
single blow' (Synge, *Playboy*, p.161). The sight of Christy, terrified by his
father's wrath, shatters the illusion of his perfect heroism. This, in turn,
causes the villagers to immediately reject him. This rejection, of course,
completely ignores the real feats of eloquence and physical prowess that
he has performed since his arrival, a fact which does not escape Christy's
attention: 'You've seen my doings this day', he cries, [*piteously*], 'why would
you be in such a scorch of haste to spur my destruction now?' (ibid.,
p.160). But Christy can no more create a heroic persona from his actions
in the village than the Mayonites can from their own, because the very
definition of the village holds that no person or action which comes from

there can be heroic. Thus, the villagers are unable to reconcile the reality of Christy's character with the destruction of his legend, and they turn their backs on him. The implications of this rejection in nationalist terms are scathing. 'It's lies you told', Peg declares, 'letting on you had him slit. And you nothing at all' (ibid., p.160). Since Christy cannot maintain the identity she helped create for him, Peg denies him any identity. In essence, Synge suggests that the pretence of heroism in the Revival will inevitably collapse when challenged by real authority, and thus that Revival rhetoric actually cements English authority rather than subverting it.

The villagers' second rejection of Christy, however, reveals the full dominance of the colonial narrative over the heroic one in which it is embedded. When Old Mahon is apparently murdered before their eyes, the villagers immediately form a mob in order to drag Christy into police custody (ibid., p.163). By attempting to realize his previously 'heroic' deed in front of them, Christy creates history rather than myth, and thus makes himself and the villagers susceptible once again to the colonial narrative of history. Consequently, the villagers become agents of colonial control. In an attempt to avoid the censure of the English authorities, they choose to enforce that authority themselves. As Michael tells Christy, 'It is the will of God that all should guard their cabins from the treachery of the law, and what would my daughter be doing if I was ruined or hanged itself?' (ibid., pp.165–6). That Michael should use this excuse to justify the actions of a mob *led* by his daughter encapsulates the crippling power of the colonial narrative that has rendered the village infertile from the beginning. The existence of male action in the past leads inevitably to the absence of male agency in the present. Declan Kiberd points out that, 'like hopeless provincials', the villagers 'have no sense of their own presence' (1995, p.184). Like Christy at the beginning of the play, they understand themselves solely as a part of an external history which strips them by design of all agency.

The audience's reaction to this scene during the play's opening performance demonstrates its accuracy as an allegory for the effects of nationalist rhetoric. According to the *Freeman's Journal*, as soon as the villagers descended on Christy, the shouts of protest which had been heard intermittently from the audience throughout the third act erupted into a sustained uproar of 'angry groans, growls, hisses, and noise' which effectively drowned out the remainder of the performance (cited in Kilroy, 1971, p.8). Just as the villagers in the play could not stand to see their heroic ideal in fallible human form, the nationalist audience could not stand to see their ideal peasantry portrayed as real subjects crippled by colonial authority. So, while the villagers try to obliterate Christy rather than amend their ideal, the audience attacked the offending image of the play rather than accept the flaws in their narrative of Irish nationality.

Synge's prescient staging of this betrayal demonstrates the futility of a nationalist myth that eludes the English narrative of post-Famine history rather than engaging it. Deane argues that,

> The failure of the community to bring the past Eden into a utopian future marks the boundary line between nationalist and romantic desire. The vagrant hero or heroine fades into legend or fantasy. The community remains; more deeply stricken, more visibly decayed.
>
> (Deane, 1985, p.53)

While the valorization of Christy momentarily brings vitality back to the village, that vitality is extinguished the moment Christy's idealized transgression translates into real action against a source of authority. Christy provides a focus for the villagers' desire for escape from the crippling absence of history, but he provides no outlet for those desires that restores history to them. This breakdown of the revolutionary impulse, the play suggests, is the end result of any national project which seeks to validate itself based on the evocation of a mythical past detached from the reality of the present.

Christy's reconception of the heroic ideal

Synge's alternative to what he saw as the self-defeating rhetoric of the Revival lies in Christy himself. While Christy's transformation may be false to the villagers, the physical and mental power it unlocks in him is quite real. He comes into the play as an inarticulate extension of the Famine-stricken land: entering the shebeen from his 'furzy ditch', he is at first so incapable of speech that he cannot even name his own crime (Synge, *Playboy*, p.118). But as he begins to embody the Playboy, Christy creates a subjectivity for himself through the myth that the villagers provide for him. Gradually, he gains control of his own narrative, first by retelling his own story, then by using his newfound subjectivity to envision a future for himself through his proposal to Peg. Kiberd observes that Christy 'rejects a false image of himself . . . and instead chooses *to be*, creating instant, improvised traditions of himself out of the shreds of popular culture' (1995, p.180) [original emphasis]. By taking on the characteristics the villagers provide, Christy is able to own his new reflection, which allows him to write the narrative of his life rather than be written by it. Through Christy, Synge demonstrates that individuals can overcome an imposed narrative that predestines them to failure and take control of their own identity.

Christy's subjugation of his father and departure from the village completes this process. By taking command of the patriarch who once dominated him, Christy creates his own legendary persona, declaring himself the 'master of fights', and promising to 'go romancing through a romping lifetime' with his father as his servant (Synge, *Playboy*, p.166). Brenda Murphy observes that this declaration 'proves through praxis the heroism [Christy] had created through mythos' (1992, p.49). The strength which Christy gained through the fiction of 'destroying' his father allows him to rise up and destroy the relationship to his father which subjugated him. Furthermore, by leaving the village he removes himself from the villagers' colonial gaze, which would demand he conform either to the static ideal of the Playboy or its emasculated negative. He achieves what neither the narrative of the villagers nor the corresponding narratives of the Revival could permit him to do: the creation of an identity that will allow him to use his heroic qualities for future activity.

This final transformation offers an alternative to the Revival's model for Irish national identity, one which overcomes the complications of Ireland's colonial history but does not ignore them. The transformation enacted through Christy essentially abandons the past as a direct source of identity and uses its decay as a source of vitality in the present. The nostalgic image of Ireland represented by Synge's Mayo village is simply too damaged by the Famine and its aftermath to be reclaimed. Individuals in the present, however, may use the distinctive aspects of Irish culture to create a subjectivity that defies the colonial narrative, as long as it is understood that those individuals are essentially separate from the society that created them. By Synge's definition, Irish nationhood cannot come from a paradoxical fixation on the past but only through a recreation of Irish history and culture which subsumes its vital qualities into a modern subjectivity.

Most importantly, the defining characteristics of that subjectivity are an understanding and command of the different narratives the past can generate and a position sufficiently outside a community to elude its current system of identification. When he enters the village, the only thing that differentiates Christy from Shawn Keogh is that he did not come from there, and thus the story which establishes his identity among the villagers can be one of heroism and not failure. Christy then comes into his own when he takes the identity that the villagers create for him and separates it from the context that would eventually destroy it. By leaving the village with the Playboy persona intact, Christy does what the villagers cannot: he travels from myth back into history.

It is easy to see why this model of Irish nationality appealed to Synge, since it defines Irishness in a way that negates the importance of heredity. The Irish revolutionary hero envisioned by the play is not determined by his class, religious heritage or ancestral connection to the people of Ireland but rather by his understanding of what it means to be Irish. This ensures the Anglo-Irish a place in the new Ireland, as long as they are willing to share in its narrative recreation. Furthermore, Synge's model actually valorizes the marginal position of Anglo-Irish authors like Synge to the society they depict. Like Christy, Synge lived in peasant communities in Wicklow, Mayo and the Aran Islands as an outsider, gathering material he would eventually use in his plays. In his Preface, which first appeared as a programme note to the inaugural performances, Synge uses his infamous metaphor of the Wicklow cottage to illustrate this relationship:

> When I was writing *Shadow of the Glen*, some years ago, I got more aid than any learning could have given me from a chink in the floor of the old Wicklow house where I was staying, that let me hear what was being said by the serving girls in the kitchen. This matter, I think, is of importance, for in countries where the imagination of the people, and the language they use, is rich and living, it is possible for a writer to be rich and copious in his words
>
> (Synge, *Playboy*, p.111)

Synge rests his art and his authority on a specific proximity to the peasantry: close enough to experience their language and culture, but not close enough to actually interact with them.[11] This passage reiterates the need for a privileged class of authors in the cause of nationalism. Synge does not suggest that the serving girls could express themselves on the national stage, or that anything could be gained by relaying their conversation directly to the national audience. Instead, a writer is needed to rearrange their words and thereby create art.

Synge's model for national rebirth, then, is a self-serving one. It preserves from the Revival the idea of a national identity which stems from the western Irish peasantry, but at the same time creates a position of eminence for the Anglo-Irish as outside observers who can refine and rearrange Western culture into a coherent national identity. It also places art and artists at the centre of this process, which effectively makes the Abbey theatre, as an Anglo-Irish institution dedicated to the creation of Irish art, the model of a nationalist institution. Self-serving or not, though, Synge's model does offer an alternative to the endless depiction of the Irish as a defeated or suffering people, which he demonstrates to be inevitably self-defeating.

Thus, *Playboy of the Western World* proposes one problematic model for Irish nationalism while satirizing another. By embodying the essence of Revival ideology in Mayo villagers and the Playboy they create, and then revealing the way this creation enforces colonial authority, the play exposes a fundamental contradiction in the dual narratives of Irish vitality and perpetual suffering employed by nationalist rhetoric. It also demonstrates the ability of narrative to create and reify identity, an ability demonstrated even more powerfully by the riots on the play's opening night. By rising up in protest to what they saw as an unflattering picture of themselves, Synge's audience became the very thing his play claimed they were, an angry mob bent on suppressing a truly revolutionary image of themselves.

References

Carleton, William. *The Black Prophet* [1847]. Poole and Washington, DC: Woodstock Books, 1996.

Deane, Seamus. *Celtic Revivals: Essays in Modern Irish Literature, 1880–1980.* London: Faber & Faber, 1985.

Deane, Seamus (ed.). 'Introduction'. *Nationalism, Colonialism, and Literature.* Minneapolis, MN: University of Minnesota Press, 1990.

Deane, Seamus. *Strange Country: Modernity and Nationhood in Irish Writing since 1790.* Oxford: Clarendon Press, 1997.

Eagleton, Terry. *Heathcliff and the Great Hunger: Studies in Irish Culture.* London: Verso, 1995.

Grene, Nicholas. *The Politics of Irish Drama: Plays in Context from Boucicault to Friel.* Cambridge: Cambridge University Press, 1999.

Hirsch, Edward. 'The imaginary irish peasant', *Publications of the Modern Language Association of America (PMLA)*, Vol.106, No.5 (1991), pp.1116–33.

Hirsch, Edward. 'The gallous story and the dirty deed: the two *Playboys.*' *Modern Drama*, Vol.26, No.1 (1993), pp.85–102.

Kelleher, Margaret. *The Feminisation of Famine: Expressions of the Inexpressible?* Cork and Durham, NC: Cork University Press and Duke University Press, 1997.

Kiberd, Declan. *Inventing Ireland: The Literature of the Modern Nation.* Cambridge, MA: Harvard University Press, 1995.

Kilroy, James. *The 'Playboy' Riots.* Dublin: Dommen Press, 1971.

Lloyd, David. 'The memory of hunger', in Tom Hayden (ed.), *Irish Hunger: Personal Reflections on the Legacy of the Famine.* Boulder, CO: Roberts Rinehart Publishers, 1997.

Morash, Christopher. *Writing the Irish Famine.* Oxford: Clarendon Press, 1995.

Murphy, Brenda. '"The treachery of the law": reading the political Synge', *Colby Quarterly*, Vol.28, No.1 (1992), pp.45–51.

Pearse, Padraic. 'To the Boys of Ireland', *Collected Works of Padraic H. Pearse*, 3 vols. Dublin, Cork and Belfast: Phoenix Publishing, 1916.

Silverman, Kaja. *The Threshold of the Visible World.* New York and London: Routledge, 1996.

Synge, John Millington. *The Aran Islands* [1907], in Alison Smith (ed.), *The Collected Plays and Poems and* The Aran Islands. London: J.M. Dent, 1997.

Synge, John Millington. *The Playboy of the Western World* [1907] in Alison Smith (ed.), *The Collected Plays and Poems and* The Aran Islands. London: J.M. Dent, 1997.

'We ought not to despair […].' *The Times* (London). 27 May, 1847.

CHAPTER 8

The Joyce of eating:
feast, famine and the humble potato in *Ulysses*

Bonnie Roos

We must bear in mind that if an article is scarce . . . a smaller quantity must be made to last for a longer time, and that high price is the only criterion by which consumption can be economized.
(Sir Randolph Routh, Commissary General to Lord Sligo, 12 October 1846)

[W]e really are all hungry and when we are hungry we are all very quarrelsome.
(James Joyce, 'The Dead', 1909)[1]

Always see a fellow's weak point in his wife.
(James Joyce, *Ulysses*, 1922)

The ending of James Joyce's *Ulysses* always troubles me. Having spent a day on the town buying food and gifts, and wishing for the renewal of affections from his wife, Molly, Leopold Bloom arrives home and asks her to make breakfast before falling asleep at her feet. Molly, having spent the day pleasuring Blazes Boylan, begins to tire of the affair, thinks back to her past life with Bloom, and considers making him this breakfast. Both characters are so admirably drawn, complicated and sympathetic, that with Molly's hint of submission, critics have desperately wanted to believe that Molly will return to Bloom and that the two will, tenuously, begin moving forward with their relationship once more. But we cannot know how the story ends because we are, like Bloom and Stephen, missing the 'key'. I do not refer to the future – the fact that the story ends before Joyce tells us what Molly does when she gets up in the morning. I refer to the past. Molly and Bloom have not had sexual intercourse since the death of their child, Rudy. Though they are both conscious of this fact, they are emotionally estranged and have not spoken of it with each other. Denied their marital intimacy, Bloom womanizes; Molly has affairs. Until their conversation begins, until they are prepared for emotional and painful 'truth-telling' about the past, they cannot lay their dead son to rest or move forward with their lives. That the 'catechetical' conversation they do have at the end of the day 'omit[s]' 'the clandestine correspondence between Martha Clifford and Henry Flower, the public altercation at . . . Bernard Kiernan and Co, Limited . . . , the erotic provocation and response thereto caused by . . . Gertrude' (Joyce, *Ulysses*, p.735), suggests Bloom, at least, is still unprepared for this level of intimacy. Not even mentioned – or entirely forgotten – are the incidents in Nighttown. Rudy remains absent. Instead, Bloom tells Molly about his meeting with Stephen Dedalus. Though the emergence of Stephen Dedalus is an auspicious emblem of friendship in an otherwise unwelcoming world, there is no evidence in this conversation that an emotional reconciliation between Molly and Leopold has begun. In this paper, I point generally to the loss of Rudy and the inability to speak of him as a metaphor for Ireland's Famine, which like Molly and Leopold, Irish writers have failed to discuss. Until this past is confronted truthfully, Ireland cannot move forward with its future. The 'truth' is made difficult to address because of hierarchical Irish traditions of Romanticism. But, Joyce suggests, if Ireland does not address this forgotten history, its continued economic reliance on British and colonial goods threatens a repetition of Ireland's Famine. Though I cannot hope to do justice in a paper this length to a text as complicated as *Ulysses*, I submit that trying to read *Ulysses* without reference to the Irish Potato Famine is to miss this 'Allimportant' key. In the reading I give of Joyce's 'Nestor' and 'Circe' chapters, I hope to set the stage for this broader reading of *Ulysses*.

How then to account for the apparent lack of reference to the Famine in *Ulysses* and in Irish writing more generally? Most post-colonial writers are historical writers. Joyce, as *Ulysses* and innumerable critical analyses show, knew his history, and in what are usually read as off-handed ways, he mentions the Famine. But the Great Famine of (approximately) 1846–51 was Ireland's defining national tragedy. It resulted in the loss of almost 30 per cent of the population in certain counties, not including those who died from complications of starvation.[2] Over 1 million emigrants, especially men, left Ireland during these inauspicious years, so that the population of Ireland by the time Joyce was writing *Ulysses* had dropped to roughly half of its pre-Famine level, though 'Cyclops's' 'citizen' sets the number at closer to one-quarter.[3] These debilitating effects of the Famine on the cohesion of the Irish nation resulted in Ireland's inability to resist the

British Empire. As Mary Lowe-Evans attests, 'The "docility" of the people was guaranteed by their indebtedness to their landlords, their colonial status, and most immediately, by their starving condition' (Lowe-Evans, 1989, p.16). The religious fervour of the Irish exacerbated perceptions of this lackluster resistance. Lowe-Evans continues,

> The Church had inculcated a scrupulousness of conscience into Irish thinking that devalued secular life and individuality. This scrupulousness manifested itself in the forms of docility, passivity, apathy, and submissiveness to the Church, the most glaring example of which was the national response to the Great Famine.
>
> (Ibid., p.21)

Thus, the English characterized the Irish as enduring the Famine and colonial empire with 'docility' and 'passivity', stereotypically feminine qualities that were perpetuated by the religious ideals of living for the hereafter rather than the present, of giving 'hospitality' even to those who deserved it least, and of the glory of self-sacrifice. It is significant that in the course of *Ulysses*, Stephen, opposing this tendency, will insist he wants Ireland to live for him, not die for him.

And yet, efforts to romanticize the plight of the seemingly martyred Irish at the mercy of the debauched English were not simple in light of documented evidence. As Christine Kinealy points out, one of the impediments of representing the Famine with historical accuracy was that

> the more unpleasant truths about the Famine [had] to be confronted and not avoided. For example, the ships that left Ireland laden with food during the Famine were doing so largely for the financial benefit of *Irish* merchants and traders. The large farmers who benefited from the availability and sale of cheap land toward the latter end of the Famine were also Irish and, sometimes, Catholic . . . Corruption, stealing, hoarding, and even cannibalism are part of the darker reality of the Famine years, and should not be forgotten in an attempt to make the Famine a simplistic morality tale about the 'goodies' (the Irish people *en masse*) and the 'baddies' (the whole of the British people).
>
> (Kinealy, 1999, p.248, original emphasis)

As Kinealy suggests, the Irish were in many ways complicit in their continuing colonization, complicit in the events that led to the Famine, which made it difficult to represent the Famine in literatures – like Revivalist sentimentalism – that tended toward idealism. Equally difficult to address in positive, progressive terms was Ireland's internalization of Britain's critique of this disaster: that Ireland required an unfortunate but necessary curbing of its population rates; that Ireland's failure to industrialize led to the Famine; that Ireland's people were too weak and lazy to prevent their own starvation; that Ireland exaggerated the Famine to better squeeze the English; that England's laissez-faire policies were designed to make Ireland a stronger nation.

The result is usually understood as a profound absence of Irish writing about the Famine. As Terry Eagleton characterizes it, Irish writing

> is marked by a hiatus between the experience it has to record, and the conventions available for articulating it. How are those conventions to take the measure of a dislocated, fantasy-ridden society in which truth is elusive and history itself reads like some penny dreadful?
>
> (Eagleton, 1995, p.224)

Irish scholars have been at pains to explain why for more than fifty years after Ireland's Great Famine, the response of the most canonical Irish writers was either to pretend it and Ireland did not exist or to romanticize Ireland with Celtic folklore revivals.[4] Thus, the Famine is only implicit in the writings of these early Modernist authors.[5] Eagleton suggests more precisely that '[t]here is indeed a literature of the Famine . . . But it is in neither sense of the word a major literature. There is a handful of novels and a body of poems, but few truly distinguished works. Where is the Famine in the literature of the Revival?' he asks, 'Where is it in Joyce?' (Eagleton, 1995, p.13).

In the following reading of Joyce's 'Nestor' chapter, I suggest that Eagleton beautifully frames the very questions Joyce addresses in *Ulysses*, and that despite our past inability to see it, *Ulysses* is all about the Irish Famine. I begin with 'Nestor' because it is the first chapter in which the issue of representing the Irish Famine is made explicit. 'Nestor' is, of course, the second part of Joyce's 'Telemachaid', a term that refers to the section of Homer's *Odyssey* that deals with Telemachus's journey and development. This journey is important not because it will be ostensibly successful; Telemachus will not find Odysseus and will have to return home alone. It is important because, in the absence of his father, the sage advice of Nestor and Menelaus helps Telemachus learn how to become a king and what such kingship entails. Though post-colonial critics have made remarkable contributions to understanding this often impenetrable text, their frequent reliance upon politics over aesthetics, post-colonialism over narrative, has left unanswered a question implied by the very structure of the story: what does Deasy/Nestor teach Stephen? If Stephen leaves his tower already knowing he must escape the kind of complicity in British colonialism represented by Buck Mulligan, what does Deasy add to the lesson? And, if we read Deasy as he is usually read – as an older version of Buck Mulligan, stingy and ignorant – is his advice then limited to teaching by opposition, to serving as the appropriate victim of Stephen's mockery? I work to develop a post-colonial argument that somewhat recuperates Mr Deasy as Homer's King Nestor, despite his faults, and as a character with the mark of complexity of a writer like Joyce. Stephen has already learned, in Joyce's 'Telemachus', that he must leave his tower, emblematic of Irish Revivalism, patriarchal Romantic ideals and Ireland's complicity in British colonialism. In 'Nestor', Stephen must learn his history (as many Joyce scholars have noted), but especially the history of the Famine, and Deasy helps him to recognize the importance of doing so. After all, Joyce suggests, it is only through this recognition and its textual articulation that Stephen can finally become Ireland's greatest epic writer, Joyce's equivalent to kingship.

Joyce's 'Nestor' begins with Stephen spending the morning teaching history, but because he lacks knowledge of his history, generally failing at his work.[6] The history his students learn, of Pyrrhus, is not Ireland's history, and is arguably irrelevant to the nationalist history that might be taught. Instead, the students learn a history and glorification of martyrdom, which students of Ireland – through Irish Revivalism and religious belief – have heard before in various forms. Stephen's students are underprepared and bored, as is Stephen, who understands their history to be 'Fabled by the daughters of memory' (Joyce, *Ulysses*, p.24).[7] Stephen, as an aspiring writer, prefers fables to history, and yet is beginning to recognize the incapacity of fable to fully encompass 'truth', the historical reality of what happened: 'And yet it was in some way if not as memory had fabled it' (ibid.). Though Irish Revivalists 'fable' Irish history – as Yeats does in 'Cathleen ni Houlihan' – they lack the realism in their tales that would allow them to serve as (Marxist) didactic tools or even as adequate expressions of national grief. Thus, avoiding real life as he once had in *Portrait*, Stephen's thoughts wander among Blake's Romantic ecstasies as his students proceed unattended to, and haltingly, with the lesson:

– I forgot the place, sir. 279 B.C.
– Asculum, Stephen said, glancing at the name and date in the gorescarred book.
(ibid.)

Stephen's student forgets, and admits it. But Stephen must check his
answers too, 'glancing at the name and date', because he does not know
his history and because this Romantic 'fabling' distracts him and makes
him forget his own history. He becomes, here, an utterly inappropriate
teacher for a history lesson. He repeatedly demonstrates to his students
that his authority comes not from knowledge but from vestiture. Also
troublingly, from a Marxist and post-colonial perspective, a lack of
knowledge of history, the inability to connect the past with the present, is
detrimental to overcoming bondage. Without knowing one's history, one
remains ignorant of one's oppression and can never resist enslavement.
Education is the ostensible solution to this problem, but Stephen, as
teacher, is as ignorant as his students and can teach them nothing.

Stephen pursues the lesson a bit further, worrying about his 'lack of
rule' in the class. And Stephen probably is more lenient than many of
Deasy's teachers. But dictatorship comes as naturally, even unconsciously,
to those authorized by the power structure as oppression does to those
without it. Thus Stephen presses Armstrong to answer a question he does
not know, embarrassing him in front of the class: '– Pyrrhus, sir? Pyrrhus,
a pier' (ibid.). Stephen mentally criticizes the other students' 'high mali-
cious laughter' at Armstrong's expense, but as we see, through mockery, he
chastises Armstrong himself as well. For Stephen is infinitely better
prepared for contests of wit and language games than he is for teaching
history, and he derives pleasure from showing off his abilities, especially in
an unthreatening environment where he already serves as undisputed
master to his young students. He is unaware that to Armstrong, his actions
border on intimidation and that they evince obvious condescension:

> – Tell me now, Stephen said, poking the boy's shoulder with the book, what is
> a pier.
> – A pier, sir, Armstrong said. A thing out in the waves. A kind of bridge.
> Kingstown pier, sir.
>
>   . . .
>
> – Kingstown pier, Stephen said. Yes, a disappointed bridge.
> The words troubled their gaze.
> – How, sir? Comyn asked. A bridge is across a river.
>
> (Ibid., pp.24–5)

Stephen's joke is funny in part because it attributes human disappointment
to the pier that wishes it were a bridge. If he does not learn his history,
Stephen tells his student metaphorically, Armstrong is destined to become

a pier, a disappointed bridge, unable to span the gaps separating his past and future. But Stephen shows off to an unappreciative, uncomprehending crowd, for his students miss the joke. More importantly, at the very moment he might enlighten his students as to his meaning – beginning a conversation about piers, bridges, London or Ireland, or even the possibilities of connections among them – Stephen's thoughts again become self-absorbed. So, preoccupied with the implications of repeating his joke to Haines for money, Stephen fails to teach the students even when, as Comyn's question indicates, they are eager to be taught. Stephen's intended lesson goes unlearned, and his class responds blankly to his jest.

Because Stephen is victim to the same problems as his class, preferring poetry to history, he undermines his lesson about the importance of history by allowing the subject to change to literature, where his own interests and strengths lie. Stephen's students interrupt the history lesson to ask for a 'ghoststory', a request that suggests that Stephen has been persuaded to set aside lessons before in order to tell a story.[8] His students' enthusiasm suggests that Stephen is a very good story-teller. But instead of telling them a story, Stephen sets aside the history lesson, a boring repetition of meaningless dates and places, and offers his students a different repetition exercise, taking Comyn's suggestion for Milton's 'Lycidas' as a starting point. An English poem about the immortalized dead, 'Lycidas' is the literary resurrection that repeats Pyrrhus's glorified martyrdom in literary terms. In its evocation of living death and virtual repetition of the (dead) history lesson, it is the very 'ghoststory' his students have requested. But if there were any question of the fate to which the students are condemned for their lack of knowledge of history, it is underscored by Talbot's broken-record reading:

> Talbot repeated:
> – *Through the dear might of Him that walked the waves,*
> *Through the dear might . . .*
> – Turn over, Stephen said quietly. I don't see anything.
> – What, sir? Talbot asked simply, bending forward.
> His hand turned the page over. He leaned back and went on again having just remembered. Of him that walked the waves.
>
> (Ibid., p.26)

Talbot recites, cheating with a paper because he cannot remember the words. Stephen knows Talbot is cheating, and when Talbot 'forgets' the next part of the poem, Stephen urges him to 'turn over' the page of his book to find the remaining part of the poem. Talbot attempts to do so discreetly, and then 'went on again having just remembered'. Though certainly Joyce mocks Talbot as much as Stephen does, Talbot also reminds us that we remember our lessons not so much through the memorization of facts, names, dates, but in written language and through meaningful context. Even though Talbot fails to 'remember' the poem and therefore cheats, because the poem is written down for him, he can 'remember' it whenever he chooses. The only time he cannot 'remember' something is when he cannot see it written down.

Of importance here is not only that failure to know their history condemns Stephen and his students to repeat it, but that the repetition itself is a source of forgetfulness. Lycidas's death is forgotten because there is no need to remember it: despite his death, he is eternally present, living again, always, in literary terms, immortal. He is also ever-present because even when Lycidas is not the topic, Pyrrhus is, and if not Pyrrus, then biblical stories, or stories of Romantic martyrdom. It is no wonder that, in relying on Romantic and Christian archetypes for a new literary aesthetic, Stephen cannot 'see anything' and becomes forgetful himself. He must be reminded that class is let out early for hockey, and so he inadvertently lets his class avoid the history lesson until the time runs out.

That time is running out concerns Stephen, and so as the students prepare to leave, Stephen valiantly makes a final attempt to reclaim the attention of the wayward class by offering them a riddle designed to capture their interest. Once again, his students eagerly fall for the ruse, desiring that Stephen teach them, if only he will:

> *The cock crew*
> *The sky was blue:*
> *The bells in heaven*
> *Were striking eleven.*
> *Tis time for this poor soul*
> *To go to heaven.*

(Ibid., p.26)

The answer, Stephen tells them, is 'The fox burying his grandmother under a hollybush' (ibid., p.27). Don Gifford and Robert J. Seidman explain that 'Stephen's riddle is a joke at the expense of riddles since it is unanswerable unless the answer is already known' (Gifford and Seidman, 1974, p.22). In other words, Stephen provides question and answer, without explaining the problem. Because Stephen's students are missing the pieces in between, the gaps and absences, they cannot figure out the riddle. By implication, Stephen reminds his students that without understanding the past, they can never understand their present or future. Indeed, had he been forced to explain it, Stephen might have 'remembered' that the answer he gives is wrong, an indication that he too misunderstands the past. Gifford and Seidman state that the answer is 'The fox burying his *mother* under a hollybush' (ibid., p.22), not 'grandmother'. Stephen's repressed memories of his mother, his personal ghost story, cause him to forget and compensate for her existence, despite and because of his guilt over his actions at her death, his idealistic refusal to pray as she asked. Even more significant, Stephen's riddle falls flat a second time. He, too, has failed to properly remember his pedagogical history: he does not recognize that he has, yet again, spoken over the heads of his students, repeated his previous mistake, and failed to turn it into an opportunity for learning, even though his students are eager to understand it. Thus, what Stephen teaches, without really meaning to, is the absolute authority of the teacher, who need not know, understand, or explain the problems or needs of his students in order to possess this authority.

Nowhere in *Ulysses* is the condemnation to repeat history until it is understood more poignantly made than in poor Cyril Sargent's repetition of sums. Stephen has no hesitation in requiring his students to recite memorized poetry they do not understand and easily forget; and he is frustrated when, giving them the question and the answer to the fox riddle, they cannot put the pieces together to make sense of them. But when he sees Deasy making the exact same mistake with his student Cyril, Stephen implicitly condemns Deasy and correctly recognizes the repetition as 'Futility':

> – Mr Deasy told me to write them all out again, he said, and show them to you, sir.
> Stephen touched the edges of the book. Futility.
> – Do you understand how to do them now? He asked.
> – Numbers eleven to fifteen, Sargent answered. Mr Deasy said I was to copy them off the board, sir.
> – Can you do them yourself? Stephen asked.
> – No, sir.
>
> (Joyce, *Ulysses*, p.27)

Even when presented with both the problem and solution, Cyril cannot understand how to work the sums by himself. But Stephen's solution to

Cyril's problem is not entirely different from Deasy's. Rather than have Cyril copy sums, he has Cyril watch him work the problem: 'Sitting at his side Stephen solved out the problem' (ibid., p.28). As with the history readings on Pyrrhus or the poem about Lycidas or his riddle to the class, Stephen shows Cyril how he can solve the problem, but stops short of explaining how the problem works, or why it works, or why it might be important for Cyril to know. And probably, if his earlier reliance on the answerbook is any indication, Stephen does not know the answers to these questions any better than Cyril. Both Stephen and Deasy teach as they were taught, and their success is both minimal and self-perpetuating.

Most scholars do not connect this danger of unlearned history repeating itself with Stephen's ensuing conversation with Mr Deasy. In his remarkable post-colonial study of *Ulysses*, Vincent Cheng points out that the verbose and condescending Mr Deasy in many ways embodies the figure of the religious Irishman complicit in his own colonization[9] (Cheng, 1995, p.164), the very problem that Stephen himself faces: thus, Deasy's walls are covered with pictures of famous English horses; a tray of Stuart coins sits on the sideboard; the twelve apostles sit in a spooncase. Obviously, Deasy's prescribed educational programme is far from Irish as well. Deasy seems willfully ignorant of the Irish colonization that sustains the British economy so that it can make what Deasy identifies as its proudest boast, '*I paid my way*' (Joyce, *Ulysses*, p.30). I believe Cheng is generally correct in his characterization of Deasy as miserly and anglophilic, for certainly Deasy is a flawed and hypocritical character – as are all the characters of *Ulysses*. But as with Buck Mulligan, whose critique of Stephen's pride and idealism is essentially correct, Deasy's advice that Stephen save his money is sound. When he pays Stephen his meagre salary, and Stephen thanks him, Deasy insists, 'No thanks at all . . . You have earned it' (ibid., p.30). If we have read 'The Dead' properly, as Vincent Pecora (1995) helps us to do, we should know here that Deasy speaks the truth:[10] he is right to correct Stephen's submissive 'thanks', and he is right to say, 'We are a generous people but we must also be just' (ibid., p.31).

But Stephen is not only put off only by Deasy's crimes of economic ignorance: Deasy advises Stephen to reserve his thanks and save his money, citing Shakespeare: '*Put but money in thy purse*' (ibid., p.30), a quote Stephen recognizes as Iago's.[11] Stephen's 'murmured'[12] attribution suggests he views Deasy as a hypocrite, knowing Deasy's savings will be spent on buying British and religious goods like those displayed in his office and thereby symbolically prostituting Ireland – just as Iago's money will purportedly be spent on prostituting Othello's Desdemona. But as we know from 'Circe' and elsewhere, Stephen's own money is generally and soon-to-be spent on prostituting as well, so his superiority is far from warranted. Stephen conceit is that he recalls the source of the quote without understanding its importance. Though better at literary memorization than his students, he has memorized without learning, a product of bad teaching. Stephen misses what Iago recognizes: despite his graces and achievements, Othello has not fully overcome his sense of himself as slave, and therefore, oppresses women just as white men have oppressed him. Othello's sexism enables Iago's manipulations, and is the source of Othello's eventual downfall. Stephen fails to realize that Deasy's advice, whether good or bad, is ambivalent because it is spoken from the same position as Othello's, spoken through the voice of one who cannot see beyond his own bondage. Instead, Stephen sneers at Deasy not because his advice is essentially incorrect, but because Stephen is a snob who knows that Deasy has ignorantly borrowed the phrase from Shakespeare's villain.[13] But Deasy's sense of spending what is earned is sage, if only Stephen and Ireland can follow it. Ireland would do well to restrain itself from buying imported luxuries like Pears soap, Malaga grapes and chocolate. To do so might mean the economic freedom from colonial oppression to which Ireland aspires.

As Deasy reminds him of all the people Stephen owes, the old, underpaid milk woman from 'Telemachus' – embodiment of the peasant backbone of Ireland – is notably 'forgotten' from his list.[14] Old Mr Deasy appropriately admonishes him, and correctly identifies without contextualizing one reason for Stephen's, and Ireland's, extravagant spending habits. He tells Stephen, 'I remember the famine. Do you know that the orange lodges agitated for repeal of the union twenty years before O'Connell did or before the prelates of your communion denounced him as a demagogue? You fenians forget some things' (ibid., p.31). Though he is not a fenian, Stephen's spending habits – the economic complicity that Buck Mulligan epitomizes – are in part caused by having forgotten the Famine: Ireland's colonial economic reliance on a single cash crop, the potato, was the cause of this famine and meant that Ireland could not support itself as it had previously when that cash crop failed. Of all of the money Stephen owes, he remembers only those debts he owes that perpetuate the legacy of British domination, payments for prostitution and luxuries, and forgets the money he spends on Irish goods, like the milkmaid's milk. Ireland is, for Stephen, a 'disappointed bridge' with a gaping hole between the past and the present that is the omission, the forgetting, of the Famine; Irish writers have failed to (re)construct this bridge through teaching of the Famine, and therefore, current economic practices seem to ignore Famine history. The danger is not only that without confronting the Famine, the Irish cannot learn to escape their bondage, but also that if unlearned, the Irish, like Cyril Sargent, may be condemned to repeating their Famine history: the continued economic dependence on England through exportation of cattle and beef makes this repetition a distinct possibility.

This fear of Famine repetition, after all, is the driving force behind the letter about 'foot and mouth' disease that Deasy asks Stephen to see published. But Deasy's letter is evidence of an inability to articulate the Famine, even as it testifies to Deasy's overt recognition of the problem. No word of Deasy's letter, we note, speaks to starvation or famine, even though the implications and urgency of his writing direct us to seek this possibility. In writing the letter, Deasy resorts to styles with which he is familiar, repeating other writers (who also failed to articulate the Famine) without learning, just as Cyril repeats his sums without understanding them. His odd letter therefore embodies many arguably inappropriate facets of Irish Revival ideals of self-sacrifice and hospitality in the context of a scientific and agricultural letter. Having admonished Stephen for being too eager to thank him for what he has earned, Deasy's own writing is hypocritically courteous and generous to the point of comedy, even where he has an exceedingly urgent message to transmit:

> May I trespass on your valuable space. That doctrine of *laissez faire* which so often in our history. Our cattle trade . . . The pluterperfect imperturbability of the department of agriculture. Pardoned a classical allusion. Cassandra. By a woman who was no better than she should be. To come to the point at issue.
>
> (Ibid., p.33)

Deasy's idealized agricultural department is at distinct odds with the fact that this same agricultural department has failed to heed the seriousness of the cattle problem Deasy discusses. Moreover, Deasy arguably adopts the language of the British colonizer, taking no apparent issue with the 'doctrine of *laissez faire*' that would become Britain's defence for doing nothing about the Famine in Ireland,[15] and is likely the agricultural department's reason for doing nothing about the cattle crisis. Thus, Deasy's condescension gets in the way of his justified critique. After apologizing for a classical allusion, Deasy appropriately references Cassandra, who, also unheeded, foretold the fall of Troy. But his connection to Cassandra is immediately undermined because of his sexist bias. Like Othello, Deasy's colonial status causes him to duplicate his own oppression by projecting it on to others. Though he shares Cassandra's plight, and though his letter will similarly go unheeded, Deasy's own domineering sexism hypocritically ignores Cassandra's 'truth-telling', referring to her not as a prophetic seer of the Trojan apocalypse, but instead as 'a woman who was no better than she should be'. Indeed, Deasy's own high ideals, representative of Irish Revivalism, perpetuate his oppression of women and others to whom he should listen, and with whom he shares colonized experience. Instead of using this experience as a basis for communication, Deasy's 'point at issue' remains wholly unclear.

Despite the lengthy preamble, we soon learn that Deasy's letter discusses 'Foot and Mouth Disease'. This illness[16] that affects pigs, sheep, goats and cattle has recurred throughout industrialized Europe but had not, by 1904, when the story of *Ulysses* takes place, yet struck Ireland (as it would in 1912). In response to outbreaks of the disease, whole herds of cattle were habitually slaughtered, and in addressing the problem, England proposed sanctions against Ireland's imports of cattle when and if it appeared there.

> Foot and mouth disease. Known as Koch's preparation. Serum and virus. Percentage of salted horses. Rinderpest. Emperor's horses at Mürzsteg, lower Austria. Veterinary surgeons. Mr Henry Blackwood Price. Courteous offer a fair trial. Dictates of common sense. Allimportant question. In every sense of the word take the bull by the horns. Thanking you for the hospitality of your columns.
>
> (Ibid., p.33)

What is at stake with this infection, given Ireland's neo-colonial economic reliance on limited agricultural exports of cattle and beef – the reliance particularly of the poor on milk and milk-products (we recall the old milkmaid from 'Telemachus') – is the same deleterious effects on Ireland that the potato blight once had. What is at stake is famine. In this sense, Joyce prophesizes about the foot and mouth disease he knows will take place in Ireland in 1912, and that may eventually cause the kind of economic and physical downfall that Ireland has already experienced in the Famine. Deasy's letter should be recognized as an impotent but heroic

attempt at the salvation of Ireland from future plagues. Indeed, Deasy's
letter echoes the letter (also virtually ignored) written by David Moore, the
curator of the Royal Dublin Society Botanic Gardens at Glasnevin. Moore
warned in 1845, a full year before the initial Famine hit, that having
spread throughout Europe, the potato blight was likely to soon hit Ireland,
and that the effects would be devastating.[17] Deasy's letter becomes in this
sense a repetition of history.

Deasy's letter suggests a possible cure for the infection from veterinarians,
via Mr Henry Blackwood Price, from Austria. But given that at the time
Joyce was writing *Ulysses*, there was still no known cure for foot and mouth
disease,[18] and that Stephen never manages to get the letter published,
Deasy's letter does not contain the correct answer to the problem. Just as
science failed to prevent or resolve the potato blight, we know that
historically, scientific help will not arrive in time to rescue Ireland from
potential devastation by foot and mouth disease.[19] Deasy's letter contains
an important clue for the cure, however: Austria and Hungary were a dual
monarchy, and so Deasy's reference implicitly foreshadows Bloom, the
hungry, Hungary man, an outsider/insider who will figure as a Joyce's
Ulyssean hero. Bloom can help Ireland move forward because, like Moses,
he has the experience of being king as well as slave.

But, for Joyce, neither science nor politics are the answer to preventing
famine; learning – and he sees Modernist literature, story, as invaluable in
this project – is the way to prevent famine. Unfortunately, Deasy is not a
good teacher. As Stephen with Cyril, Deasy shows Stephen his work, but
does not explain how he has arrived at his conclusions, what the letter has
to do with their preceding conversation, or why the letter is important to
Stephen and Ireland. These factors make Deasy's lesson difficult for Stephen
(and us, as readers) to learn, and indeed, Stephen will not recognize the
letter's importance until the 'Circe' chapter. In short, because he has not
been well-taught by Irish writers, Deasy puts his 'foot' in his 'mouth' as
soon as he tries to talk about the 'Allimportant'. Unfortunately, Stephen is
not yet a good student, either. As he was with Deasy's reference to
Shakespeare, Stephen's snobbish sensibility is affronted by the aesthetic
debacle that is Deasy's letter, and he is embarrassed to champion writing
rich in platitudes, clichés and (ironic) gratefulness for the 'hospitality of
your columns'.[20] Stephen dwells on his personal humiliation in becoming
the 'bullockbefriending bard', duty-bound to try to get Deasy's letter
published (ibid., p.36). Instead of recognizing the letter's urgency for
Ireland's future, Stephen's own unrelinquished idealism blinds him to the

importance of Deasy's message, so much so that he must work throughout the remainder of the novel to even remember the letter. Thus, in his unjustified and baseless overconfidence in the Telemachaid up to now, Stephen is demonstrably the young son who still needs to learn to become a king.

But Stephen does not leave Deasy without making progress in his journey. Deasy and Stephen part ways soon after Deasy makes an anti-Semitic remark. It is not merely the Famine history that threatens to repeat: traumatic oppression repeats itself. As much as Deasy feels himself free, he inadvertently oppresses others in lieu of challenging his bondage directly. As Bloom later puts it, 'It was a nun they say invented barbed wire' (ibid., p.155). Though Deasy knows his history, he is unable to recognize how firmly he has internalized the mindset of his oppressors. Deasy's prejudices when it comes to certain categories of people (women, Jews), is a product, as Joyce sees it, of enslavement. When Stephen challenges Deasy's anti-Semitism with 'truth' – 'A merchant . . . is one who buys cheap and sells dear, jew or gentile, is he not?' (ibid., p.34) – we know that Stephen/Telemachus has learned part of what it takes to be an artist/king. He is beginning to reject his idealizing hierarchies. Stephen, we note, though he will defend Jews as equal, does not offer the same defence of Cassandra, or Eve, or the harlot in the street. Indeed, Stephen, as we know from his assessment of the milkmaid's 'woman's unclean loins' (ibid., p.14) has the same problem that Deasy has – and that Bloom has – when it comes to women. He will need to address this prejudice before becoming the artist of his aspirations. But unlike Deasy, Stephen recognizes his failure, explaining that 'History . . . is a nightmare from which I am trying to awake' (ibid., p.34). As with Cyril, Stephen is a great way from understanding the implications of the Famine's absence in Irish writing, learning about it, and being able to solve the problem on his own. When provoked by a hunger-toothache, he will philosophically imagine a way to capture and see the shape-shifting Famine in 'Proteus', he is for the moment too much a product of his own history to awaken himself.

To find this reading of 'Nestor' convincing, however, complicates our understanding of the rest of Joyce's tale. What does the issue of women's oppression, broached in 'Nestor', have to do with Famine history? And yet it is undeniable that Joyce links the two, especially in 'Circe': Bloom carries a potato in his pocket, a clear symbol of the Famine, and exchanges it for services in prostitution, symbolic of the exploitation and oppression of women. Certainly gender is important when speaking of Famine issues: incidents of prostitution went up during Famine years;[21] and immigration left many more women than men in Ireland. But none of these facts explains the bizarre appearance of Circe in the form of Bella Cohen, the carnivalesque transvestitism and rape of Leopold Bloom,[22] Stephen's attempt to kill his mother, or Stephen's confrontation with the soldiers. Andrew Gibson offers a remarkable explanation of these events, observing, 'the phantasmagoric imagery in "Circe" is not primarily an example of modern irrationalism (expressionist, surrealist). It is a literalization of the outlandish incongruities produced by and within a colonial culture' (Gibson, 2002, p.193). I develop Gibson's premise to suggest that the incongruities are produced not merely by colonial culture, but by colonial culture's collusion with the ideologies of capitalism and Romantic idealism. This assessment invites us to read 'Circe', like all of Joyce's chapters, as a reasonably linear narrative, available for close reading. To suggest that 'Circe' is a scathing indictment of the English is, as Gibson's and Cheng's works readily attest, very clear. But even more specifically, I submit that Bloom's relations with Bella Cohen retell the story of Ireland and England's Union, which was so detrimental to Ireland's future and in many ways responsible for the Famine.[23] While Bloom represents the first generation who experience and survive the Famine, Stephen represents the second generation, who can write of the Famine, if only Bloom can learn to tell the story. Thus, Stephen's encounter with the soldiers, I argue, is an examination of the Irish response to England in the aftermath of the Famine. In tracing the role of the potato in this chapter, 'Circe' thereby becomes an examination of the causes of the Famine, which – oddly enough – Joyce attributes not only to the English, but also, in part, to patriarchy. It also reveals the absence of Irish writing about the Famine, which Joyce attributes to the rhetoric of Romanticism.

It is Leopold Bloom, Joyce's *Ulysses* figure, who has the ability to address Stephen's dilemma of how to write Ireland's Famine through the 'moly' he carries. In Homer's Circe encounter, Odysseus's men meet Circe, seductress and witch, who gives them a potion that makes them forget all thoughts of home. Circe then transforms them into pigs, for lust makes animals of men. Hermes gives Odysseus 'moly', a charm that will combat Circe's sorcery and make her considerable sexual charms available to Odysseus. Odysseus's god-given gift, his holy moly, allows him to re-establish male dominance and exploit Circe sexually without forgetting home or being reduced to an animal himself. Once conquered, Circe willingly submits her talents and possessions to Odysseus's cause. Like Homer's Odysseus, Joyce's Bloom also possesses his moly and his masculinity, in the form of a potato he carries in his pocket.[24] Indeed, the very Irish Famine that Stephen seeks, in the form of this black, shrivelled potato, Bloom's key, and our key to the text, is right where we might expect a key to be. Perhaps needless to say, Bloom's manhood is also well-placed. But Bloom does not recognize his moly for what it is. Thus, the prospect of Bloom's success in sharing his Famine story as we enter 'Circe', Joyce's most enigmatic chapter, is questionable. Up to this moment, Bloom's expressions of traditional masculinity have all utterly failed. In 'Lestrygonians', in response to his sympathetic recognition of Dilly Dedalus's imminent starvation, Bloom heroically buys bread only to feed it to the gulls;[25] in 'Sirens', though he is starving for physical nourishment from his wife, Bloom settles for his usual scraps of innards, the leftovers of the 'feast' that he has accustomed himself to 'relish', instead of courageously taking the opportunity to confront Blazes Boylan before his rendezvous with Molly; in 'Oxen of the Sun', though Bloom generously decides to 'rescue' Stephen from the company he keeps, Bloom has also bungled the job and lost track of Stephen by the time he enters Nighttown. In short, though Bloom's fragility makes him a compelling character, and though he carries around a memory of the 'Allimportant', the 'key' to *Ulysses*, Bloom remains a flawed hero.

Though Bloom speedily follows after Stephen in the opening of 'Circe', he seems initially to prepare less for valiant rescue than he does for supper. His hurried acquisition and hoarding of food is signal that the effects of the Famine are beginning to be felt. He 'appears flushed, panting, cramming bread and chocolate into a side pocket' (Joyce, *Ulysses*, p.433), followed a few moments later by the further purchase of 'a lukewarm pig's crubeen' and 'a cold sheep's trotter, sprinkled with wholepepper', one for each hand (ibid., p.434). Bloom's pausing along the way to purchase unnecessary food is the likely cause of his loss of Stephen. But waste and excess are also the initial historical symptoms of the Famine. In order to make as much money as possible from the rotten potatoes before they went completely bad, what was to become Famine first appeared as a marked glut in the market.[26] Bloom's waste of food thus indicates not only the comic difficulties of acting heroically while eating to excess, but also raises once again the spectre of Famine. Like his fellow Dubliners, Bloom has fallen under Circe's spell and has forgotten himself, his home, his history. Thus, instead of attributing his troubles to physical and cultural starvation, he suspects that the stitch in his side[27] derives from

Something poisonous I ate. Emblem of luck. Why? Probably lost cattle. Mark
of the beast. (*He closes his eyes an instant.*) Bit light in the head. Monthly or effect
of the other. Brainfogfag. That tired feeling. Too much for me now. Ow!

(Ibid., p.436)

Bloom's chase begins to repeat his actions in 'Sirens' or 'Lestrygonians' in
that as he eats and his brain fogs, he becomes too tired and overcome to
continue his heroic quest. Ironically, his inability to be a masculine hero is
probably a result of 'lost cattle', slaughtered because of infection. If
Bloom's 'lost cattle' – along with the 'pig's crubeen' and 'sheep's trotter'
(from animals similarly affected) – are in fact 'poisonous', it may be
because Deasy's warning about 'foot and mouth' disease has begun to take
its toll. Bloom, blissfully unaware of the apocalyptic danger he and Ireland
face, associates himself with the revelatory 'mark of the beast', and
continues to believe in capitalism and the false 'profit'. In this misguided
pursuit, he suspects he has been pickpocketed by Dublin's starving poor,
the dirty, impoverished Caffrey brothers. The urchins are juxtaposed with
the image of Bloom 'blessed' with excess. Indeed, worried about being
robbed,[28] he is completely unable to properly pat down his unprotected
pockets to check his possessions because his hands are too full of food –
another lost opportunity for Bloom's heroism.

Bloom's inability to be a hero at this moment of crisis arises from a long
history of Romantic idealism that pits members of different classes, races,
sexes, religions, nations, against each other. Bloom's misplaced sense of
masculinity comes at least in part from the prejudices carried by his father,
Rudolph, a name taken from Hungarian Royalty.[29] When as a child,
Bloom falls and cuts his hand while racing with the other boys, Rudolph's
critique of Bloom's (heroic) racing expresses less concern with Bloom's cut
and more concern with the company he keeps: 'I told you not go with
drunken goy ever' (ibid., p.437). Rudolph condemns the boys Bloom races
because they are poor gentiles. This contempt for the Irish gentiles, the
prejudices even oppressed peoples – especially oppressed peoples –
reproduce against others similarly oppressed, may well have contributed
to Rudolph's suicidal loneliness after the death of his wife (who was also
Irish gentile). Bloom's mother, who embodies all that Rudolph derides,
expresses the same sentiment as her husband. When she sees young
Bloom, dirty and bleeding, she swoons melodramatically:

O blessed Redeemer, what have they done to him! My smelling salts! (*She hauls
up a reef of skirt and ransacks the pouch of her striped blay petticoat. A phial, an Agnus Dei,
a shrievelled* [sic] *potato and a celluloid doll fall out.*)

(Ibid., p.438)

Ellen Bloom also accuses Dublin's poor, people like herself, of being responsible for Bloom's injuries ('what have they done to him!'). Her 'Agnus Dei' medal and her 'celluloid doll' indicate her subjection to a Romantic Christian and patriarchal sentimental ideal, one that she embraces even as it denies her power, and turns her against her own people. Both parents implicitly question young Bloom's unbiased, heroic play with the other boys.

Amidst this handful of Ellen Bloom's possessions, the black potato is anomalous. It suggests an 'unclean', Realist memory, unassociated with her bondage to the idealisms represented in the other contents of her purse. Though the potato is a symbol of Irish subjection (compared to her husband's Hungarian royalty), it is also a memory of that experience: England's exploitation; Ireland's economic culpability; and the truth behind Ireland's seeming 'docility' – women prostituted for food, infanticide and even the horrors of cannibalism, caused by the effects of starvation. Bloom's mother has clearly never told her son why she caries the potato. If he were honest with himself, Bloom would recognize that his mother's reason for carrying the potato has to do with her experience of the Famine. But, as we have seen in 'Nestor', though Bloom possesses the answer, he does not understand the problem. Instead, Bloom's pocket, with its competing clean, idealizing 'Godly' soap and dirty, rotten potato, is nearly identical to his mother's pockets with potato and Agnus Dei – another repetition of history – but with one important difference: because she has never spoken of the Famine, Bloom associates the potato with a sentimental, idealized memory of his mother rather than with the horrors of starvation. Even when he carries a conspicuous, palpable sign of the Famine in his pocket on a daily basis, Bloom sanitizes this distasteful memory. So he sees the potato as a good-luck charm from his mother, a magic moly in every sense of Homer's use of the term, but fails to recognize how it actually opposes the Circean loss of memory. To (heroically) admit the true reason his mother kept the potato, he would hold the key to Ireland's future, Ireland's 'panacea' (ibid., p.435), in the very thing it wants to 'Throwaway' (or, as Molly advocates, 'Nevertell') (ibid., p.448). For remembering this difficult and painful history is the only way for Ireland to 'win' – in its struggles against the English and against the repetition of Famine history. If Bloom does not recognize this key, it is because he, like Deasy, and like Stephen, and like Bloom's parents, has been born into a heritage that prejudices him against Irishness, Jewishness, poverty, women – any form of the 'Other'. This bias prevents the building of community that might occur through shared grief and mutual understanding, or as Bloom puts it in 'Cyclops', love. Because Bloom's parents were not good teachers, and Bloom was not a good student, he is destined to repeat his Famine history.

For Bloom adopts many of his parents' prejudices. Despite his sensitivity, Bloom – like Stephen – cannot see his oppression of women, his oppression of Molly. And so Bloom remains as divided from his wife as Ellen Bloom is divided from her Irish kin. Because he fails or is unwilling to address this 'truth', he exploits Molly as a sexual object, and Molly, who appears in Turkish garb, seems to revel in the exploitation. Molly wears exoticized Turkish clothing, 'Her ankles linked by a slender fetterchain' (ibid., p.439). She reminds us that the cycle of oppression does not begin or end with Bloom. Like Bloom, Molly exoticizes the Turkish. And, as with Bloom's adoration of innards, Molly enjoys the very objects that oppress her and reduce her to a sexual object – the Turkish clothing, sentimental literature, the gold 'fetterchain'. Mrs Breen, who flirts with Bloom in this fantasy, reminds Bloom that the result of patriarchal sentimentalism is not only its continuation, but the inability to come together, to trust, to communicate. Thus, even though Mrs Breen and Molly are best friends, Mrs Breen, in Bloom's view, would not have hesitated to take Bloom away from Molly (ibid., p.446). Similarly, Molly does not hesitate to fire their maid, Mary Driscoll, for pilfering – even though she knows Bloom is the instigator of the sexual liaison. Underscoring this point, Molly arguably even hints at a competitive jealousy she feels over the burgeoning beauty of her daughter, Milly, in 'Penelope'. Divided instead of unified by hierarchical idealism, Bloom feels little more than Molly's cruelty toward him.

Instead of confronting Molly about his feelings of rejection as an equal, who has made similar mistakes, Bloom compensates for his sense of inadequacy by invoking masculine privilege and exploiting other women. Bloom's fantasy trial is required because he must weigh the prospect of responding to this cruelty with his own affair, seeking sexual satisfaction from a prostitute for the night. Appropriately, when he stands trial, Bloom is accused by numerous women – including his maid, Mary Driscoll – of various kinds of misconduct and sexism. But Bloom defends his actions (to an all-male jury), explaining that when he propositioned Mary Driscoll, he treated her 'white', bought her nice underthings far above her station, and generously took her part when Molly accused her of stealing: perhaps most importantly Bloom explains that she wanted it, 'She counter-assaulted' (ibid., pp.460–1). Though I find Bloom generally to be a shy and sensitive man, he is so unaware of the strength of his position, because he is male and because he is rich enough to be an employer, that he understands his womanizing as innocent, even generous, and feels reasonably vindicated of his crimes. As with the starving dog to which he feeds the food, Bloom understands his treatment of women as 'Train[ing] by kindness' (ibid., p.453). By comparison to other Dubliners, as Stephen compared to other teachers, Bloom's masculine 'rule' is relatively easy; indeed, Molly chooses him because she knows she can always 'get round him' (ibid., p.782) and her 'fetterchain' is comparatively slender. But neither can undo the automatic authority granted to the masculine, authoritative positions, and so even if he is telling the truth, Bloom can never be certain on what grounds Mary Driscoll 'counterassaulted'. Blind to this power inequality, Bloom conveniently finds himself guiltless and approaches Bella Cohen's house of prostitution to seek its customary pleasures. As we will see, Bloom's betrayal of Molly is also Ireland's economic betrayal as it links its economy with England's.[30]

Like England itself, Zoe holds a number of attractions for Bloom, and unlike his reticent wife, has made herself seemingly available. Bloom is worldly enough to be unsurprised when Zoe propositions him, and her 'hand slides over his left thigh':

ZOE: How's the nuts?
BLOOM: Off side. Curiously they are on the right. Heavier I suppose. One in a million my tailor, Mesias, says.
ZOE: (*In sudden alarm.*) You've a hard chancre.
BLOOM: Not likely.
ZOE: I feel it. (*Her hand slides into his left trouser pocket and brings out a hard black shrivelled potato. She regards it and Bloom with dumb moist lips.*)
BLOOM: A talisman. Heirloom.
ZOE: For Zoe? For keeps? For being so nice, eh? (*She puts the potato greedily into a pocket, then links his arm, cuddling him with supple warmth. He smiles uneasily. Slowly, note by note, oriental music is played. He gazes in the tawny crystal of her eyes, ringed with kohol. His smile softens.*)
ZOE: You'll know me the next time.

(Ibid., p.476)

Bloom's 'nuts' have been 'off side' not only because he has not recently had sex with his wife, but because he has not been courageous enough, 'man' enough, to truthfully face up to and speak about the problems he and Molly have experienced since Rudy's death. Zoe rightly suspects that Bloom's masculinity is a threat to their potential union. But noting Zoe's 'alarm' at his 'hard chancre', Bloom assures her that this is 'Not likely'. Zoe insists on discovering the nature of Bloom's manhood and reveals a 'hard black shrivelled potato'. The potato is the key to regaining his manhood through courageously facing the truth by confronting the great absence in his life – Rudy's death and its effects on his life with Molly, the Famine and the symptomatic relations between Ireland and England. And Zoe correctly recognizes the potato as an embodiment of Bloom's masculinity, a potential threat. Again, Bloom hastens to assure her that the potato is merely a 'talisman', an 'heirloom' of a masculinity long since past; Ireland assures an uncertain England that it will never take heroic, military action against its colonial rule. But English Zoe requires all potential claims to Irish strength and manhood as payment for her services: 'For Zoe? For keeps? For being so nice, eh?' And Bloom, always seduced and comforted by traditional gender roles, 'softens' his smile and goes upstairs with Zoe as she 'puts the potato greedily into a pocket'. Like Homer's Odysseus, Bloom uses his moly to prostitute Zoe sexually. As with the Union, free trade with England initially appeared beneficial to Ireland, for it wanted to possess luxuries like those possessed by England. In reality, the Union was used to subjugate the Irish. Though Bloom offers Zoe a rotten potato, a memory in exchange for her services, he is unknowingly selling his ability to discern and express the truth. Moreover, with Ireland's Union with England, Ireland becomes complicit in the exploitation of other countries, complicit in events like the Famine. To become part of this practice of colonization and empire requires a kind of forgetting of the Famine, a willful ignorance of the truth of colonization. When Bloom exchanges the potato for Zoe's services, he unknowingly prostitutes himself, and unlike Odysseus, cedes his talisman to Circe.

With English Zoe in possession of Bloom's Irish masculinity and discernment of the 'truth', the Union agreed upon, Bloom's time is running out. Even so, Bloom maintains his now-empty performances of masculinity, his militaristic posturing. In response to the increasingly masculine Zoe's request for a 'swaggerroot', Bloom condescends disapprovingly (ibid., pp.477–8). He discourages Zoe from smoking and directs her to more traditional women's roles, especially that of a sex object: '(*Lewdly.*) The mouth can be better engaged than with a cylinder of rank weed' (ibid., p.478). Indeed, Bloom echoes 'Swaggering Dan' O'Connell[31] himself, who condescended so emphatically and chivalrously to England's 'darling little queen' Victoria.[32] Joyce posits that this Romantic rhetoric leads to lies and misconceptions about the approaching Famine, turning the conversation about the potato (Famine) into a conversation about tobacco. When Bloom gives Zoe a speech on the dangers of smoking, the subject is ironic in part because, although he downplays it, Bloom also smokes. Despite her obvious experience in the trade, Bloom lectures Zoe because she is a woman, and prefers imagining himself as her more worldly educator. But by now, Bloom can only fantasize about reclaiming his masculinity through truth-telling:

> Sir Walter Raleigh brought from the new world that potato and that weed [tobacco], the one a killer of pestilence by absorption, the other a poisoner of the ear, eye, heart, memory, will, understanding, all. That is to say, he brought the poison a hundred years before another person whose name I forget brought the food. Suicide. Lies. All our habits. Why look at our public life!
>
> (Ibid.)

Bloom's 'truths' are largely false (or ironically true) even when he does remember them. If the potato is a 'killer of pestilence by absorption', able to obstruct future famines by providing a food source for the Irish, the potato is also the source of the Famine because of Ireland's overwhelming reliance on this single crop. But even though Bloom talks extensively about tobacco, he cannot remember his potato (Famine) history. It is judged unimportant because the problem, according to Bloom, is not about the potato but about the import of tobacco, a narcotic that afflicts the 'ear, eye, heart, memory, will, understanding', and which is purchased at the expense of other colonized countries. In a comparable Famine history, discussion of the Potato Famine was sidelined when Sir Robert Peel repealed the Corn Laws, a political dispute that redirected the discussion of the Famine to questions of colonial policies (like the importation of 'Indian corn', which Joyce represents with tobacco instead).[33] Joyce's Bloom is taken in by the switch: in thinking of 'tobacco', Bloom forgets the potato. Moreover, he ignores issues of alcoholic excess, religion, prostitution, colonialism and capitalism[34] and thereby ignores the issues that are the immediate 'narcotic', causing forgetfulness among the Dubliners, and for Bloom himself even as he delivers this lecture. Appropriately, in a society that seeks to evade and defer the truth, the flaws in Bloom's argument, his inaccurate recollection, and the omissions in his narrative, are rewarded: Bloom is given high political rank by the British, who appreciate his overlooking of Famine history since it might lead to discontent and unrest[35] (ibid.); and because he has successfully skirted unpleasant truths of Ireland's complicity in colonization, he has women die for him in emulation of the Romantic revivalists (ibid., p.492). As final reward, Bloom parthenogenetically gives birth to children who trade money (ibid., p.494), become good capitalists and thereby repeat colonial and political history. Bloom's presence in a house of prostitution, and his willfully ignorant exploitation of women, signal his own repetition of Romantic patriarchal and capitalist history, that will keep Ireland subdued, will one day cause the Famine to return, and in short, is really a history of 'Suicide. Lies. All our habits.' Appropriately, the Romantic 'Daughters of Erin' repeat Bloom's unlearned mistake, adoring Bloom's holy moly – 'Potato Preservative against Plague and Pestilence, pray for us' – when, if they recognized its historical importance, the potato might actually preserve them from Famine (ibid., p.499).

Bloom becomes increasingly ambivalent with the proposed Union, and he decides to depart. But Zoe calls him back, twirling her 'neck-fillet' chains seductively, emphasizing her advantages. Bloom speaks to her of his true love of Molly, of Ireland, as the reason he cannot stay. But Zoe recognizes the Romantic idealism as falsehood and sulks: 'I hate a rotter that's insincere. Give a bleeding whore a chance' (ibid.). England claims an eagerness to work things out with Ireland, and knows Ireland's desire for the lifestyle England offers. And Bloom chivalrously realizes he has been dishonest, and so he tries to speak to Zoe more honestly about capitalist prostitution and colonial exploitation, which are, by now, their shared vices:

BLOOM: (*Repentantly.*) I am very disagreeable. You are a necessary evil. Where are you from? London?
. . . (*Feeling his occiput dubiously with the unparalleled embarrassment of a harassed pedlar gauging the symmetry of her peeled pears.*) Somebody would be dreadfully jealous if she knew. The greeneyed monster. (*Earnestly.*) You know how difficult it is. I needn't tell you.
ZOE: (*Flattered.*) What the eye can't see the heart can't grieve for. (*She pats him.*) Come . . .
Silent means consent. (*With little parted talons she captures his hand, her forefinger giving his palm the passtouch of secret monitor, luring him to doom.*) Hot hands cold gizzard.

(Ibid., pp.500–1)

Bloom's attempt at Realism and truth-telling without the potato begins with the generous admission that prostitution is a 'necessary evil'; in this light, capitalism and empire, too, are necessary. But in his white-washing of events, Bloom fails to admit that Zoe's prostitution is necessary because post-Famine Ireland's economy relies on England's desirable commodities. Bloom does not admit that he himself is one of the well-fed Irish men who objectifies, and is even considering at the very moment he speaks, the value and symmetry of Zoe's 'peeled pears'. Bloom, like Ireland, Joyce insists, desires England's colonial assets. This is, after all, why Bloom is cheating on Molly. In degrading and objectifying Zoe, Bloom unconsciously defends prostitution – capitalism, colonialism – as a 'necessary evil', adopting the rhetoric of England's laissez-faire government, which justified its refusals of Famine relief with the Malthusian claim that the Famine was an unfortunate but necessary means of depopulating Ireland.

Bloom cannot stay, he suggests, because of what he owes to Molly, to Ireland. Though he desires Zoe-England, Bloom insists that his wife would be jealous if she knew. As we know from Bloom's relationship with Mary Driscoll, Molly might be jealous (or at least self-interested) if she knew that her husband was with another woman. But Bloom does not say these words because he believes them. He says them because he wants to feel desired. Like Stephen in Deasy's school, who imagines he rules his students without severity, Bloom unconsciously and deftly pits one woman's financial self-interest against another's, one country's self-interest against another's. Having been set against her rival Molly for the financial attentions of Bloom, Zoe knows no loyalty to her sex (but every loyalty to her country) and tells Bloom that 'What the eye can't see the heart can't grieve for'. In short, she means that what Molly (Ireland) does not know cannot hurt her. This claim is false from the outset; adultery, whether it leads to guilt, lies, mistrust or unspoken suspicions, can certainly hurt a relationship. But Zoe is correct to suggest that what prostituted Ireland does not know, its own Famine history, is not seen, nor learned, nor grieved, because it is unwritten by Irish authors. Unfortunately, if the Famine that Ireland does not know leads to history repeating itself, Ireland can be hurt by it. Disguising this truth, Zoe also adopts the very language she should most loathe – that of the rapist and sexual predator – explaining that 'Silent means consent'.

If English Zoe and Irish Bloom cannot meet any more than Bloom could with Gerty, it is because they remain 'disappointed bridges', missing the very important pieces that might bring them together. These historical gaps are made clearly visible as the talk turns increasingly apocalyptic when Stephen and Bloom meet with the prostitutes upstairs. Bloom treats

Zoe chivalrously, as a lady, even though he has just agreed to buy her like an object. The other whores, drunk and on display as well, complete this illusion by hypocritically admonishing Zoe to better 'respect' herself (ibid., p.502). Bloom, in the midst of embarking on his sexual adventure with Zoe in the whorehouse, is bitterly reminded at this moment of how Molly has made a cuckold of him. Meanwhile, Stephen, drunk but trying artistically and philosophically to compose, can only repeat the gap on the piano, the oriental-sounding 'the series of empty fifths' (ibid., p.503). Stephen's philosophy of the day has involved a study of both absence and excess, but he has not yet seen the missing piece between old and new Ireland, the gap in Irish writing. Because Bloom cannot speak it, and Stephen cannot write it, tension mounts, and time is running out: the end of the world – the apocalypse, the recurrence of the Famine – is what the Irish face if Stephen cannot finish his masterpiece and learn the inexpressible and invisible in Irish literature; if Bloom and his wife cannot truthfully address the fallout over, and consequences of, Rudy's death; if the Irish cannot remember their history.

As an Irish businessman, Bloom has been trained to blindness, he is complicit, and cannot undo his own domestication. Bloom's grandfather, Virag, demonstrates how the language of Romanticism, manifested in patriarchy, conspires to befuddle the rulers as well as the oppressed. Virag transforms Bloom's impulse to humanize women into patriarchal objectification. When Bloom comments that one girl is 'rather lean', an indication of his sensitive observation that she does not get enough to eat, Virag compliments Bloom on his ability to see through the deception of her dress, which is designed to enhance her non-existent curves and deceive the male eye. When Bloom notes that one of the women seems sad, Virag tells him it is a 'Hoax', designed to entrap him (ibid., p.512). Similarly, the British response to the initial reports of the Famine was that these reports were greatly exaggerated[36] – and that the fever associated with the Famine was a hoax and unlikely to occur.[37] The tragedy is that in the context of the whorehouse, Bloom is in danger of accepting and internalizing Virag's worldview, of becoming Virag, of repeating history.

Suddenly, through the fog of absinthe/absence, Stephen begins to recognize what the absence in Irish writing is:

> Must visit old Deasy or telegraph. Our interview of this morning has left on me a deep impression. Through our ages. Will write fully tomorrow. I'm partially drunk, by the way. (*He touches the keys again.*) Minor chord comes now. Yes. Not much however.
>
> (Ibid., p.518)

In his search for the contours of the problem, Stephen now knows that what is missing in Irish literature is the Famine, and he successfully transforms the empty fifth into a three-part chord, spanning the gap with a bridge. Though it is a minor chord, and though Stephen sees it as an inauspicious beginning, he momentarily possesses the keys. But in his drunken state, playing piano in the local whorehouse, he is in no condition to write the Irish epic, to express the inexpressible. And he still does not understand why or how it is important. When Florry appears as Artifoni asking Stephen to 'sing', he insists he has 'No voice. I am a most finished artist' (ibid.). Zoe is correct to indicate that Stephen still maintains his Romantic ideals, and for this reason, is unable to love life, to write life, to 'sing' as an artist. He has thus far failed to leave his tower, and as a result, the Irish Famine, though recognized, remains unvoiced because it cannot be neatly packaged into 'goodies' and 'baddies'.

Bloom, who maintains his chivalrous but empty patriarchal conversation, is no better. Instead of heroically rescuing Stephen from the drunken debauchery of his friends, Bloom has become one of the debauched and huddles in the darkened community of the whorehouse, repeating his previous mistakes. When Blazes Boylan arrives, Bloom once more covers up his cowardice with (the last of his) food. Even with the impending Famine, Bloom passes out chocolate, a product derived from colonialism, and in a metaphor of Ireland's colonial economy, watches as it makes its way through the English prostitutes and then comes back to him; he eats it.[38] When Zoe questions the masculinity she herself has taken from him, Bloom resorts once again to an empty masculine performance and uses a master mason's secret sign, which seems to magically 'conjure' Boylan away (ibid., p.526). Ironically, because he uses a sign from a masculine society that excludes her (as Stephen tells jokes that exclude his students), Zoe is unlikely to recognize Bloom's sign; she is understandably unimpressed by his hollow display of authority.[39]

If Bloom conjures Boylan away with his sign, however, he also inadvertently brings about the appearance of Circe. Joyce undoubtedly took great pleasure in parodying Queen Victoria, a matriarch of refined, conservative and even repressive values, in the figure of Bella Cohen, 'a massive whoremistress' (ibid., p.527). As the history of 'Swaggering Dan' suggests, despite her power, Bella is exploited because she is female, but she also exploits other women and adopts the language of patriarchy, empire and domination. She is the supreme example of the oppressed projecting their oppression onto others. Confronted with Bella, Bloom suddenly regrets his decision to allow Zoe to keep his potato, his moly, his memory, his masculinity (ibid.). If he remembered the Famine, he would know that Ireland's supposed 'passivity', its 'docility', its 'submissiveness' with respect to England's colonization, is a result of the preceding events and recurring effects of Ireland's hunger. Because he does not, Bloom appears to 'relish' his bondage and seems happy eating the leftovers of others. Bloom's masochism is so conditioned, so ingrained, that he, like Molly in her Turkish clothing, appears to embrace it: 'Exuberant female. Enormously I desiderate your domination' (ibid., p.528).

Bloom's and Bella's (Bello's) inability to articulate the space between idealizing, fetishizing, objectification and the bestial cruelty eventually brings about the Famine. But initially, Bloom-as-Ireland puts England on a chivalrous pedestal while Bella-as-England insults Bloom:

BELLO: . . . Hound of dishonour!
BLOOM: (*Infatuated.*) Empress!
BELLO: (*His heavy cheeckchops sagging.*) Adorer of the adulterous rump!
BLOOM: (*Plaintively.*) Hugeness!
BELLO: Dungdevourer!
BLOOM: (*With sinews semiflexed.*) Magnificence.
BELLO: Down! (*He taps other on the shoulder with his fan.*) Incline feet forward! Slide left foot one pace back. You will fall. You are falling. On the hands down!

(Ibid., pp.530–1)[40]

Soon after, Bello weds Bloom, telling him, 'With this ring, I thee own. Say, thank you, mistress' (ibid., p.539). S/he proceeds to punish, rape, degrade and offer Bloom up for sale.[41] Bella and Bloom's relationship echoes contemporary perspectives on Ireland's Union with England which, as Woodham-Smith explains, was described in distinctly gendered terms:

Indeed, the creation of the Union was bitterly opposed; contemporaries described it not as a marriage but as a 'brutal rape', and Ireland was compared to an heiress whose chambermaid and trustees have been bribed, while she herself is dragged, protesting, to the altar.

(Woodham-Smith, 1991, pp.15–16)

Bloom's chivalrous language belies the truth about the woman, even as (self-proclaimed masculine) Ireland is personified as a feminized, protesting bride, subjected to (queen) England's 'brutal rape'. If we fail to see Bloom's enjoyment of this abuse as absurd, we miss Joyce's point.

With the introduction of the theme of cannibalism in 'Circe', Ireland's Famine has reached apocalyptic proportions. But, as in the newspapers that reported it in Ireland and England, the actual term cannibalism is never spoken. Bloom, finally '*(fainting)*' from abuse, is told he will be eaten: 'Very possibly I shall have you slaughtered and skewered in my stables and enjoy a slice of you with crisp crackling from the baking tin basted and baked like sucking pig with rice and lemon or currant sauce. It will hurt you' (Joyce, *Ulysses*, pp.530–1). Cannibalism and Famine are the economic results of the Union: England will take everything from Ireland, gobbling food that would have fed the Irish people themselves. Victoria, as woman, should understand the complexities of oppression, but instead threatens to eat Bloom, Ireland, exploiting its difficulties. And when Bloom threatens to 'tell', Bella – with help from her subjugated female conspirators, prostitutes and lower-class servants – only abuses him all the more. But despite his silence, Bloom is not coprophilic. When Bella/Bello sits on Bloom's face, forcing him to become the 'Dungdevourer' s/he had accused Bloom of being, and puts the cigar out in Bloom's ear (effectively marking the end of tobacco, the end of the importation of Indian corn), there is no sign of Bloom's pleasure in the experience. If Bloom were a woman and Bella really a man, this would be a frighteningly violent scene of rape and physical abuse. If critics have read this scene as carnivalesque (which it is) or as Bloom's feminized/masochistic enjoyment of the experience (which it is), it is only because the scene takes place in a whorehouse where, as a wealthy, paying male customer, Bloom can order anything he wants and still presumably recover his masculinity as he leaves. But the key to understanding the actions of the Dubliners lies in the self-perpetuation of their condition. Bloom is comparable to a woman who fantasizes about rape; but this fantasy does not mean she really enjoys rape when it happens, or that she wanted or asked for it. Instead, we should understand that the fantasy of rape is a product of a system of idealization that makes woman complicit in her own downfall. If Bloom fantasizes about being dominated, he does not do so because Joyce embraces sadism and masochism, but rather because Joyce condemns sadism and masochism and all kinds of controlling, dominating, hierarchical behaviour. Bello's turning the tables on Bloom is a result of the fetishizing and idealizing tendencies Bloom continues to possess and project onto women; and Ireland's O'Connell projected them onto England's queen. The subtlety of Joyce's argument is that because oppression begets oppression, Victoria, as a woman, can become the cruelest manifestation of empire in Joyce's experience. In 'Circe', Victoria projects her own sense of sexual oppression by dominating poor (masculine) Ireland because conquest and cruelty are ways she can prove her worthiness as England's reigning monarch, even though she is a woman. In this sense, patriarchy really does lead to the Famine.

And how can Ireland explain its rape? If rape is difficult for a woman to address, how much more so for a man? How does self-proclaimed masculine Ireland account for and articulate its complicity in its own ravaging, its utter subjugation? Because of his shame, and the lack of language to articulate it, Bloom cannot explain the events truthfully; he can only turn to Irish Romanticism to express the inexpressible and reclaim his masculinity. Joyce sardonically has Bloom emulate Cuchulain, a great hero of Celtic mythology and icon of Irish Romanticism. In Irish myths, Cuchulain[42] bites his thumb to the marrow to learn how to undo his predicament and gain knowledge. Thus, when Bloom emulates Cuchulain, '*He bites his thumb*' to gain knowledge about how to express what has happened to him and how justice might be achieved (ibid., p.543). Bella Cohen, England's beautiful high priest, answers on behalf of the Irish Revivalists and provides Bloom with the knowledge he implicitly seeks and already knows from stories like Pyrrhus, the story of Christ, Lycidas: 'Die and be damned to you if you have any sense of decency or grace about you' (ibid., p.543). Yet realistically, Cuchulain's biting of his own thumb is the one moment from the myths that actually hints at the extremes of hunger as the implicit problem in Ireland's past. Though like Bloom with his potato, Irish writers play up Cuchulain's thumb's magical properties, offering stories of fantastic heroism in lieu of truth-telling, Cuchulain's need to bite his thumb may speak of a practical escape from starvation in times of dire need, offering a story of cannibalism as much as it does of heroism.[43] More immediately than Bella/o him/herself, who only threatens to cannibalize Bloom, Bloom's biting of his thumb indicates that Ireland's cannibalism is a result of its actual starvation.

But this final humiliation leaves Bloom, Ireland, like Stephen, utterly voiceless, a most finished nation. As a result of his trauma-induced inability to express this truth, to admit this rape and cannibalism, Bloom loses his memory and cannot articulate or grieve for his losses: '(*Clasps his head.*) My will power! Memory! I have sinned! I have suff . . .' (ibid., p.544). As with his 'I AM A . . . ' written into the sand in 'Nausicaa', Bloom's search for identity, the expression of his suffering, cannot be told. In preference to admitting his humiliation and rape, his complicity and solicitation, his emasculation and cannibalism, Bloom takes renewed umbrage in his ability to recover the performance of patriarchy, imagining England in the form of a goddess-nymph which 'fills [him] full':

> It overpowers me. The warm impress of her warm form. Even to sit where a woman has sat, especially with divaricated thighs, as though to grant the last favours, most especially with previously well uplifted white sateen coatpans. So womanly full. It fills me full.
>
> (Ibid., p.552)

As Joyce insists, Bloom's hunger cannot really be sated by his experience with a dream in the form of a nymph. And indeed, to love her – the Virgin, the nymph, the queen, England – is, as her attempt to castrate Bloom visibly demonstrates, a denial of life: it is a denial of masculinity, sexuality, fertility, humanity. In recognition that he cannot be a man and face the truth about the Famine without it, Bloom wants to have his potato back. 'There is a memory attached to it', he explains to Zoe, 'I should like to have it' (ibid., p.555). Zoe returns the potato, reminding him that, 'Those that hides knows where to find' (ibid., p.556). If the Irish have hidden their Famine memory, only the Irish can retrieve it. Though he wants the potato and the memory attached to it, the ambivalence about whether Bloom is ready for truth-telling remains. Even with the potato returned, he imagines himself as Molly's turnkey, knows he is partially responsible for her behaviour, and is still uncertain whether he can face the truth: 'Show! Hide! Show! Plough her! More! Shoot!' (ibid., p.567). But without the potato, Bloom can never confront this truth and does not have any choice but to accept England's (and Ireland's own internalized) perception of Ireland's colonized, victimized weakness, docility and passivity.

Because Bloom, who has hidden his secrets of Famine experience, cannot speak his suffering, Stephen is not much closer to solving his aesthetic issue of writing the Famine and is reduced to symbolic canni-balism himself. Too drunk to recognize his actions, Stephen reverts to Romantic stories of his travels in exotic Parisian whorehouses. Stephen tells lurid tales about the exploitation of Parisian women for the pleasure of exploited Dublin women in order to better exploit them. It is no wonder that Stephen is wracked with guilt about women, especially his mother, who remained loyal to a Christian system that oppressed her. So internalized was her religion that when she might have told him of her love for him, Mary Dedalus could speak only of prayer in her final words with her son. Instead, she dies starving and voiceless:

(Stephen's mother, emaciated, rises stark through the floor in leper grey with a wreath of faded orange blossoms and a torn bridal veil, her face worn and noseless, green with grave mould. Her hair is scant and lank. She fixes her bluecircled hollow eyesockets on Stephen and opens her toothless mouth uttering a silent word. A choir of virgins and confessors sing voicelessly.)

(Ibid., p.579)

Her 'bluecircled hollow eyesockets' and 'emaciated' appearance speak not only of one who is ill, but also of one who is hungry.[44] Like Stephen, Mary Dedalus, ravaged bride of the Union, has no voice: she 'opens her toothless mouth uttering a silent word'. When Stephen asks for the word 'love' from his mother's ghost, she cannot answer. There is no room for love in famine: mothers sometimes stole food from their children, or murdered them in an attempt to end their suffering; prostitution became a way for a woman to feed herself and, in some cases, her husband or family. But Stephen's question is also ironic because he turns to a ghost who through her living death has become a god to him, to help him understand life. His mother's voicelessness is living death in the form of the Christianity that subjugates her, that portrays her as worth less than men, and Stephen correctly identifies her self-abnegating adherence to religion as cannibalism: 'The corpsechewer! Raw head and bloody bones!' (ibid., p.581). But Stephen's own reliance on Romantic idealism, which causes him to exploit all the women he meets, is as extreme as his mother's. Faced with reliving his mother's death, Stephen refuses to worship as she pleads with him to do; Stephen cannot come down from his idealist tower enough to demonstrate his love for her any more than she can reject her Christianity for him. The two remain disappointed bridges, and Stephen is for the moment stuck reliving his guilt, repeating history,[45] instead of understanding their complicity in the systems that have oppressed them both. Angered by his mother's voicelessness, which has become his own, Stephen, emulating Synge's Playboy Christy, kills his mother's ghost.[46] But whether he does so in recognition of his own complicity in her downfall or as a projection of violent anger at his own Irish masculine impotence onto the Irish woman he loved is unclear. For the moment, Stephen remains unawakened from the nightmare of history, and his/story. And though Bloom enacts Stephen's rescue by paying for Stephen's damages at the whorehouse and refusing to allow Bella Cohen to swindle Stephen for more money than she deserves (both good deeds in light of Irish–English relations), the method he uses to help Stephen avoid trouble with Bella and the police confirms Bloom's adherence to all the systems of oppression that he and Stephen are trying to escape. In short, to combat Bella's powers, instead of using the regained moly, instead of recognizing that he is partly responsible for making Bella what she is, instead of truth-telling, Bloom calls upon the powers of England, Church and, with his master mason signal, patriarchy, to effect their escape[47] (ibid., p.585).

If Bloom's experience with Bella is an extended metaphor for the Famine, Stephen's encounter with Privates Compton and Carr is a reflection on post-Famine Ireland. Upon leaving, Bloom finds Stephen in heated conversation with the two British soldiers about history. Stephen tells them, 'You are my guests. The uninvited. By virtue of the fifth of George and seventh of Edward. History to blame. Fabled by mothers of memory' (ibid., p.587). Like Garrett Deasy's letter, Stephen's words are now jumbled and incoherent; they express a disembodied history, a truth without context, and a context Stephen can only get from Leopold Bloom. Once again, Stephen tells the riddle and the answer, but cannot explain how he arrived at his conclusion and once more fails to understand his audience's confusion. He turns to Cissy Caffrey, perplexed: 'Some trouble is on here. What is it, precisely?' (ibid., p.589). Bloom tries to disengage Stephen from the soldiers, but Stephen will not be led: 'Why should I not speak to him or to any human being who walks upright upon this oblate orange? (*He points his finger.*) I'm not afraid of what I can talk to if I see his eye' (ibid.). Because he has no personal experience of the actual Famine, Stephen embodies an Ireland unafraid of England, but also unable to recover from the unexpressed horrors of its past experience. Instead, Stephen finds himself in further trouble as Privates Compton and Carr take his explanation for his difficulties with Romanticism as a threat of kingly assassination: '(*He taps his brow.*) But in here it is I must kill the priest and the king' (ibid.). This misinterpreted threat means there is no turning back for Stephen, and a fight is destined to ensue. Appropriately, Edward the Seventh is on hand to judge the fight, emphasizing that it be a 'clean, straight fight' (ibid., p.590). Given Stephen's hurt hand, his missing glasses, his drunkenness and his starving condition, the fight is likely to be anything but fair.

Bloom naturally fears physical brutality because of his unspoken past experiences with Bella and the threat of retribution if he tells. Given this past, his courageousness in stepping in to help Stephen once more is as laudable as his extreme fright is justified. But Bloom's response to the incident is therefore different from Stephen's: he tries to prevent and cover up the altercation between Stephen and the soldiers at all costs. So for all the most noble of reasons, Bloom undermines Stephen's moments of truth-telling. '(*To the privates, softly.*) He doesn't know what he's saying. Taking a little more than is good for him. Absinthe, the green-eyed monster. I know him. He's a gentleman, a poet. It's all right' (ibid., p.591). And soon after, he insists, '(*Terrified.*) He said nothing. Not a word. A pure misunderstanding' (ibid., p.596). When Private Carr is not mollified by his explanations, Bloom desperately begs Cissy Caffrey to speak; but once more he inadvertently uses masculine force to underscore the urgency, and in so doing, frightens her, idealizes her, into silence: '(*Shakes Cissy Caffrey's shoulders.*) Speak, you! Are you struck dumb? You are the link between nations and generations. Speak, woman, sacred lifegiver' (ibid., p.597).

The anticlimactic fight is devoid of romance or heroism, and under-scores the absence of writing about the Famine once more. Private Carr takes after Stephen: '(*He rushes towards Stephen, fists outstretched, and strikes him in the face. Stephen totters, collapses, falls stunned. He lies prone, his face to the sky, his hat rolling to the wall. Bloom follows and picks it up*)' (ibid., p.601). When the 'WATCH' – a likely reference to *The Protestant Watchman*[48] – arrives, Bloom at first tells the truth about Carr: '(*Angrily.*) You hit him without provocation. I'm a witness. Constable, take his regimental number' (ibid., p.603). But when THE WATCH ignores the truth, disperses the witnesses and tends instead toward the arrest of Stephen, Bloom backs down and asks for help from fellow mason and undertaker Corny Kelleher in covering up the situation. Corny Kelleher quickly accomplishes the task, by giving the master mason sign and making a partriarchal appeal to men and wild oats: '(*Nudges the second watch.*) Come and wipe your name off the slate. (*He lilts, wagging his head.*) With my tooraloom tooraloom tooraloom tooraloom. What, eh, do you follow me? . . . (*Winking.*) Boys will be boys' (ibid., p.604). Persuaded by Corny Kelleher's rhetoric of patriarchy, THE WATCH explain that because there are no 'corporal injuries', they need not report the incident. Stephen remains, 'stunned', silent, unconscious, with hurt arm, no glasses, drunk and hungry, but this condition is viewed by the literary authorities, the truth-tellers, as having no corporal injuries. Thus patriarchy confirms that Stephen's response to 'colonialism' is 'docility', 'passivity' and 'weakness', and indeed, denies that there ever was an incident – only 'absinthe'. Here the genial men's club ideal that Stephen and Bloom need to deny in order to embrace truth-telling and history saves Stephen certain trouble with the authorities but ultimately erases history. The fight ends with no confirmation, to Bloom, Stephen or the crowd of witnesses who are told to depart, of what has happened, or that justice will be done. No wrongs can be mourned, redressed or disputed, because they are never written. Bloom, significantly, repeatedly, *thanks* the (blind and ignorant) 'WATCH' and ironically expresses his relief about Corny Kelleher's appearance: 'Providential you came on the scene', he tells the undertaker (ibid., p.606).

While Bloom and Corny Kelleher might have bonded over the mutual rescue of Stephen Dedalus from the authorities, the potential for bonding, because it is predicated on a false ideal of masculinity, results once more in a conspiracy of lies and a general failure to communicate. Thus, Corny nervously defends his presence in the prostitution district and wants to leave without further interrogation: 'Thanks be to God we have it in the house what, eh, do you follow me? Hah! hah! hah!' (ibid., p.606). Bloom is then forced to lie about his own presence: '(*Tries to laugh.*) He, he, he! Yes. Matter of fact I was just visiting an old friend of mine there. Virag, you don't know him (poor fellow he's laid up for the past week) and we had a liquor together and I was just making my way home' (ibid., p.606). Because he has an ideal to uphold, one that he does not want others to question him about, Corny Kelleher abandons Bloom, who is stuck with the unconscious Stephen and no ride home. Like the well-trained beasts he whips 'encouragingly', whose harnesses jingle so cheerfully, Bloom and Corny Kelleher are unable to shed their domestication; they, too, have been 'trained by kindness'. So, 'mirthfully', they proceed with the world as it has always been, remaining 'mute', history destined once more to repeat itself. Stephen, drunk, blind, lame, starving, beaten and unconscious, is, Bloom's generosity tells him, better off asleep:

> (*The jarvey chucks the reins and raises his whip encouragingly. The car and horse back slowly, awkwardly and turn. Corny Kelleher on the sideseat sways his head to and fro in sign of mirth at Bloom's plight. The jarvey joins in the mute pantomimic merriment nodding from the farther seat. Bloom shakes his head in mute mirthful reply. With thumb and palm Corny Kelleher reassures that the two bobbies will allow the sleep to continue for what else is to be done. With a slow nod Bloom conveys his gratitude as that is exactly what Stephen needs. The car jingles tooraloom round the corner of the tooraloom lane. Corny Kelleher again reassuralooms with his hand. Bloom with his hand assuralooms Corny Kelleher that he is reassuraloomtay. The tinkling hoofs and jingling harness grow fainter with their tooraloolooloo lay. Bloom, holding in his hand Stephen's hat festooned with shavings and ashplant, stands irresolute. Then he bends to him and shakes him by the shoulder.*)

(Ibid., pp.607–8)

Hope remains for Stephen, since the undertaker decides Stephen and
Bloom are too much a part of the living to take a ride, and because we
know the conversations in 'Eumaeus' and 'Ithaca' constitute the beginnings of a friendship, a love of the kind that distinguishes humans from
idols or animals – a love that might set the stage for Bloom to tell Stephen
what happened. But the 'Circe' chapter ends on a decidedly bleak note,
with Bloom 'murmuring' secrecy to Stephen, 'swear[ing] that I will always
hail, ever conceal, never reveal, any part or parts, art or arts' about what
happened (ibid., p.609). It is upon this promise that the ghost of Rudy
appears to him, as his son, the progeny of Ireland, reading a book. But as
an unnourished, unvoiced, unmanned artist, Stephen is left with no book
to write. Thus Rudy reads '*inaudibly, smiling, kissing the page . . . Gazes unseeing
into Bloom's eyes and goes on reading*' without hearing Bloom's call (ibid.). The
ghost cannot be laid to rest, cannot be mourned, and history cannot be
learned, because Stephen cannot write it if Bloom cannot help him. Since
Bloom erased and promised never to tell history, he has condemned,
rather than rescued, Ireland's future. And at the end of 'Circe', as the
appearance of Rudy confirms, the ghost story is likely to continue.

If Bloom and Molly are able to recover their lost marriage, the recovery
happens not from Bloom's alleged rescue of Stephen in 'Circe', but from
a willingness to confront distasteful truths about their past lives and their
actions since the death of their son. If the Irish are to reclaim their nation,
Irish writers too must be willing to confront distasteful truths – about
Ireland's complicity and victimization in the Famine. But until the generation of Bloom can speak – and Bloom, with the potato in his pocket is
one of the only people who can tell Stephen the story – and until the
generation of Stephen can write on these issues, Stephen and Bloom will
remain flawed teachers and patriarchs, unaware of the subtleties of their
authority and domination, and destined to repeat their history, to repeat
the Famine. Part of the subtlety of Joyce's argument is the complexity with
which he imagines the problem: the Union emasculates Ireland; capitalism
and the rhetoric of Romanticism that belies reality, manifested for Bloom
in the chauvinist dismissal of a woman queen, cause the Famine. But
because Joyce is more astute than his alter-ego Stephen, representation of
hunger forms not only the problem, but the solution: economic freedoms
are to be gained from living less exorbitantly, from being 'hungry'; starving
Stephen, will one day turn this absence of cultural nourishment into a
national epic. Hope exists because, after all, Joyce does talk about the
Famine if we are attentive readers and know our history. And the birth of

Molly's voice, the adoption of stream-of-consciousness as a deliberately female style, and Bloom's O/other child, Milly, Ireland's future, all present Joyce's sense of possibility for something new to happen.

References

Cheng, Vincent J. *Joyce, Race and Empire*. Cambridge: Cambridge University Press, 1995.

Cusack, George. "'In the gripe of the ditch": Nationalism, famine and *The Playboy of the Western World*', in George Cusack and Sarah Goss (eds), *Hungry Words: Images of Famine in the Irish Canon*. Dublin: Irish Academic Press, 2006, pp.133–58.

Dwyer, June. 'Feast and famine: James Joyce and the politics of food', *Proteus: A Journal of Ideas*, Vol.17, No.1 (2000), pp.41–4.

Eagleton, Terry. *Heathcliff and the Great Hunger: Studies in Irish Culture*. London: Verso, 1995.

Gibson, Andrew. *Joyce's Revenge: History, Politics, and Aesthetics in* Ulysses. Oxford: Oxford University Press, 2002.

Gifford, Don and Robert J. Seidman. *Notes for Joyce: An Annotation of James Joyce's* Ulysses. New York: E.P. Dutton, 1974.

Gonne MacBride, Maud. *A Servant of the Queen: Reminiscences*. Bury St Edmund: Boydell & Brewer, 1983.

Harris, Ruth-Ann M. 'Introduction', in Arthur Gribben (ed.), *The Great Famine and the Irish Diaspora in America*. Amherst, MA: University of Massachusetts Press, 1999.

Joyce, James. *A Portrait of the Artist as a Young Man*. (The definitive text corrected from the Dublin holograph.) New York: Viking Press 1973.

Joyce, James. *Ulysses*. (The complete and unabridged text, as corrected and reset in 1961.) New York: Vintage International, 1990.

Joyce, James. 'The Dead', *Dubliners*. New York: Signet Classics of Penguin Books, 1991.

Kelleher, Margaret. *The Feminisation of Famine: Expressing the Inexpressible?* Cork and Durham, NC: Cork University Press and Duke University Press, 1997.

Kinealy, Christine. *A Death-Dealing Famine: The Great Hunger in Ireland*. Chicago, IL: Pluto Press, 1997.

Kinealy, Christine. 'The Great Irish Famine – a dangerous memory?' in Arthur Gribben (ed.), *The Great Famine and the Irish Diaspora in America*. Amherst, MA: University of Massachusetts Press, 1999.

Kissane, Noel. *The Irish Famine: A Documentary History*. Dublin: National Library of Ireland, 1995.

Lowe-Evans, Mary. *Crimes Against Fecundity: Joyce and Population Control*. Syracuse, NY: Syracuse University Press, 1989.

McGee, Patrick. *Joyce Beyond Marx: History and Desire in* Ulysses *and* Finnegans Wake. Gainesville, FL: University Press of Florida, 2001.

Merritt, Robert. 'Faith and betrayal: the potato in *Ulysses*', *James Joyce Quarterly*, Vol.1, No.28 (1990), pp.269–76.

Osteen, Mark. *The Economy of Ulysses: Making Both Ends Meet*. Syracuse, NY: Syracuse University Press, 1995.

Paul-Dubois, L. *Contemporary Ireland*. Dublin: Maunsell, 1908.

Pecora, Vincent P. *Self and Form in Modern Narrative*. Baltimore, MD: Johns Hopkins University Press, 1989.

Walzer, Michael. *Exodus and Revolution*. New York: Basic Books, 1985.

Woodham-Smith, Cecil. *The Great Hunger: Ireland 1845–1849*. London: Penguin, 1991.

CHAPTER 9

'Buried! Who would have buried her?': Famine 'ghost graves' in Samuel Beckett's *Endgame*

Julieann Ulin

For he knew how the dead and buried tend, contrary to what one might expect, to rise to the surface, in which they resembled the drowned.
(Samuel Beckett, *Malone Dies*)[1]

Ghost graves . . . Never but the one matter. The dead and gone.
(Samuel Beckett, 'A piece of monologue')[2]

The last desperate stake for life had been played, and all was lost.
(A.M. Sullivan, *New Ireland*)[3]

In an article in the *Irish Times*, dated 3 November 1969, following Samuel Beckett's Nobel Prize, Con Leventhal, Beckett's close friend and Trinity colleague, noted with surprise the lack of attention paid to the Irish influences in Beckett's writing. Citing the debate over whether France could claim Beckett as her eleventh Nobel Prize winner, or Ireland as her third, Leventhal wrote:

There is no one here to make the full Irish case. Few to talk of the kinship with Swift, though more to tie the Dubliner in a Joycean knot. No one, however, is sufficiently aware of the background to notice the Irishness of the *Godot* tramps . . . How few French people were able to realise the added humour and pathos to the French version of *Fin de Partie* when in its English form it was acted by Patrick Magee and Jack Magowran in the author's own production! The French, ignorant of the exciting possibilities of an 'Endgame' played by the right Irish actors, are likewise unfamiliar with the revelatory new touches which these two actors can give to their interpretation of a Beckett text on radio and television.[4]

Over three decades later, few have tried to make the 'full Irish case'. While
the issue of Beckett's Irishness has been the subject of book-length studies
such as John P. Harrington's *The Irish Beckett* as well as a number of articles
that argue the importance of understanding the Irish context of Beckett's
work, no sustained close reading has attempted to address the question
Leventhal invites but never answers. What are the uniquely Irish possibilities of *Endgame?*

Despite the critical reluctance to consider the influence of Irish history
on Beckett, reviewers were quick to note the Irish elements of his plays. In
addition to Leventhal's piece, which suggests an Irish element in *Endgame*,
reviewers noted Irish resonances in *Waiting for Godot* and its Irish language
version, *Ag Fanacht le Godot*, which premiered at the Peacock in Dublin for
two nights in 1972. In his famous review of *Waiting for Godot*, which
appeared in the *Irish Times* under the title 'The Uneventful Event', Vivian
Mercier writes that 'Mr. Beckett's own English version of "En attendant
Godot" has two points of special interest for the Irish reader. On the one
hand, it is an adaptation rather than a translation, in which Irish allusions
have sometimes been substituted for French ones.' He goes on to note the
'local flavour' given off by the Dublin production.[5] Dominic Ó Riordain
writes of the Irish language version of *Godot*, '*Go bhfaca mé Godot i nGaeilge
níor thug me i gceart conas chomh cruinn is a thugann Beckett dúchas litríochta na
Gaeilge leis. Mar is gobán saor an ghrínn é, greann gnéasach, macabre atá chomh
seanda leis an Táin agus chomh úr le Finnegans Wake.*'[6] Thus, there appears to
be a discrepancy between what the Irish audiences experienced watching
Beckett and what the critics have read as Beckett's universalism.

Beckett's Anglo-Irish background and education, his prolonged absence
from Ireland, and his adoption of a foreign tongue refute any reductive
attempt to read Ireland into Beckett, and even those who accept Beckett
as an Irish writer caution against any simplistic definition of his Irishness.[7]
If Beckett's relationship to Ireland is considered by critics to be a complex
one, his relationship to Irish history is even more problematic. In 'Young
Beckett's Irish Roots', J.C.C. Mays argues that Beckett does indeed have
an Irish background, 'but Ireland is most important to Beckett as an
inheritance to deny, or a set of appearances to go behind, or a range of
authorities to disagree with' (Mays, 1984, p.21). Yet Declan Kiberd points
out, as have Beckett's biographers, the significance of the Easter 1916
Rebellion for the 10-year-old Beckett, whose father took him and his
brother to the top of a local hill from where they could see Dublin burning
(Kiberd, 1995, p.530).[8] Beckett's relationship with Ireland is the subject of

John P. Harrington's *The Irish Beckett*, in which he argues that while Beckett's humanism is a well-charted problem, his Irishness remains uncharted. Harrington's own treatment stays above the text, and when he deals with Irish history it is in a brief aside having to do with *Endgame*:

> In *Endgame*, evocation of the residue of a past is one form of the terminal maneuvers suggested by its title. As is often the case in Beckett's drama, *Endgame* offers only suggestions of the past of its characters, a past rather more accommodating than their present, and a past, imagined or not, with some historical relevance to Ireland.
>
> (Harrington, 1991, p.183)[9]

While a number of critics have linked Beckett's fragmented narration and preoccupation with displacement, exile and alienation to an Irish sensibility, most have been content to strand any historically specific reverberations at the level of the paradigmatic. Harrington argues that tropes such as home and away, and travelling and wandering, have a peculiarly Irish resonance: 'Beckett's work elaborates a paradigm of orientation and disorientation, of place and individual, and of context and imagination that is analogous to, among other things, the particular historical complex of modern Ireland' (ibid.).[10] Even attempts to read *Endgame* in a post-colonial frame fail to engage with Irish history as a possible prototype for the desolation of Beckett's universe.[11] This critical impulse prevents even those who defend an Irish Beckett from seeing the implications of *Endgame*, Beckett's most Irish play, in which there are significant textual correspondences with Famine Ireland that would have been readily available to an Irish audience.

Samuel Beckett's Ireland, as it has been treated by critics, is an Ireland without the Famine. Beckett's Ireland is contested territory, and even those who venture into it make little mention of the cultural trauma of the previous century, even when considering historical models for the terrestrial catastrophe at the back of *Endgame*.[12] Ronan McDonald writes,

> It is true that Beckett's skeletal characters and desolate landscape are haunted by the ghosts of Auschwitz. Yet it is also the case that the fragmentary narratives, the splintered memories, and the refusal of a dominant narrative voice betoken the fractured consciousness of a country with a traumatic history of famine, displacement, persecution and lost language.
>
> (McDonald, 2002, p.142)

But McDonald neglects to follow this point with the implications it has for reading Beckett in terms of Irish cultural memory. In 'Joyce and Beckett', Seamus Deane points out a number of references to the loss of the Gaelic language in Beckett, arguing that these references come from an author who 'has seen the disappearance of the Gaelic language as an historical premonition of his own plight' (Deane, 1984, p.63).[13] Ireland for Beckett is the historical correlative of the state that the Beckettian character desires: 'Silent, ruined, given to the imaginary, dominated by the actual, it is the perfect site for a metaphysics of absence' (ibid., p.64). Deane goes on to argue that Beckett repudiates Ireland in the same manner in which he repudiates history: 'While Joyce's writing is heavy with the weight of history, Beckett's is weightless.' Repudiation, however, demands an initial engagement, and in *Endgame* the Irish history of the Famine, the disaster that was the major contributing factor to the decline of the Irish language, offers itself as one 'historical premonition' for the catastrophe outside the door.

The memory of the Famine appears throughout *Endgame* in the connection between Beckett's imagery and Hamm's narrative to the tropes associated with the Famine. Hamm's characterization as an absentee landlord in control of the food supply and his advocating of laissez-faire economics strongly evoke Famine history, and it is in the failure of his chronicle to contain the trauma of the memory of death and starvation that the Famine is most present. The magnitude of the catastrophe is the driving force and also the defeat of Hamm's chronicle; the deprivation that permeates the play cannot be contained within Hamm's narrative framework. A close analysis of the Famine's presence in *Endgame* reveals the extent to which it may be seen as one historical prototype of the human condition that Beckett depicts.

The original French version of *Endgame*, *Fin de Partie*, was published in 1957, a year after Edwards and Williams's monumental *The Great Famine: Studies in Irish History, 1845–1852*. While the Famine tropes in *Endgame* were widely available in a number of popular nineteenth-century histories of Ireland, I will refer to this collection because it is contemporary with Beckett's play and because it illustrates the degree to which the Famine remained ingrained in the Irish consciousness a century later.[14] While I am not identifying Edwards and Williams's study as a source text for Beckett, my intention in citing it alongside his play is to identify the correlation between the conditions as described in *Endgame* and the significant tropes that reappear in the Irish memory of the Famine over a century after its onset. *The Great Famine* was widely reviewed, and the initial print run of 2,000 sold out within two years. Roger J. McHugh's chapter in particular, 'The Famine in Irish Oral Tradition', which deals with the legacy of the Famine in folklore, and William P. MacArthur's chapter, 'Medical history of the Famine', resonate to such a degree with Beckett's play as to support the argument that a catastrophe that critics have typically identified as abstract and universal had a recognizable antecedent for Irish audiences.

Endgame centres on a devastated and depopulated landscape. The catastrophe outside the house in which Hamm, Clov, Nell and Nagg are entombed is marked by the general collapse of nature. When Hamm says, 'Nature has forgotten us', Clov replies, 'There's no more nature' (Beckett, 1991, p.262). The landscape is one of continual deprivation, and the play is punctuated by a refrain of what is 'no more': bicycle-wheels, decency, pap, sprouting seeds, sugarplums, tides, navigators, rugs, pain-killers and coffins.[15] The failure of Clov's garden and seeds correlates with the general impoverishment of the land in suggesting a famine:

HAMM: Did your seeds come up?
CLOV: No.
HAMM: Did you scratch round them to see if they had sprouted?
CLOV: They haven't sprouted.
HAMM: Perhaps it's still too early.
CLOV: If they were going to sprout they would have sprouted. (*Violently*) They'll never sprout. (*Pause*)

(Ibid.)

Roger McHugh remarks that the oral tradition of the Famine has many anecdotes of 'men who dug all day, often in vain, to find enough potatoes for one meal' and 'of farmers of formerly fertile acres who now starved' (McHugh, 1994, p.397).

In addition to the desolation of the earth, it is clear throughout the play that the people who once lived there have been 'extinguished'. When asked by Clov why Hamm keeps him, Hamm answers, 'There's no one else' (Beckett, 1991, p.261). Hamm and Clov's discussion of other former inhabitants of the land hints at a mass death. When confirming the death of the doctor, Hamm speaks in a manner that suggests that the doctor could not be anything but dead:

HAMM: That old doctor, he's dead, naturally?
CLOV: He wasn't old.
HAMM: But he's dead?
CLOV: Naturally.

(Ibid., p.265)

The language ties nature to the death of the doctor, as if it is the natural 'course' which is responsible. In discussing the class distribution of Famine-related deaths, MacArthur points out the high fatality rate among doctors working with victims of Famine fever. MacArthur quotes from a medical report, 'which could be multiplied many times', that 'the number of persons who contracted the disease, whose duties brought them constantly into contact with fever patients, such as physicians, clergymen, and hospital nurses, clearly shows the contagious nature of the late epidemic' (MacArthur, 1994, pp.278–9). Towards the end of the play, when a small boy is sighted, Clov calls him a 'potential procreator', pointing again to the supposed human annihilation. The two possibilities that Hamm identifies for the boy are exposure and death or begging for shelter and food: 'If he exists he'll die there or he'll come here' (Beckett, 1991, pp.276–7). This threat of an exposed death strikes a particular chord in Famine history.

The implication that the dead remain where they die, without the cover of burial, appears in Clov's description of the landscape and recalls one of the prominent horrors of the Famine continually remarked upon in the folklore:

HAMM: (*Normal voice*) . . . All is . . . all is. . . all is what? (*Violently*) All is
          what? (*Violently*) All is what?
CLOV: What all is? In a word? Is that what you want to know? Just a
          moment. (*He turns the telescope on the without, looks, lowers the telescope,
          turns towards* HAMM) Corpsed. (Pause) Well? Content?

(Ibid., p.266)

In describing the world as 'corpsed', Clov alludes to the widespread nature of this disaster, but he also suggests the presence of unburied corpses visible on the landscape. Beckett's preoccupation with issues of burial and mourning is outlined by Phil Baker in 'Ghost stories: Beckett and the literature of introjection' in his *Beckett and the Mythology of Psychoanalysis*: 'Beckett's writing is marked less by the absence of the dead than by the ghostly presence of their "tenacious trace" (Baker, 1997, p.145). Baker treats the ghostly figures that psychically return to haunt Beckett's texts as voices or as watchers in light of Freud's 1917 paper 'Mourning and Melancholia' (Freud, 1989, pp.584–9). Baker's analysis may be extended to *Endgame*, where Hamm's fear of not being buried, the lack of coffins in which to bury the dead, and the implied chaos all recall the improvised burial methods during the Famine.

In one of the two passages in the play that concerns the deceased neighbour Mother Pegg, Hamm's own fear of not being buried emerges:

HAMM: Is Mother Pegg's light on?

CLOV: Light! How could anyone's light be on?

HAMM: Extinguished!

CLOV: Naturally it's extinguished. If it's not on it's extinguished.

HAMM: No. I mean Mother Pegg.

CLOV: But naturally she's extinguished! (*Pause*) What's the matter with you today?

HAMM: I'm taking my course. (*Pause*) Is she buried?

CLOV: Buried! Who would have buried her?

HAMM: You.

CLOV: Me! Haven't I enough to do without burying people?

HAMM: But you'll bury me.

CLOV: No I shan't bury you.

(Beckett, 1991, p.269)

In the above passage, the repetition of the word 'naturally' again links nature to death, this time Mother Pegg's. Possible answers to Clov's question, 'Who would have buried her?' are haunting ones. Either no one survives to bury her or those who do survive are as indifferent as Clov. Examples of both scenarios may be found in primary Famine accounts.

Roger McHugh writes that as the Famine worsened, coffin burial became exceptional, and improvised methods of burial replaced them. Often a sheet replaced a coffin and McHugh records a poem attributed to a Clare poet which reads: '*Is dána an rud domh-sa a bheith a' súil le cómhra / Is maith an rud domh-sa má dh'fhuighim bairlín / Is a Rí na glóire, tabhair fuascailt domh-sa / Go dteigh mé im chómhnuidhe san gcill úd.*'[16] Gradually the starving families and neighbours became too weak to bury the dead, and burial rituals and funerals declined and in some places completely vanished. *Endgame* registers this same preoccupation with the lack of coffins:

CLOV: (*Imploringly*) Let's stop playing!
HAMM: Never! (*Pause*) Put me in my coffin.
CLOV: There are no more coffins.
HAMM: Then let it end!

(Ibid., p.276)

When Nell dies, the dustbin in which she lived serves as a makeshift coffin. The reliance on crude coverings after the coffins 'ran out' during the Famine is well-recorded in the Irish Folklore Commission reports.[17] It should be noted that as a last favour from Clov, Hamm requests covering. The counterpart to Hamm's coffin is his sheet:

HAMM: It's we are obliged to each other. (*Pause.* CLOV *goes towards door*) One thing more. (CLOV *halts*) A last favour. (*Exit* CLOV) Cover me with the sheet. (*Long pause*) No? Good.

(Ibid., p.277)

The undercurrents in this conversation, and the great offence of not burying, might be attributed to Hamm's continual need to be covered, perhaps in retribution for the sin of his Biblical namesake who refuses to cover his father and instead looks upon his nakedness in Genesis 9:18–28. Just as Hamm threatens to withhold food to maintain power, Clov's agency comes from his ability to deny burial despite his own obsession with order: 'I love order. It's my dream. A world where all would be silent and still and each thing in its last place, under the last dust' (ibid., p.272). Inseparable from Clov's notion of an ordered world is a return to burial practices, and his own refusal to enforce these practices appears either a resignation to the chaos of the world outside or an attempt to exert some power over Hamm. But in addition to this purely textual reading, Hamm's fear of not being buried and Clov's refusal to bury Mother Pegg and Hamm evoke the deepest horrors of the Irish memory of the Famine, a dimension of the play which would be available to an Irish audience familiar with Famine history. In recognizing these correlations, a reading of the play emerges in which the Famine offers a prototype for the modern condition.

Famine accounts continually refer to the paralysis of the starving Irish, and critics have argued that this legacy of the Famine persisted in various forms into the modern era.[18] The wasted, paralyzed and decaying bodies of Beckett's *Endgame* imprison the characters within their own bodies as well as in the house. Beckett crafts the body of each of the four inhabitants of the house as incapable of leaving; they are together because none has the strength to 'get on' without the other. Each of the characters is paralyzed in a certain position: Hamm cannot stand, Clov cannot sit, and Nell and Nagg will die in their dustbins, unable to even scratch one another. Nagg's legs are stumps, Nell is freezing, Hamm is wheelchair-bound and cannot move himself. Many of the ailments that afflict the characters appear in William P. MacArthur's chapter, 'Medical history of the Famine', in Edwards and Williams's study. A description of the diseases arising from food deficiencies emphasizes many of the same medical afflictions from which Hamm, Clov, Nell and Nagg suffer:

> Two non-infectious conditions arising from food deficiencies were rife among the hunger-stricken – scurvy and famine dropsy . . . [Scurvy] gave rise to spongy swellings and ulcerations of the gums, with eventual loss of teeth. Haemorrhagic blotches appear in the skin – the 'purpula' so often recorded in the famine – and in advanced cases there are massive effusions of blood into the muscles and under the skin, causing tension and great pain. The legs may be completely black up to the middle of the thigh; it was such discolourations that gave rise to a colloquial name for scurvy, *cos dhubh* (black leg). There are also painful effusions around and into the joints.
>
> (MacArthur, 1994, pp.269–70)

The arrival of the Famine had disastrous consequences for conditions of hygiene and sanitation: 'The lack of cleanliness, the unchanged clothing and the crowding together, provided conditions ideal for lice to multiply and spread rapidly' (ibid., p.271). The relapsing fever that ravaged the weakened population is described in a manner that recalls Hamm's body: 'a fatal complication was suppression of urine. Inflammation of the iris occurred occasionally, and "in one or two instances" blindness' (ibid., p.284). All of the above conditions are present in *Endgame* in Hamm's blindness and eyes that 'have gone all white', in his problems urinating, in Nagg's lost teeth, in the unchanged sawdust of Nell and Nagg's dustbins, in Clov's flea or crablouse, and in the pains in Clov's legs: 'The pains in my legs! It's unbelievable! Soon I won't be able to think anymore' (Beckett, 1991, pp.261, 265, 263, 267 and 270).

Clov appears to be the only character with a chance of escaping the confines of the house, but he describes his attempt to escape as ending in certain collapse and death: 'I open the door of the cell and go. I am so bowed I only see my feet, if I open my eyes, and between my legs a little trail of black dust. I say to myself that the earth is extinguished, though I never saw it lit. (*Pause*) It's easy going. (*Pause*) When I fall I'll weep for happiness. (*Pause. He goes towards door*)' (ibid., p.277). Hamm's earlier taunting of Clov with the possibility of fertile land elsewhere is especially vicious because of the impossibility of Clov surviving the journey:

HAMM: That here we're down in a hole. (*Pause*) But beyond the hills? Eh? Perhaps it's still green. Eh? (*Pause*) Flora! Pomona! (*Ecstatically*) Ceres! (*Pause*) Perhaps you won't need to go very far.
CLOV: I can't go very far.

(Ibid., p.268)

Paralysis characterizes the house and each character's movement within it. Staying in the house will only defer the inevitable, and Hamm describes Clov's eventual end in terms of this paralysis:

HAMM: . . . One day you'll say to yourself, I'm tired, I'll sit down, and you'll go and sit down. Then you'll say, I'm hungry, I'll get up and get something to eat. But you won't get up. You'll say, I shouldn't have sat down, but since I have I'll sit on a little longer, then I'll get up and get something to eat. But you won't get up and you won't get anything to eat. (*Pause*) You'll look at the wall a while, then you'll say, I'll close my eyes, perhaps have a little sleep, after that I'll feel better, and you'll close them. And when you open them again they'll be no wall any more. (*Pause*) Infinite emptiness will be all around you, all the resurrected dead of all the ages wouldn't fill it, and there you'll be like a little bit of grit in the middle of the steppe. (*Pause*) Yes, one day you'll know what it is, you'll be like me, except that you won't have anyone with you, because you won't have had pity on anyone and because there won't be anyone left to have pity on. (*Pause*)
CLOV: It's not certain. (*Pause*) And there's one thing you forget.
HAMM: Ah?
CLOV: I can't sit down.
HAMM: (*Impatiently*) Well, you'll lie down then, what the hell! Or you'll come to a standstill, simply stop and stand still, the way you are now. One day you'll say, I'm tired, I'll stop. What does the attitude matter?

(Ibid., p.267)

The centrality of food in this play emerges in the repeated emphasis on food as a instrument to control others. The above passage, in which Hamm's description of Clov's paralysis is bound up with his inability to get up or 'get anything to eat', recalls Hamm's earlier threat to starve Clov to death:

HAMM: Get me ready. (CLOV *does not move*) Go and get the sheet. (CLOV *does not move*) Clov!
CLOV: Yes.
HAMM: I'll give you nothing more to eat.
CLOV: Then we'll die.
HAMM: I'll give you just enough to keep you from dying. You'll be hungry all the time.
CLOV: Then we shan't die. (*Pause*) I'll go and get the sheet. (*He goes towards the door*)

(Ibid., p.261)

What surfaces here is not only mutual dependence, but the individual weapons of coercion. Hamm holds food as currency with which he demands obedience, and Clov has the power of refusal to bury.

Famine accounts detail paralysis as an effect of the failure of the crops and the slow starvation of the people dependent upon them. As they realized their predicament, 'Blank stolid dismay, a sort of stupor, fell upon the people . . . It was no uncommon sight to see the cottier and his little family seated on the garden-fence gazing all day long in moody silence at the blighted plot that had been their last hope. Nothing could arouse them' (Sullivan, 1878, p.85). The paralysis that pervades *Endgame* is the result of continual deprivation, the characters' inability to leave the house, and the waiting for 'the end', precisely the condition of many Famine victims in Ireland of the previous century. The dominance of the confining interior space and the association of the outside with death evoke the sole method of burial available to many Famine victims, a self-entombing within the home. Asenath Nicholson talks of 'the more revolting sights of families found in the darkest corner of a cabin in one putrid mass, where, in many cases, the cabin was tumbled down upon them to give them a burial' (Nicholson, 1998, p.38). Sullivan also mentions that 'by levelling above their corpses the sheeling in which they died, the neighbours gave them a grave' (Sullivan, 1878, p.93). Whether or not Clov leaves at the end of the play, the fate of those who remain in the house may well be the same fate experienced in this Famine account:

A cabin was seen closed one day a little out of town when a man had the curiosity to open it, and in a dark corner he found a family of the father, mother, and two children, lying in close compact. The father was considerably decomposed; the mother, it appeared, had died last and probably fastened the door, which was always the custom when all hope was extinguished, to get into the darkest corner and die where passers-by could not see them. Such family scenes were quite common, and the cabin was generally pulled down upon them for a grave.

(Nicholson, 1998, p.118)

The folklore reports that the enclosure of the starving and paralyzed family within the house, awaiting certain death, resulted in psychological changes that were manifest in an indifference to death and suffering.

One of the most lamented consequences of the Famine was its effect on the relations among family members. McHugh cites an anecdote of a Donegal woman:

Things were so bad at that time that no one cared how the other was . . . Families began to die and the rest were so weak and far spent that they could do nothing for them but leave them until the last one in the house died. All in the house died and the bodies lay here and there through it. They were never moved from it.

(McHugh, 1994, p.417)

The effects of prolonged hunger and starvation destroyed even the most basic human sympathy, and a similar indifference appears in the reaction of Clov and Hamm to Nell's death. While Nagg cries, Clov merely 'bottles' Nell's body in the dustbin, which will serve as her makeshift coffin. The relationship between Hamm and Nagg is one marked by mutual cruelty. Hamm calls his father 'Accursed progenitor!' and 'Accursed fornicator!' (Beckett, 1991, p.262). Upon learning that there is no more 'pap' for his father, Hamm taunts him, 'Do you hear that? There's no more pap. You'll never get any more pap.' He instructs Clov to 'Bottle him!' and 'Sit on him!' In retaliation, Nagg tells his son that he was neglected as a child. Hamm's voice in the stage directions is described as 'cold' on several occasions, and he appears unmoved by the prospect of Clov's death or of leaving:

HAMM: Yes, but how would I know, if you were merely dead in your kitchen?

CLOV:　　Well . . . sooner or later I'd start to stink.
HAMM:　　You stink already. The whole place stinks of corpses.
CLOV:　　The whole universe.

(Ibid., p.270)

For an Irish audience familiar with the prolonged effects of starvation, the entrapment within the house, the indifference with which Hamm views the possibility of Clov's 'mere' death, and the stench of corpses with which Clov identifies the universe recall the condition of Ireland during the Famine. The primary accounts found in McHugh's chapter, for example, depict a similar breakdown of familial relationships in response to the catastrophic conditions brought about by the Famine. The only creatures that thrive in such circumstances are the scavengers.

The characters of *Endgame* are especially preoccupied with rats, the scavenger animals of Famine Ireland. MacArthur quotes from a representative 1846 letter to the Duke of Wellington: 'the same morning the police opened a house on the adjoining lands, which was observed shut for many days, and two frozen corpses were found lying upon the mud floor *half devoured by the rats*' (MacArthur, 1994, p.275). McHugh relates a similar story from the folklore: 'The hunger brought on the sickness – the fever – God bless us – and the two sons were buried . . . the poor mother was not able to go to the graveyard with them. Some time after . . . when some neighbour went to see the old woman, she was found dead and her body almost eaten away with the rats' (McHugh, 1994, p.418). The rat lurks in the background of *Endgame*, waiting:

CLOV:　　There's a rat in the kitchen!
HAMM:　　A rat! Are there still rats?
CLOV:　　In the kitchen there's one.
HAMM:　　And you haven't exterminated him?
CLOV:　　Half. You disturbed us.
HAMM:　　He can't get away?
CLOV:　　No.
HAMM:　　You'll finish him later. Let us pray to God.

(Beckett, 1991, p.271)

Clov fails to exterminate the rat, whose presence incites prayer and who reappears at the close of Hamm's chronicle. Hamm cannot forget the presence of the rat: 'All kinds of fantasies! That I'm being watched! A rat!'

(ibid., p.275). The rat escapes both Clov's attempts to kill it and the plague that has claimed the lives of the inhabitants of the world outside the house:

HAMM: Outside of here it's death! (*Pause*) And the rat?
CLOV: He's got away.
HAMM: He can't go far. (*Pause. Anxious*) Eh?
CLOV: He doesn't need to go far.

(Ibid., p.276)

If the rat does not need to go far it is because there will be food for him soon enough. Even the flea, the only other live animal mentioned in the play, is a parasite that feeds off the body.

Numerous Famine accounts discuss a madness that was the result of continual deprivation and the hopelessness of the people. Clov appears to be bordering on a type of madness to which he is driven by the inability of his incessant 'ordering' to combat the chaos of the world outside. He lashes out at Hamm, 'You drive me mad, I'm mad!' and disappears into his kitchen to stare at the wall. Clov muses, 'Sometimes I wonder if I am in my right mind. Then it passes over and I'm as lucid as before . . . Sometimes I wonder if I'm in my right senses. Then it passes off and I'm as intelligent as ever' (ibid., p.275). While Clov appears to border on madness, Hamm is able to escape into his mind, where he re-establishes himself as the landlord of the estate despite the death of his paupers and the sterility of the land.

It is in his position as landlord and the chronicle he fashions that Hamm most explicitly recalls the conditions of Famine Ireland. Hamm's confusion with the state of the world is that of the absentee landlord: 'Absent, always. It all happened without me. I don't know what's happened' (ibid., p.276). His confusion leads to violent outbursts as he attempts to understand the decimation around him:

HAMM: Do you know what's happened?
CLOV: When? Where?
HAMM: (*Violently*) When! What's happened! Use your head, can't you! What has happened?
CLOV: What for Christ's sake does it matter? (*He looks out of window*)
HAMM: I don't know.

(Ibid.)

In addition to wielding the threat of imposing starvation, both within and outside the space of his chronicle, Hamm possesses the power to aid those around him. He repeatedly returns to his belief in letting nature take its course, recalling the disastrous consequences of the ideology of laissez-faire economics espoused by Charles Trevelyan. Hamm's failure to control his chronicle and restrict it within the framework he constructs suggests the trauma and lack of resolution of the catastrophe, which he attempts to escape through his reliance on a central position.

Throughout *Endgame*, Hamm obsesses over the central position of his chair rather than what Freud terms 'the actual, important thing' (Freud, 1989, p.435).[19] Hamm's attempts to understand what has taken place in his absence cannot be separated from his insistence on remaining in the centre:

HAMM: Back to my place! (CLOV *pushes chair back to centre*) Is that my place?

CLOV: Yes, that's your place.

HAMM: Am I right in the centre?

CLOV: I'll measure it.

HAMM: More or less! More or less!

CLOV: (*Moving chair slightly*) There!

HAMM: I'm more or less in the centre?

CLOV: I'd say so.

HAMM: You'd say so! Put me right in the centre!

CLOV: I'll go and get the tape.

HAMM: Roughly! Roughly! (CLOV *moves chair slightly*) Bang in the centre!

CLOV: There! (*Pause*)

HAMM: I feel a little too far to the left. (CLOV *moves chair slightly*) Now I feel a little too far to the right. (CLOV *moves chair slightly*) I feel a little too far forward. (CLOV *moves chair slightly*) Now I feel a little too far back. (CLOV *moves chair slightly*) Don't stay there (*i.e. behind the chair*), you give me the shivers.

(Beckett, 1991, p.265)

And later:

HAMM: (*Anguished*) Don't leave me there! (*Angrily* CLOV *restores the chair to its place*) Am I right in the centre?

(Ibid., p.276)

The degree to which Hamm clings to routine and ritual throughout the play, and his anguish when that routine is threatened, recall Freud's treatment of the repressed, in which repression is not an event that takes place once, but requires a continual afterpressure to be exerted. The cessation of this afterpressure threatens to bring the repressed into the forefront of consciousness.[20] This afterpressure makes itself felt in Hamm's resistance to a rupture in order, seen in his fury at being interrupted:

HAMM: Nothing stirs. All is –
CLOV: Zer –
HAMM: (*Violently*) Wait till you're spoken to!

                                                    (Ibid., p.266)

When asked by Clov, 'Why this farce, day after day?' Hamm replies, 'Routine. One never knows.' That which is unknown, the catastrophe for which Hamm violently demands an explanation and continually attempts to measure, can be combated only through an over-reliance on what is known. If, as Rene Girard argues in *Violence and the Sacred*, 'the sole purpose of ritual is to ensure total immobility, or failing that, a minimum of disturbances', since 'if the door is opened to admit change, there is always the risk that violence or chaos will force an entry', then Hamm's obsession with order and routine may be seen as an attempt to shield himself from the disaster outside (Girard, 1977, p.284). If read in the context of Irish history, the landlord's attempts to remain in control despite the chaos around him and the continual petitions for aid correspond with the Famine conditions and the questions raised about the distribution of charity and relief.

   In addition to his obsession with his 'place' and the central position of his chair, Hamm's relationship with his stuffed dog betrays a desperate desire to reconstruct from the meager props around him the societal structure that preceded his absence. When he instructs Clov to take him for a turn around the room, he may well be re-enacting the surveying of his paupers, with the dog standing in for the begging supplicants:

HAMM: (*His hand on the dog's head*) Is he gazing at me?
CLOV: Yes.
HAMM: (*Proudly*) As if he were asking me to take him for a walk?
CLOV: If you like.
HAMM: (*As before*) Or as if he were begging me for a bone. (*He withdraws his hand*) Leave him like that, standing there imploring me.

CLOV *straightens up. The dog falls on its side.*

(Beckett, 1991, p.268)

The collapse of the imploring dog immediately after Hamm 'withdraws his hand' recalls Hamm's relationship with Mother Pegg and the begging man in his chronicle.

In this identification of Hamm with the absentee landlord, an interesting connection between McHugh's study and Beckett's play emerges. The coincidence of voice in the following two passages is striking when compared to McHugh's description of a landlord:

CLOV: When there were bicycles I wept to have one. I crawled at your feet. *You told me to get out to hell.*

(my emphasis, ibid., p.261)

And later:

CLOV: (*Harshly*) When old Mother Pegg asked you for oil for her lamp and *you told her to get out to hell,* you knew what was happening then, no? (*Pause*) You know what she died of, Mother Pegg? Of darkness.

HAMM: (*Feebly*) I hadn't any.

CLOV: (*As before*) Yes, you had.

(my emphasis, ibid., p.276)

'Anecdotes about evicting landlords still keep their memories alive', McHugh writes, before reporting a landlord with remarkable similarities to Beckett's Hamm:

A third [landlord] used to shout 'get away to hell!' to people who sought relief, until the poorhouse was built, when he substituted 'get away to the poorhouse!' to which an old woman replied that the poorhouse had been a great saviour of souls.

(McHugh, 1994, pp.428–9)

Hamm justifies his withholding throughout the play by advocating the same principles used to discourage giving aid in violation of the laws of political economy during the Famine.

Hamm's repeated emphasis throughout the play on letting things take their course recalls the disastrous policies of laissez-faire economics. The

English elite of the 1840s concluded 'that the Irish famine was God's will, an inevitable event, which should be permitted to take its course' (Daly, 1995, p.126). Sullivan writes, 'In a few cases, I am sorry to say, the horrible idea seemed to seize the land-owners . . . that, as their imposition would result only in ruining "property", it was well to *"let things take their course"*' (Sullivan, 1878, p.90, my emphasis). Hamm speaks the language of the landlord and advocates the economic ideologies which allowed for mass starvation, and his chronicle may be seen as bound up with Irish issues of landlords and starving tenants from which it cannot generate narrative coherence.

The presence of the unnamable catastrophe outside is the driving force and also the defeat of Hamm's chronicle, and the anxieties present in his story are intimately bound up with questions of culpability and evoke the discourses of the Famine. The repetitive speech of Hamm's chronicle refuses to advance plot or confer meaning, and despite Hamm's compulsion to tell and retell, all the while demanding an audience, this retelling never results in a resolution. Beckett's familiarity with the effects of trauma and repression stems from his own experience being analyzed by Dr Wilfrid Bion for about two years. The methods used by Bion were those of dream analysis, memory work and free association, all methods used to bring the repressed into consciousness and identify and reconcile the origins and agencies of repression (Dukes, 2001, p.47). Both Clov's obsession with order and Hamm's anxious attempts to recreate his previous surroundings within the house may be seen as reactions to the trauma of the disaster that has destroyed the world outside. While much has been written about Beckett and notions trauma and repression, there is a reluctance to consider these issues in relation to Irish history. Famine memory is inextricably bound up with issues of trauma and a repression of that which cannot be articulated, what Adorno terms 'the presupposed terrestrial catastrophe' (1980, p.161) that is constantly measured and noted, but never identified.

Hamm's 'chronicle' echoes Irish history of the Famine era and has interesting implications when read in the frame of relief efforts. The story centres on the plight of the hungry and starving and on the narrator, who is in a position to provide aid. Hamm tells the story in the first person, assuming the voice of the possessor of food and shelter with the power to fulfill or deny petitions. Hamm's narrative, by its refusal to end and its tendency to get repeatedly 'stuck' at the same place – the moment at which a petition for aid must be answered either with human sympathy or an economic system that allows for nature to take its course – is clearly linked up with trauma and repression. It is significant that the chronicle halts with the word 'Enough' rather than with 'The End'. Hamm is also guilty of a refusal to bury. While Clov withholds the promise of burial from Hamm, it is Hamm who cannot bury the narrative, which refuses to be contained within his framework, instead surfacing repeatedly in the play's dialogue.

Hamm begins his story several times with various instruments of measurement, a heliometer, an anemometer and a hygrometer, illustrating both his continual attempts to piece together what has gone on in his absence, as well as the failure to measure the catastrophe. In his chronicle, Hamm is in a position of wealth and prosperity and apparent physical wholeness, and he describes being petitioned by labourers as a typical event. MacArthur mentions as one of the three major classes affected by the Famine 'labourers who had no fixed employment and no land, living in hovels and hiring yearly a scrap of land from some farmer' (MacArthur, 1994, p.264). Hamm describes the labourer's home as 'the hole', which is a three-day journey away. The figure of the labourer haunts Hamm even with the supposed narrative distance: '(*Pause*) I can see him still, down on his knees, his hands flat on the ground, glaring at me with his mad eyes, in defiance of my wishes' (Beckett, 1991, p.271). The looming madness of Clov may be seen as prefigured in the madness of the glaring beggar, aligning Clov with the petitioner and keeping Hamm in the position of the landlord. Hamm fears being looked at by the begging labourer: 'He raised his face to me, black with mingled dirt and tears . . . No, no, don't look at me, don't look at me. He dropped his eyes and mumbled something, apologies I presume.' In a section detailing stories about landlords, McHugh records a landlord named 'Foster, who used to turn away his head when speaking to a Catholic' (McHugh, 1994, p.429). Hamm's role as receiver of petitions and his own emphasis on his superior English differentiates him from the labourer on whom he cannot stand to look.[21]

Despite Hamm's prosperity within the space of the chronicle, the landscape already shows the effects of the catastrophe: 'the sun was sinking down into the . . . down among the dead' (Beckett, 1991, p.271). The man has left his child 'deep in sleep', and states that the two are the sole survivors in the area from which he has travelled. Hamm is aware that the devastation has swept away the population in other areas. He asks the petitioner, 'What are you insinuating? That the place is still inhabited? No no, not a soul, except himself the child – assuming he existed. Good. I inquired about the situation at Kov, beyond the gulf. Not a sinner. Good. And you expect me to believe you have left your little one back there, all alone, and alive into the bargain? Come now! (*Pause*).' Hamm wants the labourer to hurry up and finish his appeal so that Hamm can 'put up his holly' in time for the Christmas festivities. The man's petition is for food for his child: 'Well to make it short it fatally transpired that what he wanted from me was . . . bread for his brat. Bread? But I have no bread, it doesn't agree with me. Good. Then perhaps a little corn? (*Pause. Normal tone*) That should do it. (*Narrative tone*) Corn, yes, I have corn, it's true, in my granaries.' The three types of food mentioned in Hamm's chronicle – bread, corn and porridge – are among the main foods distributed in Famine relief efforts. Hamm's position as food distributor throughout *Endgame* takes on a new dimension in his chronicle, where he appears to be a seen as a possible source of relief by a starving community. Hamm begins to refuse the man's request based on what he feels to be the permanence of the disaster: 'But what in God's name do you imagine? That the earth will awake in spring? That the rivers and seas will run with fish again? That there's manna in heaven still for imbeciles like you? (*Pause*).' At least part of the reason for Hamm's refusal to aid the petitioners appears to be the hopelessness of the catastrophe.

The lifespan of the child of Hamm's chronicle has been marked by Famine, and it is clear that the child has known nothing else. The impossibility of the child thriving beyond the nourishment of a single meal infuriates Hamm because it merely extends the suffering death a while longer:

> But use your head. I give you some corn, a pound, a pound and a half, you bring it back to your child and you make him – if he's still alive – a nice pot of porridge (NAGG *reacts*), a nice pot and a half of porridge, full of nourishment. Good. The colours come back into his little cheeks – perhaps. And then? (*Pause*) I lost patience. (*Violently*) Use your head, can't you, use your head, you're on earth, there's no cure for that!
>
> (Ibid.)

The manuscript versions of the play identifies Clov as the child of the story,[22] and the chronicle tells of Hamm's consenting to take in the child, although not before trying to tempt the father into forgetting the child, who has known nothing but cold and hunger anyway: 'Well? (*Pause*) Well? Here if you were careful you might die a nice natural death, in peace and comfort. (*Pause*) Well? (*Pause*) In the end he asked would I consent to take in the child as well – if he were still alive. (*Pause*) It was the moment I was waiting for. (*Pause*) Would I consent to take in the child . . .' (ibid., p.271). When Hamm returns to the narrative outside the constraints of his chronicle, it is to return to this point, and the question which haunts the play is whether there is a point to extending suffering through keeping one (barely) alive, or whether it is better to let nature run its course, precisely the conclusion reached by nineteenth-century advocates of laissez-faire economics. Even in his final monologue, Hamm must return to the chronicle: 'It was the moment I was waiting for. (*Pause*). You don't want to abandon him?' (ibid., p.278). This inability to contain the narrative within Hamm's framework underscores the trauma at its core.

Hamm has the power to alleviate suffering, a power he attempts to retain in *Endgame*. He is not in the position of the starving man, yet he returns to the narrative continually, and it is worth considering if this hints at the vexed response of the Anglo-Irish to Irish history. There appears to be no hope that the story will end, and at the prospect of finishing, Hamm looks for a way to continue the story: 'I'll soon have finished with this story. (*Pause*) Unless I bring in other characters. (*Pause*) But where would I find them? (*Pause*) Where would I look for them?' (ibid., p.274). The story lives on not in a continual invention, but in a continual return. It can neither be controlled nor laid to rest.

If Hamm's story is an example of a repressed or coded memory of Famine Ireland, which has been transformed by a creative effort into a 'chronicle', the reverberations of the story's content may be seen throughout the play when Hamm returns to the chronicle outside its frame. The two competing voices in Hamm's head, his guilt and the economic belief in 'the course', appear in this section beyond the boundaries Hamm attempts to construct:

HAMM: All those I might have helped. (*Pause*) Helped! (*Pause*) Saved. (*Pause*) Saved! (*Pause*) The place was crawling with them! (*Pause. Violently*) Use your head, can't you, use your head, you're on earth, there's no cure for that! (*Pause*).

(Ibid.)

Even now, Hamm tries to reason with the dead. His own attempts to aesthetically control the narrative repeatedly fail, along with his reasoning that the condition of being on earth subjects one to certain unavoidable catastrophes for which there are no 'cures'. It is clear that those who request aid are requesting food, again placing Hamm in the position to distribute food, and thus in the centre of the same controversies surrounding Famine relief efforts. In an aside punctuated by violence, Hamm returns to his position as a landlord in possession of an English food source:

HAMM: When it wasn't bread they wanted it was crumpets. (*Pause. Violently*) Out of my sight and back to your petting parties! (*Pause*) All that, all that!

(Ibid.)

These asides defer the ending of Hamm's story, which stands as a contrast to Nagg's joke. Here there is no punch line, no closure, only a history that refuses containment or the sanctuary of creative distance.

In his last monologue, Hamm returns to the events of the story. He is unable to stop himself from slipping into the narrative tone indicated by the stage directions:

(*Pause. Narrative tone*) If he could have his child with him . . . (*Pause*) It was the moment I was waiting for. (*Pause*) You don't want to abandon him? You want him to bloom while you are withering? Be there to solace your last million last moments? (*Pause*) He doesn't realize, all he knows is hunger, and cold, and death to crown it all. But you! You ought to know what the earth is like, nowadays. Oh, I put him before his responsibilities! (*Pause. Normal tone*) Well, there we are, there I am, that's enough.

(Ibid., p.278)

The story, like the memory itself, will never end but must be recalled 'enough' for each day. Questions of whether disasters can be 'helped' or must be considered a function of 'what the earth is like, nowadays' receive no definitive resolution. Even when Hamm announces, 'Moments for nothing, now as always, time was never and time is over, reckoning closed and story ended', this statement is immediately followed by '(*Pause. Narrative tone*) If he could have his child with him . . . (*Pause*)' (ibid.). Despite his repeated return, Hamm achieves no mastery over the events in the chronicle. While Hamm's narrative has been treated in terms of its incompleteness, its reflection of his desire for control, and the insight it offers into the relationship between Hamm and Clov,[23] it also strongly evokes the relationships between landlords and tenants in Famine Ireland and the central political doctrines of laissez-faire economics. The traumatic legacies of both refuse narrative closure.

Samuel Beckett's review of MacGreevy's *Jack B. Yeats: An Appreciation and an Interpretation* appeared in the *Irish Times*, 4 August 1945. In it, Beckett takes issue with MacGreevy's identification of Yeats as a national artist:

> The national aspects of Mr. Yeats' genius have, I think, been overstated, and for motives not always remarkable for their aesthetic purity. To admire painting on other than aesthetic grounds, or a painter, *qua* painter, for any other reason than that he is a good painter, may seem to seem to some uncalled for. And to some also it may seem that Mr. Yeats's importance is to be sought elsewhere than in a sympathetic treatment (how sympathetic?) of the local accident, or the local substance. He is with the great of our time . . . because he brings light, as only the great dare bring light, to the issueless predicament of existence, reduces the dark where there might have been, mathematically at least, a door.
>
> (Beckett, 1945, p.2)

Similarly, one must be careful not to overstate the national aspects of Beckett's own work. Within a week of the appearance of this piece, two atomic bombs had forever altered conceptions of nations, boundaries and decimation. To regard Beckett in a purely Irish context is to ignore the unprecedented world events of his lifetime, and his reaction to them, as well as the fact that Beckett spent most of his life in France. In an address given on 10 June 1946 to Irish listeners on Radio Erin called 'The Capital of the Ruins', Beckett gestured toward the human condition as opposed to the national. He discussed his six months' working at the Irish Red Cross station at Saint-Lô, stating that such an experience granted 'a vision and sense of a time-honored conception of humanity in ruins, and perhaps even an inkling of the terms in which our condition is to be thought again' (Harrington, 1991, p.145). Too often, however, reviews and addresses such as these, which rail against confinement within the national and the local, have prevented the exploration of the Irish in Beckett.

My aim here has not been to restrict Beckett to the 'local accident'. Indeed, the Famine could never be considered one. Beckett's Irishness, as Eoin O'Brien cautions, 'should not be seized upon by the patriotic purveyors of national character and genius for public display' (O'Brien, 1986, p.xix). While Beckett's preoccupation with hunger, disease and a suffering body long past dignity or hope of recovery corresponds to conditions during the Famine, the play ultimately depends on a horror that is not culturally specific. Yet how strange that the greatest catastrophe to befall Ireland in the nineteenth century, accounts of which centred on many of the same horrors that appear in *Endgame*, should not be considered as a possible prototype for the impoverished condition of the modern world as depicted by Beckett. The ways in which the Famine appears through the imagery and rhetoric in *Endgame* suggest that the world of deprivation depicted in these plays, and the terrifying consequences of letting nature 'take its course' in the face of such suffering, have a particular resonance in Irish history and for an Irish audience.

Read as a comment upon a universal human condition, Beckett's *Endgame* presents a horrifying picture, but this horror multiplies with the realization that the play has a literal counterpart in Irish history. The deprivation, paralysis, the inability to mourn or bury the dead, as well as the sense of living in a world that could only be described as 'corpsed', subject to economic doctrines which espoused letting nature take its course regardless of the human cost, describe both *Endgame* and the conditions of Famine Ireland. When the full Irish case is made for Beckett's *Endgame*, his depiction of the relationship between landlord and starving, begging subject, would, especially when played on an Irish stage with Irish actors and for an Irish audience, have rendered a scene far from abstract, universal or absurd.

References

Adorno, Theodor W. 'Reconciliation under duress', in Ronald Taylor (trans. and ed.), *Aesthetics and Politics: Theodor Adorno, Walter Benjamin, Ernst Blobs, Bertold Brecht, George Lukas*. London: Verso, 1980.

Baker, Phil. 'Ghost stories: Beckett and the literature of introjection', *Beckett and the Mythology of Psychoanalysis*. New York: St Martin's Press, 1997.

Beckett, Samuel. 'MacGreevy on Yeats', *Irish Times*, 4 August 1945.

Beckett, Samuel. *Three Novels: Molloy, Malone Dies, The Unnamable*. New York: Grove Press, 1955, 1956, 1958.

Beckett, Samuel. 'A piece of monologue', *Kenyon Review*, (1979), in *Collected Shorter Plays*. London: Grove Press, 1984.

Beckett, Samuel. *Endgame*, in Seamus Deane (ed.), *The Field Day Anthology of Irish Writing*, Vol.3. Derry: Field Day Publications, 1991.

Daly, Mary E. 'The operations of famine relief, 1845–1847', in Cathal Póirtéir (ed.), *The Great Irish Famine*. Dublin: Mercier Press, 1995.

Deane, Seamus. 'Joyce and Beckett', *Irish University Review*, Vol.14, No.1 (1984), pp.57–68.

Doll, Mary A. 'Rites of story: the old man at play', in Katherine H. Burkman (ed.), *Myth and Ritual in the Plays of Samuel Beckett*. Rutherford, NJ: Fairleigh Dickerson University Press; London and Cranbury, NJ: Associated University Presses, 1987.

Dukes, Gerry. *Illustrated Lives: Samuel Beckett*. Harmondsworth: Penguin: 2001.

Freud, Sigmund. 'Obsessive actions and religious practices', in Peter Gay (ed.), *The Freud Reader*. New York: W.W. Norton & Co., 1989.

Freud, Sigmund. 'Repression', in Peter Gay (ed.), *The Freud Reader*. New York: W.W. Norton & Co., 1989.

Gibbons, Luke. 'Have you no homes to go to?: James Joyce and the politics of paralysis', in Derek Attridge and Majorie Howes (eds), S*emi-Colonial Joyce*. New York and Cambridge: Cambridge University Press, 2000.

Girard, Rene. *Violence and the Sacred*, Patrick Gregory (trans.). Baltimore, MA: Johns Hopkins University Press, 1977.

Harrington, John P. *The Irish Beckett*. Syracuse, NY: Syracuse University Press, 1991.

Kenner, Hugh. *A Colder Eye: The Modern Irish Writers*. New York: Knopf, 1983.

Kiberd, Declan. 'Beckett's texts of laughter and forgetting'. *Inventing Ireland*. Cambridge, MA: Harvard University Press, 1995.

Leventhal, A.J. 'Nobel prizewinner', *Irish Times*, 3 November 1969.

Lloyd, David. 'Writing in the shit: Beckett, nationalism, and the postcolonial subject', *Anomalous States: Irish Writing and the Post-Colonial Movement*. Durham, NC: Duke University Press,1993.

MacArthur, William P. 'Medical history of the famine', in R. Dudley Edwards and T. Desmond Williams (eds), *The Great Famine: Studies in Irish History, 1845–1852*. First Published Dublin: Brown & Nolan, 1956. Reprinted Dublin: The Lilliput Press, 1994.

McCormack, W.J. *From Burke to Beckett: Ascendancy, Tradition and Betrayal in Literary History*. Cork: Cork University Press, 1994.

McDonald, Ronan. *Tragedy and Irish Writing: Synge, O'Casey, and Beckett*. New York: Palgrave, 2002.

McHugh, Roger J. 'The famine in Irish oral tradition', in R. Dudley Edwards and T. Desmond Williams (eds), *The Great Famine: Studies in Irish History, 1845–1852*. First Published Dublin: Brown & Nolan, 1956. Reprinted Dublin: Lilliput Press, 1994.

Mays, J.C.C. 'Young Beckett's Irish roots', *Irish University Review*, Vol.14, No.1 (1984), pp.18–33.

Mercier, Vivian. 'Beckett and the search for self', *New Republic*, 19 September 1955.

Mercier, Vivian. 'The uneventful event', *Irish Times*, 18 February 1956.

Mercier, Vivian. *Beckett/Beckett*. Oxford: Oxford University Press, 1977.

Nicholson, Asenath. *Annals of the Famine in Ireland*, Maureen Murphy (ed.). Dublin: Lilliput Press, 1998.

O'Brien, Eoin. *The Beckett Country: Samuel Beckett's Ireland*. Monkstown, Co. Dublin: Black Cat, 1986.

Ó Riordain, Dominic. '"Ag Fanacht le Godot" sa Pheacoig', *Irish Times*, 1 March 1972, p.10.

Pearson, Nels C. '"Outside of here it's death": Co-dependency and the ghosts of decolonization in Beckett's *Endgame*', *English Literary History* (*ELH*), Vol.68, No.1 (Spring 2001), pp.215–39.

Sullivan, A. M. *New Ireland*. Philadelphia, PA: Lippincott, 1878.

PART THREE:

THE STRUGGLE FOR CONTEXT

CHAPTER 10

Frank O'Connor and the Irish Holocaust

Robert C. Evans

Frank O'Connor's published comments on the 'Great Famine' leave little doubt about the intensity of his views. In *The Backward Look*, the history of Irish literature he composed near the end of his life, he wrote that '"Famine" is a useful word when you do not wish to use words like "genocide" or "extermination"' (O'Connor, 1967a, p.133). He argued that Irish literature 'came to a dead halt with the Famine' (ibid., p.140) and contended that 'behind Irish history for the last fifty years of the nineteenth century looms the shadow of the Famine – not the Famine as historians see it but as ordinary people saw it' (ibid., p.141). He blamed the Famine (and the British government, at whose feet he laid much of the blame) for killing off not only millions of Irish people but also much of the Irish spirit, including the musical traditions that had previously exercised such a strong and positive influence on Irish culture. Indeed, in a fiercely worded review of Cecil Woodham-Smith's famous book on the Famine published in 1962, O'Connor even compared the event to the Jewish holocaust recently perpetrated by the Nazis.

In the pages that follow I seek to achieve several objectives. First, I will bring together and examine O'Connor's scattered remarks on the Famine (a task no one has undertaken to date). Second, I will examine O'Connor's own life (especially his poverty-stricken and often hungry youth, as well as the youth of his destitute and orphaned mother) in order to explore why the Famine may have had a particular personal resonance for him. Third, I will briefly survey a number of stories in which hunger, poverty or emigration to America play prominent roles (especially the hauntingly beautiful tale entitled 'The Bridal Night'). Finally, this essay will examine a relatively neglected story by O'Connor – entitled 'Ghosts' – in which the Famine and its enduring consequences are dealt with most movingly and explicitly.

O'Connor on the Famine

O'Connor's most widely available comments on the Famine occur in *The Backward Look: A Survey of Irish Literature*, published in 1967, not long after his death and at the height of his international fame.[1] Chapter 11, 'The Background of Modern Irish Literature', is full of comments on this topic. In addition to making the remarks already quoted, O'Connor also offered a number of others. He contended, for instance, that the Famine was a turning point in the development of Irish culture: 'If Irish literature can be said to have continued after this period, it can have done so only in a very different way' than had previously been the case (O'Connor, 1967a, p.132). He described three successive waves of Irish emigrants to America in the first half of the nineteenth century, arguing that each wave was more desperate than the one before it and that the 'third wave, after the Famine, was practically hopeless – illiterate, drunken, and despairing' (ibid., p.133). O'Connor highly recommends a book written by an American woman evangelist who visited Ireland just before and during the Famine; her account, he says, helps us realize that 'debased, hungry, and ragged as they were, the Irish were still a race of artists' (ibid., p.136) before the full effects of the hunger hit. 'It was not', O'Connor continues, 'that the people were too simple to realize the Dachau-like nightmare of their circumstances', but that even during their direst times they were still hungry for music (ibid.). O'Connor goes on to note that when the historian 'George Petrie . . . tries to tell us what the effect of the Famine really was, he does not speak of the shrunken population, the hundreds of gutted villages, the Famine pits or the emigration boats' (ibid., p.137). Instead, O'Connor points out, what most struck Petrie and others was the stark, unaccustomed, and nearly universal silence that descended on a country formerly brimming with music (ibid.). For O'Connor, then, among the worst effects of the Famine was not only its horrific physical toll but also the fact that it nearly killed the Irish spirit, and with it, Irish culture.[2]

By far the most incendiary of O'Connor's comments on the Famine occur, however, in a long book review first published in 1962 and never since reprinted. Tracking down the review is a difficult task even for dedicated scholars, not only because it now survives mainly in rare microfilmed archives, but also because its original date of publication is misreported in the standard scholarly sources.[3] The review, which discusses Cecil Woodham-Smith's book *The Great Hunger: Ireland 1845–1849*, appeared in the 10 November 1962 edition of the *Irish Times*. James Matthews,

O'Connor's somewhat unsympathetic biographer, has called the piece 'unexplainably harsh and vitriolic'; he suggests that O'Connor 'seemed bent on hearing more stories of the Famine's horrible effects, rather than a historian's balanced explanation of the forces and attitudes that caused it' (Matthews, 1983, pp.350–1). In any case, the review ('Murder Unlimited') offers our most detailed insight into O'Connor's views of the Famine – views he expressed in his full maturity, when his place in Irish and international literature was solidly established and when he had had nearly six decades to reflect upon the matter.

O'Connor begins by immediately comparing the Famine to 'the extermination of the Jews by Hitler's Government'. He likens the writings of one nineteenth-century British official to those of Eichmann and then instantly asks about Woodham-Smith,

> Is it, perhaps, supreme tact on the author's part that she does not mention [Eichmann's] name, and, when the moment comes, drops the nasty word 'genocide' only to dismiss it? It is as though Miss Woodham-Smith were aware of more sinister interpretations than she can admit – interpretations that need not the cool piety of the historian but the maddened poetry of some Biblical prophet.[4]

O'Connor calls the volume 'a book about racialism that leaves the problem of racialism untouched'. He continues: 'For reasons which the author cannot explain, and which, perhaps, no civilised human being could explain, a majority of Englishmen hated the Irish as a majority of Germans hated the Jews, and would not oppose a policy of extermination.' He quotes from comments by English officials that seem to support this view and then asks whether such officials 'were devils or merely madmen'.

According to O'Connor,

> None of the whys and wherefores of the Famine can be rationally explained; it was merely the culminating point in a campaign of frightfulness that had been going on for hundreds of years . . . and would have happened if the potato had never failed. Long before the Famine America was flooded with illiterate, destitute Irish – 'White Niggers' as the Negroes called them.

O'Connor rejects explanations of the Famine that blame the religious differences of the English and Irish, and he argues that when English peasants faced hunger, they were given Irish bread while the Irish themselves were left to die.

Perhaps the most moving paragraph in the whole review is also the most personal, when O'Connor writes as follows:

> For one of my generation this is not an easy book to read. I remember my grandmother's stories of what she saw round Cork Harbour when she was a girl; [the historian] Petrie's description of how Ireland, the most music-loving country in Western Europe, suddenly fell silent almost overnight; an tAhair Peadar's [*sic*] of the kindly young couple he knew, who – separated in Macroom workhouse – heard of the death of their two children and decided to die at home themselves. He describes in a way that has haunted me since I was sixteen how the young couple – the wife dying of typhus – went to weep at the famine pit where their children had been dumped, walked the six miles back to their little cabin, and were found next day by the neighbours, the dead wife's feet inside the dead husband's shirt to warm them until the end.

'You will find nothing like this', O'Connor sarcastically notes, 'in Miss Woodham-Smith's immensely valuable book. She, no doubt, will forgive me if I fail to respond to the views of Sir Charles Eichmann-Trevelyan on the subject.' The review ends with a recommendation that the Arts Council put up a small sum of money to reprint the book of the American evangelist who visited Ireland just before the Famine – a book O'Connor considers more significant than a dry, scholarly study.

The depth of O'Connor's passion in this little-known review is astonishing – not because the subject fails to merit passion, but because O'Connor, during his long career preceding this article, had never before written so vehemently on this topic. None of his stories deals directly with the Famine (perhaps because he tended not to write historical fiction), and indeed his most famous and seminal story ('Guests of the Nation') had presented English characters in such a sympathetic light that he had been scathingly attacked himself for his allegedly lukewarm Irish nationalism (see, for example, Kavanagh, 1947). He detested the kind of hyper-nationalism associated with the government of de Valera; he was ashamed that the Irish had stayed neutral during the Second World War; he earned much of his income from radio work for the British Broadcasting Corporation; he had a dependable publisher and a wide and appreciative readership in Britain during years when many of his works were banned in Ireland; and in general his attitudes toward Britain, from the time of his youth, seem to have been moderate and in fact often favourable.[5] Like most people of his generation he was a fervent patriot, but his patriotism never seems to have spilled over into wholesale contempt for England or the English. His review of Woodham-Smith's book, therefore, seems surprisingly intense in its language and emotions. He places most of the blame for the Famine, it is true, at the feet of English officials, but (in a passage already cited) he does not exempt the English as a whole from responsibility: 'a majority of Englishmen hated the Irish as a majority of Germans hated the Jews, and would not oppose a policy of extermination'. Never before had O'Connor put the matter quite so bluntly or forcefully, and he would never do so again.[6] Although one might have expected such strongly expressed views to have surfaced previously in O'Connor's fiction or essays, the record suggests otherwise. Nevertheless, his reading of Woodham-Smith's book had obviously touched a highly sensitive nerve. Perhaps O'Connor's passionate reaction was rooted, in part, in his own personal familiarity with poverty and hunger.

Personal dimensions

By the early 1960s, when O'Connor issued his review of Woodham-Smith, he was famous not only for having written some of the finest short stories in the English language but also for having penned many highly affecting pieces of autobiography; these essays eventually resulted in two book-length volumes: *An Only Child* and *My Father's Son*.[7] In the former book, O'Connor describes in searing detail his childhood as the son of a saintly, self-sacrificing mother who had herself suffered from extreme poverty in her own youth; O'Connor also details his ambivalent relations with a father whose alcoholism led him to abuse his wife and drink away most of the family income, including the pittance O'Connor's mother earned as a charwoman. Describing the constant cycle of his father's drunken irresponsibility, O'Connor notes that it

> always ended in the same way – only when we were completely destitute; when the shopkeepers refused Mother even a loaf of bread, and the landlord threatened us with eviction, and Father could no longer raise the price of a single pint. At that point only did he give in – 'cave in' better describes what really happened to him. Sour and savage and silent, he began to look for another job.
>
> (O'Connor, *An Only Child*, 1988a, p.37)

O'Connor, then, knew personally what it meant to go hungry, and so it is little wonder that he found tales of the Famine so emotionally compelling. Nevertheless, the parts of *An Only Child* that are most harrowing are not the sections that describe O'Connor's own deprivations but the sections that describe the sufferings of his beloved mother. These sufferings occurred not only at the hands of her drunken husband but especially during her own childhood as an orphan. In one of the most moving passages of the whole book, O'Connor describes how his maternal

> Grandmother took Mother and [her sister] Margaret to the Good Shepherd Orphanage, and when Mother realized that they were being left behind, she rushed after my grandmother, clinging to her skirts and screaming to be taken home. My grandmother's whispered reply is one of the phrases that haunted my childhood – indeed, it haunts me still. 'But, my store, I have no home now.' For me, there has always been in imagination a stage beyond death – a stage where one says 'I have no home now.'
>
> (Ibid., p.44)[8]

The isolation, suffering and literal hunger of his mother touched O'Connor far more deeply than any deprivations of his own; he realized that, compared to her, he had enjoyed a relatively easy life. At one point, for instance, he describes her experiences as an adolescent, working as a household servant in another woman's boarding-home: 'After each meal served to the lodgers, Mrs. Joyce rushed in to gather up the scraps, so that there was nothing left to eat. Hunger was no new thing to any of the orphanage children, but starvation was a new thing to Mother' (ibid., p.55). Little wonder, then, that O'Connor's mother married at the first opportunity, and little wonder, too, that even after years of abuse from her husband, she still felt some deep gratitude to him for rescuing her from a life of utter, devastating poverty. In one of the most resonant moments in *An Only Child* O'Connor describes how, as an adult, he visited his delirious mother as she lay babbling on her sick-bed. Referring to O'Connor's father, she simply muttered, "'God! God! . . . He raised me from the gutter where the world threw me. He raised me from the gutter where the world threw me!'" (ibid., p.39).

Poverty in O'Connor's fiction

Given O'Connor's personal familiarity with poverty and hunger, and given his outrage at the Famine and its consequences for Irish culture, including the mass exodus of Irish to America in the decades preceding and following his own birth, one might have expected these topics to play a much greater role in O'Connor's fiction than is actually the case. Many characters in O'Connor's fiction are poor, but hunger per se is not a major theme. 'Achilles Heel' deals with hunger only lightly and comically (O'Connor, 1982, pp.592–602), while 'The Late Henry Conran' (ibid., pp.13–19) offers a similarly light-hearted treatment of Irish emigration. In his early and little-known story 'The Awakening', a young woman does plan to depart for America, but neither hunger nor poverty is strongly stressed.[9] Emigration is touched on in 'My Da' (O'Connor, 1952, pp.61–71), but poverty is not emphasized as a reason. Likewise, emigration is an issue in the wonderful tale 'Peasants' (O'Connor, 1982, pp.313–20), but in that case expulsion to America is contemplated as punishment for theft rather than as a result of hunger or financial need. Movement between the United States and Ireland is a major theme of 'The American Wife' (O'Connor, 1969, pp.32–45), but neither hunger nor poverty plays a major role. Emigration (or, rather, the return of an emigrant) is a chief concern of the touching tale 'Michael's Wife', but the characters, though not rich by any means, are not especially needy.[10] Financial need is a minor factor in the splendid story 'Lady Brenda', but its lower-middle-class characters face no absolutely pressing need.[11] Hunger *is* a major concern of the affecting story entitled 'Pity', an under-appreciated tale that has rightly been called a 'small gem' by James Matthews (1983, p.298). O'Connor writes, concerning the main character, that 'Denis was always hungry . . . When he was not dreaming of home, he dreamt of food . . . [One] day [he and a friend] were passing the priests' orchard and he suddenly saw that for once there wasn't a soul in sight. At the same moment he felt the hunger-pains sweep over him like a fever' (O'Connor, 1982, pp.221–34, esp. pp.223–4). Even in this story, however, the characters are lower middle class, and the protagonist is never seriously threatened with anything approaching starvation. Neither O'Connor's own experiences with hunger and poverty as a youth, nor the prior experiences of his mother, nor his later vehement feelings about the Famine, nor even his vivid memory of the couple who starved to death during the Great Hunger, seems to have had much impact on the vast majority of his stories.[12]

However, one story in which true poverty and hunger are serious concerns is also one of O'Connor's masterpieces: 'The Bridal Night' (O'Connor, 1982, pp.19–25). Although the story touches on the issue of mass emigration (the narrator, a male visitor to a remote coastal village, notes in passing that 'It is to America all the boys of the locality go when they leave home' [p.19]), the tale's main concern is the unrequited love felt by a poor rural lad named Denis Sullivan for a financially comfortable, friendly schoolteacher named Winnie Regan, who takes up residence in the tiny hamlet where Denis lives with his mother.[13] Denis's infatuation with Winnie is doomed from the start, not only because Winnie, though amiable, seems rather indifferent to men in general, but also because the lonely Denis is poor; as his mother tells the narrator, 'he . . . was maybe without the price of an ounce of 'baccy – I will not deny it: often enough he had to do without it when the hens would not be laying, and often enough stirabout and praties [i.e. porridge and potatoes] was all we had for days. And there was she with money to her name in the bank!' (p.21). Gradually Denis's obsession with Winnie – an obsession obviously fed by his emasculating poverty – drives him mad.[14] When his condition becomes desperate, neighbours help his mother restrain him with ropes in his bed until attendants from a mental asylum can come the next day. When Denis begs his mother to untie the ropes, she does, against the neighbours' advice, and when Denis insists that Winnie be called to his bedside, the mother and neighbours reluctantly ask her to come. To everyone's astonishment, she not only agrees to visit Denis in the middle of the night, thereby calming him, but also agrees to lie with him in his bed, allowing him to sleep peacefully. The story ends with three splendid paragraphs, the first two spoken by Denis's mother, the last added by the unnamed narrator:

> It was a great ease to us. Poor Denis never stirred, and when the police came he went along with them without commotion or handcuffs or anything that would shame him, and all the words he said to me was: 'Mother, tell Winnie I'll be expecting her.'
>
> And isn't it a strange and wonderful thing? From that day to the day she left us there did no one speak a bad word about what she did, and the people couldn't do enough for her. Isn't it a strange thing and the world as wicked as it is, that no one would say the bad word about her?
>
> Darkness had fallen over the Atlantic, blank gray to its farthest reaches.
>
> (O'Connor, 1982, p.25)

The climax of this story, especially the ironic juxtaposition of the gathering darkness of nature and the bright glimmer of compassion and humanity demonstrated both by Winnie and by the villagers, helps make this one of O'Connor's most memorable tales. The few critics who have discussed the story have praised it highly (see Evans and Harp, 1998, p.304), but O'Connor himself unfortunately later turned away from the style of story-telling he had perfected in this early work (see Matthews,

1983, pp.155 and 176). Interestingly enough, in one of the stories in which he most frankly confronted Irish rural poverty and hunger he also achieved one of his greatest successes. One cannot help but wish that he had taken up these topics more often.

'Ghosts'

One story in which O'Connor *does* deal most explicitly with poverty, emigration and even the Famine itself is also one of his very finest works – the posthumously published tale 'Ghosts' (O'Connor, 1982, pp.694–702).[15] This relatively neglected story is one of the best examples of O'Connor's art; it delicately balances – and blends – humour and pathos, and its complex ending packs a strong emotional punch. The story is told by an Irish shop-owner, Tim Clancy; he and his wife Nan, over the years, have employed various servants from a family of Irish peasants, the Sullivans. One day Mary Sullivan, the matriarch of the peasant clan, informs Tim that an American cousin is due to pay the family a visit; Nan instantly volunteers Tim and his car to retrieve the cousin from the rail station. When Tim arrives at the station, however, he discovers not only that the American has brought his wife, son and daughter with him, but that the Americans are immensely wealthy – owners of a firm called Sullivan's Shoes. It emerges that Jer Sullivan, the father, has returned to the land of his ancestors to pay homage, in particular, to two of his grandparents who emigrated during (or following) the Famine. Nan and Tim drive the rich Americans out to the remote and run-down cottage owned by the peasant Sullivans. Nan is obviously embarrassed to have the Americans witness the poverty that abounds in the countryside. Jer, though, seems genuinely pleased by his encounter with the effervescent Mary and her family and genuinely moved by his visit to the ruins of his grandfather's cottage. Nevertheless, on the drive back to town, Nan (despite Tim's unexplained resistance) finds a pretext to ensure that the car will stop at the estate of the wealthy Hopkins family; Nan wants the Americans to realize that not everyone in the vicinity is impoverished. Although the Sullivans quickly befriend Major and Mrs Hopkins and their teenaged daughter, with whom they have much in common, Tim seems increasingly agitated and even angry. When (during the drive back to town) the American Sullivans and Nan lament the poverty of the Irish peasantry, Tim can stand Nan's condescension no longer: he angrily reveals that the Hopkins family are descendants of the very landlords who long ago evicted Jer Sullivan's grandparents from their land. Jer's wife and children seem 'delighted' by the odd coincidence, but Jer himself seems anything but pleased. The story ends by emphasizing Jer's deep discomfort and his worry that he has somehow betrayed his ancestors by letting his money lead so instantly to a friendship with the wealthy descendants of the people who had forced his grandparents to emigrate.

Several passages from 'Ghosts' seem especially relevant to issues of the Famine. In the first such segment, Tim describes the road the group travel on their way to the cottage in Oorawn owned by the impoverished Sullivans:

> On a fine evening the sea road is grand. The sea was like a lake, and the mountains at the other side had a red light on them like plums.
>
> 'Is there only this road from Oorawn to Cove?' he [i.e., Jer Sullivan] asked me.
>
> 'There's only this road from Oorawn to Hell', said I. 'Why?'
>
> 'I was thinking', said he, 'this must be the road my grandfather travelled on his way to America. He used to describe himself sitting on their little tin trunk on the back of an open cart. My grandmother was having her first baby, and she was frightened. He sang for her the whole way to keep her courage up.'
>
> 'There was many a homesick tear shed along this road', I said, because, damn it, the man touched me the way he spoke.
>
> 'Count the ruined cottages, and you'll see your grandfather wasn't alone.' Then the road turned off up the valley and over the moors, a bad place to be on a winter's day.
>
> (O'Connor, 1982, p.697)

O'Connor skillfully frames this vignette with contrasting images of nature. The opening reference to the calm sea implies nature's beauty and even its beneficence, but the closing reference to the 'moors . . . on a winter's day' reminds us that nature (as the potato famine proved) can be harsh, punishing or (at the very least) indifferent to human suffering. The reference to the boggy, weed-filled 'moors' suggests an unforgiving, inhospitable landscape – land reclaimed by nature from any effort to farm it or make it productive or life-sustaining. Such landscapes may have a wild beauty, but they are not fit places for people to live. Meanwhile, the reference to 'Cove' is similarly double-edged. By itself, the word suggests a small inlet from the sea, providing ships with much-desired safety and protection; many of O'Connor's readers, however, would have known that he is here referring to the famous Irish port of Cove (i.e., Cobh), near the city of

Cork, from which numerous poverty-stricken emigrants left their homeland for America. Thus a name apparently associated with peace and
tranquillity was, historically, associated with loss, homelessness, social
disruption and the origins of the Irish diaspora. O'Connor's effective use
of irony and ambiguity continues in Tim's joking reference to 'Hell': on
one level the comment is simply funny, but on a deeper level it not only
reminds us of the hellish fate of many of the people who had to flee the
Famine but also foreshadows the bleak ending of the present tale: Jer, the
American visitor, will be enmeshed in a personal hell of his own when he
later travels back along this same road. And, ironically, it will be Tim (who
at this early moment in the story seems quite appealing and sympathetic)
who will plunge the American visitor into this personal torment.

O'Connor deftly implies everything we need to know about Jer
Sullivan's grandparents: the fact that their trunk was made of 'tin' (a weak,
cheap metal) suggests their poverty; the fact that they ride on an 'open
cart' makes them seem vulnerable and literally exposed; while the fact that
they sit at the 'back' of the cart helps us realize that they did not even own
the vehicle transporting them: literally and symbolically, they were not in
control of their own movement. Nor, presumably, were they the only
passengers being transported. Their humble 'cart' contrasts symbolically
with the comfortable 'car' in which their descendants now ride. O'Connor
enhances the poignancy of the scene by referring to the grandmother's
pregnancy, subtly reminding us that the Famine and its aftermath affected
not only adults but even (or perhaps especially) innocent and helpless
children. At the same time, the reference to the pregnancy may suggest a
sense of new beginnings for a new generation of Irish people who would
grow up in more prosperous conditions in lands far from their ancestral
home. Jer's grandmother is 'frightened', obviously, not just for herself but
for her unborn child, and indeed her implied concern for her offspring
nicely foreshadows an important moment later in the tale. However,
perhaps the most intriguing aspect of this scene, especially in view of
O'Connor's later explicit comments about the Famine, is Jer's description
of how his grandfather sang to the grandmother 'to keep her courage up'.
This detail, touching in itself, seems even more resonant when we recall
O'Connor's preoccupation with the silence, the sudden loss of music, that
descended on Ireland as the Famine tightened its grip. Deliberately or not,
O'Connor in this scene shows us the departure of music (and the spirit
and 'courage' music can inspire) from the Irish countryside. The closing
reference to the 'ruined cottages' is depressing not only because of the

physical collapse of these former homes but because of the ghostly silence the image implies.

Like almost everything else in this story, Tim's suppressed exclamation ('damn it') is effectively double-edged. On the one hand it powerfully implies, in a potently unsentimental fashion, the depths of his own sentiments and empathy; on the other hand, it also suggests his capacity for anger – an anger that will express itself quite memorably by the end of the tale. There as here, Tim's capacity for sympathy will ironically find expression in a seemingly bitter way. For the moment, however, his profanity actually makes us admire him; it implies his own vulnerability and tenderness and his growing fondness for Jer. His reference to the ruined 'cottages' shows O'Connor's facility for choosing just the right word: the term implies smallness, poverty and humility in a way that the word 'homes' (for instance) would not. Meanwhile, Tim's statement that Jer's grandfather 'wasn't alone' implies the immense social dimensions of this otherwise private event: O'Connor goes out of his way to remind us that there 'was *many* a homesick tear shed along this road' (emphasis added). This social dimension helps make 'Ghosts' perhaps the most explicit of O'Connor's fictional treatments of the Famine.[16]

Despite (or perhaps because of) the poverty and suffering of Jer Sullivan's grandparents, O'Connor goes out of his way to emphasize their dignity, nobility and bravery. These are not the 'illiterate, drunken and despairing' emigrants described in *The Backward Look* (O'Connor, 1967a, p.133) or the 'White Niggers' mentioned in the Woodham-Smith review. The Sullivan grandparents are depicted as homeless but noble, and any literal hunger they may have felt is not mentioned. They are hungry, if anything, for the music O'Connor himself so highly valued, and his tone here is not the 'maddened' tone 'of some Biblical prophet' he would call for in his Woodham-Smith review; instead, the tone is poignantly, powerfully elegiac. Certainly it is far more effective than any shrill, unsubtle, propagandistic tone would have been; in his story O'Connor shows himself, paradoxically, a far more skillful rhetorician and propagandist than in his review: readers put off by the tone and substance of the latter would presumably have little objection to the subtle touch employed in 'Ghosts'.

Another of the particularly poignant moments of 'Ghosts' comes when Tim Clancy notices how two of Mary Sullivan's daughters stare in wonder at Rose, their well-dressed and attractive American cousin:

The two younger girls were standing in front of Rose with their fingers in their mouths, looking at her as if she were a shop window.

'That's right', I said. 'Have a good look at your cousin, and stick to the books and maybe ye'd be like her some day.'

'Wisha, how in God's name would they, Mr. Clancy?' said Mary, really upset at last. 'And don't be putting foolish notions into the children's heads . . . Your daughter is a picture, Jer', she said with the tears of delight standing in her eyes, and then she took Rose's two hands and held them. 'You are, treasure,' she said. 'I could be looking at you all day and not get tired.'

(O'Connor, 1982, p.698)

The fact that the girls are 'younger' makes them seem even more innocent and vulnerable, while the fact that they stand 'with their fingers in their mouths' is funny but also touching: it suggests their wonder, naivete, shyness and inarticulateness, and perhaps it even suggests that they are also illiterate. Meanwhile, the fact that they look at Rose 'as if she were a shop window' not only suggests that she is not quite real to them (partly because she is thereby associated with cities and towns) but also implies their poverty, their unfamiliarity with the finer things of life. Tim Clancy's comment that if they 'stick to [their] books' they can become like Rose seems one of his few verbal missteps in the entire story; the remark is unintentionally cruel (unlike his later intentionally biting comments to Jer Sullivan). The peasant Sullivans, undoubtedly, have little access to books, either at home, at school, or at the local library (if one even exists).[17] And, even if books and education were freely available, and even if the Sullivan girls knew how to read, Mary's sharp response suggests that an abundance of books would make little difference in the actual lives her girls are likely to experience. By abruptly calling Tim 'Mr. Clancy', the normally relaxed and friendly Mary implies respect but also a sudden anger, a formality that is also a form of defiance, distance and self-assertion. Her invocation of 'God's name' likewise implies the quick shift to a highly serious tone: moved to protect her children, she suddenly becomes assertive and aggressive. When she indicts Tim for trying to put 'foolish notions' into the heads of her offspring, she implies that the future, for her and for them, will not be much different from the present or the past; in that one phrase she suggests the enduring poverty, the continually limited horizons, of people such as herself and her girls. (Significantly, no husband, father or other mature, responsible male is ever mentioned when O'Connor describes the Irish Sullivans. Presumably Mary's husband has emigrated, died or abandoned her.)

Mary, though, is not self-pitying or maudlin: her own 'tears of delight' as she looks at Rose imply her fundamental lack of jealousy and envy and thus make her seem all the more admirable. (At the same time, the tears may be more complex than the explicit phrasing implies: perhaps they also derive in part from the sorrow and anger she has just been feeling.) The fact that Mary instantly takes 'Rose's two hands' into her own implies her normal and basic affection for other people, especially children; she communicates in a way more intimate than speech, reassuring Rose (by actually touching her) that Rose is not to blame for the tension that has just arisen. Ironically, it is the poverty-stricken Mary who focuses on Rose's physical beauty while it is Tim, the middle-class shop-owner, who has just focused on Rose's wealth. The whole incident implies, once more, the fundamental dignity of Irish peasants: Mary not only stands up for her own girls but immediately seeks to comfort Rose as well. She emerges, perhaps, as the best-mannered character in the entire tale; certainly she is more thoughtful and more fundamentally considerate than either Tim or Nan, who are nominally superior to her in the normal social scale. The Famine and its after-effects have left people like Mary poor in wealth but not in spirit. The whole vignette implies the real and enduring financial poverty of the Irish Sullivans, but it also shows that they are hardly poor in other respects.

The enduring effects of the Famine are stressed even more explicitly in an ensuing scene, when Jer Sullivan finally revisits the now-dilapidated cottage that once belonged to his grandparents:

> The sun was going down when we reached the ruin of the little cabin. It was all overgrown, and a big hawthorn growing on the hearth. Sullivan's face was a study.
>
> 'Grandfather used to say that the first Sullivan to come back should lay a wreath on the grave of the landlord that evicted us', he said in a quiet voice.
>
> 'A wreath, is it?' cried Mary, not understanding his form of fun. 'I know what sort of wreath I'd lay on it.'
>
> 'Now,' he said gently, a little embarrassed by us all, 'I'd like to stay here a few minutes by myself, if you won't think it rude of me.'
>
> 'Don't stay too long,' said his wife. 'It's turned quite chilly.'
>
> We left him behind us, and made our way back over the fields.
>
> (O'Connor, 1982, p.699)

Jer's first epiphany occurs, ironically but appropriately enough, in the midst of gathering darkness. The cabin, already 'little' to begin with, is now a 'ruin', while the fact that it is 'overgrown' reinforces the story's earlier emphasis on nature as innately wild and potentially threatening: the balance between man and nature that defines civilization has here been overturned, and nature has begun reclaiming its own, partly because of human neglect. The literally thorny (and thus symbolically painful and threatening) 'hawthorn' – which can take the form either of a tree or of a bush – has long usurped the very centre (the symbolic 'heart') of the cabin, the 'hearth', which is normally the focal-point of family life, of warmth, togetherness and, sustenance and of human comfort and protection. Jer Sullivan is now in a 'study', a word which the *Oxford English Dictionary* defines as meaning both a 'state of mental perplexity and anxious thought' and a 'state of reverie or abstraction', and when Sullivan finally speaks of his 'Grandfather', the word he chooses (unlike, say, 'granddad') implies respect, formality, humility and obeisance. The 'wreath' Sullivan mentions, unlike the wild 'hawthorn', is a plant shaped for human purposes, but it is also, by its very nature, dead vegetation that symbolizes mortality. His ironic, sardonic reference to the 'wreath' shows a mental sophistication and subtlety of which Mary, his Irish cousin, is incapable, while his reference to 'the landlord that evicted *us*' (emphasis added) implies his deep identification with his ancestors as well as his general capacity for empathy. Yet there is no overt trace of bitterness or anger in his tone, while his sudden desire to be left by himself implies O'Connor's ever-present emphasis on the theme of human loneliness, of each person's fundamental isolation from his fellows.[18] Jer's worry that his desire for isolation may seem 'rude' shows, once more, his fundamental concern for others, whether it be his present companions or his distant ancestors. Meanwhile, his wife's concern that it is growing 'quite chilly' not only reminds us that nature is not always beneficent but also ironically foreshadows the deeper, far more significant psychological chill that will descend on Jer by the end of the story.

That chill falls most heavily after the Clancys and the American Sullivans have left the manor home of the wealthy Hopkins family. Interestingly, O'Connor describes the Hopkinses, who are themselves English or at least of English ancestry, not as the monsters depicted in his review of the Woodham-Smith book but merely as slightly snobbish (Mrs Hopkins) or even as a bit of a buffoon (her husband, 'the major'). Although 'the major's' association with the military might have given O'Connor all the ammunition he needed to score obvious points against British imperialism, he once again works, instead, in more subtle ways: the drunken, selfishly amiable major is an object of the narrator's ridicule; however much damage the major's ancestors may once have visited upon the Sullivan family, their present-day descendant seems merely ridiculous. He has no Nazi-like hate for the Irish; his main concern is his whiskey. It is, ironically, Tim Clancy himself who causes the most pain to Jer Sullivan by suddenly revealing the identity of the Americans' new friends:

> 'That was a delightful end to a remarkable day', he [i.e., Jer] said.
> 'It was', I said. 'Almost as remarkable as the day.'
> 'You probably can't appreciate what it meant to me', he said.
> 'You might be surprised', I said.
> 'All my life', he said, 'I wanted to stand in the spot where the old couple set off on their journey, and now I feel something inside me satisfied.'
> 'And you laid a wreath on the grave of the man who evicted them as well', said I. 'Don't forget that.'
> The funny thing was, it was his wife that knew what I meant.
> 'What's that?' she said, leaning forward to me. 'You mean the Hopkins were the landlords who evicted them?'
> 'They were', said I. 'And cruel bad landlords, too.'
> I knew 'twas wicked of me, but the man had roused something in me. What right had any of them to look down on the Sullivans? They were country people as I was, and it was people like them that had gone crying down every road in Ireland to the sea. But they were delighted, delighted! Mrs. Sullivan and Nan and Bob and Rose, they couldn't get over the coincidence of it. You'd think 'twas an entertainment I put on for their benefit. But Sullivan wasn't delighted, and well I knew he wouldn't be. The rest were nice, but they were outside it. They could go looking for ghosts, but he had ghosts there inside himself and I knew in my heart that till the day he died he would never get over the feeling that his money had put him astray and he had turned his back on them.
>
> (O'Connor, 1982, pp.701–2)

This passage, like the rest of the story, is full of subtle phrasing. Thus, when Tim tells Jer, seemingly casually, that Jer 'might be surprised', his comment is double-edged: Jer *will* be surprised to a degree and with a force he can't anticipate. Meanwhile, Tim's remark is laced with a kind of bitter sarcasm and biting irony that was totally absent in Jer's own earlier gently ironic comment about laying a wreath on the grave of the evicting landlords. Meanwhile, Jer's reference to his grandparents as the 'old couple' is, of course, appropriate in one respect, but in another respect it helps bring the story full circle, since the last time we saw them – as Jer and Tim travelled on the way *toward* Oorawn – they were depicted as a young couple, sad but literally full of life. O'Connor thus subtly implies the inevitable mutability of human existence. And, just as Jer's grandparents once felt an immense sense of loss as they travelled the road on which he now rides, so Jer will shortly experience a similar sense of profound depression. Jer refers, with effective imprecision, to the 'something inside' him that now feels satisfied (alternative phrasing, such as 'soul' or 'spirit', would have seemed too maudlin or pretentious), but that 'something' will soon be disturbed at its core.

Tim's apparently casual admonition about laying the wreath – 'Don't forget that' – is more ominous than it seems: Jer probably never *will* forget what Tim is about to spell out; indeed, he will be scarred by the revelation forever, as Tim clearly realizes. Tim justifies his biting revelation by saying that Jer had 'roused something' in him, thus reminding us, ironically, of the much earlier scene in which Jer's tender comments about his grandparents had roused an answering tenderness in Tim. Here, however, Tim's tone is bitter, and although he justifies it by identifying with the 'country people' he thinks the American Sullivans and Nan have implicitly disparaged, he behaves with sophisticated, cutting sarcasm and irony that seem distant from the obvious gentleness and forbearance we have earlier seen a countrywoman such as Mary Sullivan display. (Mary, it is true, is roused to defend her children, but she does so openly, without Tim's urbanely ironic indirection.) Tim here is fully conscious that he is wounding Jer ('Sullivan wasn't delighted, and well I knew he wouldn't be'); the pain Tim inflicts at this moment, unlike the pain he had earlier caused Mary Sullivan, is deliberate and intentional. Tim confesses that he 'knew in [his] heart' that Jer would be forever scarred and haunted by Tim's comments – a confession that, ironically, makes Tim seem simultaneously cruel and regretful: even as he admits his 'wicked' behaviour, he thereby seems partly to atone for it. Indeed, the ironies of this closing paragraph quickly accumulate: Tim, having disturbed Jer, seems also to have disturbed himself by doing so; Tim, as much as Jer, is likely to be 'haunted' by this chance encounter (as the very existence of the narrative implies); Tim, who accuses Jer of having 'turned his back' on his ancestors, seems in a sense to have turned his back on Jer; and Tim, who indicts Jer for having been put 'astray' by money, is perhaps guilty here of having been put 'astray' himself by envy, jealousy or class resentment. His motives – as the ostensible defender of 'country people' – may not be as pure as he thinks, and it is part of the richness of O'Connor's story that all these potential complications emerge just as the story ends. As readers, we – like Jer and Tim – are left with much to think about: 'ghosts' of all sorts abound in the story's final paragraphs.

Further ironies emerge: incapable really of ever hurting 'the major', whom he despises, Tim can and does hurt the gentle-souled Jer, whom he largely admires. Jer, intending the journey to his ancestral home-place to be a way of paying homage to his grandparents, leaves with the feeling that he has betrayed them: the trip he hoped would bring him satisfaction instead leaves him deeply disturbed. Jer, indeed, may feel even worse than the grandparents who once travelled this same road: they, at least, were young and had a new baby and a new life to look forward to, and they had no reason to feel guilt about their circumstances. Jer, in contrast, is at the very least middle-aged; his future, far from being full of promise, is now likely to be always darkened by his memory of this visit, and he leaves Oorawn with an overwhelming sense of shame and remorse. Jer's grandparents at least had the hope of starting over; Jer will not have that option: he has become, in a sense, an internal exile – a condition that may be worse, in its own way, than being actually forced from one's home. Finally (to add one further irony), although it is Tim who literally gets the last word, and although that word (or phrase) is passed in judgement of Jer, perhaps it is Jer for whom we ultimately feel the most sympathy and concern, and perhaps it is Tim whom we judge most harshly. O'Connor's story leaves us stewing in moral complications – complications of the sort that typify the work of a fine writer and a profound thinker.

The fundamental plot of 'Ghosts' would easily have provided a lesser artist with plenty of opportunities to score propagandistic points and to turn the story into a gussied-up version of a political pamphlet. It is easy to imagine how O'Connor could have written the story in the heated style, the 'maddened poetry' of the 'Biblical prophet', he commended in his review of the book by Woodham-Smith. Instead, he here chooses the wiser, subtler route of the great artist, and what we are left with is not a mere, shrill indictment of the Famine and its effects, but an exceptionally thought-provoking, and moving, meditation on an important chapter in the history of Ireland and the world. The most explicit treatment of the Famine in O'Connor's short fiction is simultaneously the most profound and, for that reason, also the most politically effective.

References

Angley, Patricia, *et al.* 'Ways of reading: Frank O'Connor's "Lady Brenda" and the possibilities of criticism', in Robert C. Evans and Richard Harp (eds), *Frank O'Connor: New Perspectives*. West Cornwall, CT: Locust Hill, 1998.

Barcroft, Stephen. Letter. *Irish Times*, 13 November 1962, p.7.

Bowden, Curtis, *et al.*, 'Selected stories of Frank O'Connor: synopses and quick critiques', in Robert C. Evans and Richard Harp (eds), *Frank O'Connor: New Perspectives*. West Cornwall, CT: Locust Hill, 1998.

Boyd, Andrew. Letter. *Irish Times*, 28 November 1962, p.9.

Dunalley, Beatrix. Letter. *Irish Times*, 22 November 1962, p.9.

Durrer, Kathleen B., *et al.* 'Theories and practice: "Guests of the Nation" and "The Bridal Night" from diverse critical perspectives', in Robert C. Evans and Richard Harp (eds), *Frank O'Connor: New Perspectives*. West Cornwall, CT: Locust Hill, 1998.

Evans, Robert C. (ed.). *Frank O'Connor's 'Ghosts': A Pluralist Approach*. Montgomery, AL: Court Street, 2003.

Evans, Robert C. and Richard Harp (eds). *Frank O'Connor: New Perspectives*. West Cornwall, CT: Locust Hill, 1998.

Kavanagh, Patrick. 'Coloured balloons: a study of Frank O'Connor.' *The Bell*, 3 December 1947, pp.11–21.

Kerr, John. Letter. *Irish Times*, 16 November 1962, p.9.

McKeon, Jim. *Frank O'Connor: A Life*. Edinburgh and London: Mainstream, 1998.

Matthews, James. *Voices: A Life of Frank O'Connor*. New York: Atheneum, 1983.

Mulloy, Charles. Letter. *Irish Times*, 24 November 1962, p.13.

Nisbet, T. Letter. *Irish Times*, 28 November 1962, p.9.

O'Connor, Frank. *Bones of Contention and Other Stories*. [1936] Great Neck, NY: Core Collection Books, 1978.

O'Connor, Frank. [under the pseudonym 'Ben Mayo']. 'Pouring millions down the drain of artificial idleness', *Sunday Independent*, 2 January 1944, p.10.

O'Connor, Frank. *The Stories of Frank O'Connor*. New York: Knopf, 1952.

O'Connor, Frank. *Domestic Relations*. New York: Knopf, 1957.

O'Connor, Frank. 'Murder unlimited', *Irish Times*, 10 November 1962, p.8.

O'Connor, Frank. *The Backward Look: A Survey of Irish Literature*. London: Macmillan, 1967a.

O'Connor, Frank. *A Short History of Irish Literature: A Backward Look*. New York: Putnam, 1967; also New York: Capricorn Books, 1967b.

O'Connor, Frank. *A Set of Variations: Twenty-Seven Stories*. New York: Knopf, 1969.

O'Connor, Frank. *Collected Stories*. New York: Vintage Books, 1982.

O'Connor, Frank. *An Only Child and My Father's Son*. London: Pan, 1988a.

O'Connor, Frank. *Irish Miles*. [1947] London: Hogarth, 1988b.

O'Connor, Frank. *Dutch Interior*. [1940] Belfast: Blackstaff, 1990.

O'Connor, Frank. *A Frank O'Connor Reader*. Michael Steinman (ed.). Syracuse, NY: Syracuse University Press, 1994.

Riordan, Maura. Letter. *Irish Times*, 17 November 1962, p.12.

Sheehy, Maurice (ed.). *Michael/Frank: Studies on Frank O'Connor*. New York: Knopf, 1969.

Woodham-Smith, Cecil. *The Great Hunger: Ireland 1845–1849*. London: Penguin, 1991.

CHAPTER 11

Tom Murphy: famine and dearth

Nicholas Grene

A reader, picking up *The Great Hunger* for the first time in 1942 and reading through the opening lines, might well have misinterpreted the subject of Kavanagh's long poem:

> Clay is the word and clay is the flesh
> Where the potato-gatherers like mechanized scarecrows move
> Along the side-fall of the hill – Maguire and his men.
> If we watch them an hour is there anything we can prove
> Of life as it is broken-backed over the Book
> Of Death?
>
> (Kavanagh, 1996, p.18)

The title, the scene in the potato field, the image of the 'mechanized scarecrows', would all have led such a reader to suppose this was a narrative of the terrible Irish Famine of almost a century before. That misassociation is part of Kavanagh's design for the poem. He invokes memories of the worst disaster in Irish history, the resonance of catastrophe, to enforce his polemical point. These 'mechanized scarecrows' do not suffer from hunger; blight has not affected their potatoes. They are deprived not of food but of life, sex, any sort of fulfilment of the body or the spirit. The poem will claim polemically – stridently at times – that the deprivation experienced by Maguire and his men in Free State rural Monaghan has a right to its fearsome title. This is a metaphorical, not a literal, Great Hunger.

Strangely, though, it may have been this metaphorical application of the idea of famine that first gave the phrase its currency in English. The 'Great Hunger', a literal translation from the Irish *An Gorta Mór*, was apparently not widely used as an appellation for the Famine before Kavanagh. Indeed, when Cecil Woodham-Smith published her best-selling history *The Great Hunger* in 1962, Kavanagh angrily maintained that she had stolen his title (Quinn, 2001, p.179). Whichever came first, the metaphorical or the literal application, the two are arguably linked historically. The tradition of deferring marriage by the male heir, and enforcing celibacy or emigration on other siblings, had its origins in the need to avoid subdivision in landholdings by small farmers ever conscious of the memory of famine (Lyons, 1971, p.39). Maguire's mother in Kavanagh's *The Great Hunger*, who 'praised the man who made a field his bride' (Kavanagh, 1996, p.20), has a century's history of obsession with the land and terror of imprudent reproduction behind her. The metaphoric needs of a Paddy Maguire are in a sense descendants of the physical needs of his ancestors.

For Tom Murphy, writing *Famine* in the 1960s, there was comparable interplay between the historic and the contemporary, the literal and the figurative, the past and the present. In his introduction to the play, Murphy comments on different ways of seeing it:

> There are three broad approaches from which one can look at *Famine* and its genesis. It is historical and, I believe, accurate in the historical facts that it presents to the degree of my ability and my judgement in writing a play of this kind. It is autobiographical, the subject offering me the opportunity to write about myself, my private world and my times. It has, as a play, a life of its own, and tired of history, tired of me, it continues its own process of discovery to its own conclusions, now with me, the author, not in the ascendancy but in pursuit.
>
> (Murphy, *Plays: 1*, p.ix)

Famine is certainly a remarkable effort of the historical imagination, based on extensive reading of most of the major sources on the subject. Though it does not attempt the impossible task of a 'realistic' representation of the set of events in which a million people died of starvation, it does go out to the experience of one imagined family in one village standing in for the country as a whole. In fact, Murphy's task was to find a theatrical idiom that would be appropriate to rendering that experience. But the play is imaginatively connected with other works of the playwright with a contemporary setting, including *A Crucial Week in the Life of a Grocer's Assistant* (Murphy, *Plays: 4*), written just a few years before *Famine*. For his twinned 1980s plays, *Bailegangaire* and *A Thief of a Christmas* (Murphy, *Plays: 2*), Murphy went back to a non-defined period that must be supposed as a folkloric time of memory between his own mid-twentieth century and the Famine of a century before. The fact of famine, the consequences of famine and the idea of deprivation interlink this sequence of Murphy's plays. My aim in what follows is to look at *Famine* itself as the most ambitious treatment of the subject in Irish theatre, to explore its conception, form and dramatic realization. I want then to go on to consider the way the play imagines the Famine in a continuum of Irish history, relating it to other plays both by Murphy himself and by his contemporaries. Finally, I will try to tease out the relationship in Murphy's drama between the literal and the metaphorical, famine and dearth.

Staging the famine

Murphy tells about how he first read the history of the Famine in Woodham-Smith: '*The Great Hunger* was a major event in the publishing world (1962) and I expected it to inspire a half-dozen plays on the subject of the Irish Famine. I'm still surprised that they did not materialise' (Murphy, *Plays: 1*, p.x). Christopher Morash has commented, in fact, on how few Irish dramatizations of the event there have been. As against the outpouring of novels and poems about the Famine from the time of the event itself, it was not until 1886 that the first play appeared, and across the span of the twentieth century only five playwrights took it as their setting. Margaret Kelleher has highlighted the general problem of representation that recurs in so much famine literature: 'can the experience of famine be expressed; is language adequate to a description of famine's horrors?' (Kelleher, 1995, p.232).[1] This problem is all the more acute in the theatre because of the immediacy of representation and the palpable limitations of the medium. These are live actors before us, in a restricted stage space that cannot possibly reproduce the extent of countrywide desolation. It is perhaps suggestive that, in what appears to have been the first draft of the play, Murphy began in discursive form as though starting on a nineteenth-century style novel (Murphy, unpublished papers, TCD, MS 11115 3/2, fols. 85v–90v), before breaking into dialogue.[2]

A prolonged period of historical research had preceded the writing of the play. It was Woodham-Smith's 1962 book that made the first impact on the young dramatist, whose play *A Whistle in the Dark* (Murphy, *Plays: 4*) had given him a major West End success the previous year at the age of just 25. But he diligently read and took detailed notes on a whole series of other historical sources: the major scholarly volume *The Great Famine*, edited by R. Dudley Edwards and T. Desmond Williams from 1956; James Connolly's *Labour in Ireland* (1916); the nineteenth-century histories of John O'Rourke, *The History of the Great Irish Famine of 1847* (1875), and Sir

Charles Gavan Duffy, *Four Years of Irish History, 1845–1849* (1883), as well as Sir Charles Trevelyan's contemporary account, *The Irish Crisis*, originally published in 1848 (Murphy, unpublished papers, TCD MS 11115 3/2). Murphy's initial struggle was to find a means of incorporating this historical information into the play itself. At one point, he considered intercutting, as ironic counterpoint to the dramatic action, spoken excerpts from Trevelyan's *The Irish Crisis*; one notebook was filled with extensive quotations keyed to the scenes in which they were to be used (Murphy, unpublished papers, TCD MS 11115 3/1/1–13). A number of scenarios for the play involved an alternation between scenes in the starving village and vignettes of the public debates elsewhere: Lord John Russell, Prime Minister at the outbreak of the Famine, speaking in the House of Commons, or the disputes between Young Ireland and followers of Daniel O'Connell (Murphy, unpublished papers, TCD MS 11115 3/2 fol. 117v). But in the end Murphy felt he had to narrow the focus down to a single situation and mediate all the history through the voices of the people themselves.

Literary and oral sources were vital to the development of a style for *Famine*. Murphy read no less than three novels of William Carleton – *Valentine McClutchy*, *The Emigrants of Ahadarra* and *The Black Prophet* – in each case noting passages of dialogue and colloquial phrases. One line from *The Black Prophet* that he jotted down evidently struck him as especially significant: 'This world has nothing good or kind in it for me – and now I'll be equal to it' (Murphy, unpublished papers, TCD MS 11115 3/1 fol. 80r.).[3] A version of this line appeared already in a very early scenario for the play (Murphy, unpublished papers, TCD MS 11115 3/2 fol. 118r.) and becomes the crucial concluding statement of Maeve, the one surviving daughter of the Connor family, in the last scene of the play: 'There's nothing of goodness or kindness in this world for anyone, but we'll be equal to it yet' (Murphy, *Plays: 1*, p.89). Even more important were Murphy's researches in the collections of the Irish Folklore Commission.[4] It was there he found the words of the 'Colleen Rua', the fantastical ballad that Liam and Maeve sing exultantly in Scene 4, one of the brief moments of exhilarated happiness in the play (Murphy, *Plays: 1*, p.47). And it was from the same source that he transcribed the words of a traditional keen that was to provide the play's opening. This is how the original text begins:

> Cold and silent is thy bed. Damp is the blessed dew of night; but the sun will bring warmth and heat in the morning, and dry up the dew. But thy heart

cannot feel heat from the morning sun: no more will the print of your footsteps be seen in the morning dew, on the mountains of Ivera, where you have so often hunted the fox and the hare, ever foremost among young men.

(Murphy, unpublished papers, TCD MS 11115 3/2, fol. 75r.)[5]

In Scene 1 of *Famine*, these lines are distributed between two speakers, the mother of the dead Connor daughter and a neighbour, identified only as Dan's Wife, with a chorus of mourners providing antiphonal responses:

DAN'S WIFE. Cold and silent is now her bed.
OTHERS.   Yes.
DAN'S WIFE. Damp is the blessed dew of night,
             But the sun will bring warmth and heat in the
             morning and dry up the dew.
OTHERS.   Yes.
MOTHER.   But her heart will feel no heat from the sun.
OTHERS.   No!
DAN'S WIFE. Nor no more the track of her feet in the dew.
OTHERS.   No!
DAN'S WIFE. Nor the sound of her step in the village of Connor,
    Where she was ever foremost among young women.

(Murphy, *Plays: 1*, pp.5–6)

With the keen for John Connor's dead daughter, Murphy brings us into the community of Glanconor in August 1846. Mourning is still expressed through the ritual forms of the keen, giving a collective voice to grief, a dignity and solidarity to the experience of death. But already at the edges of this scene there is a very different kind of language, the broken exchanges of the men, desperately anxious about the potatoes:

MARK.   (*nervous staccato voice*). But – but – but, ye see, last year the first
         crop failed but the main crop was good, and this year the first
         crop failed, but the main crop will be – will be – will be . . .
DAN.   Hah?
BRIAN.   Oh, you could be right.

(Murphy, *Plays: 1*, p.8)

By the end of the play, Dan will be left alone to repeat the keen over his dead wife Cáit, who had led the original lament, without the support of other mourners. And overlaying Dan's intoned words are the last violent confrontations between Mother and her daughter Maeve, Mother and her husband John Connor, the final breakdown of the family. Murphy's play dramatizes, enacts, what the economic historian Cormac Ó Gráda sums up as the general effect of large-scale famines on the poor: 'kinship and neighbourhood ties eventually loosen or dissolve, theft becomes endemic, collective resistance yields to apathy, and group integrity is shattered' (Ó Gráda, 1999, p.46).

Murphy had originally planned to make Malachy O'Leary the central character in tracing this collapse of communal values, the young man who returns from England to find both his parents dead from starvation and is driven to violence by despair. But he chose instead to focus on the figure of John Connor, as the unelected leader of the village. Connor, baffled and beaten down by suffering, places his faith in a dogged, unwavering adherence to the laws of God and man. When the assembled villagers demand 'What are we going to do?', his answer comes as if an inspiration:

JOHN.   What's right!
         The statement seems to surprise himself as much as it does the others.
         . . . What's right. And maybe, that way, we'll make no mistakes.
                                               (Murphy, *Plays: 1*, p.22)

Throughout the action John acts on this self-validating principle of righteous action, restraining violence, stopping the men from attacking the convoy of corn-carts leaving the village, insisting on providing hospitality even when his own family is starving. And it gets him nowhere. Mother is the articulate voice of the contrary point of view: 'What's right? What's right in a country when the land goes sour? Where is a woman with children when nature lets her down?' (Murphy, *Plays: 1*, p.32). The play's drama consists in the clash between her desperate pragmatics and his monolithic, blind idealism.

Vivian Mercier has written on the resonance of the Book of Job for Murphy's work, but John Connor is a Job whom God has forgotten. In the face of his afflictions, John affirms his belief:

Welcome be the holy will of God. No matter what He sends 'tis our duty to submit. And blessed be His name, even for this, and for anything else that's to come. He'll grace us to withstand it.

                                               (Murphy, *Plays: 1*, p.16)

But he is not given that grace. Instead the violence that he has barely restrained in others and repressed in himself is used as his 'sacred strength' in the terrible act of killing his own wife and young son. For this Job there will be no second set of wives, camels and maidservants to replace the first. By any normal standard of judgement, Mother is right and John is wrong throughout the play, but his deluded mistakenness has an element of the heroic in it. It is this that makes him a convincingly tragic figure. He is an Oedipus or a Lear, central to his community yet distinct from it in the individuality of his conviction, a conviction that we in the audience know to be disastrously misplaced yet have to respect for its massive integrity.

Famine, however, is no *Oedipus Rex* or *King Lear*, Murphy gives his play none of the grand afflatus of tragedy. Even though John Connor may be considered a descendant of Ireland's high kings, he is a bewildered, reluctant leader, inarticulate in his anguished struggle to deal with the situation. The distanced alienation in the play's style has frequently been attributed to the influence of Brecht. Murphy had seen a number of Brecht plays in London in the 1960s, including *Baal* and *Mother Courage*, and he admits that at this stage of his career he was 'impressionable and impressed' by the theatre he saw at the time. Certainly the play has been produced in Brechtian mode from its premiere in the Peacock in Tomás Mac Anna's production in the round, to its most recent major revival, directed by Garry Hynes at the Abbey. This last production divided the critics evenly. Emer O'Kelly, the *Sunday Independent* reviewer, objected to the 'cloak of Brechtian alienation', complaining that 'there is no inclination to weep for the one-dimensional black shadows Hynes gives us on the Abbey stage' (O'Kelly, 1993). Lorcan Roche, if a little doubtful, was more positive about the hallmark Brechtian signboards: 'Hynes' use of projected-on, introductory headings to each scene will undoubtedly be questioned – but they crystallised things, even if they were initially intrusive' (Roche, 1993). But it was Fintan O'Toole, here as so often Murphy's most persuasive interpreter, who responded most appreciatively to the political implications of the play in this version:

[John Connor] is, from the start, incapable of grasping, much less altering, what is happening to his society. To take action, he would need to be able to get his bearings, but this world of famine is a world without reference points. Culture, all the accumulated associations by which people understand themselves, has been wiped away by hunger. By showing us its absence, Murphy shows us its importance.

(O'Toole, 1993)

This is to read John Connor as Mother Courage, Mother Courage as Brecht himself saw her, an object lesson in failed understanding. Scene 5, 'The Relief Committee', certainly does give a powerful representation of the political forces at work in the Famine: the landlords keen to offer assisted emigration as a means of clearing the land for more profitable purposes, the silently collusive merchant who has been benefiting from high grain prices, the parish priest, seeing the ulterior purposes of the others, but powerless to stop them or help the suffering people. This is the one scene in the play that takes place outside the village community itself, putting before the audience what John Connor and the villagers so signally fail to comprehend. Yet the play is hardly as politically tendentious, nor its vision as alienated, as O'Toole makes it appear. The experience of *Famine* is the experience of the people themselves; it is expressed in their own language and we are drawn in to their suffering. Its terrible climax, with the killing of Mother and Donaill by John Connor, is some sort of dreadful act of defiance, an affirmation of the only freedom left to them, as Mother herself says in urging her husband on to the murder:

> They gave me nothing but dependence: I've shed that lie. And in this moment of freedom you will look after my right and your children's right, *as you promised*, lest they choose the time and have the victory.
>
> (Murphy, *Plays: 1*, p.88, original emphasis)

To choose the time and manner of one's death is no more than a profoundly tragic consolation. Yet it represents the urge within the play to render the inalienable human dignity of the people, not to allow them to appear merely the unknowing victims of a historical calamity beyond all human scale or imagining.

Looking before and after

As a young boy, Murphy was taken by his mother to a performance by a local amateur group in Tuam of Gerard Healy's Famine play *The Black Stranger*. It made a big impression on him. Although he deliberately avoided reading the play as an adult, fearing it might interfere with his own imaginative project, some features of Healy's work may have stayed with him when writing *Famine*. The choric figure of Sean the Fool, for example, who announces the 'black stranger on the roads' whose 'first name is Hunger' (Healy, 1950, p.24), has some sort of equivalent in Murphy's grotesque truth-teller, the hunchback Mickeleen. The contrasts between the two plays, however, are more striking than the similarities. *The Black Stranger*, first performed in 1945, the centenary of the start of the Famine, is trapped within the traditional mode of the well-made Abbey play: the realistically rendered family cottage, crossed love affairs, standard naturalistic dialogue, all worlds away from Murphy's radically innovative theatrical style. What is more significant is the legacy of the Famine as the two playwrights render it. The hero of *The Black Stranger* is Michael Corcoran, political militant and trade union activist before his time, who is driven by the extremity of famine to a suicidal one-man attack upon the British soldiers: 'I've strength in me yet – strength enough to send a few of the red-coats ahead of me before I go' (Healy, 1950, p.39). Bridie, who was in love with Michael, at the end of the play will marry his less radical brother Bart: 'He has Michael's blood in him an' a son be Bart could be taught to take the place of the son that Michael'll never have' (ibid., p.52). The political implications are clear. The descendants of the victims of Famine will be the freedom fighters who are to liberate Ireland from its colonial yoke.

Malachy O'Leary is Murphy's version of Michael Corcoran, the figure who rejects John Connor's doctrine of passive resistance. There is an early notebook sketch of Malachy, when he was still envisaged as the play's central character: '28, tall, well-built, a good deal of cunning, a survivor, lucky, violent' (TCD MS 11115 3/2, fol. 106v.). We see these characteristics in the play as the wordless violence of his reaction to famine is turned into action: he lures two policemen to a quarry, kills them, and takes their gun, with which he then kills the JP supervising the relief works. At the end of the play, he has disappeared. Liam remarks, 'Some say Malachy is dead . . . I don't know. Some say he's in America, a gang to him. Whichever, this country will never see him again.' To which Maeve replies darkly, 'It'll see his likes' (Murphy, *Plays: 1*, p.89). Murphy supplies a gloss on this open ending to Malachy's story as the

> violent *consequence* of famine . . . I saw Malachy as a foretaste of the atrocities that were to follow in the Land Wars; I saw him, also, as a precursor in a direct line that led to Michael Collins, the great, decisive, guerrilla leader who came seventy-or-so years later.
>
> (Ibid., p.xvii, original emphasis)

But in this vision of the militant there is none of Healy's unqualified political celebration. Malachy may just as well have ended up as one of the Irish gangsters who warred on the New York streets in the 1850s, a

lawless violence ethically undifferentiated from the guerrilla action of a
Michael Collins.

Murphy's treatment of Malachy O'Leary is closer to his counterparts in
Brian Friel's *Translations* (Friel, 1984), the never-seen Donnelly twins. In the
encounters between the 1830s Irish-speaking community of Baile Beag and
the British soldiers making the Ordnance Survey map, the Donnelly twins
are always somewhere offstage as the threat of violence. Just as Malachy in
Famine kills the well-intentioned JP, so in Friel it is the innocent Hibernophile
Yolland who is missing, presumed killed by the Donnellys for his cross-
community relationship with Maire. *Translations*, as the inaugural production
of the Field Day Theatre Company in 1980, placed the Donnelly twins as
the forerunners of the Republican paramilitaries, the figures of violence who
fill the vacuum when efforts at political understanding break down. And even
if Murphy, by his own 1992 account, had not planned to expound the
message 'that the result of a shameful present is a violent future . . . the play
keeps coming up with it. (Even – though undesignedly – anticipating the
outbreak of hostilities in Northern Ireland)' (Murphy, *Plays: 1*, p.xvii).

Friel and Murphy are at one in regarding troubled twentieth-century
Irish politics as the outcome of the disasters of nineteenth-century history.
But they see the pre-Famine period differently. Though *Translations* is set a
decade before the Famine, it is repeatedly trailed as the catastrophe
waiting to happen, with talk of the 'sweet smell' that is the first sign of
blight. Maire's spirited defiance of such anxieties – 'did the potatoes ever
fail in Baile Beag? Well, did they ever – ever? Never!' (Friel, 1984, p.395)
– we know will be overtaken by events. Friel links the coming Famine in
the play to the Anglicization of the Ordnance Survey map-making and
the institution of the National Schools as the factors that destroyed the
Irish language and the pre-colonial society it expressed. In his comparison
of *Translations* and *Famine*, Fintan O'Toole points out that Friel's play
'depends on a notion of history as a fall from a golden age, a time when
people spoke Irish and were happier' (O'Toole, 1987, p.91). By contrast,
Murphy's view of pre-Famine Ireland is anything but Edenic.

In Scene 1, already, we get glimpses of earlier famines, like in Dan's
grotesque reminiscence: 'Well, I remember in '17 – and the comical-est
thing – I seen the youngsters and the hair falling out of their heads and
then starting growing on their faces.' This starts off a competition in
horror stories, with each of the men trying to outshout the others in their
testimony to the bad years of the past: 1822, 1836, 1840, 1841. Once
again it is Dan who tops all his competitors in ghastly memory:

In '22 – In '22 – In '22! I counted eleven dead by the roadside and my own father one of them. Near the water, Clogher bridge, and the rats. I'm afeard of them since.

(Murphy, *Plays: 1*, p.13)

It is Dan, the oldest character in the play, who provides a long-term retrospective on the course of Irish history before the Famine in his rambling speech through the penultimate Scene 11:

What year was I born in? 1782 they tell me, boys. There's changes since, Brian? There is, a mac. And Henry Grattan and Henry The Other and prosperity for every damned one. Hah? Yis – Whatever that is. (*Laughs.*)

(Murphy, *Plays: 1*, p.84)

The Volunteer Parliament, in which the leading figures were Henry Grattan and Henry Flood, meant little liberation for the likes of Dan. It is the same with the later landmark events of his time: the 1798 Rebellion – 'we had the sport, 1798 yis, out all hours under the bushes' (Murphy, *Plays: 1*, p.84) – or Catholic Emancipation in 1829.

Emancy-mancy – what's that, Nancy? – Freedom, boys! Twenty-nine was the year and it didn't take us long putting up the new church. The bonfires lit, and cheering with his reverence. Father Daly, yis. And I gave Delia Hogan the beck behind his back. I had the drop in and the urge on me.

(Murphy, *Plays:* 1, p.88)

The official narrative of Irish history with its epoch-making dates is transformed into a series of carnival occasions for drink and illicit sex.

Murphy's play encourages few illusions about the situation of the people before the Famine, demystifying any view of Irish history as a long march towards freedom. When writing the play, rather, Murphy came to feel that the depressed condition of his own time in mid-twentieth-century Ireland was a product of the events of the previous century. In an interview with Michael Billington during the Abbey Theatre season of his plays in 2001, Murphy reflected on 'the culture that I grew up in, how repressed, how harsh I thought Irish womanhood was'.

How the natural extravagance of youth, young manhood, young womanhood was repressed, while the people preaching messages of meekness, obedience, self-control I observed had mouths that were bitter and twisted. And I began to feel that perhaps the idea of food, the absence of food, is only one element of famine: that all of those other poverties attend famine, that people become

silent and secretive, intelligence becomes cunning. I felt that the hangover of
the 19th century famine was still there in my time; I felt that the Irish mentality
had become twisted.

(Murphy, 2002, p.101)

Repressiveness, enforced conformism, secrecy – these are the inherited
characteristics of the community Murphy portrayed in *A Crucial Week in the
Life of a Grocer's Assistant* (*Plays: 4*).

A Crucial Week, known at one point as *The Fooleen*, was Murphy's second
full-length play, written immediately after *A Whistle in the Dark*, although it
had to wait until 1969 for its première at the Abbey. *Whistle* dramatized
the ethos of socially deprived Irish emigrants in Britain with their
compensatory heroics of male violence. *A Crucial Week* dealt with those left
behind in Ireland, those who had too little gumption to make it to Britain
or America. The play is a small-town version of Kavanagh's *The Great
Hunger* with the grocer's assistant of the title, John Joe Moran, a younger
counterpart of Paddy Maguire, cowed into celibate submission by his
mother and Mother Church. Aged 33, John Joe still lives at home,
financially and emotionally dependent, incapable of consummating his
rather tepid love affair with the middle-class girl who works in the bank.
He has fantasy dreams of escape or of sexual fulfilment; he has nightmares
of his employer and the priest coming to operate on him to remove his
soul. But each time, he wakes up to the reality of his mother in his
bedroom rousing him to go to his hated job.

Mother in *A Crucial Week* is the latter-day equivalent of Mother in
Famine. Murphy's stage description of her makes this all but explicit. She
is 'harsh in expression and bitter; a product of Irish history – poverty and
ignorance; but something great about her – one could say "heroic" if it
were the nineteenth century we were dealing with' (Murphy, *Plays: 4*,
p.94). The Mother of *Famine* is heroic in her determination to save her
family at all costs, even though that means stealing a neighbour's turf to
exchange for meal. The Mother of *A Crucial Week* makes ends meet by
taking in washing and ironing, and informs on her own brother in an
effort to secure the inheritance of a small shop for her beloved son. Father
is no tragic John Connor but an almost catatonically inert unemployed
gravedigger. The profession is no doubt significant. The town itself was
luridly characterized as a cemetery by one of its more disenchanted
inhabitants: "'This town", he said, "is like a graveyard with walking pus-
eaten corpses, and fat maggots jumping from one corpse to the next,
looking for newses'" (Murphy, *Plays: 4*, p.131). It is the priest Father Daly

who reports this ghoulish simile – laughingly remembering it, to assuage the mutinous John Joe – as the youthful outburst of one of his parishioners, who has now settled down into contented family life. The priest of *Famine*, also Father Daly, is a genuinely intelligent and compassionate man, desperately conscious of his impotence in the face of hunger and political manipulation. The Father Daly of post-colonial Ireland in *A Crucial Week* is himself the manipulator, the complacent controller of his people.

Ó Gráda described the effects of famine in a passage quoted earlier: 'kinship and neighbourhood ties eventually loosen or dissolve ... collective resistance yields to apathy, and group integrity is shattered' (Ó Gráda, 1999, p.46). For Murphy, these consequences are still being felt in 1950s Ireland; the small-town denizens of *A Crucial Week* are the overdetermined creatures of their history. Economic enforced emigration in *Famine* was the means used by the landlords to clear the land; John Connor's resolution to resist and stay in Glanconor was seen as a dogged, if ultimately hopeless, commitment to home and homeland. The disheartened survivor world of *A Crucial Week* presents a diminished version of this choice of evils. As John Joe exclaims in the climactic Scene 11,

> It isn't a case of staying or going. Forced to stay or forced to go. Never the freedom to decide and make the choice for ourselves. And then we're half-men here, or half-men away, and how can we hope ever to do anything.
>
> (Murphy, *Plays 4*, p.162)

In this scene, John Joe publishes at the top of his voice all the secrets of the town in a one-man doomsday revelation, all the hidden scandals and meannesses that everyone knows and no one will acknowledge, including the fact that his own brother who did emigrate has been to prison. John Joe here speaks for the play itself, for the need to tell it like it is, and so perhaps redeem this lifeless life from the grip of its inherited history. He is a tragicomic counterpart to the fully tragic John Connor, whose murder of his wife and child is his only means to defy the historical events that he can neither understand nor resist.

Famine and dearth

The word 'dearth' has an interesting semantic history. Formed as an abstract noun from the adjective 'dear', on the model of 'warmth', 'health', 'wealth', it started by signifying 'dearness, costliness, high price' (*OED* 2). Its primary meaning then shifted to indicate what generates such costliness, 'a condition in which food is scarce and dear . . . a time of scarcity with its accompanying privations, a famine' (*OED 3*). From there it was transferred to a more figurative general meaning: 'scarcity of anything, material or immaterial' (*OED 4*). Murphy's plays considered here traverse these senses of dearth from the physical to the metaphorical. The townspeople of *A Crucial Week* are more poor-spirited than actually poor; they are driven as much by fear of social disgrace as by the lack of resources. The characters in *Bailegangaire* (Murphy, *Plays: 2*), set in 1984, the year of its composition, are positively affluent by the standards of the past. Dolly receives a regular £85 a week from her husband working in England and hardly knows what to do with it. She arrives on a motorcycle, crash-helmet in hand, and describes her well-to-do lifestyle: 'I've rubber-backed lino in all the bedrooms now, the Honda is going like a bomb and the *lounge*, my dear, is carpeted' (Murphy, *Plays: 2*, p.107). Her sister Mary is one of the emigrant success stories, having made a career as a nurse and risen to 'Assistant Matron at the age of thirty' (ibid., p.148). Yet the lives of both the sisters are grimly unhappy. Dolly, a grass-widow for most of the year, is visited only at Christmas by her husband, who brutalizes her for her casual promiscuity. At the time of the play's action, she is pregnant and desperate to dispose of the baby, the visible proof of her infidelity. Mary has returned from England, lost and directionless, seeking in the care of her senile grandmother some home of attachment, but Mommo refuses to recognize her, and treats her like a paid servant.

It is a dysfunctional family that is represented in *Bailegangaire* and its dysfunction has its roots back in the past time narrated in Mommo's unending story. This story, 'of Bailegangaire and how it came by its appellation' (the play's subtitle), is dramatized in the companion play *A Thief of a Christmas*. *A Thief*, produced by the Abbey Theatre in 1985, the same year that Druid Theatre Company produced *Bailegangaire* in Galway, is set 'about 50 years ago' (Murphy, *Plays: 2*, p.171); the age gaps of the characters in *Bailegangaire*, on the other hand, would imply a date for Mommo's story of the 1950s. In fact, no fixed date can be assigned to this tale of a laughing competition: this is a folklorized back-projection into an archaic past. The milieu is sketched in by Murphy in the opening stage direction of *A Thief* – 'we are dealing with a neglected, forgotten peasantry' (Murphy, *Plays: 2*, p.175) – and elaborated in his description of the people who have crowded into the pub by Act 2 to watch the laughing contest:

Those who have arrived in the last two hours are shaped and formed by poverty and hardship. Rags of clothing, deformities. But they are individual in themselves. If there is a beautiful young woman present she, too, looks freakish because of her beauty. The sounds of sheep, goats, sea-birds can be heard in their speech and laughter.

(Ibid., p.215)

The miseries of the semi-modernized Ireland of the 1980s, of a Mary or a Dolly, have their origins in these antecedents two or more generations back, 'shaped and formed by poverty and hardship'.

The scene of *A Thief* is the village of Bochtán (= 'the poor man'), and the time is Christmas. But a very bad market in the neighbouring town of Tuam (Murphy's own home town) means that it will not be the festive occasion the villagers in the pub were anticipating but 'a thief of a Christmas' instead. It is when the Stranger and the Stranger's Wife, Mommo of *Bailegangaire*, find themselves there, stranded on their way home because of the frost, that the substitute entertainment of the laughing competition is devised. The Stranger, on a whim, challenges the large local man with the infectious laugh: 'I'm a better laugher than your Costello' (Murphy, *Plays: 2*, p.201). What follows is a contest fuelled by local partisanship and heavy betting on both sides that is continued literally to the death, as Costello collapses at the end, and the Stranger (as we learn from *Bailegangaire*) dies shortly afterwards of injuries sustained in the following melée. To make this bizarre story the more grotesque, the subject proposed by the Stranger's Wife/Mommo to stimulate the laughers' laughter is 'misfortunes'.

There have been plenty of misfortunes in Mommo's own life: her dead marriage – 'forty years an' more in the one bed together an' he to rise in the mornin' (and) not to give her a glance' (Murphy, *Plays: 2*, p.140) – the children she has lost to death or driven to emigration by her ferocious rapacity in the home. It is the memory of all this that drives her on aggressively to force her husband to compete in the laughing contest, to propose that they laugh at misfortunes. But it is a collective accumulation of communal disasters that pours out when they get going, beginning with 'potatoes, the damnedable crop was in it that year'.

'Wet an' wat'rey?', says the stranger.
'Wet an' wat'rey', laughing Costello.
'Heh heh heh, but not blighted?'
'No ho ho, ho ho ho, but scabby an' small.'

(Murphy, *Plays: 2*, p.163)

'*Not* blighted': it is not memories of the Famine we are dealing with here, but of the routine rural afflictions, the oats 'lodged in the field', the turf 'still in the bog', the chickens 'the pip', the sheep 'the staggers, an' the cow that just died, an' the man that was in it lost both arms to the thresher' (Murphy, *Plays: 2*, p.140).

The laughing competition is like one of the wake games that accompanied the traditional mourning vigil. In the opening scene of *Famine* we see 'Preparations begin for the festive side of the wake. Talk grows louder, people laugh, smoke, eat and drink. Off, behind house, the FIDDLER is playing a tune and the dancing has begun' (Murphy, *Plays: 1*, p.16). One interpretation of this carnival practice represents it as the affirmation of life in the face of death, 'a kind of defiant gesture by those who took part, to show that, unlike the corpse, which lay dead in their presence, they were still "alive and kicking"' (Ó Súilleabháin, 1997, p.167). But the laughing contest is a wake-game with a difference, something closer to a *danse macabre*:

> The stories kept on comin' an' the volleys and cheers. All of them present, their heads thrown back abandoned in festivities of guffaws: the wretched and neglected, dilapidated an' forlorn, the forgotten an' tormented, the lonely an' despairing, ragged an' dirty, impoverished, hungry, emaciated and unhealthy, eyes big as saucers, ridiculin' an' defying of their lot on earth below – glintin' their defiance – their defiance an' rejection, inviting of what else might come or *care* to come! – driving bellows of refusal at the sky through the roof.
> (Murphy, *Plays: 2*, pp.164–5)

This black exultation, however, this mockery of misery, does not exorcise the horrors it evokes. Rather it becomes its own trauma. The village where it happens is cursed with its new name, Bailegangaire, 'the town without laughter'. The laughing contest not only results in the deaths of the contestants, but also the tragic sequel that we only learn about in *Bailegangaire*, the accidental death of Mommo's small grandson Tom, left with his two sisters alone in the house while his grandparents were waylaid in the pub. The two surviving sisters are Mary and Dolly. Their lives, Mommo's pathological incapacity to tell out her story to its end, are the unresolved consequences of the actions of long ago. In *Bailegangaire* Murphy figures Ireland's past history as a memory of dearth that lives on and constitutes its own sort of deformation in the present. Only the completion of the story, the reconciliation of Mary with Dolly, Mommo with Mary, offers the possibility of healing closure.

Bailegangaire uses the device of the endlessly deferred conclusion to the story, Mommo's 'unfinished story', as a metaphor for the unending narrative of Irish history. As in *A Crucial Week*, as in *Famine*, Murphy feels the need to tell out that story to some sort of point of comprehension. He does not treat the Famine simply as one historical catastrophe; he places it within the context of generations of poverty and deprivation stretching before and after. Even when material poverty is alleviated, the psychological and emotional disabilities remain. He speaks of the autobiographical aspects of *Famine*, the opportunity it afforded 'to write about myself, my private world and my times'. To represent the conditions of the Famine that were beyond representation required the playwright to work back from the darkest parts of his own experience and his own imagination. He did not live through famine, but he had felt the dearth in Irish society intuited as the legacy of famine. *A Crucial Week*, *A Thief*, *Bailegangaire* and many more of his plays are created out of that sense of the gaps, the absences, the communal dysfunction of post-Famine Ireland. But as he stresses also in that passage quoted at the start of this essay, a play has 'a life of its own' and 'continues its own process of discovery'. *Famine* so lives on, not just as a powerful and moving dramatization of its terrible subject, but as a vital part of the collective act of Irish self-representation.

References

All information about *Famine* in this essay for which no other source is given is taken from a personal interview with Tom Murphy, 23 August 2004. I am most grateful to Mr Murphy for his generous help in answering my questions.

Carleton, William. *The Black Prophet*. [1847] New York and London: Garland, 1979.

Carleton, William. *The Emigrants of Ahadarra: a Tale of Irish Life*. London: Simms & McIntyre, Belfast, 1848.

Carleton, William. *Valentine McClutchy, The Irish Agent*. London: Henry Lea, [ca. 1850].

Connolly, James. *Labour in Ireland* [1916]. Dublin: The Sign of The Three Candles, 1949.

Duffy, Sir Charles Gavan. *Four Years of Irish History, 1845–1849*. London and New York: Cassell, Petter, Galpin [1883].

Edwards, R. Dudley and T. Desmond Williams. *The Great Famine: Studies in Irish History 1845–52*. Dublin: Published for the Irish Committee of Historical Sciences by Browne & Nolan, 1956.

Friel, Brian. *Selected Plays*. London: Faber, 1984.

Healy, Gerard. *The Black Stranger*. Dublin: James Duffy, 1950.

Kavanagh, Patrick. *Selected Poems*. Antoinette Quinn (ed.). Harmondsworth: Penguin, 1996.

Kelleher, Margaret. 'Irish famine in literature', in Cathal Poírtéir (ed.), *The Great Irish Famine*. Cork and Dublin: Mercier Press, 1995.

Lyons, F.S.L. *Ireland since the Famine*. London: Weidenfeld & Nicolson, 1971.

Mercier, Vivian. 'Noisy desperation: Murphy and the Book of Job', *Irish University Review*, Vol.17, No.1 (1987), pp.18–23.

Morash, Christopher. 'Sinking down into the dark: the Famine on stage', *Bullán*, Vol.3, No.1 (1997), pp.75–86.

Murphy, Tom. *Plays: 1*. London: Methuen, 1992.

Murphy, Tom. *Plays: 2*. London: Methuen, 1993.

Murphy, Tom. *Plays: 4*. London: Methuen, 1997.

Murphy, Tom. 'In conversation with Michael Billington', in Nicholas Grene (ed.), *Talking about Tom Murphy*. Dublin: Carysfort, 2002.

Murphy, Tom. Unpublished papers in the Library of Trinity College, Dublin. TCD MS 11115.

Ó Gráda, Cormac. *Black '47 and Beyond: the Great Irish Famine in History, Economy and Memory*. Princeton, NJ: Princeton University Press, 1999.

O'Kelly, Emer. 'Abbey: *Famine*', *Sunday Independent*, 10 October 1993.

O'Rourke, John. *The History of the Great Irish Famine of 1847: with Notices of Earlier Irish Famines*. Dublin: n.p., 1875.

Ó Súilleabháin, Seán. *Irish Wake Amusements*. Cork and Dublin: Mercier Press, 1997.

O'Toole, Fintan. *The Politics of Magic: the Work and Times of Tom Murphy*. Dublin: Raven Arts, 1987.

O'Toole, Fintan. 'Second opinion: down to zero', *Irish Times*, 9 October 1993.

Quinn, Antoinette. *Patrick Kavanagh: a Biography*. Dublin: Gill & Macmillan, 2001.

Roche, Lorcan. 'Hynes' classic *Famine* simply mesmerizing', *Irish Independent*, 7 October 1993.

Trevelyan, Sir Charles. *The Irish Crisis: Being a Narrative of the Measures for the Relief of the Distress Caused by the Great Irish Famine of 1846–7*. London: Macmillan, 1880.

Woodham-Smith, Cecil. *The Great Hunger: Ireland 1845–1849*. London: Penguin, 1991.

CHAPTER 12

Irresponsible anorexia: the ethics of Eavan Boland's Famine

Nieves Pascual

More than 800 million people all over the world know what it means to go to bed hungry every night. About 25,000 people die from the effects of hunger each day. That is about one person every four seconds.

(United Nations' WFP)

The story is familiar: an underprivileged country supplies its agricultural raw materials to an industrialized nation. Peasants devote their lives to growing food that passes into the landowners' hands. The surplus extracted from the peasants does not find its way into investment. Local industry withers while the existing resources remain underused.

The result is death or else migration for the dispossessed, although the list of possibilities is open. At times illegal traffic networks encourage thousands of immigrants to die on the daily treacherous journey to a rich country in rubber rafts. In January 2004 sixteen would-be immigrants were killed when their boats capsized off Fuerteventura. In

In 1841 the population of Ireland had been 8,175,124. Given a normal rate of increase it could have been expected by 1851 to have reached 9,018,799. But the census of 1851 gave the population of Ireland as 6,552,385. If the figure of about 1,500,000 who emigrated during the five years 1845–9 is added to the 1851 census total the result is just over eight million – or one million short of the anticipated population figure for that year. Deaths from the Famine years 1845–9 can therefore be estimated approximately at one million. Modern Irish historians whose objectivity is exemplary usually put the figure at around 800,000.

(Kee, 1982, p.101)

How did this gigantic loss of life come to pass? On 1 January 1801, 'the Act of Union between Ireland and England became operative', writes Cecil Woodham-Smith in her formidable account of the Irish Famine, first published in 1962 (p.15). The consequences of the covenant did not wait. On the one hand, Catholic emancipation did

April 2004 at least 14 suspected immigrants drowned at sea off the coast of Spain's Canary Islands. Some other times governments favour the exodus of skilled labour on condition that they send home foreign exchange to help repay international aid loans: '[E]xporting labour which is needed at home is like exporting food when people are hungry: resources go where the profits are highest, not where the needs are greatest' (Hartmann and Boyce, 1982, p.35). But if starvation brings suffering to many, it also benefits a group of Westernized people who 'know how to operate the mechanisms, (and) how to talk to the government', if we are to believe Michael Maren, who has been in numerous famine situations over the years (Hubbell, 1997). Native merchants, moneylenders, and large landowners who are now able to buy land cheap from their impoverished neighbours make a profit. Governments, in need of the support of the rural and urban elites, are more than willing to meet the interests of the rich. Significantly, foreign aid from official government agencies and international organizations is also big business both for the recipient and donor countries: 'There's never been a famine situation that didn't make somebody rich, and it's not always just local people on the ground; there's foreign contractors and shipping companies.

not follow immediately on the Union, as expected. It was only achieved in 1829. On the other hand, Ireland started to be used as a market for surplus English goods: 'In the eighteen-forties, after nearly seven hundred years of English domination, Irish poverty and Irish misery appalled the traveller' (ibid., p.19). Rapidly the situation worsened because the Irish system of landholding and the methods of growing food were antique. Irish peasants lived off small plots of land for which they paid such a high rent that they had to sell the crops grown on them simply to pay the weight of the rents.

When the potato disease devastating Europe reached Ireland, her peasants, largely dependent on the potato for survival, died in droves. Hunger oedema, swelling limbs, distended jaws, growth of hair on the face, typhus fever, scurvy, diarrhoea and dysentery ravaged the Irish. And yet, throughout the Famine years the produce of Ireland was streaming out of the country. Most outrageously, Ireland did not stop importing grain. The entire famine was unnatural, 'a preventable tragedy', says Boland (1995b, p.164), due not to excusable mismanagement but to scandalous indifference to human life.

Those who did not die migrated across the Irish Channel to Great Britain, Liverpool, Glasgow and

Most of the money that goes into it ends up back in the U.S. in the form of cash, contracts and salaries', says Maren in the interview conducted by Stephen Hubbell, Middle East correspondent for *The Nation*.

Maren's declarations are logical. On the one hand, the recipient government is responsible for the implementation of developing programmes. Usually money is skimmed to its own advantage. On the other hand, charities 'get government contracts to do the stuff, and the more they do, the more money they get. Contracts . . . [are] cash flowing through the organization' (ibid.). Since development is done in terms of contracts that do not often exceed a three-year period, contractors are unable to gauge results, correct mismanagement or shift the norms guiding negotiations. 'Most aid projects', Maren insists, 'are absolute failures, complete wastes of money that succeed primarily at keeping Westerners employed' (ibid.). Hartmann and Boyce agree. Seemingly aid only feeds the problems and stifles the economy: 'Instead of feeding needy people, food aid often strengthens the very forces which create hunger – bolsters the elite and undermines any impulse towards self-reliance' (Hartmann and Boyce, 1982, p.48). And on yet another hand, starvation satisfies the donors' economic and political interests. In 1964 a prominent aid official wrote:

ports of South Wales (Woodham-Smith, 1991, p.206). Seventy-five per cent (Kee, 1982, p.97) crossed the Atlantic to the United States. Thousands expired during their journey in the coffin ships.

'It is not easy to understand why the British government did not foresee what would happen,' says Woodham-Smith (1991, p.155). Maybe easier to understand are the reasons that goaded the English government into minimizing its involvement in Famine relief. The Free Trade doctrines that had made England rich proved inadequate to maintain the starving in Ireland. The effects of the public works scheme, the Soup Kitchen Act, the Poor Law legislation and the Quarter-Acre Clause were dreadful. Charitable projects 'attracted large sums from prominent people in England . . . But of course the real responsibility remained with the government, and the principles on which that responsibility was assumed did not primarily include compassion' (Kee, 1982, p.94). The landless poor, landlords and emigrants bore heavy casualties, but wealthy tenants and the Catholic middle class profited from the calamity.

Although as Christopher Morash demonstrates in *Writing the Irish Famine* (1995) and this anthology ratifies, representations of the Famine have existed in Irish canonical literature since the 1840s into the present, Eavan Boland imagines Irish literature

In the most general sense, the main objective of foreign assistance, as of many other tools of foreign policy, is to produce the kind of political and economic environment in the world in which the United States can best pursue its own social goals . . . The second objective, which concerns the immediate future, is internal stability, which is sought by giving politically popular types of aid to existing governments, by the prevention of internal disorders . . . The third major objective of foreign assistance is security of the United States and its allies from external aggression.

(Chenery, 1984, p.81)

Since within the logic of utilitarian practice administrable benefits come before needs, and the needs of others rarely coincide with administrable needs, 'norms for disappointment in performance or the expectations of it' (Walker, 1998, p.44) are already regulated in our social context of moral relations. In this economy of responsibility – in the etymological sense of *respond_re*, 'to promise in return of a crime or debt regardless of outcome' – it is no wonder that the aid community is more concerned with fund-raising and image than with beneficial impact: 'With a camera in a refugee situation, you can compress the hunger. You can package it, frame it . . . It looks like you are taking part in the liberation of Buchenwald, when in fact it's a lot more complicated. The starving body picture is a lie', because it is as an inhibitor of its remembrance. Justifications for the inaccessibility of this literary legacy exist in abundance. On the one hand, hunger is a narcotic that nourishes forgetfulness: 'Caged so/I will grow angular and holy/. . . as will make me forget', Boland writes in 'Anorexic' (1989, pp.35–6). On the other hand, in Boland's view, 'language . . . holds out . . . amnesia' to fend off unpleasure (1995b, p.152). In effect, the press at the time wrote the Irish as assassins and murderers (Woodham-Smith, 1991, p.105). Oblivion of its language prevented contagion. It kept the picture from growing stale and deprived the colonizer of the power of naming. Oblivion also minimized religious controversy. Charles Trevelyan, Head of the Treasury, vehemently defended, before consuming his time in writing a history of the Irish Famine, that it had pleased the Protestant God to inflict famine on the Catholic lazy (ibid., p.177). At a time when historical events reflected the will of God, victory was a sign of one's rectitude, and defeat a warning of sin.

If the sin was nameable, its effects were often described as beyond the realm of representation. On 15 December 1846 – Woodham-Smith reports – Mr Nicholas Cummins, the well-known magistrate of the County of Cork, addressed a letter to the Duke of Wellington, and also presented as an infant unable to take care of herself, Maren vehemently claims (Hubbell, 1997).

Seemingly, hunger advertisements sell awareness and truth by signifying a non-coded, non-artificial, and non-perverted reality. However, technology can only simulate an unmediated reality. Operators, trained in angles and poses, employ the conventions of the photographic art associated with the spectacle of compassion. Beautiful famished women and children in black and white are depicted close-up and in full face, looking out of the image at the viewers, depending upon us. But there is no threat of protest, because the look is often absent and vulnerable. The text that normally accompanies the image participates in this fabricated objectivity turning hunger into a commodity fetish. The picture is thus domesticated, tamed, 'its realism remains relative, tempered by aesthetic or empirical habits' (Barthes, 1981, p.119), 'its vision oneiric, not ecmnesic' (ibid., p.117), a dream that drives memory off.

Because the images do not provide discomfort, they move us to sympathy. Some consumers, fascinated by the image as the supreme illustration of suffering, and erotically stimulated by the pleasure of power they feel through helping the empained, are moved to act. Others do not react, because in repeatedly picturing the horrors in our societies

sent a copy to *The Times*. It was published on 24 December 1846:

> I accordingly went on the 15th instant to Skibbereen, and to give the instance of one townland which I visited, as an example of the state of the entire coast district, I shall state simply what I there saw . . . Being aware that I should have to witness scenes of frightful hunger I provided myself with as much bread as five men could carry, and on reaching the spot I was surprised to find the wretched hamlet apparently deserted. I entered some of the hovels to ascertain the cause, and the scenes which presented themselves were such as no tongue or pen can convey the slightest idea.
>
> (Ibid., p.162)

Paradoxically, he then proceeds to describe the facts that exceed description. Indeed, the details of a helpless people's frantic search for food are so sickening that the subject was logically deemed unfit for bardic poetry. In an interview conducted by Elizabeth Schmidt in 1997, Boland explains that Irish poetry has a history of poets unmaking history through odes, ballads and elegies written for the flattery of wealthy patrons. On 2 February 2004, Boland confirmed that: '[In the nineteenth century] you could go through Irish poetry and not find any real references to the Irish famine . . . the poetry kept up its heroism, its resistance to ordinariness . . . I fell into some kind of disagreement with that [traditional] poem – or, at least, with its without alteration in plot and form, we deprive these images of their meaning and dilute the harshness of the reality they are meant to uncover. In both cases, however, the profusion of images erodes the original, speeds up forgetfulness, and feeds our complacency. And inasmuch as '[T]o witness suffering does one good', says Nietzsche (Nietzsche, 1996, p.48) it cannot be otherwise. So, having enjoyed for a minute both the pity we have for others' pains and the happiness that liberates us from those pains, we lean back with satisfaction and regain a good conscience. As Maren claims, in advertising the goal is not to make us think about hunger and poverty, but to relieve us of the burden of having to think about it (Hubbell, 1997). After all, health abides by the capacity to forget. In the words of Nietzsche:

> Forgetfulness is no mere *vis inertiae*, as the superficial believe; it is rather an active – in the strictest sense, positive, inhibiting capacity, responsible for the fact that what we absorb through experience impinges as little on our consciousness during its digestion (what might be called its 'psychic assimilation') as does the whole manifold process of our physical nourishment, that of so-called 'physical assimilation'.
>
> (Nietzsche, 1996, p.39)

However, it so often happens that those witnesses who can give first-history' (Quinn, 2004). In *Object Lessons* Boland recalls that she went to Achill for Easter years before the book's publication in 1995. She lived in a cottage. It 'had no water, and every evening the caretaker, an old woman . . . would carry water up to me . . . She was the first person to talk to me about the famine. She kept repeating to me that they were great people, the people of the famine. *Great people*. I had never heard that before. She pointed out the beauties of the place. But they themselves, I see now, were a subtext' (Boland, 1995b, p.124). Since then Boland has been writing extensively on the Famine and the subtext of its great people. In 'Quarantine', included in *Against Love Poetry* (2001c), a sequence of songs that refute the conventions of traditional love poetry, a man and a woman leave the workhouse at the time of the 1847 famine. 'It was in Carrigstyra in West Cork', Boland comments. '[T]hose were very desperate times – there was famine fever and starvation. The incident must have been like hundreds of others and would probably have been forgotten but it was left as an anecdote by a man writing sixty years later' (*Caffeinedestiny*). In 'The Journey' she remembers: '"Cholera, typhus, croup, diptheria"/she said, "in those days they racketed/in every backstreet and alley of old Europe./Behold the children of the plague"' (Boland, 2001b, p.94).

hand evidence of the actual reality are fated to remember and may therefore 'be compared to a dyspeptic' (ibid.). I am one of those witnesses and here I can only tell the story of my dyspepsia. The story of my indigestion, my hunger and my mother's and others'. A story of mine and still not solely mine. Hunger is here all over, consuming these words, feeding on them as I feed on them because words are what anorexics consume:

> July 1984: Where did you learn to do anorexia? From seeing others. She looked at me. She grew thin. I was eating into her. Yet I had all the symptoms of an eating disorder: ceasing of menstruation, growth of lanugo, constipation, hiding feelings, excessive exercising, use of laxatives, and self-induced vomiting.
>
> (my personal record)

This was my mother's question after my first year at the university, far from home. It was 1984. My answer made her sick. Even though 'every daughter's experience of hunger will be shaped to some extent by that of her mother' (Knapp, 2003, p.73), this one time I shaped hers. At the Catholic residence I stayed in we all learned to do anorexia, and do bulimia, and contemplated every other combination from watching TV, conversing and reading. The activity spread during the 1990s. It continues to be reinvented.

'The Making of an Irish Goddess' is still another picture of agony: 'the famished harvest,/ the fields rotting to the horizon/the children devoured by their mothers' (ibid., p.39). Incidentally, Kee also records the anecdote of a mother driven to eat the flesh of her own dead daughter during the Famine, consuming her in the attempt not to consume herself (Kee, 1982, p.100).

In the article: 'Famine? What Famine? Ireland Ponders its Nineteenth Century Catastrophy' published in *The Economist* in June 1995 on the occasion of the big commemoration of the Great Famine to be held in Dublin in 1997, the author notes that most people in Ireland are not keen to talk about the Famine because they 'feel that their subservience at the time was inglorious'. He adduces that 'barely a finger was raised between 1803 and 1848'. This same view is shared by Kee, who writes that Irish peasants 'were almost pathetically peaceful' (Kee, 1982, 87). The picture disclaims the romantic version of history that prevailed in Catholic Ireland for most of the past century: 'that of the "martyr" nation – pure, Gaelic, heroically resistant to alien, above all, British influence'. Paradoxically, this interpretation of history was upheld by '[T]he Catholics who did well out of the Famine' and who became 'the backbone of the land movement, of Parnell's electorate,

The words in my diary resonated in 1994 after the irresponsible death by hunger of an old female acquaintance. She also saw and copied. She learned how to copy and became 'a passable imitation of what went before' (Boland, 2001b, p.79), just a copy of a copy of a copy: 'I don't want to be an imitation,' says the anorexic woman in Chernin's *The Obsession*, 'I want to make my own name, cut my own image, set my own trend' (Chernin, 1981, p.102). She insists on singularity, yet we are born imitators.

To Andrew Meltzoff humans are 'the consummate imitative generalist(s)' (Meltzoff, 1998, p.59); they imitate almost everything and anything when the reinforcement is sufficient. Following psychologist Thorndike, Susan Blackmore in 1998 differentiates imitation from contagion, individual learning and non-imitative social learning. In her view imitation only refers to a novel action. It must exhibit three necessary conditions: Heredity (the form and the details of the behaviour are copied), variation (they are copied with errors and embellishments), and selection (only some behaviours are copied). When these three conditions apply, there 'is true evolutionary process', she concludes (Blackmore, 1998). Contagion, by contrast, is associated with innate actions: 'When we start laughing', she explains, 'when everyone else is

of the Catholic laity and clergy, of the Gaelic Athletic Association, and of all subsequent nationalist agitation' (Killen, 2003, p.48). Now it is being disputed by revisionist Irish historians:

> So-called 'revisionist' Irish historians, both Catholic and Protestant, have striven to present a less black-and-white view. They deride the traditionalists as unduly romantic and parochial . . . They debunk the notion of history espoused by Irish nationalists in their battle to erase British rule – and ideology – from the island . . . some of them tend to stress the role of well-meaning and earnest Britons in the provision of relief. One well-known nationalist writer, irritated by the latest treatment of the famine, says – in bitter jest – that the revisionists will soon be explaining it as a 'mass outbreak of anorexia nervosa'.
> (Ibid.)

The jest is indeed bitter. It is immoral to establish connections between the hunger of those living in poverty and the copycat hunger of eating disorders. 'Worrying about losing a few pounds is not at all the same as worrying about survival', says Caroline Knapp in *Appetites*, her autobiography on anorexia (Knapp, 2003, p.18). And yet, imposed hunger and self-willed starvation metabolize in Boland's work into oppressive ideologies that weigh the lives of women down. In 'Contingencies' from *Outside History*, 'women spoke . . . /with a private hunger in laughing we have not learned how to do the act. We already knew how to act, and the kind of laugh we made is not modelled on the laugh we hear.' Within the category of individual learning Blackmore includes both 'classical conditioning' – 'when two stimuli become associated by repeated pairing' – and 'operant conditioning' – 'when a behaviour . . . is either rewarded or punished and therefore either increases or decreases in frequency' (ibid). Social learning, in turn, is learning about the environment through observing others. It includes 'stimulus enhancement', when the action has already been learned but it is triggered by a new motivation, 'local enhancement', when attention is directed towards the goal, and 'goal emulation', when the outcome of some other's behaviour is copied without copying the form of the behaviour itself. These distinctions, however, blur into each other within anorexia.

Certainly, anorexia is not a novel behaviour. It was practiced by women in medieval times to achieve holiness. It continued to be practiced during the eighteenth and nineteenth centuries to attain femininity and spur creativity. In the twentieth century it was performed to deconstruct the binary masculine/feminine and incorporate those qualities that tradition has assigned to men, that is autonomy, independence and identity. In this regard,

whispered kisses' (Boland, 2001b, p.58). In 'A Woman Painted on a Leaf', from *In a Time of Violence*, her 'dried-out-face' is all '[C]heekbones. Eyes', she, an invisible witness looking without being looked at (Boland, 1995a, p.69). In 'A False Spring', female bodies are emaciated, cadaverous ghosts (Boland, 2001b, p.37) that 'haunt the Irish present', (Boland, 1995b, p.171). In 'The Photograph', 'a woman holds her throat like a wound' (Boland, 2001b, p.43), unable to speak, aphasic, muzzled by silence because speech hurts. In 'A Ballad of Beauty and Time', another woman believes she will achieve beauty by 'getting thin' (ibid., p.122), still one more 'paragon of dispossession' (Boland, 1995b, p.171). In 'Anorexic' the same woman deprives herself of food in the attempt to achieve purity and make herself holy. On the experience of anorexia Boland has constructed a new language to possess the forgotten story of the Irish Famine: 'a new language/is a kind of scar/and heals after a while/into a passable imitation of what went before', Boland writes (2001b, p.79). Anorexia is, in fact, a passable imitation of the Famine, an imperfect copy of a copy because, as Christopher Morash ingeniously claims, it is only through images and words that we learn the history of the Famine:

> Like all past events the Famine is primarily a retrospective textual

Susan Bordo explains that women 'feel themselves deeply attracted by the aura of freedom and independence suggested by the boyish body ideal' (Bordo, 1998, p.44). Nevertheless, before 1984 it was no part of my own behavioural repertoire. It was a novel action in a novel situation within a novel context. I learned the details, but I had my own tricks. I perfected my selected ability till it offered the most effective rewards, otherwise I would have renounced it, or so I thought before being full of hunger and unable to give it up. Food: rejection: reward. Anorexia allowed you to become a member of a co-operative group, an 'elite fraternity' (Chernin, 1981, p.14), a sect, a nation, without the cost of reciprocation. It gave you a sense of control over your life and body. It gave you agency and identity. It fostered social acceptance and solved your self-esteem conflicts. In a month you came to be happy, thin and beautiful. 'Where did you learn to do anorexia?' When my mother asked this, she revealed her belief that I had learnt by conditioning and imitation. As Blackmore concedes, '[I]n practice, we may not always be able to tease out those things we have individually learned by conditioning from those we have learned by imitation, and very often both are involved' (Blackmore, 1998). Indeed, both were involved. The social stimulus was, further-

creation. The starvation, the emigration, and the disease epidemics of the late 1840s have become 'the Famine' because it was possible to inscribe those disparate, but interrelated events in a relatively cohesive narrative. For all of us born after the event, the representation has become the reality.

(Morash, 1995, p.3)

Boland inscribes thus the representation of history in the narrative of anorexia: 'the present tense . . . instructed by the past' (1995b, p.173), the retrospective textual creation supplemented by the twentieth-century reality in Ireland. In effect, some recent research studies in Ireland suggest that up to 70 per cent of teenage girls have attempted to slim. And yet, history is flesh and flesh is history (Weil, 1987, p.18). So, if you renounce history, you renounce flesh. If you deprive yourself of food, you deprive yourself of history. As it is, history by itself already falls into oblivion: 'history/is one of us who turns away while the other is turning the page' (Boland, 2001b, p.45). After all, health abides by the capacity to forget. In this logic, there is no possibility of fleshing out history in the process of discarnation.

Intriguingly, Boland deciphers the difference between history and the past: 'In a country like Ireland it was possible to see the difference between the past and history – how one was official and articulate and more, endless and the goals of our sacrifice – whatever methods we used to increase quality – beneficial and successful for us all. That was true evolutionary adaptation!

Nevertheless, it is not entirely clear to me what an innate action is. In the first substage of Piaget's theory, children are supposed to enter the world equipped with a set of inherited action patterns and reflexes through which they experience their environment. These natural schemata form the basis for more complex future developments. But, how to distinguish innate behaviour from instruction when children begin learning from the moment of birth? Much evidence is complex and controversial. Daniel le Grange, Ph.D., of the Eating Disorders Clinic in the Department of Psychiatry at the University of Chicago, remarks on the importance of exploring the biological roots of anorexia (le Grange *et al.*, 1997). Blake Woodside, at the Division of Behavioral Science and Health in the Toronto General Research Institute, says that anorexia is caused by a combination of genes that are currently being uncovered (Woodside *et al.*, 1998). Scans, in fact, seem to have revealed structural abnormalities in the brains of many anorexic women. Hilde Bruch, however, in *The Golden Cage* suggests that anorexia depends on the experience of satiation the baby has, its satisfaction or its frustration at the

the other was silent and fugitive. I suppose I was drawn to the past, rather than to history', she declares (*Caffeinedestiny*). As unofficial and unwritten, the past transfers 'its available resources from memory to allegory' (Boland, 1995b, p.9) and becomes myth, the myth of 'the women of a long struggle and a terrible survival' (ibid., p.135). To Boland myth is the unedited truth of humiliation, marginality, daily grief and ordinariness: 'Sometimes on a summer evening . . . I could imagine . . . that such lives as mine and my neighbors were mythic, not because of their strangeness but because of their powerful ordinariness' (ibid., p.167). Myth, she says, is 'the wound we leave in the time we have' (Boland, 2001b, p.39), and heals with food. Food=oblivion. Boland resists food, oblivion and health. She chooses the past (1995b, p.163). If hunger, as Maud Ellmann argues, is a hieroglyph that 'both immures and disenthralls' (1993, p.93), Boland keeps in the dailiness of the past and the inventory of the forgotten dead and in the same movement excretes history. She chooses out of history, out of 'the toxins of a whole history' that has ignored the Great Famine and its consequences: 'I won't go back to it/my nation displaced/into old dactyls/oaths made/by the animal tallows/of the candle . . . / No. I won't go back', she sings in 'Mise Éire' (2001b, p.78), the title of mother's breast (Bruch, 1978). That explains why some children as young as three have a psychological fear of food. Connan, Katzman *et al.*, for their part, have been working on a neurodevelopmental model for anorexia that examines how a genetic predisposition combines with early attachment experiences to produce changes in appetite regulation that may lead an individual to anorexia nervosa (Nasser *et al.*, 2003). Be anorexia the result of an imbalance of chemicals in the brain or be it not, regardless of whether there is an anorexia gene, this condition surely is a pre-programmed behaviour that the individual is able to relearn through looking at another individual. Anorexia is thus simultaneously contagious and new, in the Latin sense of *novus*: 'the second, the other, repeated or reiterated to renovate'.

Of necessity, observing others activates the need to hunger. The observation triggers the transmission of symptoms to viewers organically predisposed to contract them, 'such as those with pre-existing depression or anxiety, low self-esteem in childhood, a history of weight preoccupation, and perhaps genetic predispositions' (Connan *et al.*, 2003, p.2). If observation involves, as Williams *et al.* maintain, 'translating from the perspective of another individual to oneself' (Williams *et al.*, 2001, p.288), imitation must be built on intersub-

which is taken from an older Irish poem by P.H. Pearse in which Ireland speaks as a woman.

Nevertheless, Boland goes back to the history of the Irish writing community and its traditional use of the feminine body to represent the Irish nation. Within Irish literary tradition woman becomes, Ailbhe Smyth says, 'a symbol of civic power, not because she stands for "woman" but because "woman" stands for something else' (Smyth, 1989, p.9). In 'Anorexic' Boland vomits the hungers of the female body, reducing the Old Woman of the Roads, Caitlín Ní Houlihán, Dark Rosaleen, Anna Livia Plurabelle, Banba, Eiriú, Red Rose, Róisín Dubh and Mother Machree to 'skin and bones' (Boland, 1989, pp.35–6) – their bodies discarnated, yet beautiful, yearned for and 'sinless', as Catholic orthodox tradition and nationalism demand, because 'flesh is heretic'. The performance of this belief drove many women to hunger in medieval times. In 1985 Rudolph Bell coined the term 'holy anorexics' for women like Saint Catherine of Siena, Saint Mary Magdalene of Pazzi and Saint Teresa of Avila. Bell convincingly argues that 'the suppression of physical urges and basic feelings – fatigue, sexual drive, hunger, pain – frees their bodies to achieve heroic feats and the souls to commune with God' (Bell, 1985, p.15), or 'slip back into him again', as Boland puts it.

jective understanding, fellow empathy, compassion and responsibility for things and to others. If this is so, imitation plays a crucial role in the development of a moral sense. With great acuity Meltzoff and Moore explicate that:

> The apprehension of others like me is the foundation on which our mature folk psychology is constructed. Even our moral sense is anchored there. We 'do unto others' in a special way because there is a deeply felt equivalence between self and other. Without a sense of like-me-ness, we do not think our folk psychology and moral judgements would take the form they do.
>
> (Meltzoff and Moore, 1999, p.11)

In so far as '"[A]utonomous" and "moral" are mutually exclusive' (Nietzsche, 1996, p.41), following a model improves one's virtue. But, which is the model in anorexia? In whose shoes do anorexic imitators stand? What kind of moral sense or responsibility or intersubjective understanding or fellow empathy or compassion is involved in their behaviour? Is imitation not founded also on the desire to be transported out of ourselves (Rousseau, 1979, p.104), not to be one's self?

For Rousseau the discrepancy between desire and the power to satisfy desire is the fundamental recipe for individual unhappiness:

> Everything that pleases him tempts him; everything others have, he

Here God is the lover, the father who cannibalizes the flesh of her daughter in a final act of compassion. God, the creator, the supreme poet. To Boland the poet, she writes in 'Colony' from *The Lost Land*, 'is a man . . ./He has no comfort, no food' (Boland, 1999, p.15).

But, is not Boland disowning women in this heroic feat of suppression, in this progress toward nothingness? If in 'Making the Difference' Boland asserts that the erotic object is an old prescription of the image system in the Irish poem (1995b, p.212), is she not proving to be unable to displace it? Is she not fixing women as erotic objects in simplifying them out of existence? Yet, by scrupulously applying the equation 'Ireland (=) Absence' (1999, p.38), Boland demonstrates its absurdity. She writes the poem away from the traditional erotic object by making the created create herself and granting her the task of expression. In so doing, she allows the woman poet a privileged perception of the 'forces of reaction in Irish poetry' (1995b, p.151) and grants her true authority: 'The authority grows the more the speaker is weakened and made vulnerable by the tensions he or she creates' (ibid., p.186). Paradoxically, in this movement of subversion she satisfies her urgent need to locate herself in the Irish literary tradition (ibid., p.138). As it is, Ireland has a long history of wants to have. He covets everything; he is envious of everyone. He would want to dominate everywhere. Vanity gnaws at him . . . He comes home discontented with himself and others. He goes to sleep . . . troubled by countless whims. And even in his dreams his pride paints the chimerical goods, desire for which torments him and which he will never in his life possess.

(Ibid., pp.228–9)

The copy improves the model or is inferior to it, but in either case unequal to it. Therefore, since no copy is perfect, we are condemned to perpetual dissatisfaction. 'What he is, is nothing; what he appears to be is everything for him' (ibid., p.230), Rousseau says of the envious person tormented by the desire for goods that he will never possess. 'Where did you learn to do anorexia? From seeing others.' Envy = identification = emptiness = hunger.

Desire for what others are, or envy of what they appear to be, is bolstered by modern capitalism. Society wants us to believe that we can be most ourselves by expelling our history, driving out fat, looking like someone else. Within the same movement, envious desire is condemned as morally wrong. We are taught, however, that the vice of envy can be redistributed into compassion, which – and even though compassion is just one more hidden expression of envy itself – is the only moral imperative of modern hungry poets with a visionary compulsion. Yeats thought that poets had to be thin because poetry consumed their potency and their maleness. In effect, hunger impacts sex drive (Claude-Pierre, 1997, p.108). Beckett compressed his body into a minimal number of words, stripping literature to the barest monosyllables. Joyce aimed at a kind of anorexia in his prose and preached hunger (Heywood, 1996, p.89). Kavanagh confessed that as a poet he 'was born in or about nineteen fifty-five', only then did he 'become airborne and more', he 'achieved weightlessness' (2003, pp.314–15): 'Who owns them hungry hills/That the waterhen and snipe must have forsaken? A poet/ then by heavens he must be lean' (ibid., p.284), he writes. Through suppression Boland joins in, because only through discarnation is a poet able to be in Ireland. Maybe the body of Ireland, the 'geological weakness' (Boland, 1995b, p.152) of a small island of permeable boundaries, surrounded by a mass of water that eats into her cliffs, catalyzes the inanition of her national writers. It so happens that in Ireland 'the place . . . happens to you' (ibid., p.154). Interestingly, in *The Parasite* Michael Serres conceives of writing as the transfusion of the living body into language:

What is a work? It eats its worker, devouring his flesh and his time; it is democracies: 'Our society', says René Girard, 'is the most preoccupied with victims of any that ever was' (Girard, 2001, p.161). It is precisely by redistributing and redescribing human actions that we express our sense of responsibility (Walker, 1998, p.10). But responsibility must be articulate if it is to be understood by spectators.

I have arrived at this writing through my anorexia. I arrived at my anorexia through my desire not to be myself, to be like the beautiful images I consumed. My excess of zeal consumed me instead. Inasmuch as I lost self-control I abdicated my responsibility. Inasmuch as I forgot others I renounced my responsibility. Inasmuch as I forced my mother to assume responsibility for my starvation my story is one of irresponsibility. In the second stage of my anorexia, when I was victimized by my bodily habits, vividly attuned to the experience of being that vulnerable person who is helped, and mimicking the great love for others displayed by the super-thin fashion models of the media through their conspicuous involvement in charity projects, I overtly projected myself into visual representations of hunger victims and revelled in them as *causa fiendi*. This transvaluation of values gave meaning to meaningless hunger. But, what's more, in so far as '[P]ractices of responsibility include

slowly substituted for his body. The invasion causes fear. Who am I? This, there, written in black on white, fragile, and this is my body, has taken the place of my body, frail. This is written in my blood; I am bleeding from it, and it will stop only with the last drop. The work para- sites the worker; no, soon he no longer exists. He dies of it. And he can do nothing about it.

(Serres, 1982, p.131)

Boland strips reality to its naked bones, her written poem as minimal as the androgynous body of the poet. She dissolves her 'I' into hungry stanzas, her writing emptying her body, consumed by her words in her identification with the starving:

My lips now are as blue as hers [a hungry woman, client of one of her ancestors], the shallow blue of those shrubs. I have no house, no room in which I write, no books. My children are not healthy and noisy. They are fractions of my own grief which cling at my skirt, their expressions scarred with hunger and doubt. Instead of bright cotton and denim – clothes they pick out and array themselves in – they wear fustian and the hated flannel. And they, like me, are ripe for the fevers which come in off the marshes and stagnate the water of the town.

(Boland, 1995b, p.171)

If she had not identified herself, she would not have emptied herself and

. . . setting terms of . . . excusability, and exculpation for what is . . . done, and for some of what ensues as a result' (Walker, 1998, p.93), I was now ready to take responsibility for my mother's starvation and my own hunger. 'The acute anorexic', writes Claude-Pierre, 'believes she is responsible for everything' (1997, p.146). In this belief I filled both our hungers with compassion just '[T]o silence the envy in my thought', as Yeats ingeniously puts it in 'Meditation in Times of Civil War'. I was not alone. Other anorexics also gorge on *les nostalgies de la croix*. Alice, who in *The Passion of Alice*, an anorexic story by Stephanie Grant, trips into fantasies of her own saint-liness, mimics the agonies of Christ, 'the first anorexic' (1995, p.37). Sarah in Shute's *Life-Size* (1992) stands in the shoes of Mahatma Gandhi and Simone Weil. Convinced that hunger gives gender and gender gives hunger, Josephine in *Hunger Striking* by K. Brenan puts the face of ema-ciated Third World women on her pain: 'How beautiful the bone-mother, sheltering in the sweep of her scarf her child's fleshless corpse' (Brenan, 1999, p.155). Lori Gottlieb identifies with the picture of a famished girl on one collection box 'that said, PLEASE HELP THE HUNGRY' (Gottlieb, 2001, p.92). In the process she flattens differ-ences into sameness:

she would never have been hungry. By slimming her words and subscribing to the aesthetics of starvation, Boland fattens the list of Irish canonical authors who pared their writings to essentials.

'[A] new language/ is a kind of scar/ and heals after a while/ into a passable imitation/ of what went before' (Boland, 2001b, p.79). But hunger is a formula and the language of anorexia is not new (Pascual, 2001). Anorexia imposes its own closed-loop system onto its narratives, reducing every story to the repe-tition of another one. There is no possibility of a new language in anorexia. And inasmuch as language conditions experience, there is not even a possibility of an original anorexia. '[M]y speech will not heal. I don't want it to heal' (Boland, 2001b, p.46), says Boland. In fact, it cannot heal. It will neither heal herself nor others. She chooses to remember hunger as the pathway to hell: 'angular and holy . . ./in a small space/into forked dark/into python needs/heaving to hips and breasts/ and lips and heat/and seat and fat and greed' (Boland, 1989, p.36). She writes a story of indiges-tion, hers and still not hers, a private story that inevitably is universal because '[O]ne part of the poem in every generation is ready to be com-munally written' (Boland, 1995b, p.177). 'Anorexic' is a beautiful poem made of 'beautiful . . . words' that

[T]he secret on the girl's lips was pretty obvious. 'People think I need help because I'm hungry, but they're the ones who need help. At least I'm thin.' I could tell that's what she was thinking . . . She had the kind of big round eyes that Mom and her friends always say are so beautiful, if you add a little mascara to the upper lashes. I wish I was that beautiful.

(Ibid., 93)

Clearly hers, like mine, is a compassion grounded on envy, but compassion nonetheless. So, fed on beautiful sights we, my mother and I, nourished pity and incorporated morality, 'morality as consequence, symptom, mask, Tartufferie, illness' (Nietzsche, 1996, p.8). We took in the past and the inventory of the forgotten dead by hunger in underprivileged countries. They remained in for a while.

I am not anorexic anymore. I now write on anorexia to experience the experience, because 'at the time of writing', like Sheila MacLeod herself, 'I had begun to become anorexic again' (MacLeod, 1982, p.7). On writing I willingly assumed the risk. I knew that anorexia grows with its performance, I knew that writing mimes the act of fasting, and I knew that morality is illness. As Morash concludes: 'There is always the danger that having recognized there is no direct access to an empirical historical reality other than through textual traces, the dream of such access will reemerge in the literary text' (Morash, 1995, p.4). I wanted to catch the dream and I did.

'honour the dead' because words 'are the dead' (Boland, 2001b, pp.53–4). If '[W]hatever calls one to memory calls one to responsibility', as Derrida writes (1989, p.xi), Boland is called to responsibility by the starving. Responsibility = intersubjective understanding = fellow empathy = compassion = morality = illness.

Nevertheless, Boland was never known to be anorexic (Crnovich). She imitates anorexia. She writes 'not to recall our lives/but to imagine them' (Boland, 2001a, p.18). She imagines imitation. 'Instead of getting poems about experience, I am getting poems that are experiences', she writes quoting Adrienne Rich (Boland, 1995b, p.131). She experiences her imagined imitation, willingly running the risk of experience. 'There is always the danger that having recognized there is no direct access to an empirical historical reality other than through textual traces, the dream of such access will re-emerge in the literary text', says Morash (1995, p.4). On reading Boland we recognize in her national experience our story of deprivation and come to feel part of her community of the hungry. On reading her poems we develop our responsibility.

The two-column format reflects my desire to tell two stories simultaneously. They start and end the same, yet their plots differ.

References

Barthes, Roland. *Camera Lucida: Reflections on Photography*. Richard Howard (trans.). New York: Hill & Wang, 1981.

Bell, Rudolph M. *Holy Anorexia*. Chicago, IL: The University of Chicago Press, 1985.

Blackmore, Susan. 'Imitation and the definition of a meme', *Journal of Memetics: Evolutionary Models of Information Transmission*, Vol. 2 (1998) <http://jom-emit.cfpm.org/1998/vol2/blackmore_s.html>.

Boland, Eavan. *Selected Poems*. Dublin: Carcanet, 1989.

Boland, Eavan. *In a Time of Violence*. New York and London: W.W. Norton, 1995a.

Boland, Eavan. *Object Lessons. The Life of the Woman and the Poet in Our Time*. New York and London: W.W. Norton, 1995b.

Boland, Eavan. *The Lost Land*. New York and London: W.W. Norton, 1999.

Boland, Eavan. *Code*. Manchester: Carcanet, 2001a.

Boland, Eavan. *Outside History*. New York and London: W.W. Norton, 2001b.

Boland, Eavan. *Against Love Poetry*. New York and London: W.W. Norton, 2001c.

Bordo, Susan. 'Anorexia nervosa: psychopathology as the crystallization of culture', in Deane W. Curtin and Lisa M. Heldke (eds), *Cooking, Eating, Thinking. Transformative Philosophies of Food*. Bloomington, IN: Indiana University Press, 1998.

Brenan, Kit. *Hunger Striking*. Winnipeg: Nuage, 1999.

Bruch, Hilde. *The Golden Cage. The Enigma of Anorexia Nervosa*. Cambridge, MA: Harvard University Press, 1978.

Caffeinedestiny. Interview with Eavan Boland (2001), <http://www.caffeinedestiny.com/boland.html>.

Chenery, Hollis B. 'Ojectives and criteria for foreign assistance', in Gustav Ranis (ed.), *The United States and the Developing Economies*. New York and London: Norton 1964.

Chernin, Kim. *The Obsession. Reflections on the Tyranny of Slenderness*. New York: Harper, 1981.

Claude-Pierre, Peggy. *The Secret Language of Eating Disorders: The Revolutionary New Approach to Understanding and Curing Anorexia and Bulimia*. New York: Times, 1997.

Connan, Francis, Ian C. Campbell, Melanie Katzman, Stafford L. Lightman and Janet Treasure. 'A neurodevelopmental model for anorexia nervosa', *Psychology and Behavior*, Vol. 79 (2003), pp.13–24.

Crnovich, Amber. 'A portrait of Eavan Boland', <http://domin.dom.edu/students/crnovam201/boland.html>.

Derrida, Jacques. *Mémoires: For Paul de Man*. Cecile Lindsay, Jonathan Culler, Eduardo Cadava and Peggy Kamuf (trans.). New York: Columbia University Press, 1989.

Ellmann, Maud. *The Hunger Artists. Starving, Writing and Imprisonment*. London: Virago, 1993.

'Famine? what famine?: Ireland ponders its nineteenth century catastrophy', *The Economist*, 24 June 1995, <http://www.swan.ac.uk/history/teaching%20resources/An%20Gorta%Mor>.

Girard, René. *I See Satan Fall Like Lightning*. James G. Williams (trans.). New York: Orbis, 2001.

Gottlieb, Lori. *Stick Figure: A Diary of my Former Self*. New York: Berkeley 2001.

Grant, Stephanie. *The Passion of Alice*. New York: Houghton Mifflin, 1995.

Hartmann, Betsy and James Boyce. *Needless Hunger. Voices from a Bangladesh Village*. Oakland, CA: Food First Books, 1982.

Heywood, Leslie. *Dedication to Hunger. The Anorexic Aesthetic in Modern Culture*. Berkeley: The University of California Press, 1996.

Hubbell, Stephen. Interview with Michael Maren. 'The big lie of foreign aid and international charity', *Might Magazine* (March/April 1997), <http://www.netnomad.com.might.html>.

Kavanagh, Patrick. *A Poet's Country. Selected Poems*. Antoinette Quinn (ed.). Dublin: Lilliput, 2003.

Kee, Robert. *Ireland: A History*. London: Abacus, 1982.

Killen, Richard. *A Short History of Modern Ireland*. Dublin: Gill & Macmillan, 2003.

Knapp, Caroline. *Appetites*. New York: Counterpoint, 2003.

le Grange, Daniel, C.F. Telch and W.S. Agras, 'Eating and general psychopathology in a sample of Caucasian and ethnic minority subjects', *International Journal of Eating Disorders*, Vol. 21 (1997), pp.1025–30.

MacLeod, Sheila. *The Art of Starvation. A Story of Anorexia and Survival*. New York: Schocken, 1982.

Meltzoff, Andrew N. 'Imitation, objects, tools, and the rudiments of language in human ontogeny', *Human Evolution*, Vol. 3 (1998), pp.45–64.

Meltzoff, Andrew N. and M. Keith Moore. 'Persons and representation: why infant imitation is important for theories of human development', in J. Nadel and G. Butterworth (eds), *Imitation in Infancy*. Cambridge: Cambridge University Press, 1999.

Morash, Christopher. *Writing the Irish Famine*. Oxford: Clarendon Press, 1995.

Nasser, Mervat, Melanie Katzman and Richard A. Gordon. *Eating Disorders and Cultures in Transition*. New York: Roultedge, 2001.

Nietzsche, Friedrich. *On the Genealogy of Morals*. Douglas Smith (trans.). Oxford: Oxford University Press, 1996.

Pascual, Nieves. 'Depathologizing anorexia: the risks of life narratives', *Style*, Vol. 35, No. 2 (2001), pp.341–53.

Quinn, Alice. Interview with Eavan Boland. *The New Yorker*, 4 February 2004, <http://www.newyorker.com/online/content/?011029on_online only01a>.

Rousseau, Jean-Jacques. *Émile*. Allan Bloom (trans.). New York: Basic Books, 1979.

Schmidt, Elizabeth. Interview with Eavan Boland. 1997, <http://www.poets. org/poems/Prose.cfm?prmID=2088>.

Serres, Michael. *The Parasite*. Lawrence R. Schehr (trans.). Baltimore, MD: Johns Hopkins University Press, 1982.

Shute, Jenefer. *Life-Size*. New York: Houghton Mifflin, 1992.

Smyth, Ailbhe. 'The floozie in the jacuzzi', *Irish Review*, Vol.6 (1989), pp.7–24. United Nations' World Food Programme. <http://www.wfp.org>.

Walker, Margaret Urban. *Moral Understandings. A Feminist Study in Ethics*. New York and London: Routledge, 1998.

Weil, Simone. *Gravity and Grace*. New York and London: Routledge, 1987.

Williams, J.H.G., A. Whiten, T. Suddendorf and D.I. Perret. 'Imitation, mirror neurons and autism', *Neuroscience and Biobehavioural Reviews*, Vol.25 (2001), pp.287–95.

Woodham-Smith, Cecil. *The Great Hunger: Ireland 1845–1849*. London: Penguin, 1991.

Woodside, Blake, L.L. Field, P.E. Garfinkel and M. Heinmaa. 'Specificity of eating disorder diagnoses in families of probands with anorexia nervosa and bulimia nervosa', *Comparative Psychiatry*, Vol.39, No.5 (1998), pp.261–4.

CHAPTER 13

'It was a life-changing book': tracing Cecil Woodham-Smith's impact on the canon of children's literature of the Irish Famine

Karen Hill McNamara

Let us debunk the notion that children's books are less worthy candidates for literary discourse, cultural analysis and critical respect. Traditionally regarded as academically inferior, writing designated especially for children has lacked the status of adult literature. Until recently, children's writers and books were not considered part of the official cultural heritage – typically absent in national histories of literature, rarely mentioned in encyclopedias or lexicons, receiving comparatively less serious, systematic study and certainly not solicited by scholarly anthologies illuminating the works of canonical authors.

Today the field of children's literature is flourishing. Sales are at a record high with over 5,000 new titles published annually in the United States, and children's book reviews are routinely printed in newspapers and magazines. As the economics (profitability) of the discipline has risen, so has the respect and the acceptability. No longer viewed sceptically by the official pedagogical establishment, academic interest is surging. Children's literature is now taught at hundreds of universities (where such classes are typically oversubscribed), the Modern Language Association has given the field legitimacy as a division and hosts numerous panels at its annual convention, and there is a growing body of provocative scholarship on all aspects of the topic (Griswold, 2002, p.237). Cognizant of its literary, social, political, historical and cultural value, researchers have elevated the field in academia. With a more prominent and secure stature, children's literature 'rightfully deserves its place at the banquet table with other kinds of literary study' (ibid., p.239).

Children are extremely impressionable, and what they read has an impact on the way they view the world. Much has been researched on the role of narrative in the development of a reader's historical understanding, and authorities are clear about its value in children's social and intellectual development. Children's books are powerful vehicles for delivering cultural awareness and national identity. The plots and themes act as a 'cultural barometer', measuring trends in society. Juvenile literature helps define the character of the people it portrays, provides a sense of nationality, and acts as a guide to the history and development of the country that produced it.

One of the most popular literary genres published for children in Ireland is historical fiction. Novels set in the past communicate a sense of complexity and constant change, yet they also connect history seamlessly with the present. The books tend to focus on the human side of history and give young readers a sense of how life was lived in an earlier time. Irish children's literature scholar Celia Keenan notes that this genre is valuable in colonial and post-colonial cultures and that the growth of Irish historical novels for young readers reflects 'a new confidence in Irish society emanating from widespread popular belief that if we understand the past, we might behave better in the future' (Keenan, 1997, p.369). A watershed in Ireland's past is the Great Irish Famine of the mid-nineteenth century, and this essay examines the inspiration and the context for the creation of a canon of children's literature presenting this calamitous period.

Children's literature of the Great Famine is relatively young; the earliest book, *The Search of Mary Katherine Mulloy*, was written by Carole Bolton and published in 1974, 129 years after the start of the Famine. This extraordinary time gap is significant in that children's writers have readily addressed other monumental and traumatic events in human history as worthwhile topics. It appears that novelists are infatuated with certain historical eras, such as the Holocaust or slavery, yet uninterested in others, like the Irish Famine. What explains this delay? Why were the Irish late in addressing this defining event in their history? The answers are complicated and relate to a 'silence' that has surrounded the Famine. Historians are cognizant of this silence, and it has recently received a fair amount of attention.[1] Contributing factors to the silence are feelings of deep shame associated with being perceived as passive victims and feelings of guilt associated with being perceived as ruthless survivors.

What initially motivated the pioneering authors to portray such a controversial and catastrophic historical event to children? Most of the authors are still living, and I was able to conduct primary research and ask them. The novelists I interviewed cited Cecil Woodham-Smith's *The Great Hunger: Ireland 1845–1849* (1962) as the silence breaker.[2] Nearly every author had emotive connections to Woodham-Smith's work and several were inspired to write about the Irish Famine for children as a direct result of reading the book. *The Great Hunger* inspired the 'founding fathers' to create a canon of Irish Famine literature for children.

Cecil Woodham-Smith

While Cecil Woodham-Smith is usually referred to as an English historian, closer inspection reveals that she is the product of famed Irish roots. Born in 1896 into the widely known FitzGerald family, she has been referred to as the 'Irish daughter of a colonial general' (Hayden, 2001, p.13). Although Woodham-Smith's mother was Welsh, her father was Irish, a descendant 'from one of the leaders of the United Irishmen's plot to collaborate with the French to free Ireland from British Rule' (Small, 2004). A meticulous researcher, she wrote several famous historical texts, including *The Reason Why* (1953), which examines the Charge of the Light Brigade at Balaclava during the Crimean War, and detailed biographies of Florence Nightingale and Queen Victoria. However, it was *The Great Hunger*, originally published by Hamish Hamilton in 1962, that many consider her most influential work.

One can only speculate what initially inspired Woodham-Smith to research such a politically charged, complex and dark subject. At the time, there was a universal silence surrounding the Great Famine with few scholarly published accounts available. Marginalized by the academic community, the Famine was not included by most schools and universities in their curriculum. Perhaps Woodham-Smith's Irish ancestry first sparked her interest in the topic. Her participation in an Irish Republican demonstration caused her to be dismissed from Oxford University (Small, 2004, p.3). In addition, the fact that she lived outside Ireland may have allowed her the academic breathing room needed to address this taboo subject considered too controversial in Ireland. Christine Kinealy has acknowledged that 'the impetus to remember the Famine was often strongest outside of Ireland' (Valone and Kinealy, 2002, p.2). Whatever the motivations for Woodham-Smith's writing, *The Great Hunger* was the first mainstream factual account of the Irish Famine and clearly a ground-breaking book.

With its narrative flair and readability, *The Great Hunger* was an immediate commercial success. Woodham-Smith's flowing literary style combined with her moral passion made the book an international bestseller. Tim Pat Coogan, in *Wherever Green is Worn* (2000), called it a 'gripping read, which burst on a new generation of Irish readers in the 1960s like a thunderbolt' (p.172). Coogan also quoted Dr Conor Cruise O'Brien as saying Woodham-Smith's 'just and penetrating mind, her lucid and easy style, and her assured command of the sources have produced one of the great works, not only of Irish nineteenth-century history, but of nineteenth-century history in general' (ibid.). The book was well-received by the popular press in North America and Europe, with reviewers acclaiming it as intelligent, thought-provoking and a masterly account of a terrible tragedy in human history.

The Great Hunger's exposure of the British government's culpability, along with presenting horrifying images of human suffering, made an indelible impression on readers, most of whom had little knowledge of the Irish Famine. According to Valone and Kinealy, 'It informed an entire generation of people about the tragedy' (2002, p.6). The realities of the catastrophe, such as the mass evictions, starvation, disease, and death, were conveyed in week-by-week accounts. Woodham-Smith revealed haunting descriptions of the human trauma and wrote comprehensive reports of how the Irish endured during the Famine. It is important to emphasize that this was the first time the scale of the tragedy was thoroughly exposed and readily available to the general public. Previously uninformed readers now had an understanding of this significant event in world history. In fact, a more positive attitude toward Ireland among Americans has been attributed to *The Great Hunger*. According to Aedan O'Brerne of the Irish Embassy in Washington in 1963, it won 'a sympathy and a respect for the Irish emigrant who was the victim of the Famine and its consequences in the ensuing Century' (quoted in Daly, 2002, p.10).

Despite its wide appeal and undisputed popular acclaim, however, Irish historians vilified *The Great Hunger*. Kinealy points out that 'While Woodham-Smith's book captured the public imagination . . . the Irish academic establishment derided or ignored her publication' (quoted in Gribben, 1999, p.246). Many in the academy criticized Woodham-Smith's work, claiming her descriptions were too emotive and her accusations against the British government too damning. Most likely, the scathing remarks resulted from additional factors. The unique situation of having a historical text achieve a massive audience and enjoy lucrative success may have given plenty of scope for jealous disdain in the Dublin historical community. Interestingly, outside Ireland reputable scholars received *The Great Hunger* more favourably; however, historians left the topic relatively untouched for the next three decades. Perhaps embroiled in the tradition of denial or intimidated by *The Great Hunger*'s dominance, it was not until the commemoration of the Irish Famine's 150th anniversary that scholars began producing new research and texts on the subject.

While scholars of Irish history may differ on some interpretive points of *The Great Hunger*, all would agree on its tremendous influence. It clearly struck a chord with readers around the world and influenced the writings of poets, such as Seamus Heaney and Eavan Boland, playwrights, such as Tom Murphy, novelists, such as Frank O'Connor, and historians and scholars. Woodham-Smith's work had a particular impact on writers for children, and inspired them to create a canon of historical Irish Famine novels. This seminal text is often reflected within the narratives, educating today's young people about the Famine and constructing the way children view their cultural identity and heritage.

Authors inspired by Cecil Woodham-Smith

Consider Michael Morpurgo, a prolific author of 100 books, many of which have received literary awards. A great storyteller of critical acclaim, he was named a Children's Laureate in 2003 and is a leading figure in the field of children's literature. It is not surprising that Morpurgo, who often pushes the boundaries in his books for children and young adults by tackling perplexing historical topics, was among the first to address the Irish Famine in a novel for young people. During our interview in London, he explained that his son, a student at Trinity College Dublin, introduced him to *The Great Hunger* during a heated discussion about the Irish Republican Army (IRA).

'He was very angry with me', Morpurgo said. 'He wasn't inclined to get angry; this was unusual for my son. Suddenly, there was this great big twenty-year-old telling me I knew nothing about anything!' The results of this father-son conversation made an indelible mark on the author:

> He said that if I wanted to make comments about the Irish situation, I had to know something about what has been happening to Ireland over the past five hundred years. 'Had I read anything? Did I know anything?' Yes, like most people in England what I know of Ireland is what began in the 1960s, the troubles. Anyway, he said 'I want you to read these books.' One of the books was called *The Great Hunger* by Cecil Woodham-Smith. He said, 'Right, when you have read that we'll have a discussion about Ireland and why Ireland is

and why people do what they do.' I read this book. I was horrified. Pretty horrified. I wasn't aware of the nature or the intensity of the effects of it . . . I read this book and thought, why don't we know anything about this?

(Morpurgo, 2001)

Although reluctant to write a historical novel, the devastating details described in *The Great Hunger* compelled Morpurgo to tackle the topic to make young readers aware of the consequences of the Famine. Morpurgo's *Twist of Gold*, published in 1983, was the first children's book published in England on the Irish Famine. An adventure tale, the story revolves around Sean and Annie, the two surviving children of the O'Brien family during the Irish Famine. The misery of the Famine is left behind as the children set off to America in search of their father.

Ann Pilling echoes similar sentiments to Morpurgo's in the postscript to her Famine book for children, *Black Harvest* (1983): 'Books can change your life, and a book that changed mine was *The Great Hunger* by Cecil Woodham-Smith' (Pilling, 1983, p.188). Pilling told me how emotionally Woodham-Smith's words affected her during our interview in Oxford: 'I was very unnerved by it. I mean, I wept. When I got to the end of it, I wept. It was a life-changing book for me. I could never again think of the history of Ireland in the same way. I was deeply moved by it' (Pilling, 2001). Pilling spoke about the book's harrowing descriptions of how the people suffered as they succumbed to starvation and death. In the novel's postscript, she explains to the reader:

> Most agonizing in *The Great Hunger* are the descriptions of children. Starvation turned them into wizened monkey-like creatures covered all over with fine down; hospitals were silent places, filled with iron bedsteads where children opened and shut their mouths noiselessly, waiting for death. Unable to pay the rent, whole families were driven from their pathetic hovels, which were then razed to the ground to prevent their return.

(Pilling, 1983, p.188)

When Pilling finished Woodham-Smith's book, she slowly began to formulate the ideas for her children's narrative. Commissioned to write a ghost story, Pilling decided to use a horrible event in history in order to have the tale rooted in reality. In *The Great Hunger*, Pilling found a story more chilling than anything she could invent. Part horror story, part time-slip, *Black Harvest* is the tale of three modern-day English children who are vacationing in the Irish countryside and become possessed by ghosts who died during the Famine. The children take on the suffering of the starving family.

Meticulous about historical facts, Pilling pulled true stories directly from Woodham-Smith's work, such as the skeletal women combing the barren fields for crumbs of food and the cruel eviction scenes. Also included in *Black Harvest* is the particularly desperate incident of a young mother in a shop who tried to pay for bread with her dead child, a description Pilling found in *The Great Hunger* (ibid., 176).

Well-received when first published, *Black Harvest* has remained in print for over twenty years, is now considered a 'Collins Modern Classic', and has the distinction of being the longest-selling Irish Famine narrative written for children. Pilling noted the value of children's literature of the Famine and likes to think that *Black Harvest* will enlarge the sympathies and understanding of those who turn its pages (ibid., 192). Following *Black Harvest*, Pilling wrote four additional ghost stories, all with the same characters embedded in historical episodes. She insists that *Black Harvest*, her first published book, is also her best because no other tragic event has ever affected her as much as the Great Famine. During our interview she explained, 'I never had the same "kick" from writing any other book, because I was very moved by the plight of the Famine children' (Pilling, 2001).

Along with Morpurgo and Pilling, Eve Bunting remains greatly indebted to Woodham-Smith's work. Born and educated in Ireland, Bunting immigrated to the United States with her husband and children from Northern Ireland in 1958. A Caldecott Medal winner, she has written over 230 books for children. One of Bunting's first children's novels was *The Haunting of Kildoran Abbey* (1978), an adventure tale portraying the Great Famine. During our interview, Bunting told me that she was introduced to Woodham-Smith by her husband, who has a library 'that you wouldn't believe, everything with the word "Ireland" in the title is on his shelf!' Once Bunting started *The Great Hunger*, she became 'really obsessed' and was unable to stop reading it:

> I felt of all the books I read at that time, this was the one that really gave me the most heartache and when a book does that to you, well, then I know I love it and want to do something myself. That is just a tremendous book, and I learned so much from that book. The more I immersed myself in what had happened in Ireland all those years ago, the more intent I became in writing something about it for children.
>
> (Bunting, 2001)

After reading *The Great Hunger*, Bunting, for the first time in her life, understood the reality of the Famine and began to comprehend fully how horrendous life was for the Irish in the 1840s. 'I learnt nothing about the Famine in school', Bunting explained to me. She went on to say that reading *The Great Hunger* also made her feel homesick and even more Irish. Bunting explained:

> I was very much into all things Irish and it is so strange because when you live in Ireland you don't think a bit about being proud of being Irish and when you leave – that's when you begin to realize it! I will always be glad I was born in Ireland and lived in Ireland and all my children were born in Ireland. There is always that tug because of Ireland.
>
> (Ibid.)

The Haunting of Kildoran Abbey centres around eight homeless and orphaned Irish youths in 1847. Columb and Finn Mullen, 15-year-old twins, are the leaders of the group who band together to feed their starving village by capturing a barge filled with food en route to England. The adventure novel is fast-paced and contains various political, economic and historical details derived from Woodham-Smith's text.

Another author from Ireland influenced by *The Great Hunger* is Marie-Louise Fitzpatrick. An accomplished illustrator and writer for children, she holds the distinction of being the first person to have twice won the coveted Bisto Award, the annual children's book prize in Ireland awarded to an author or illustrator born or residing in Ireland. During our interview in her downtown Dublin studio, Fitzpatrick recalled her initial reluctance to read Woodham-Smith's text:

> I was afraid that I was going to find out that we were a lazy people who laid down and died, you know. I finally went out and picked up *The Great Hunger*, and when I read it, I understood completely how it happened. It is wonderful! I cried. It is a history book, but I cried. She is a factionist. She doesn't tell you what to think at all. You know, when you read you just want the facts.
>
> (Fitzpatrick, 2001)

Fitzpatrick wrote and illustrated *The Long March: A Famine Gift for Ireland* (1998), which has won numerous accolades, such as the 1998 Parents' Choice Gold Award and the 1999 Bisto Book of the Year Merit Award. Part parable, part history, the picture book tells the story of how the impoverished American Choctaw Indians sent aid to the Irish during the Famine.

Arthur McKeown, Irish author of *Famine* (1997), was 15 years old when he first read Woodham-Smith's book. He reread the text as an adult and was even more astounded by the information. During our interview in Dublin, McKeown told me he intentionally inserted a phrase from *The Great Hunger* – 'Who knows if this great hunger will ever end?' – into his easy-reader children's narrative. *Famine*, illustrated with black and white sketches and written with a simple vocabulary, centres on 8-year-old Maggie Campbell and her father Joe. The Irish Famine forces them to leave their homeland and sail to America.

Malachy Doyle is another Irish author who wrote a Famine book targeted for younger readers; it was published during the same time period as *Famine*. Doyle told me that he 'drew strongly' on Woodham-Smith's research. In fact, he even borrowed the title, *The Great Hunger* (1998), for his children's book. Set in Northern Ireland, the narrative centres on two young siblings, Maggie and Art Ryan. They witness the failure of the potato crop and are eventually forced to emigrate from Ireland.

James Heneghan, a Canadian author born in England, also told me that *The Great Hunger* was an 'especially valuable' resource while researching his time-travel narrative, *The Grave* (2000). His young adult novel concludes with an author's note that devotes a paragraph to Woodham-Smith's book (Heneghan, 2000, p.244). Conspiracy and intrigue lie at the centre of this mystery adventure tale, which revolves around 13-year-old Tom Mullen, who is living in 1970s Liverpool. Falling into a grave, Tom travels back in time to 1840s Ireland, where he experiences the cruelties and injustices of the Famine. *The Grave* has won numerous awards, including the 2001 Sheila A. Egoff B.C. Book Prize for Children's Literature and the 2000 Mr Christie's Book Award Silver Seal.

Several other children's writers I interviewed commented on the effect Woodham-Smith had on their Irish Famine novels: Carol Drinkwater, *The Hunger: The Diary of Phyllis McCormack* (2001), Laura Wilson, *How I Survived the Irish Famine* (2001), Soinbhe Lally, *The Hungry Wind* (1997), and Lynne Kositsky, *Rebecca's Flame* (1998). Some of the recent writers of the Irish Famine primarily gather their research from internet sources, and, unromantically, their impetus to create a Famine story for children is often market-related. Publishers, aware of the new teaching mandates regarding the Famine as part of the Holocaust curriculum in New York, New Jersey and other parts of the United States, are starting to commission children's authors to write on the subject. These formula-driven, word-controlled, series-type books continue the growth of Irish Famine literature but lack the passion displayed by the early authors on this historical topic.

Basic plot formula

Historical novels portraying the Great Famine to children and adolescents tend to follow predictable plot patterns. Generally, there is a reliance on two traditional conventions. The first is the quest, which is to survive the Famine, and the second is the initiation into adulthood, demonstrated by emigrating from Ireland. While some novels present the Famine from a slightly non-traditional angle and may insert unique twists and turns into the narrative, overall there is a remarkable consistency in the way the catastrophe is portrayed. In order to illustrate the representation of the Irish Famine in children's books, the general plot sequence is worth examining.

'As they drew near the lane they noticed a strange smell, a smell of something rank and putrid' (Lally, 1997, p.12). The typical story opens with the stench of the rotting potatoes in the field of a small farm, the desperate attempts to salvage any unspoiled potatoes, and the ultimate resignation that blight has occurred.[3] The reader vicariously feels the vast hunger the young girl and her family experience as they seek to survive. Most tales contain the historically accurate portrayal of the cruelty meted out to the peasants by the merciless and predatory landlords. Eviction scenes show the suffering and deprivation of thousands who were callously evicted from their homes by English soldiers.[4] Inevitably, each story includes the tumbling of a poor widow's cottage.

With their homes demolished, the main character and her family are left destitute, and the quest for food and work begins. There are depictions of wretched labourers working for a pittance and the contemptuous export of corn and cattle from Ireland while the poor starve.[5] Workhouses feature in these accounts, usually as places to be dreaded and feared.[6] To survive, sometimes the family must enter a workhouse, but disaster often strikes in the form of disease or other dire consequence.

Death is omnipresent. These are not cheery tales, as they deal with cruelty and hardship and are heart-wrenching at times. The young heroine often loses her parents and a baby sister to Famine fever.[7] Yet however desperate the situation may appear, the key to survival is usually found in the predictable escape from Ireland.[8] During the long walk to the docks, the protagonist has a series of encounters with the starving along the road. The initiation into adulthood now unfolds. Eventually the young woman reaches the docks and makes the horrendous passage to North America in a 'coffin ship'. There are similarly graphic descriptions of the crowded, stench-filled steerage pit where she comes face to face with illness and death.[9] In fact, the plots are somewhat repetitive. The central character befriending another family, an older passenger dying of fever and being cast overboard, and the storm at sea are all viable plot points. Sometimes the story concludes with the central character's arrival in America and the completed passage into adulthood. These narratives offer the Irish immigrant a fresh start, and the story is able to conclude on a happier or more hopeful note.[10] Sequels set in America follow several of these novels.[11]

Heroic characters

These are survival stories. The resourcefulness and inner courage necessary in escaping starvation and fever under horrendous circumstances lie at the centre of these novels. While adult Famine literature is often centred on passive victimization or active resistance, children's Famine literature is focused on the will to survive incredible hardships. The main characters are consistently courageous, spirited, quick-witted and independent. Determined to create new and better worlds for themselves, these young heroes learn to endure and to seize every chance for survival.

Nearly every author I interviewed purposely depicted confident and positive Irish characters in his or her Famine narrative. The protagonists remained strong throughout the storyline by enduring emigration from Ireland and battling bigotry and intolerance in America. These attributes are rooted in historical fact, as Hasia Diner describes in *Erin's Daughters in America* (1983). Her research reveals that thousands of Irish women were able to utilize ambition, energy and ability that would otherwise have remained stifled by the effects of the Great Famine. Diner describes these educational and occupational successes and emphasizes that the qualities that enabled many Irish to prosper can be found in Ireland's cultural traditions. The personality traits that Diner articulates are repeated in the central characters of children's fiction of the Famine. Themes of resiliency, gallantry, love and loyalty, commonly portrayed in Famine novels, are interpreted by youngsters as typically Irish.

Novels about the Great Famine allow readers to experience vicariously the devastating effects that famine, poverty and homelessness can have on people and provide an understanding of human resilience. Children, who are beginning to form their own values and principles, can learn from the bravery and hope of the protagonists who persevered against the odds. I believe these stories allow young readers today to relate to these Irish protagonists as heroes, thus counteracting potential guilt and shame that may have plagued the generations before them.

Why didn't the Irish just fish?

Consider this personal memory relating to the theme of guilt and shame. I have vague recollections of my social studies teacher remarking that it was ludicrous that the Irish never fished the seas, implying that they were responsible for starving. This sentiment is not unique, and some of my American contemporaries have similar recollections that the Irish were too lazy, too stupid to save themselves. 'It is difficult at first to understand why the Irish people, thousands of whom lived near the coast, did not fish', Woodham-Smith acknowledges (Woodham-Smith, 1991, p.289). Certainly, it is unflattering for a nation to perceive itself as passive victims.

Contemporary Irish children's literature has changed this misconception. Embedded in numerous narratives are various reasons explaining why Ireland, an island surrounded by water, failed to take advantage of its maritime wealth. Novels such as *Twist of Gold* (Morpurgo, 1983) educate children by portraying their characters taking risks by fishing illegally. *The Hungry Wind* (1997), by Irish author Soinbhe Lally, also reveals the hardships endured during the Great Famine:

> Each day the women and girls went to the rocks to gather seaweed and shellfish. At one end of the strand there were stretches of muddy sand, encrusted with acres of mussels, but they were not allowed to pick those. For fear that hunger would tempt them the landlord's agent, Mister Hamilton, sent his men to warn tenants, that the mussel beds were not included in their shore rights.
>
> (Lally, 1997, p.14)

A passage from the fantasy novel *Knockabeg: A Famine Tale* (2001), written by Mary E. Lyons, gives additional information regarding this issue: 'The shilling go to Lord Armitage Shank for his bloody rent! Many families have even sold their hide canoes and fishing nets to pay the fee' (Lyons, 2001, p.5).

These narratives do not correlate laziness with Irishness. Instead, the books educate young readers by illustrating the varied and complex circumstances surrounding the fishing problem, such as fishermen being forced to sell their gear to buy food for their families and fishing rights belonging to the English landlords. Shame, which may have been associated with passive victimization, has now been replaced by an accurate historical understanding of this issue. Children's literature of the Irish Famine, non-existent during my childhood, sheds new light on complicated issues and educates children by weaving historical information through the narrative.

Significance of children's literature of the Famine

Irish Famine novels ignite a historical consciousness and provide an ideal way to help children learn about the most dominant cultural and societal event in Irish history, as well as about the consequential tidal wave of emigration it produced. 'The vivid descriptions of the conditions and suffering endured by people at this time help children come to grips with the enormity of the tragedy', observes children's literature scholar John Savage (1999, p.162). This literature is particularly important in educating children about the Great Famine because there is limited mention of the event in history textbooks. The lack of reference in American, Irish and English school texts has been documented by various scholars.[12] Writers for children have imaginatively represented the Irish Famine by bringing the event to life in a way that informational books cannot. Several Irish Famine novels are regularly used in the classroom, and *Under the Hawthorn Tree* (1990) by Marita Conlon-McKenna is on the national curriculum and read by every Irish primary student. Young people, rarely represented in traditional textbooks, are the main protagonists in juvenile fiction. Famine novels help children understand the greatest crisis in Irish history by personifying it through fictional characters with whom they can identify, thus making the history of the Great Famine real to them. The protagonists are heroes, surviving by any means they can, whether it is fishing illegally on the landlord's land or emigrating from their homeland. A more confident Irish identity results from this new understanding and awareness.

Historical children's novels depicting the Irish Famine provide linkages between the past and the present. Understanding the human impact of the Irish Famine can help young readers understand the political side of the world hunger issue today. These novels reveal the root causes of famines, which include the reality that politics often prevent the distribution of food to the victims. Amarta Sen, the 1998 Nobel laureate economist, has argued that modern famines are not about food but about a lack of will in its distribution. According to Cormac Ó Gráda, Sen stresses that 'a major problem with food aid is that much of it never reaches the starving' (Ó Gráda,1999, p.47).

There are frequent references in children's Famine narratives to silent Irish villages where dogs are no longer heard barking because they are either too weak to bark or have been killed and eaten by the starving peasants. This eerily parallels a *Sixty Minutes* segment profiling the ongoing famine in North Korea; Mike Wallace reported that birds could no longer be heard singing because the famished North Koreans have eaten them

all. Also, scenes in Famine novels of Irish children scavenging the coast-
lines for food are identical to the *Sixty Minutes* footage of the North
Koreans foraging the beaches for scraps of maritime leftovers. In addition,
many texts detail the drastic steps taken by those desperate to escape
starvation. Stowaways are referenced, their plight often resulting in
disastrous consequences. Do children realize that similar ill-fated attempts
still occur? This valuable literature enables readers to make the connection
that many people today, similar to the Irish Famine emigrants, face leaving
their homelands as a result of sheer necessity. Young readers should be
aware that the extremes of famine and poverty during the 1840s are still
pervasive in many parts of the world. The Irish Famine should be
remembered so that future famines can possibly be prevented.

Conclusion

Cecil Woodham-Smith's serendipitous impression on children's literature
has long been unacknowledged, though it is perhaps her most significant
legacy. Her groundbreaking book *The Great Hunger* provided the emotional
spark and historical information necessary for authors to create authentic
historical fiction that accurately represent the events of the Irish Famine
to children. Young readers, who often identify with the characters in the
storyline, relate to the perseverance of these protagonists and believe that
they too can successfully learn to handle difficult situations. Reading about
the Great Famine in historical fiction encourages children, both in Ireland
and globally, to construct new definitions of Irishness, which result in a
richer cultural identity and a deeper historical understanding of their
ancestral homeland.

Clearly, what initially compelled many authors to take the risk of
addressing traumatic details of the Irish Famine was their reading of
Woodham-Smith's *The Great Hunger*. Her work resonated deep within these
maverick children's authors, inspiring them to write against the mainstream
publishing mindset of the time about a historically significant, but socially
taboo, subject. Cecil Woodham-Smith provided the inspiration and context
for the creation of a canon of children's literature of the Irish Famine.

References

Bolton, Carole. *The Search of Mary Katherine Mulloy*. New York: Thomas
    Nelson, 1974.
Branson, Karen. *The Potato Eaters*. New York: G.P. Putman's Sons, 1979.

Branson, Karen. *Streets of Gold*. New York: G.P. Putman's Sons, 1981.

Bunting, Eve. *The Haunting of Kildoran Abbey*. New York: Frederick Warne, 1978.

Bunting, Eve. Telephone interview, 28 November 2001.

Conlon-McKenna, Marita. *Under the Hawthorn Tree*. New York: Holiday House, 1990.

Conlon-McKenna, Marita. Personal interview, 21 August 2001.

Coogan, Tim Pat. *Wherever Green Is Worn*. London: Arrow Books, 2000.

Daly, Mary E. 'Nationalism, sentiment, and economics: relations between Ireland and Irish America in the postwar years', *Eire-Ireland: Journal of Irish Studies*, Spring–Summer (2002), 25 March 2004 <http://www. findarticles.com/cf_dls/m0FKX/2002_Spring- Summer/87915677/ p10/article.j>.

Diner, Hasia R. *Erin's Daughters in America*. Baltimore, MA: Johns Hopkins University Press, 1983.

Doyle, Ann. 'Ethnocentrism and history textbooks: representation of the Irish Famine 1845–1849 in history textbooks in English secondary schools', *Intercultural Education*, Vol.13 (2002), pp.315–30.

Doyle, Malachy. *The Great Hunger*. London: Franklin Watts, 1998.

Doyle, Malachy. 'The Famine', e-mail to author, 7 August 2001.

Drinkwater, Carol. *The Hunger: The Diary of Phyllis McCormack*. London: Scholastic, 2001.

Drinkwater, Carol. 'Re: the hunger – the diary of Phyllis McCormack', e-mail to author, 8 January 2002.

Drinkwater, Carol. 'Re: interview', e-mail to author, 11 January 2002.

Fitzpatrick, Marie-Louise. *The Long March: A Famine Gift for Ireland*. Dublin: Wolfhound Press, 1998.

Fitzpatrick, Marie-Louise. Personal interview, 22 August 2001.

Giff, Patricia Reilly. *Nory Ryan's Song*. New York: Delacorte Press, 2000.

Giff, Patricia Reilly. *Maggie's Door*. New York: Wendy Lamb Books, 2003.

Gribben, Arthur (ed.). *The Great Famine and the Irish Diaspora in America*. Amherst, MA: University of Massachusetts Press, 1999.

Griswold, Jerry. 'The future of the profession', *The Lion and the Unicorn*, Vol.26, No.2 (2002), pp.236–42.

Hayden, Tom, (ed.). *Irish Hunger: Personal Reflections on the Legacy of the Famine*. Boulder, CO: Roberts Rinehart Publishers, 1997.

Hayden, Tom. *Irish on the Inside*. New York: Verso, 2001.

Heneghan, James. *The Grave*. New York: Frances Foster Books, 2000.

Heneghan, James. 'Re: children's literature of the Irish Famine', e-mail to author, 28 July 2001.

Keenan, Celia. 'Reflecting a new confidence: Irish historical fiction for children', *The Lion and the Unicorn*, Vol.21, No.3 (1997) pp.369–78.

Kinealy, Christine. *This Great Calamity: The Irish Famine, 1845–52*. London: Pluto Press, 1994.

Kinealy, Christine. *A Death-Dealing Famine: The Great Hunger in Ireland*. London: Pluto Press, 1997.

Kinealy, Christine. 'The Great Irish Famine: a dangerous memory', in Arthur Gribben (ed.), *The Great Famine and the Irish Diaspora in America*. Amherst, MA: University of Massachusetts Press, 1999.

Kinealy, Christine. 'The Famine killed everything: living with the memory of the Great Hunger', in David A. Valone and Christine Kinealy (eds), *Ireland's Great Hunger*. Lanham, MD: University Press of America, 2002, pp.1–40.

Kositsky, Lynne. *Rebecca's Flame*. Montreal: Roussan Publishers, 1998.

Kositsky, Lynne. Telephone interview, 24 September 2002.

Litton, Helen. 'The Famine in schools', in Tom Hayden (ed.), *Irish Hunger*. Boulder, CO: Roberts Rinehart Publishers, 1997.

Lyons, Mary E. *Knockabeg: A Famine Tale*. Boston, MA: Houghton Mifflin, 2001.

Lyons, Mary E. Personal interview, 10 November 2001.

Lally, Soinbhe. *The Hungry Wind*. Dublin: Poolbeg Press, 1997.

Lally, Soinbhe. Personal interview, 27 August 2001.

Lutzeier, Elizabeth. *The Coldest Winter*. London: Oxford University Press, 1991.

Lutzeier, Elizabeth. *Bound for America*. London: Oxford University Press, 2000.

McCormack, Colette. *Mary-Anne's Famine*. Cork: Attic Press, 1994.

McCormack, Colette. *After the Famine*. Dublin: Attic Press, 1995.

McKeown, Arthur. *Famine*. Dublin: Poolbeg Press, 1997.

McKeown, Arthur. Personal interview, 2 February 2002.

McNamara, Karen Hill. 'Telling Bridget's tale of hunger: Children's literature of the great Irish famine.' Ph.D. dissertation, available at <http://www.il.proquest.com>

Morpurgo, Michael. *Twist of Gold*. London: Kaye & Ward, 1983.

Morpurgo, Michael. Personal interview, 3 July 2001.

Murphy, Maureen, Maureen Militia and Alan Singer (eds). *New York State Great Irish Famine Curriculum Guide*. Albany, NY: State Department of Education, 2001.

Ó Gráda, Cormac. *Black '47 and Beyond: The Great Irish Famine in History, Economy, and Memory*. Princeton, NJ: Princeton University Press, 1999.

Pilling, Ann. *Black Harvest*. London: Armada, 1983.

Pilling, Ann. Personal interview, 5 July 2001.

Savage, John F. 'Integrating Irish children's literature into a multicultural curriculum', *New Advocate*, Vol.12, No.2 (Spring 1999), pp.155–67.

Small, Hugh. 'Florence Nightingale's 20th-century biographers', 14 April 2004, <http://www.florence-nightingale-avenging-angel.co.uk/biograph.htm>.

Valone, David and Christine Kinealy (eds). *Ireland's Great Hunger*. Lanham, MD: University Press of America, 2002.

Wallace, Mike. 'North Korea', *Sixty Minutes*. CBS, 2 February 2003.

Wilson, Laura. *How I Survived the Irish Famine: The Journal of Mary O'Flynn*. New York: HarperCollins, 2001.

Wilson, Laura. Personal interview, 6 July 2001.

Woodham-Smith, Cecil. *The Reason Why*. New York: McGraw-Hill, 1953.

Woodham-Smith, Cecil. *The Great Hunger: Ireland 1845–1849* [1962]. London: Penguin, 1991.

CHAPTER 14

An afterword on silence

Christopher Morash

It is now almost twenty years now since I first began thinking about Irish Famine literature. Back in the mid-1980s, when I told colleagues about my work, the response was almost always the same. I would get a quizzical look, followed by: 'There's not much to study, is there?'

Of course, at that time there was a good basic reason for questioning the existence of a body of Irish Famine literature. Apart from a few well-known examples (principally Carleton's *The Black Prophet* and some of Mangan's poetry), nineteenth-century Irish writing was of marginal scholarly interest, studied only as the unlikely loam out of which the Literary Renaissance flowered, and hence almost entirely out of print. Without this background of contemporary literary responses to the Famine, it was difficult to see how more recent works, such as Tom Murphy's *Famine*, could fit within a wider context of something called 'Irish Famine Literature'.

There was a palpable shift in Irish Studies in the late 1980s and early 1990s, and for those of us writing about nineteenth-century Irish cultural history, there was an equally palpable sense of excitement, of breaking new ground. Among the many changes that took place in the critical landscape as the 150th anniversary of the Famine approached was an erosion of the disciplinary boundaries between literary criticism and other forms of historical and cultural enquiry. This 'turn to history', as it was sometimes called, was, of course, by no means unique to Irish Studies and has now become so much the norm in all aspects of literary studies that it is easy to forget that in the late 1980s, amidst the roar of post-structuralist textual critics locking horns with an earlier generation of textual critics, those of us who wanted to recover the referent often had to cling to the thinnest of theoretical ledges. But cling we did, buoyed by a growing recognition that a theoretically sophisticated recovery of history was absolutely necessary in a literary culture in which the authority of the author had long been an almost unquestioned orthodoxy (not least among authors themselves). In time, this reshaping of the critical landscape was given a distinctively Irish theoretical shape by writers like Terry Eagleton, Seamus Deane and David Lloyd, and with the emergence of post-colonial theory in the mid-1990s, there was at last a critical context in which nineteenth-century Ireland seemed less like a quaint antiquarian interest and more like a paradigm of one of the defining struggles of modernity.

The other major tectonic shift that took place in those years was the permission – borrowed from the wider field of cultural studies – to consider literary texts as cultural artefacts rather than as aesthetic objects to be assessed. Personally, the initial excitement of nineteenth-century Irish studies for me came not from the unexpected and rare discovery of a forgotten work of a real quality, but from the ephemera: the tracts, the sermons, the newspapers that collapsed after three issues, the ballads. Indeed, for me the paradigmatic work of nineteenth-century Irish Famine literature is not Carleton's best known novel, *The Black Prophet*, but *The Squanders of Castle Squander*, a vital mess that starts out as an Irish Victorian novel and ends up as an exploded archive of miscellaneous writing, somewhere far beyond the limits of narrative resolution. It has never been reprinted and probably never will be; but in its disorder it has that 'touch of the real', to use Stephen Greenblatt's phrase, that remains one of the central, unattainable goals of the study of Famine writing (Greenblatt, 1997, p.14). So, when Katherine Parr, in the current collection, argues that two writers in the *Nation* are 'major nineteenth-century Irish poets' (Parr, this volume, p.30), I am not sure that I would agree with her; but that may be because I do not think it is necessary for a writer to be 'major' to be worth our time. Indeed, for a period after the publication of David Lloyd's influential *Nationalism and Minor Literature* in 1987, being a 'minor' writer conferred a certain street credibility in the field of nineteenth-century Irish writing.

And so a corpus of Famine writing began to take shape; the *Nation* poetry, Carleton's wayward but mesmerizing fiction, and plays such as Hubert O'Grady's *The Famine* all began to take their place in an archive whose value derived from a common referent – the Famine – rather than from the aesthetic qualities of the signifying text. In some regards, *Hungry Words* continues this process of canon formation, with Parr making a place for the *Nation* poets Ellen Mary Downing and Mary Anne Kelly, and Karen Hill McNamara breaking new ground with her survey of children's Famine literature (although each of these contributors, it should be noted, still want to make claims of literary value for their subjects). And there are, of course, essays re-evaluating recognized milestones of Famine literature: Nicholas Grene's reassessment of Tom Murphy's *Famine*, drawing for the first time on Murphy's manuscripts (now in the library of Trinity College, Dublin); Margaret Scanlan's return to Trollope's *Castle Richmond*; and Jerome Day's contextualization of Yeats's Famine play, *The Countess Cathleen*.

At the same time, *Hungry Words* marks a shift in the study of Famine literature in that it contains a stream of essays whose agenda is to relocate the Famine at the heart of a traditional, aesthetically defined, Irish literary canon. So, we have Bonnie Roos continuing the work begun by Cheryl Herr in *Joyce's Anatomy of Culture* (1986) by unravelling references to the Famine in Joyce's *Ulysses*; Julieann Ulin making the case for Beckett's *Endgame* as a Famine play; George Cusack hearing echoes of the Famine on the dark Mayo roads of Synge's *Playboy of the Western World*; and Sarah Goss arguing that Stoker's *Dracula* 'stands for the Famine dead who will not stay buried' (this volume, p.105). *Ulysses*, *Playboy of the Western World*, *Endgame* and *Dracula*: these are all almost certainly works on anyone's list of a mainstream Irish literary canon. Add to this Nieves Pascual's reading of Eavan Boland's anorexia poems as Famine texts, Bob Evans's recovery of the importance of the Famine in Frank O'Connor's understanding of Irish history, and Margaret Kelleher's look back to Maria Edgeworth (a writer we would usually consider to have pre-dated the Famine), and we see a new development in Famine studies. Here we have critics extending the range of Famine writing not by recuperating ever-more obscure writers, but by becoming more sensitively attuned to traces of the Famine at the heart of mainstream literary culture.

From Beckett to obscure nineteenth-century ballads churned out on hand-presses, from Eavan Boland to evangelical sermons and Victorian economic tracts – the body of Irish Famine writing has grown and spread in all directions over the past two decades, from the ephemeral and non-literary to texts that satisfy even the most demanding definition of high culture. And yet, one thing remains unchanged in the study of Famine literature: the assumption that there has been a literary silence concerning the Famine. This assumption – sometimes spoken, sometimes implicit – was there all those years ago when my colleagues and I were asked if there was any Famine literature worth studying; and it is present today, in a different form, not least in some of the essays included here.

Over the years, that silence has itself become an object of inter-pretation, filtered through a variety of views of agency in human history.

For some commentators, it is a deliberate evasion: on the part of the British government and British people, who could have done more; on the part of the rural middle classes in Ireland, many of whom profited from the redistribution of land; or on the part of Irish people as a whole, ashamed at what had happened. Indeed, the essay by Christine Kinealy in the current collection provides a useful survey of the continuing debates over cause and culpability that continue to shape historical understanding of the Famine, reminding us that in spite of extensive archival scholarship over the past couple of decades, key issues remain unresolved. The politics of the interpretation may vary; nonetheless, there is a widely-shared belief that the Famine remained taboo for more than a century, the great unwritten event of Irish history.

On the face of it, it may seem like time that this particular idea was laid to rest: if nothing else, the essays contained here, and the whole body of Famine scholarship on which they draw, have brought to our view a tradition of Famine writing, which, if it was not always overt, was nonetheless sustained. However, we may well be overly hasty in dismissing the silence. While the notion of silence as an absence of representation (at least in terms of quantity) may fly in the face of the evidence, over the years the notion of silence has mutated into something less literal. While it may no longer be possible to argue that there is a lack of literary response to an event whose traces can be found in Beckett, Joyce and Yeats, at the same time, the adequacy of that response is still very much an open question. It has long been recognized that as an historical event in which matters such as causality, duration and agency look increasingly unresolvable, the Famine lacks a recognizable narrative shape. Indeed, one of the surprising threads running through the current collection is the persisting importance of Cecil Woodham-Smith's *The Great Hunger*, which emerges as a defining influence on children's literature in Karen Hill McNamara's essay as well as on Tom Murphy's *Famine* in Nicholas Grene's essay. It could be argued that in spite of the criticism that has been levelled at Woodham-Smith's book as history, its continuing appeal – like the appeal of John Mitchel's *The Last Conquest of Ireland (Perhaps)* in the nineteenth century – is its ability to confer a structured historical narrative on the events of those years.

However, the question of adequate representation goes beyond configuring events into a narrative form. The question goes further, to what Paul Ricoeur has called 'the paradox of the trace'. 'On one hand, the trace is visible here and now, as a vestige, a mark', he writes. 'On the

other hand, there is a trace (or track) because "earlier" a human being or
animal passed this way. Something did something . . . Where then, is the
paradox? In the fact that the passage no longer is, but the trace remains'
(Ricoeur, 1985, p.119). For Ricoeur, this is a foundational paradox for all
forms of historical writing; in the case of the Famine we confront it in an
extreme form. The events of the past are gone. To state the situation this
bluntly is, however, to diminish what is meant here. The lives, the
sufferings, the consciousnesses of thousands, of millions, of human beings
were here; but now they are gone. In their place, we have traces: marks on
paper, marks on landscape, fragments in memory. And these traces must
bear the burden of the reality of all those past lives; they must, to borrow
another phrase from Ricoeur, perform the function of 'standing for' that
which is no longer present. And this function, as Ricoeur reminds us, is
not aesthetic; it is an ethical obligation. In retrospect, it becomes clear that
it was this substitution of the ethical for the aesthetic that created the
initial necessity in Irish Studies of putting aside questions of artistic value
to study the minor and the ephemeral when creating a corpus of Famine
literature.

In the current collection, the aesthetic re-enters the equation in a
number of different guises. There is the continuing attempt to make
claims for forgotten writers as 'major' figures, and there is the new drive to
locate traces of the Famine in the established canon whose aesthetic value
is unquestioned. But there is a more subtle thread running through many
of the essays contained here, as they attempt in their varying ways to
define with greater clarity this task of 'standing for' by considering the
Famine as metaphor. While all of the essays here deal with this issue to
some extent, the opening of Nicholas Grene's essay on Tom Murphy
helps us to pin it down precisely. Grene is writing about Patrick
Kavanagh's long poem *The Great Hunger*, the title of which, he notes,
would lead a reader 'to suppose this was a narrative of the terrible Irish
Famine of almost a century before'. Of course, Kavanagh is writing not
about the Famine of the 1840s at all, but about the hungers that gnaw at
the life of a small farmer in rural Monaghan in the 1940s; at the same
time, 'he invokes . . . the resonance of catastrophe to enforce his polemic
point . . . Strangely, though, it may have been this metaphorical application of the idea of famine that first gave the phrase [the Great Hunger]
its currency in English' (Grene, this volume, p.245).

In fact, it may not be strange at all that the phrase 'the great hunger'
gained currency in English through metaphor. Collectively, the essays

gathered here remind us of the extent to which traces of the Famine are caught in nets of metaphor. 'Dracula represents the potential that the horrors of the Famine will not remain buried in the past,' argues Sarah Goss (this volume, p.105). For Bonnie Roos, the 'shrivelled black potato' that Bloom carries in his pocket throughout *Ulysses* becomes a metaphor for the Famine, carried secretly through the streets of Dublin; similarly, for Julieann Ulin, all of those elements of Beckett's *Endgame* that theatre-goers would identify as most purely Beckettian can be read as metaphors for the Famine: 'The paralysis that pervades *Endgame* is the result of continual deprivation, the characters' inability to leave the house, and the waiting for "the end", precisely the condition of many Famine victims in Ireland of the previous century' (this volume, p.207). In Nieves Pascual's essay, the structure of metaphor takes a physical form on the page itself, as her essay splits into two columns, through which meditations on contemporary subsistence crises, the Irish Famine of the 1840s, and the poems of Eavan Boland weave together. 'For Tom Murphy, writing *Famine* in the 1960s', continues Nicholas Grene, 'there was comparable interplay between the historic and the contemporary, the literal and the figurative, the past and the present', and he goes on to quote from comments made by Tom Murphy in a public discussion during the 2001 Murphy retrospective at the Abbey Theatre:

> I began to feel that perhaps the idea of food, the absence of food, is only one element of famine: that all of those other poverties attend famine, that people become silent and secretive, intelligence becomes cunning. I felt that the hangover of the 19th century famine was still there in my time . . .
>
> (this volume, pp.255–6)

These comments tell us about more than Tom Murphy's *Famine*; they describe a technique common to many of the essays gathered here.

For the scholars contributing to *Hungry Words*, the 'hangover' (a word much more evocative than 'trace') of the nineteenth-century Famine continues to exist, not simply in their own time, but also in the time of the writers whose work they are considering, from Beckett in the 1950s, to Frank O'Connor in the early 1960s, to Yeats in the 1890s, retrospectively to (in the case of Margaret Kelleher's essay) Maria Edgeworth. Collectively, these essays remind us of the power of metaphor to dislodge an event from the linear flow of time. Indeed, one of the characteristics shared by a number of the key texts here – *Endgame, Playboy of the Western*

World and *The Countess Cathleen* – is their lack of any clear historical
referent. Jerome Day makes a particular point of this in his reading of
Yeats's play, pointing out that while the manuscript version of the play
indicates that it is set in the seventeenth century, Yeats's comments to
Lionel Johnson place it in the sixteenth century (Day, this volume, p.120).
By the same token, George Cusack notes that the world of Synge's *Playboy*
is 'removed from the dominant historical continuity' (this volume, p.145),
and the play could, effectively, take place in any century from the seventeenth to the twentieth. Such works – like Kavanagh's *The Great Hunger* –
both refer, and do not refer, to the Famine of the 1840s. Dislodging an
event from 'the dominant historical continuity' may not be the way in
which to understand the historical past for an empiricist historian; indeed,
such a practice runs the risk of transforming history into myth. At the
same time, this disruption of the flow of history through metaphor is part
of the process through which the Famine becomes part of an internalized
– but analyzable – historical identity. If the metaphors through which the
Famine appear to us are sometimes blatantly ahistorical – as in the case of
Kavanagh's poem, or Murphy's comments – we are presented with a kind
of Brechtian alienation effect, reminding us that we are not confronting
the Famine itself, but something which performs the function of 'standing
for' the Famine. The Famine, by necessity, is elsewhere.

     This in turn brings us back to the defining feature of the Famine: it is
not hunger, or disease, or emigration, or displacement or land ownership;
it is not colonialism, or resistance or culpability: it is absence. There is the
absence of food, the absence of the culture that was uprooted, and most
of all, the absence of the human beings who died or who emigrated. As
such, the Famine presents an historiographic problem which is by no
means unique. Quite the contrary, it could be said to be exemplary. In
historical writing, the past, which is by definition absent, must become the
subject of a text in the present, by means of the 'standing for' function, of
which Ricoeur speaks. In the case of the Famine, absence is multiplied; for
that which is absent in the past is, in itself, an absence.

     As the Famine settles into a recognized place within Irish cultural
studies, as the essays gathered here collectively testify, it might be argued
nonetheless that these traces are becoming fainter with time. Margaret
Scanlan certainly challenges us to consider this possibility in her essay,
when she reminds us that for the past decade Ireland has had one of the
highest rates of economic growth in the world, opening an ever-wider gulf
between an Ireland in which people died in ditches and an Ireland with

the highest *per capita* Mercedes sales in Europe. 'The contemporary Irish person, like the contemporary American, occupies the position that middle-class English people occupied in the 1840s', she writes.

> They are not victims of the dominant economic system, but its beneficiaries, an uneasy moral position for anyone contemplating its human costs. Such people may wish to empathize with the starving, yet the leap is such that empathy risks seeming sentimental or presumptuous.
>
> (Scanlan, this volume, pp.66–7)

From this perspective, it is true that the Famine is less of a living metaphor now than it was for an earlier generation of Irish writers, such as Patrick Kavanagh or Tom Murphy (much less for the writers of the nineteenth century), and Scanlan does well to warn us that a certain kind of writing about the Famine courts a dangerous and deceptive sentimentalism, feeding a desire to cling to the status of victim amid the spoils of economic success. In this regard, we would do well to recall a play that was a contemporary of Tom Murphy's *Famine*: Hugh Leonard's *The Patrick Pearse Motel* (1966), set in 'Dublin's vodka-and-bitter lemon-belt', and featuring 'The Famine Room' restaurant ('best steaks in Ireland'). There is an argument to be made, for instance, that keeping the Famine alive through renewing its metaphorical language performs an ethical function in the present, creating a communal conscience that provides a necessary historical context for dealing with issues such as economic refugees in contemporary Ireland, or Ireland's responsibility towards the developing world. At the same time, it could well be that as the Famine recedes from the world of contemporary Ireland, it becomes more purely an absence, approached only through the misdirections of metaphor. As such, it returns to the state in which it most fully bears witness to the lives of those who are gone.

Silence.

References

Carleton, William. *The Squanders of Castle Squander*. London: Office of the Illustrated London Library, 1852.

Carleton, William. 'Extract from *The Black Prophet*', in Seamus Deane (ed.), *The Field Day Anthology of Irish Writing*, Vol.2. Derry: Field Day Publications, 1991.

Greenblatt, Stephen. 'The touch of the real', *Representations*, 59 (1997), pp.14–29.

Herr, Cheryl. *Joyce's Anatomy of Culture*. Urbana, IL: University of Illinois Press, 1986.

Leonard, Hugh. 'The Patrick Pearse Motel', in SF. Gallagher (ed.), *Selected Plays: Hugh Leonard*. Gerrards Cross: Colin Smythe, 1992.

Lloyd, David. *Nationalism and Minor Literature: James Clarence Mangan and the Emergence of Irish Cultural Nationalism*. Berkeley, CA: University of California Press, 1987.

Mitchel, John. *The Last Conquest of Ireland (Perhaps)*. (1861); reprinted London: Burns, Oates & Washbourne, n.d.

O'Grady, Hubert. *The Famine* (1886); rpt *Journal of Irish Studies*, Vol.14, No.1 (January 1985), pp.25–49.

Ricoeur, Paul. *Time and Narrative*, Vol.3. Chicago, IL: University of Chicago Press, 1985. 3 vols.

NOTES

NOTES to Chapter 1

1. This was the original title of a poem written by Speranza, which was subsequently renamed 'The Famine Year'.

NOTES to Chapter 2

1. In Christopher Morash's *A Hungry Voice*, we find an unnamed poet whose lament approximates the traditional *caoine* (p.48). The poem 'Lay of the Famine: the Irish Husband to his Wife' is initialed 'W.C.B.'
2. The Field Day series on Irish writers omits poetry by the *Nation's* women poets, only including essays by Lady Wilde and Downing. Furthermore, histories of nineteenth-century Ireland written by men acknowledge these women only in notations to the men with whom they were romantically linked: Ellen Downing with Joseph Brennan and Mary Kelly with Kevin Izod O'Doherty.
3. Eileen O'Connell's 'The Lament for Art O'Leary' appears in Sean O'Tuama's explication of the poem and in the fourth volume of the *Field Day Anthology of Irish Writing*.
4. In March 2004, I visited the North Presentation Convent and was graciously received by Sr Dolarosa, Sr Marie Gaetti, Sr DeLourdes Keane and Sr Rosarei, who confirmed that the annals of the convent record Downing's reception to the convent 29 May 1850, and her reluctant departure on 16 September of the same year.
5. Kelly attributes the verse to Jeremiah 49:17.

NOTES to Chapter 3

1. An earlier version of this essay was published in *Éire-Ireland*, Vol.32, No.1 (1997), pp.41–62. I gratefully acknowledge the permission of the Irish American Cultural Institute for its republication; my thanks also to Vera Kreilkamp for her invaluable assistance.
2. Key studies are Marilyn Butler's ground-breaking *Maria Edgeworth: A Literary Biography* (Oxford: Oxford University Press, 1972); Michael Hurst's treatment of Edgeworth's politics in *Maria Edgeworth and the Public Scene: Intellect, Fine Feeling and Landlordism in the Age of Reform* (London: Macmillan, 1969); Tom Dunne's *Maria Edgeworth and the Colonial Mind* (Dublin: National University of Ireland, 1985); and W.J. McCormack's discussion of Edgeworth in *Ascendancy and Tradition in Anglo-Irish Literary History from 1789 to 1939* (Oxford: Clarendon, 1985). Significant contributions to Edgeworth criticism in recent years range from Claire Connolly's edition of *Letters for Literary Ladies* (London: Everyman, 1993) to, most recently, Sharon Murphy's *Edgeworth and Romance* (Dublin: Four Courts, 2004).

3. The phrase is that of Homi Bhabha; see Colin Graham's application of Bhabha's theory to *Castle Rackrent* in his 'History, gender and the colonial moment', in Margaret Kelleher and James H. Murphy (eds), *Gender Perspectives in Nineteenth-Century Ireland: Private and Public Spheres* (Dublin: Irish Academic Press, 1997), pp.93–103.

4. From 1986–87, as part of the 'Mothers of the Novel' series, Pandora Press (London) republished *Belinda, Patronage* and *Helen*. The Pickering twelve-volume series was completed in 2003.

5. Maria Edgeworth to Michael Pakenham Edgeworth, 19 February 1834, reproduced in Frances Edgeworth, *A Memoir of Maria Edgeworth*, 3 vols. (privately printed, 1867), Vol.3, pp.87–8, and in Augustus J.C. Hare, (ed.) *The Life and Letters of Maria Edgeworth*, 2 vols. (London: Arnold, 1894), p.202.

6. Terry Eagleton, *Heathcliff and the Great Hunger: Studies in Irish Culture* (London: Verso, 1995), p.176; David Lloyd, *Anomalous States: Irish Writing and the Post-Colonial Moment* (Dublin: Lilliput, 1993), p.134; the other example of this 'consensus', cited by Lloyd, is that of Sydney Owenson (Lady Morgan).

7. Maria Edgeworth to Michael Pakenham Edgeworth, 19 February 1834, reproduced in Hare (ed.) *The Life and Letters of Maria Edgeworth*, p.202, and in Edgeworth, *A Memoir of Maria Edgeworth*, Vol.3, pp.87–8.

8. See Grace A. Oliver, *A Study of Maria Edgeworth, with Notices of her Father and Friends* (Boston, MA: Williams, 1882); see also Helen Zimmerman, *Maria Edgeworth*, Eminent Women Series (London: Allen, 1883).

9. Anna Maria (Mrs S.C.) Hall's recollections of her 1842 visit to Edgeworthstown were published in *Art Journal*, Vol.1 (1849), pp.225–9, and Vol.18 (1866), pp.345–9. See also Zimmern, *Maria Edgeworth*, pp.207–9.

10. Michael Hurst, in *Maria Edgeworth and the Public Scene* (London: MacMillan, 1969), characterizes her politics as 'enlightened conservatism' (pp.29–30) and Edgeworth herself as a 'highly intelligent and voluble instance of the upper-class reformer with limited ends' (p.18).

11. Edgeworth's famine account thus differs significantly in form, and in outlook, from the diary of her contemporary Elizabeth Smith, a County Wicklow landowner. Two editions of Smith's diaries are available: Patricia Pelly and Andrew Tod (eds), *The Highland Lady in Ireland: Elizabeth Grant of Rothiemurchus* (Edinburgh: Canongate, 1991), and David Thomson and Moyra McGusty (eds), *The Irish Journals of Elizabeth Smith: 1840–1850* (Oxford: Clarendon, 1980).

12. Since 1995, the Edgeworth letters held by the Bodleian Library and National Library Dublin are available on microfilm. The series of two parts, totaling 45 reels, is entitled *Women, Education and Literature: The Papers of Maria Edgeworth, 1768–1849* (Reading: Adam Matthew, 1995). References to Bodleian holdings (part I) are drawn from this series; the abbreviation WEL will be used, and the relevant reel number provided. Although National Library Dublin holdings have been consulted in their original form, a cross-reference to the WEL series (part II) will also be provided.

13. Jones (1790–1855) was professor of political economy in King's College London from 1833 to 1835 and, from 1835, Malthus's successor as chair of political economy and history at the East India College in Haileybury. Eighteen letters from Edgeworth to Jones, written between 1833 and 1849, are collected in the Edgeworth Papers, Ms. 22,822, National Library Dublin; WEL, part II, reel 17. (Jones and Edgeworth shared a deep passion for roses, as much of their correspondence shows.)

14. Louisa Moore was mother of George Henry Moore, the nationalist MP, and grandmother of novelist George Moore. Typescript copies of six letters from Edgeworth to Moore are available in the Edgeworth Papers, Ms. 495, National Library Dublin; see WEL, part II, reel 19. Selections from these letters also appear in Joseph Hone, *The Moores of Moore Hall* (London: Cape, 1939).

15. Selections from Edgeworth's and Cruger's correspondence are contained in the Edgeworth Papers, Ms. 18,995, National Library Dublin; reproduced in WEL, part II, reel 15.

16. For Edgeworth's correspondence with the Society of Friends, see Edgeworth Papers, Ms. 989, National Library Dublin; reproduced in WEL, part II, reel 19. Three Edgeworth letters, on related topics, are included in the Ballitore Papers, National Library Dublin. References to this correspondence also occur in letters written by Maria to family members; see Edgeworth, *A Memoir of Maria Edgeworth*, Vol.3, p.250.

17. Selections from family letters appear in Frances Edgeworth's memoir and in Augustus Hare's volumes; references to some of Edgeworth's letters to Jones also appear in Michael Hurst's study. Many of the extracts referenced in this article, however, have not been previously published.

18. In terms of average excess mortality between 1846 and 1851 (that is, deaths attributable to famine), County Longford recorded between 20 and 30 deaths per 1,000; in national terms, the county is thus ranked among those counties less severely affected. See Peter Gray, *The Irish Famine* (London: New Horizons, 1995), p.94. However, as Christine Kinealy notes, for 1847, County Longford's mortality was well above the average, matching that experienced in Galway, Kerry and Roscommon; see Christine Kinealy, *This Great Calamity: The Irish Famine, 1845–1852* (Dublin: Gill & Macmillan, 1994), p.170. As Edgeworth herself warns, however, such estimates are very general in nature and fail to account for the great variations between localities; see note 19.

19. Maria Edgeworth to Honora Beaufort, 8 May 1847; reproduced in WEL, part I, reel 6. Part of this letter is reproduced in Edgeworth, *A Memoir of Maria Edgeworth*, Vol.3, p.254. In 1838 Honora had married Captain Francis Beaufort, Hydrographer Royal to the Navy and later Admiral; Captain Beaufort was brother to Honora's stepmother Frances Beaufort Edgeworth.

20. By spring 1847, the delay in opening soup kitchens, following the closure of public works, added significantly to the distress; see Kinealy, *This Great Calamity*, pp.123–36.

21. Maria Edgeworth to Honora Beaufort, 8 May 1847; reproduced in WEL, part I, reel 6.

22. Ms. 989, Edgeworth Papers.

23. Society of Friends Relief of Distress Papers, National Archives Dublin, ref. no: 2/506/36 [note: emphasis is Edgeworth's]. On 14 February, in a letter to her sister Fanny, Edgeworth observes that the poor have suffered dreadfully from the cold, the price of turf having trebled; see WEL, part I, reel 9.

24. Ms. 989, Edgeworth Papers.

25. Ibid.; see also letters from Edgeworth to Harvey and others in Ballitore papers, National Library Dublin – these letters are not included in the WEL series.

26. Maria Edgeworth to Dr Joshua Harvey, 1 February 1847; Ms. 989. For a wider discussion of women's philanthropy and famine work, see Margaret Kelleher, *The Feminisation of Famine* (Cork: Cork University Press, 1997), pp.86–100.

27. Bewley and Pim to Maria Edgeworth, 5 February 1847; Maria Edgeworth to Bewley and Pim, 5 February 1847; Ms. 989.

28. Maria Edgeworth to Bewley and Pim, 5 May; Ms. 989.

29. See *Transactions of the Central Relief Committee of the Society of Friends during the Famine in Ireland* (Dublin: Hodges & Smith, 1852; facsimile edition printed in Dublin: Éamonn de Búrca, 1996), pp.249–50; see also Ms. 989. The 'friend' alluded to by the committee appears to be a Miss Ryan, an Irishwoman living in America who lobbied her colleagues on the Irish relief committee in Cincinnati to send the balance of its funds to Edgeworth. A letter of thanks from Edgeworth to Ryan, written 1 January 1848, is included in Ms. 8,145, Edgeworth Papers, National Library Dublin; see WEL, part II, reel 20.

30. Maria Edgeworth to Bewley and Pim, 20 December 1847; Ms. 989.

31. Maria Edgeworth to Bewley and Pim, 29 December 1847; Ms. 989. In their letter of 22 December, Bewley and Pim alert Edgeworth, pointedly, to the measures they have taken to spare charges of transit and delay and to their inclusion of 84 lbs excess cornmeal in a total order of 4.5 tons.

32. Maria Edgeworth to Harriet Butler, 26 April 1847; see WEL, part 1, reel 10. The emphasis is Edgeworth's. A version of this letter also appears in Edgeworth, *A Memoir of Maria Edgeworth*, Vol.3, pp.252–3. Harriet's husband, Richard Butler, was Rector of Trim and afterwards Dean of Clonmacnoise.

33. Maria Edgeworth to Emmeline King, 17 July 1847; reproduced in WEL, part I, reel 6. Ticknor was Professor of Modern Literature at Harvard; he and his wife visited Edgeworthstown in the 1830s and remained in correspondence with the Edgeworth family. See Isabel Clarke, *Maria Edgeworth: Her Family and Friends* (London: Hutchinson, 1950), pp.166–71.

34. Maria Edgeworth to Emmeline King, 13 December 1847; reproduced in WEL, part 1, reel 6. In a letter to Fanny Wilson, 25 July 1847, Edgeworth mentions that she and family members are engaging in knitting 'chains' (headbands) as 'souvenirs or tokens of gratitude' for these young people and children; see WEL, part I, reel 9. Another anecdote, frequently cited by biographers, concerns the porters in America who, in 1847, refused to accept payment for transporting relief supplies and for whom Edgeworth and family members also knitted woollen comforters; writing to Miss Ryan on 1 January 1848 (Ms. 8,145), Edgeworth asks her advice on suitable gifts for these 'cartmen'. See also Edgeworth, *A Memoir of Maria Edgeworth*, Vol.3, p.290.

35. Maria Edgeworth to R.B. Forbes, 22 April 1847, reproduced as preface to R.B. Forbes, *The Voyage of the Jamestown on her Errand of Mercy* (Boston, MA: Eastburn, 1847).

36. Forbes, 'Note to Introduction', *The Voyage of the Jamestown*.

37. Harriet Cruger to Maria Edgeworth, 8 February 1847, reproduced in Ms. 18,995, Edgeworth Papers.

38. Maria Edgeworth to Harriet Cruger, 30 May 1847; Ms. 18,995.

39. Harriet Cruger to Maria Edgeworth, 7 February 1849; Ms. 18,995.

40. A copy of this circular is included in the Edgeworth–Cruger correspondence, Ms. 18,995.

41. The work of Christine Kinealy is particularly significant in this regard. See her study, *A Death-Dealing Famine: The Great Hunger in Ireland* (London and Chicago, IL: Pluto, 1997), pp.106–17.

42. Maria Edgeworth to Miss Ryan, 1 January 1848, in Ms. 8,145, Edgeworth Papers. In a letter to her sister Emmeline King, 13 December 1847, Maria

described how the money was disposed of: 'Mrs Edgeworth has the money and is disposing of it to the best advantage in employing men, women and children – and preventing them from being mere beggars standing with their hands before them and their mouths open at soup shop doors or our doors'; see WEL, part I, reel 6.

43. Following her marriage to Lestock Wilson in 1829, Fanny [Frances Maria] lived in London.

44. Maria Edgeworth to Fanny Wilson, 31 January 1847; see WEL, part I, reel 9. Two weeks later, on 14 February, Maria returned to the same theme, in a letter also addressed to Fanny: 'I felt myself bound in honour to do something for the poor of our parish and now that so much has been done for them in consequence of my begging and I adhere to the subject of *charity* which I think I can make useful and entertaining'; see WEL, part I, reel 9.

45. Maria Edgeworth to Fanny Wilson, 14 February 1847; see WEL, part I, reel 9.

46. *Orlandino* was published in 1848 by William and Robert Chambers, Edinburgh. According to Edgeworth, some 2,500 copies were published; a second edition of the story appeared in 1853, with an American edition in 1848 and a French edition in 1849.

47. *Orlandino*, p.59. In a letter written to Honora Beaufort, 21 March 1847, Edgeworth praises highly 'those poor Irish emigrants who have sent home so much of their earnings constantly, constantly to their parents and friends – not only in this distress – but regularly for years'; see WEL, part I, reel 6.

48. Edgeworth's address book for 1846 (Ms. 18,754, Edgeworth Papers, National Library Dublin; WEL, part II, reel 13) and other sources, such as her stepmother's memoir, testify to the many letters she forwarded to America from local people, through a London intermediary Mr Millar also mentioned in *Orlandino*.

49. Maria Edgeworth to Fanny Wilson, 5 February 1847; see WEL, part 1, reel 9.

50. Edgeworth, *Orlandino*, p.169. This was a topic which greatly exercised Edgeworth herself in correspondence with Jones, even as late as April 1849, the month before her death; see Ms. 22,822, Edgeworth Papers.

51. Maria Edgeworth to Honora Beaufort, 8 May 1847; see WEL, part 1, reel 6. See also notes 18 and 19 above.

52. For references to Frances Edgeworth's and Vicar Powell's aid to the poor, see Maria Edgeworth to Fanny Wilson, 9 March 1849; reproduced in WEL, part I, reel 9.

53. As Christine Kinealy observes, the Temporary Relief Act of February 1847 and the succeeding Poor Law Extension Act (June 1847) allowed outdoor relief, which had been prohibited by the 1838 Irish Poor Law, for the first time. See Kinealy, *A Death-Dealing Famine*, pp.98–106 and 119–30.

54. Maria Edgeworth to Richard Jones, 14 June 1847; see Ms. 22,822, Edgeworth Papers.

55. Maria Edgeworth to Louisa Moore, 29 November 1845; see Ms. 495, Edgeworth Papers.

56. Maria Edgeworth to Dr Joshua Harvey, 1 February 1847; see Ms. 989, Edgeworth Papers.

57. Edgeworth to Jones, 14 June 1847; see Ms. 22,822, Edgeworth Papers.

58. Gray, *The Irish Famine*, p.58; Kinealy, *A Death-Dealing Famine*, p.105.

59. Edgeworth to Jones, 14 June 1847; see Ms. 22,822, Edgeworth Papers.

60. Edgeworth to Jones, 2 April 1837; see Ms. 22,822, Edgeworth Papers. George Nicholls, author of the English poor-law report in 1834, visited Ireland in 1836–37; his reports were to lay the foundation for the Irish Poor Law Act of 1838. Writing to Jones on the subject of Nicholls' Irish report, Edgeworth explained how Nicholls had changed her mind from previous opposition 'to any poor law for Ireland' to support of 'the workhouse system . . . guarded by the destitution test'.

61. Harriet Martineau's *Illustrations of Political Economy* (London: Fox, 1832–34) and *Poor Laws and Paupers Illustrated* (London: Fox, 1833) were stories written in illustration of contemporary principles of political economy.

62. Edgeworth to Jones, 2 April 1837; see Ms 22,822, Edgeworth Papers. Some controversy concerns the dating of this extract. Michael Hurst dates it 4 May 1844 (*Maria Edgeworth and the Public Scene*, p.134); however, a number of pieces of internal evidence, including a reference to Captain Beaufort's son, Francis Lestock, then a student of Jones's at Haileybury, clearly indicate that these pages belong to the 1837 letter.

63. Maria Edgeworth to Fanny Wilson, 5 February 1847; see WEL, part I, reel 9.

64. Elizabeth Smith, diary entry, 21 January 1849. See Thomson and McGusty (eds), *The Irish Journals of Elizabeth Smith: 1840–1850*, p.211.

65. Maria Edgeworth to Louisa Moore, 30 July 1847; see Ms. 495, Edgeworth Papers. This letter includes an admonishing by proxy of Louisa's son, George Henry, MP – 'I do not quite agree with Mr Moore in his anger against the English government for their conduct towards Ireland through these late distresses' – Edgeworth's own opinion being that, in spite of 'plenty' of mistakes made by Peel and Russell's administrations, 'they have meant well for Ireland'.

66. See Thomson and McGusty, *The Irish Journals of Elizabeth Smith*, pp.182 and 199.

67. Maria Edgeworth to Louisa Moore, 31 October 1848; see Ms. 495, Edgeworth Papers.

68. See Edgeworth, *A Memoir of Maria Edgeworth*, Vol.3, pp.277–85. The list's conclusion makes striking reading: 'End with examining whether Time does, or does not, do justice at least, in fairly apportioning moral or literary fame' (p.285). Edgeworth died on 22 May 1849, at the age of 81.

69. Born to a Scottish labouring family and raised in deep poverty, Somerville became famous for his rural commentaries and was employed by the *Manchester Chronicle* to report on conditions in Ireland in 1847. His *Letters from Ireland during the Famine of 1847* were published in volume form in 1852.

70. *Transactions of the Central Relief Committee of the Society of Friends during the famine in Ireland* (Dublin: Hodges & Smith, 1852; facsimile edition printed Dublin: Éamonn de Búrca, 1996), Appendix 24, p.454.

71. See Joe Lee's recent observations as to the need for practitioners of both historical and literary studies 'to become more sensitive to the perspectives of the other'; J.J. Lee, 'The Irish diaspora', in Laurence M. Geary and Margaret Kelleher (eds), *Nineteenth-Century Ireland: A Guide to Recent Research* (Dublin: University College Dublin Press, 2005), p.218.

72. David Fitzpatrick, 'The failure: representations of the Irish Famine in letters to Australia', in E. Margaret Crawford (ed.), *The Hungry Stream: Essays on Famine and Emigration* (Belfast: Institute of Irish Studies, 1997), p.161.

NOTES to Chapter 4

1. Trollope knew very well that the rural Irish southwest was Irish-speaking at the time. In *The MacDermots of Ballycloran* (1847), for example, a landlord wanted for murder takes shelter with an 'old man [who] could not speak a word of English; but Thady could talk Irish' (p.243). In this earlier novel, as in *The Kellys and the O'Kellys* (1848), Trollope occasionally adds a bit of demotic Irish to dialogue, e.g., Mrs Kelly's habit of calling Anty Lynch *alanna*, 'my child'. In these novels, Irish Catholic characters include the old gentry and an ambitious lower middle class, as well as the rural poor we see in *Castle Richmond*, and the narrative enters their minds about as often as it enters the minds of the Anglo-Irish.

2. There are other examples; the competition between Mollett *père* and Mollett *fils* for Fanny the barmaid repeats the pattern at the level of low comedy. In a marvelously Freudian line, one of Herbert's acquaintances remarks that 'I should go mad if my mother turned out to be somebody else's wife' (*Castle Richmond*, p.853). Patrick, Clara's brother, seems to dote on Owen almost as much as his mother does, exclaiming, 'By heavens – If I were her, I know whom I should love' (ibid., p.753). It is he who goes off with Owen in the end.

3. Similarly, 'the horrible catastrophe' to which the narrator refers on p.595 is the revelation that Lady Fitzgerald's first husband is alive, not the Famine.

4. Trollope defends the Irish against the implicit English reader's belief that they are inclined to revolution or violence (*Castle Richmond*, pp.122 and 373). 'One would think that starving men would become violent, taking food by open theft – feeling, and perhaps not without some truth, that the agony of their want robbed such robberies of its sin. But such was by no means the case. I only remember one instance in which the bakers' shops were attacked . . . ' (ibid., p.640).

5. Morash says the scene 'both demands and denies the possibility of empathy. And it is this tension which generates the desire for an ethics of empathy, even if that project must be founded on its own failure'. Christopher Morash, *Writing the Irish Famine*. Oxford: Clarendon Press, 1995. I would argue that the scene also illustrates the character's humility before a suffering so much more basic than his own that he does not imagine that he can wholly understand or identify with it. Both language and the law fail to address it.

6. 'And so in one sense those who were the best . . . who worked the hardest for the poor and spent their time most completely among them, became the hardest of heart, and most obdurate in their denials. It was strange to see devoted women neglecting the wants of the dying, so that they might husband their strength and time and means for the wants of those who might still be kept among the living' (*Castle Richmond* p.763). Asenath Nicholson, an American evangelical who spent the Famine years in Ireland, took a different view: 'The principle of throwing away life lest means to protect it tomorrow might be lessened, was fully and practically . . . carried out'. Asenath Nicholson, *Annals of the Famine in Ireland*. 1851, Maureen Murphy (ed.). Dublin: Lilliput, 1998.

NOTES to Chapter 5

1. See, for example, the end of *Castle Daly*: 'The valley had never looked fairer', but 'there was something wanting; the old sights were there, but not the old sounds.

A strange silence reigned all about the place that felt like an ache on Ellen's heart'. Annie Keary, *Castle Daly: The Story of an Irish Home Thirty Years Ago*. New York: Garland Publishing, 1979 [1875], Vol.3, p.332. When Connor returns to Ireland after his post-1848 exile, he asks Ellen urgently, 'Where *are* the people? that is what I cannot make out . . . I say again where *are* the people?' (ibid., p.349).

2. In the case of her second victim, for example, the child is left 'terribly weak, and looked quite emaciated' (Bram Stoker, *Dracula*. Maud Ellman [ed.]. New York: Oxford University Press, 1998, p.178). Seward describes Lucy as 'a dim figure in white, which held something dark at its breast . . . . We could not see the face, for it was bent down over what we saw to be a fair-haired child. There was a pause and a sharp little cry' (ibid., p.210). Moments later, Lucy is again holding the child to her breast, as if to feed it or feed on it, when she is interrupted by the men: 'With a careless motion, she flung to the ground, callous as a devil, the child that up to now she had clutched strenuously to her breast, growling over it as a dog growls over a bone. The child gave a sharp cry, and lay there moaning. There was a cold-bloodedness in the act which wrung a groan from Arthur' (ibid., p.211).

3. *The Black Prophet* draws mainly on the author's experiences of the famines of 1817 and 1822, but it was meant to provide insight into the events of the 1840s. Carleton dedicated the book to Lord John Russell for his callous laissez-faire principles 'which have brought our country to her present calamitous condition' (William Carleton, 'Extract from *The Black Prophet*', in Seamus Deane [ed.], *The Field Day Anthology of Irish Writing*, Vol.2. Derry: Field Day Publications, 1991, p.124), and is elsewhere in his novel explicit in his blame of the English government.

4. There is a similar evolution in the pattern of Mina's symptoms. Her mouth is emphasized: 'She was very, very pale – almost ghastly, and so thin that her lips were drawn away, showing her teeth somewhat prominently' (Stoker, *Dracula*, p.294). But it relieves Harker to note that despite the paleness and the prominence of her gums and teeth, 'As yet there was no sign of the teeth growing sharper' (ibid.).

5. For example, he writes, 'all sense of becoming restraint or shame was now abandoned, and the timid girl, or modest mother of a family . . . goaded by the same wild and tyrannical cravings, urge their claims with as much turbulent solicitation and outcry as if they had been trained since their very infancy to all the forms of impudent cant and imposture' (Carleton, 'Extract from *The Black Prophet*', p.126).

6. The Wanderer's visit to Stanton's cell resembles the scenes we imagine occurring between Dracula and Renfield. We can only assume that Renfield accepted the 'devil's bargain' that Stanton manages to avoid: Melmoth enters Stanton's cell through supernatural means, but this is only possible because of the invitation that Stanton has unconsciously given him by desiring and pursuing him, much as Renfield invites Dracula in as a prelude to becoming his victim. The master/slave relationship that ensues between the Wanderer and Stanton is replicated in Renfield's relationship with his 'Master'.

7. The question of Home Rule brought together different denominations in Protestant Ireland in unionist solidarity, and historical events important in Protestant memory were more widely commemorated, parades and church

services attended by more people. Walker points out, for example, 'the growing significance of the Derry story in the new political and religious confrontations of post-1886 Ireland' (Brian Walker, *Past and Present: History, Identity and Politics in Ireland*. Belfast: The Institute of Irish Studies, Queen's University of Belfast, 2000, p.17). Events like the siege of Derry, and the remembrance of the rebellion of 1641 in which many Protestants were killed, had, according to Walker, taken on new and greater significance in the late nineteenth century because of the heightening of sectarian tensions over the issue of Home Rule (1886 was the year of the first proposed Home Rule Bill).

8. As I have discovered, Michael Moses's article on Parnell as a model for Dracula makes a very similar argument about Renfield's function in the novel. Moses writes, 'More than any other figure in *Dracula* the character of Renfield serves as a stand-in for the Irish adherents of Parnell and the nationalist cause' (Michael Valdez Moses, 'The Irish vampire: *Dracula*, Parnell, and the troubled dreams of nationhood'. *Journal X: A Journal in Culture and Criticism*, Vol.2, No.1 (1997), p.84). Moses points out that in the absence of direct supervision by the English Seward, Renfield is monitored by an *Irish* doctor, Patrick Hennessey; 'Renfield's erratic conduct follows a pattern that Parnell's detractors detected in his most troublesome Irish Catholic and Fenian followers' (ibid., p.84). His 'worshipful self-abasement' (ibid., p.85) to his Master echoes the reported behaviour of Irish peasants who knelt in the presence of Parnell, and Moses argues that Renfield's attack on Seward with a knife recalls the 'sensational details' of the Phoenix Park murders. Renfield 'at least *believes*' he is fighting 'against institutional oppression and for his political rights' (ibid.).

9. To give just a few of many possible examples, the alliance refer to 'the plans formed for the campaign' (Stoker, *Dracula*, p.326) and 'our plan of battle' (ibid., p.236). Van Helsing declares, 'We have here much data, and we must proceed to lay out our campaign' (ibid., p.241).

10. They are glad the Count's body is likely to dissolve to dust because 'In such case there would be no evidence against us, in case any suspicion of murder were aroused. But even if it did not, we should stand or fall by our act, and perhaps some day this very script may be evidence to come between some of us and a rope' (Stoker, *Dracula*, p.335).

11. There are many examples of this idea in the novel: Seward records, 'At present I am going in my mind from point to point as a mad man, and not a sane one, follows an idea' (Stoker, *Dracula*, p.193). Introduced to his mentor's plans for the first time, he asks, 'Dr. Van Helsing, are you mad?' (ibid., p.194) and Arthur echoes, 'Are you mad that speak such things, or am I mad that listen to them?' (ibid., p.206). Seward speculates, 'I sometimes think we must all be mad and that we shall wake to sanity in strait-waistcoats' (ibid., p.274).

12. Seward muses, 'Yesterday I was almost willing to accept Van Helsing's monstrous ideas . . . I wonder if his mind can have become in any way unhinged. Surely there must be *some* rational explanation of all these mysterious things. Is it possible that the Professor can have done it himself?' (Stoker, *Dracula*, p.204).

13. In *The Last Conquest of Ireland (Perhaps)* (1861), for example, Mitchel wrote, 'the Almighty, indeed, sent the potato blight but the English created the Famine' (Christine Kinealy, *A Death-Dealing Famine: The Great Hunger in Ireland*. Chicago, IL: Pluto Press, 1997, p.6). Morash writes, 'For Mitchel, the "institutions" which had

been established by the state, ostensibly for the prevention of suffering, were in fact instruments of imperial hegemony' (Christopher Morash, *Writing the Irish Famine*. Oxford: Clarendon Press, 1995, p.66).

14. Harker writes, 'Dr. Seward said to us, when we were alone, that he did not wish to go into the matter; the question of an inquest had to be considered, and it would never do to put forward the truth . . . As it was, he thought that on the attendant's evidence he could give a certificate of death by misadventure in falling from bed' (Stoker, *Dracula*, pp.289–90).

15. Swales, though a minor character, articulates an idea central to *Dracula*: that authorized monuments, like official versions of history, often lie to hide the culpability of the victors. The tombstones in Whitby are 'simply tumblin' down with the weight o' the lies wrote on them' (Stoker, *Dracula*, p.65). In a novel preoccupied with who gets to tell the stories of the dead – from Renfield's forged death certificate to Van Helsing's careful foresight in protecting the band of men from the possibility of future allegations that they murdered Lucy (ibid., p.202) – Swales provides satirical commentary on the way the common dead are remembered. The graves often contain no bodies, he declares, a point that would have resonated with those who remembered the coffin ships during and after the Famine. Those who died in the hellish passage were given burials at sea. As a sailor, Swales has many such examples to relate: 'Why, I could name ye a dozen whose bones lie in the Greenland seas . . . or where the currents may have drifted them. There be the steans around ye. Ye can, with your young eyes, read the small print of the lies from here' (ibid., p.66). On the surface, of course, Swales's words are meant to convey his simplicity in misunderstanding the purpose of gravestones. However, although his speech is 'deformed' by thick dialect, Swales expresses a powerful critique of history as recording only the testimony of the winners and of the assumption that victory bequeaths moral superiority.

16. Carleton, for example, describes a 'famine crowd' as 'wild and wolfish', 'like creatures changed from their very humanity by some judicial plague, that had been sent down from heaven to punish and desolate the land' ('Extract from *The Black Prophet*', p.128).

17. Annie Keary also places emphasis on the eerie silence over the land in the years after the Famine.

18. Carleton describes the howling of dogs as blending in with the wails of the people: 'Both day and night, but at night especially, their [the dogs'] hungry howlings could be heard over the country, or mingling with the wailings which the people were in the habit of pouring over those whom the terrible typhus was sweeping away with such wide and indiscriminating fatality' ('Extract from *The Black Prophet*', p.129).

19. John Mitchel wrote, in a quote worth repeating here, 'Britain being in possession of the floor, any hostile comment upon her way of telling our story is an unmannerly interruption' (quoted in Morash, *Writing the Irish Famine*, p.70), a mere 'howl'.

NOTES to Chapter 6

1. References to *The Countess Cathleen*, first written in 1892, come from the 1953 edition of *The Collected Plays of W.B. Yeats* (New York: Macmillan), originally

published in 1934. Where variations from the 1899 performances occur, they are noted in the text.

2. Cf. Letter from Edward Martyn to WBY, 28 March 1899, n1.
3. Cf. Letter to T.P. Gill from WBY, 25 March 1899, n1.
4. Cf. Letter from the Reverend William Barry enclosed in Letter from WBY to Lady Gregory, 27 March 1899.
5. Ibid.
6. Cf. Letter to Lady Gregory, 1 April 1899, n2.
7. Cf. Letter to May Whitty, ? 23 April 1899, n4.
8. Ibid.
9. Cf. Letter to the editor of the *Morning Leader*, 13 May 1899.
10. Ibid.
11. Ibid.
12. Cf. Letter to Lady Gregory, 27 March 1899, n2.
13. Cf. J.G.A. Pocock's 'Verbalizing a political act: towards a politics of speech', in Michael J. Shapiro (ed.), *Language and Politics*. New York: New York University Press, 1984, pp.27–43.

NOTES to Chapter 7

1. An earlier version of this essay appeared in *Modern Drama*, Vol.45, No.4 (Winter 2002), pp.567–92. I would like to acknowledge *Modern Drama* for their permission to reprint the essay here and to extend my particular thanks to Anna Racette for her assistance.
2. The name 'Revival' has at least two distinct meanings in relation to this period. It sometimes refers to the 'Gaelic Revival', which includes the Gaelic League and various related movements that sought Irish independence through the re-gaelicization of Ireland. 'Revival' can also refer more generally to the 'Irish Revival', which places under one banner the National Theatre, the Gaelic League, and all other artistic movements in Ireland at the turn of the century. Kelleher uses the latter definition in her book, but her examples in this case apply equally well to both. Throughout this paper, I use the former, more restrictive definition of Revival, which I present as a political project that differs in many significant ways from the goals of the National Theatre.
3. In this context, the term 'Malthusian' does not necessarily refer to the actual theories of Malthus, but rather to the kinds of social discourse that his works created after their publication, as the basic framework of his theories was extended into areas which the author never intended. Morash explains: 'as Malthusian ideas begin to migrate beyond the texts which generated them, they move beyond the confines of demography and economics, and enter that realm of truth which masks its origins under the guise of "common sense" (Christopher Morash, *Writing the Irish Famine*. Oxford: Clarendon Press, 1995, p.22). In England, these discourses, which extended far beyond Malthus's readership, combined with the prevailing belief in England's national superiority and divine favour in order to add scientific reinforcement to the existing social paradigm.
4. Eagleton offers the Famine's obliteration of history as an explanation for why, to his mind, Irish authors at the turn of the twentieth century seem to thoroughly

avoid engaging with the Famine. It is Eagleton's belief in this absence of Famine representation that leads to his now famous question, 'Where is the Famine in the literature of the Revival?' Terry Eagleton, *Heathcliff and the Great Hunger. Studies in Irish Culture*. London: Verso, 1995, p.13. I do not seek to directly refute Eagleton's claim in this paper, if for no other reason than numerous other scholars have done so already. Margaret Kelleher, for example, presents her analysis of Famine rhetoric in the Revival as a direct contradiction to Eagleton's claims. Furthermore, I fully agree with Eagleton that the atemporality of the trauma induced by the Famine makes direct engagements with it problematic for authors seeking to create a national narrative, as this is exactly the problem Synge addresses by critiquing the use of Famine imagery in nationalist rhetoric.

5. 'Properly mourn the dead' is a rather subjective term here. Upon returning from the wake in Act 3, Michael describes the event to Christy thus: 'you'd never see the like of it for flows of drink, the way when we sunk her bones at noonday in her narrow grave, there were five men, aye, and six men, stretched out retching speechless on the holy stones', J.M. Synge, *The Playboy of the Western World* [1907] in Alison Smith (ed.), *The Collected Plays and Poems and* The Aran Islands. London: J.M. Dent, 1997, p.157. Synge's critics saw this as yet another example of the author perpetuating colonial stereotypes of the Irish peasantry for comedic effect, a charge that is not without merit. Michael's description of the wake as little more than a drinking contest does, indeed, resonate rather uncomfortably with the stage-Irish convention of the drunken Paddy. In the context of the play, however, this description also serves as one more example of the discontinuity between symbol and reality in the villagers' lives. Although Michael's desire to attend the wake would seem to have very little to do with his grief over the death of Kate Cassidy, the wake itself still represents a communal obligation to him. Thus, his inability to simultaneously attend the wake and care for his daughter and his eventual solution to this dilemma – leaving his daughter in the care of a confessed murderer – both point to the desperation with which the Mayonites try to maintain the appearance of a functional community, no matter how absurd the results.

6. It should be noted that, while Synge agreed with Gaelic Revival's assertion that the peasant culture in western Ireland had a vital and unique spirit, he also believed that this spirit was inevitably dying. The full sentence excerpted above asserts that,

> In Ireland, for a few years more, we have a popular imagination that is fiery, and magnificent, and tender; so that those of us who wish to write start with a chance that is not given to writers in places where the springtime of local life has been forgotten, and the harvest is a memory only, and the straw has been turned into bricks. (Synge, 'Preface', in *Playboy*, p.112)

Thus, while many of the Revivalists asserted that the culture of western Ireland could and should be brought back whole cloth into mainstream of Irish life, Synge contended that it could only serve as a direct source of inspiration to the current generation of writers.

7. Synge derived this understanding of Irish criminality during his travels in the west of Ireland. In *The Aran Islands*, he suggests that 'The impulse to protect the criminal is almost universal in the west. It seems partly due to the association between justice and the hated English jurisdiction' (J.M. Synge, *The Aran Islands*

NOTES TO CHAPTER 7 321

[1907] in Alison Smith (ed.), *The Collected Plays and Poems and* The Aran Islands.
London: J.M. Dent, 1997, p.298). In this text, Synge sympathizes with the
islanders' desire to subvert English law, although this sympathy largely drops out
of *Playboy*, as the play's satirical focus leads the author to ridicule the heroism that
his villagers associate with law breaking.

8. It is also surely no coincidence that the crimes associated with these local heroes
   – attacking an agent of English law and mutilating livestock – are traditional acts
   of political violence. By having his village girls valorize these men without
   establishing whether their actions were politically motivated or not, Synge
   suggests that the distinction between violence in the service of one's nation and
   violence for any other purpose is largely irrelevant here, which further explains
   the villagers' readiness to accept Christy's patricide as a demonstration of
   heroism. Nicholas Grene argues that much of the nationalists' objection to
   Synge's play stemmed from this lack of distinction: '[according to Synge's critics]
   The Irish people are traduced in being charged with sympathy for *all forms of
   crime*. It was crucial to the nationalist position to discriminate between forms of
   crime which were legitimate, in so far as they represented a justifiable struggle
   against an oppressive colonial power, and those which had no such legitimacy'
   (Nicholas Grene, *The Politics of Irish Drama: Plays in Context from Boucicault to Friel*.
   Cambridge: Cambridge University Press, 1999, pp.89–90) [original emphasis].
   Synge's refusal to make the distinction between political violence and any other
   kind further demonstrates his desire to undermine violence as a tool for
   rebuilding Irish identity.

9. The villagers' belief that a severe crime must be accompanied by a compelling
   motive also comes directly from Synge's experience on the Aran Islands. Synge
   comments on 'the primitive feeling of these people, who are never criminals but
   always capable of crime, that a man will do no wrong unless he is directly under
   the influence of a passion which is as irresponsible as a storm on the sea' (Synge,
   The Aran Islands, p.298). Synge seems entirely unaware of the irony that this belief
   in 'uncontrollable' Irish passion was the primary reason offered by English
   authorities that the Irish could not be trusted to govern themselves. Synge's first
   audience, however, clearly did not overlook this, as it was during this scene that
   the first angry voices were heard on opening night.

10. Michael does indicate shortly after this exchange that this 'practical' effect of
    Christy's presence will also be largely symbolic: 'the peelers in this place is decent,
    drouthy poor fellows wouldn't touch a cur dog and not give warning in the
    middle of the night' (Synge, *Playboy*, p.123). While the villagers clearly hate and
    fear the peelers as an institution (as their final rejection of Christy illustrates), they
    seem to have little concern for the actual policemen in their district.

11. This is not meant to be taken literally; Synge did, in fact, interact with those he
    defined as the peasantry a great deal on his trips to the west, which he documents
    at length in his travel writing. It is significant, though, that he does not mention
    this in the Preface, which was written largely to defend the play's authenticity and
    his credentials as an author. It seems that, for these purposes, Synge actually
    preferred to characterize his relationship to the peasantry as that of an unknown
    eavesdropper.

NOTES to Chapter 8

1. Comments like these in Joyce's 'The Dead' point to Joyce's earlier work on the Famine, and his critique of Irish post-Famine economies: Gabriel Conroy's Irish are 'quarrelsome', and with each other, because they are not 'hungry' (at the Morkan feast, with its lavish, imported foods), in contrast to Famine years when the Irish were not 'quarrelsome' enough to fight the British, due to the severe and debilitating effects of hunger.

2. See Mary Lowe-Evans, *Crimes Against Fecundity: Joyce and Population Control*. Syracuse, NY: Syracuse University Press, 1989, p.11. Lowe-Evans borrows this statistic from early twentieth-century estimates, particularly L. Paul-Dubois's *Contemporary Ireland*. Dublin: Maunsell, 1908, which cites the number as 729,033 (p.72). This statistic has more recently been called into question. See also Ruth-Ann M. Harris, 'Introduction', in Arthur Gribben (ed.), *The Great Famine and the Irish Diaspora in America*. Amherst, MA: University of Massachusetts Press, 1999, p.8.

3. See Christine Kinealy, *A Death-Dealing Famine: The Great Hunger in Ireland*. Chicago, IL: Pluto Press, 1997, p.151: 'The population continued to fall [after the Famine] throughout the remainder of the century, a combination of emigration, delayed marriages and celibacy. By 1900, it had fallen to approximately half of its pre-Famine level. The population decline did not finally reverse until the 1960s.'

4. As June Dwyer comments, 'A generation later, the reaction of many revival thinkers and writers to the ugliness of the past was to ignore Ireland's colonial history entirely and instead to base the nation's claim to identity on folklore and legend' ('Feast and famine: James Joyce and the politics of food', *Proteus: A Journal of Ideas*, Vol.17, No1 (2000), p.41).

5. Joyce sees more Famine in canonical writers than critics have previously seen. For example, Stephen writes a vampire-poem in 'Proteus', which probably references what Joyce saw as Lord Byron's Famine symbolism, (though, I believe, Joyce uses this poem as an example of what Stephen should not write). Stephen also conjures up Oscar Wilde's 'love that dare not speak its name', which Joyce may see as related as much to an absence of speaking about the Famine as it is to homosexual love. For Joyce, the only canonical writer who took on the Famine 'truthfully' was Synge, in his *Playboy of the Western World* – mentioned by Stephen Dedalus in the very middle of the 'Scylla and Charybdis' chapter. Especially its use of excesses of food as bespeaking an absence, Joyce's *Ulysses* is in many ways a homage to Synge's *Playboy*. For further details on Synge as a Famine writer, see Cusack, this volume, pp.133–58.

6. See also McGee's chapter 'Pedagogy and Theory' in *Joyce beyond Marx: History and Desire in* Ulysses *and* Finnegans Wake. Gainsville, FL: University Press of Florida, 2001, pp.17–30. McGee is speaking more theoretically about Stephen's particular use of language as signifier and 'history's echo' (p.19) at these given moments. He writes:

   > Stephen . . . teaches his students that understanding involves more than effacing words in order to grasp a referent. It involves seeing or hearing words as iterative, as self-reflexive. If we are blind or deaf to this dimension of language, then we become susceptible to every kind of mystification and block our own capacity for creative self-invention. We surrender our positions as subjects and become the objects of another's subjectivity; we

become the unwitting puppets of the discourse of the master . . . instead of generating our own master signifiers through critical use of language within the dynamic process of cultural transformation.

(Ibid., p.20)

7. Throughout the story Joyce will point to a weakness only to turn it into a strength. In this case, the 'fabling' of history is problematic, as is Stephen's mental reference to Blake's Romantic poetry in the 'daughters of memory'. But on the other hand, Bloom's daughter Milly, as the 'Circe' episode begins to suggest, will become the appropriate carrier of memory.

8. Irish Romantic writers are famous for stories of ghosts, the walking dead or vampires, and in one sense, Stephen's students ask for a repetition of a story they already know. But in another sense, the 'ghoststory' refers directly to the Famine, which was often linked with ghosts. In a series of poems on Famine Ireland, for example, H.D., one of the few English artists to tackle the subject, entitles her works 'Spectre'. Other descriptions of the Famine liken even the living to ghosts.

9. Cheng's beautiful reading of this chapter provides a far more elaborate discussion of Deasy's persona than I do here. His book is by now the seminal post-colonial discussion of *Ulysses*. As such, Cheng focuses on the school as perpetuating 'cultural hegemony', and most often compares Deasy's 'English ruling class' values to those of the Englishman Haines (Vincent Cheng, *Joyce, Race and Empire*. Cambridge: Cambridge University Press, 1995, p.164). I think Cheng is correct in this reading of Deasy's character, but I would like to develop the idea that there are further possible layers of meaning, many that are somewhat more redemptive, that overlay Deasy's depiction and explain Deasy's dependence on English values.

10. Pecora calls into question Joyce's use of the terms 'generous' and 'hospitable' in one of the most remarkable and lucid essays ever written on 'The Dead' (Vincent Pecora, *Self and Form in Modern Narrative*. Balitmore, MD: John Hopkins University Press, 1989). Pecora suggests that Joyce opposes the ideals of (Romantic) self-sacrifice.

11. Shakespeare's Iago to Roderigo on the promise of Desdemona's eventual prostitution: 'It cannot be that Desdemona should long continue her love to the Moor, – put money in thy purse, – nor he his to her: it was a violent commencement, and thou shalt see an answerable sequestration; – put but money in thy purse. – These Moors are changeable in their wills; – fill thy purse with money: *the food that to him now is as luscious as locusts, shall be to him shortly as bitter as coloquintida*' (my emphasis). Joyce is interested in Iago's sexism, which prompts him to compare Desdemona to food. Bloom also compares women to food, appreciating the servant-girl's 'hams', always connecting Molly to seedcake, and as we see in 'Circe', admiring Zoe's 'peeled pears'.

12. Joyce uses the term 'murmuring' throughout *Ulysses*, and the word serves to reference the story of Moses, in which it is also used repeatedly. Michael Walzer's *Exodus and Revolution* (New York: Basic Books, 1985) gives a nuanced reading of this biblical story that closely allies it with post-colonial thinking: he describes the Israelites as afraid of freedom, so that when Moses began petitioning Pharaoh for their release, and Pharaoh increased their workload, they began their complaints. But they continue it into the wilderness, where they must face up to the idea that freedom entails responsibility, and they must now search for their own food, water

and shelter. The complaints of the Israelites are registered to Moses as 'murmuring'. In the end, the Israelites have so internalized their bondage that new generations must be born before they can enter the promised land. Integral to this reading is that Moses is chosen by God because the only man who can free the Israelites is one who is an outsider, one who has not internalized his bondage. See also Andrew Gibson's chapter, 'Only a foreigner would do: Leopold Bloom, Ireland, and Jews' in *Joyce's Revenge: History, Politics and Aesthetics in* Ulysses. Oxford: Oxford University Press, 2002, pp.42–59.

13. As critics, we should be careful not to make the same mistake with Deasy, assuming that because the advice comes from a hypocrite that it is invalid. Because they are Irish, circumscribed by their bondage, everyone in *Ulysses* is a hypocrite, including, frequently, Bloom and Stephen.

14. Mark Osteen writes, 'Mulligan pays the milkwoman but, typically, hedges. He slides a florin along the table, with Stephen acting as middleman, but underpays her by twopence (they owe 'two and two')' (*The Economy of Ulysses: Making both Ends Meet.* Syracuse, NY: Syracuse University Press, 1995, p.43). Possibly Stephen includes this money in what he owes Mulligan, but clearly he does not feel any responsibility to the old woman who was cheated of her money.

15. Cecil Woodham-Smith in *The Great Hunger: Ireland 1845–1849*, London: Penguin, 1991, writes:

> This theory, usually termed *laissez faire*, let people do as they think best, insisted that in the economic sphere individuals should be allowed to pursue their own interests and asserted that the Government should interfere as little as possible . . . The influence of *laissez faire* on the treatment of Ireland during the famine is impossible to exaggerate. Almost without exception the high officials and politicians responsible for Ireland were fervent believers in non-interference by Government, and the behaviour of the British authorities only becomes explicable when their fanatical belief in private enterprise and their suspicions of any actions which might be considered Government intervention are borne in mind.
>
> (1991, p.54)

16. A virus that is spread through feces to cloven animals.

17. Moore writes the following in his letter of 5 November 1845 to the Royal Dublin Society:

> From the first intimation given by Dr Lindley of the potato crop in England being attacked, my attention was turned to the subject, as I fully expected it would reach the country, judging from the progress it had made from the Continent to the Channel Islands, thence to the southern counties; and considering it, as I still do, epidemic, I was consequently watching the appearance of the potato fields here, and observed the first symptoms on the 20th of August. On the first week in September, I accompanied a gentleman to see a field on the Earl of Charlemont's demesne, which was then a good deal affected, and at the same time received communications on the subject and samples of diseased potatoes from several persons in this neighborhood, affording proofs that the disease was beginning to be general about Dublin at that period, as I stated in a letter published in the *Irish Farmers' Journal* on the 10th September, and also my opinion of the nature of the disease, which subsequent events have, to a great extent, corroborated to have been correct.

Quoted in Noel Kissane, *The Irish Famine: A Documentary History*. Dublin: National Library of Ireland, 1995, p.20. Obviously, Moore's letters were not viewed as requiring an immediate response.

18. A vaccine came about in 1938, but until then, the only treatment in use was mass slaughtering of infected animals.

19. Another interesting historical corollary occurs here. Joyce's Dr Henry Blackwood Price may be a reference to Dr Lyon Playfair. According to Cecil Woodham-Smith in *The Great Hunger*,

> [Ireland's Prime Minister Sir Robert] Peel had been on friendly terms with Dr. Lyon Playfair, a scientist and chemist of considerable reputation . . . He now advanced a theory that potatoes which were apparently sound, or almost sound, when dug could be given a chemical treatment to prevent them from rotting . . . Peel decided to set up a Scientific Commission in Ireland to investigate what science could do to save the potato . . . [But in the end, n]o deliberation was necessary. The briefest possible enquiry was sufficient for the professors to become alarmed, and after two days Playfair wrote to Peel that 'the account is melancholy and it cannot be looked upon in other than a most serious light. We are confident that the accounts are under-rated rather than exaggerated . . . I am sorry to give you so desponding a letter, but we cannot conceal from ourselves that the case is much worse than the public supposes.
>
> (1991, pp.43–4)

20. Joyce's puns on the word 'columns', a reference to the sentimental columns of *titbits* whose style Deasy cannibalizes, and on Bloom's corresponding columns of shit, a marker of the quality of Deasy's writing.

21. Margaret Kelleher discusses these facts especially in conjunction with famines in Bengal, but is also referencing the Irish Famine: 'Maria Luddy notes that records for arrests for prostitution in Dublin show that the greatest number of arrests occurred during the famine years' (*The Feminisation of Famine: Expressing the Inexpressible?* Cork and Durham, NC: Cork University Press and Duke University Press, 1997, p.160 n.120).

22. The number of recent post-colonial critics who, in lengthy discussions of *Ulysses*, simply do not mention Bloom's transvestitism and rape, which occupies a full third of this extensive chapter, surprises me. Gibson's otherwise brilliant book demonstrates what appears to me to be a clear tendency among writers who are very sensitive to issues of race to avoid gender issues altogether. As Gibson puts it, for example,

> The situation in 'Circe' can be expressed in a nutshell: in 'The King versus Bloom' (15.859), Bloom has to be on both sides; or rather, he can only promote his own 'side' by trying to join the other side, too. In this respect, the Dublin unconscious is not so much wild or turbulent as subdued, and therefore in large measure conformist. It is caught in contradictions and complicities.
>
> (Gibson, *Joyce's Revenge*, p.193)

Gibson's reading, though apt, omits gender issues to the point of misreading. I will develop the idea in this section, based on the scene of Bloom's rape and the pre-Famine history to which *Ulysses* speaks, that Bloom's situation might be better expressed as 'the queen verses Bloom'. Because he is part of the later generation, *Stephen* must do battle with 'the king'.

23. As Woodham-Smith explains,

> On January 1, 1801, an event of enormous importance had taken place –
> the Act of Union between Ireland and England became operative. The two
> countries were made one, the economy of Ireland was assimilated into the
> economy of England . . . At first sight it seemed that Ireland had everything
> to gain. Free Trade between Ireland and England meant that the discrimi-
> nation hitherto practiced by England against Irish industry would come to
> an end; united with English riches Ireland would gain the capital she
> desperately needed for development, while the hundred Irish Members who
> were to sit at Westminster would give Ireland, for the first time, a voice in
> Imperial affairs. Further, an impression had been created that when the
> Union became law Catholic emancipation would immediately follow.
> Catholics (and three-quarters of the population of Ireland were Catholics)
> would be assured of justice from the wide and unprejudiced views of the
> Imperial Parliament, and the laws which, amongst other restrictions,
> prevented Catholics from becoming Members of Parliament or Judges or
> being appointed King's Counsel would be repealed . . . The reality, however,
> was very different. The primary object of the Union was not to assist and
> improve Ireland but to bring her more completely into subjection.
>
> (Woodham-Smith, *The Great Hunger*, pp.15–16).

24. For further readings on the function of the potato in Joyce's *Ulysses*, see Robert
Merritt, 'Faith and betrayal: the potato in Ulysses', *James Joyce Quarterly*, Vol.1,
No.28 (1990), pp.269–76.

25. In a wonderful Marxist metaphor, Bloom notes that the birds he feeds live by
their wits and do not mistake paper for food (James Joyce, *Ulysses*, New York:
Vintage International, 1990, pp.152–3).

26. According to Woodham-Smith,

> The soundness of the potato when first dug was responsible for bewildering
> contradictions. Optimists, delighted to witness the digging of what seemed
> a splendid crop, hastened to send off glowing accounts . . . In almost every
> case, hope was short-lived. Within a few days the fine-looking tubers had
> become a stinking mass of corruption, and growers began to flood the
> market with potatoes, anxious to get rid of them before the rot set in.
>
> (Woodham-Smith, *The Great Hunger*, pp.43–4)

Completing the visual irony, those who were starving possessed distinctively large
bellies as a symptom of fever and malnutrition.

27. Critics have rightly suggested that Bloom's resulting sideache is an indication of
his Christocentric characteristics; but for Joyce, Bloom as Christ – as evidenced
in the resurrection and second coming – is Joyce's extreme example of history
repeating itself.

28. Kissane writes, 'The rate of crime doubled during the Famine, but the increase
mainly consisted of crimes against property. The focus was on food or the money
to provide it; crime ranged from poaching or siphoning blood from cattle, to
burglary, attacks on shops and armed robbery' (*The Irish Famine*, p.56).

29. 'Rudolph' is derived from the Germanic elements *hrod* 'fame' and *wulf* 'wolf'. It was
also the name of rulers of the Burgundy, the Holy Roman Empire and Austria.

30. Instead of looking for Stephen, Bloom is in Nighttown to accommodate his own
sexual needs – if not in actual consummation, then in finding himself (his

masculinity, his money, his authority) desired. Having vindicated himself, Bloom enters Bella Cohen's whorehouse with every intention of finding himself a prostitute for the evening. He does not know for certain that Stephen is inside; indeed, it is not where he had expected Stephen to go. Thus, if he is ostensibly following Stephen, the pursuit is really a pretext for Bloom's interest in Nighttown, whether or not he acknowledges it.

31. Gibson writes, citing Maud Gonne's *A Servant of the Queen*, 'According to Gonne, O'Connell Street was soon full of redcoats walking their girls [prostitutes], "with the result that almost every night there were fights"' (*Joyce's Revenge*, p.184).

32. Daniel O'Connell, Woodham-Smith writes, despite his 'lawyer's respect for the law' and 'horror of armed rebellion',

> gave up a brilliant career at the bar to devote his life to Ireland. Adopted by a Catholic uncle . . . a fluent speaker of the Irish language, with a magnificent voice and presence, a quick wit, a superb gift of invective, and a flamboyance his enemies called vulgarity, he was nicknamed 'Swaggering Dan'. Self-government, not separation from England, was O'Connell's aim; and he cherished a romantic admiration for Queen Victoria, 'the darling little queen'.
>
> (*The Great Hunger*, p.16)

33. As Woodham-Smith comments,

> The entanglement of the Irish famine with the repeal of the Corn Laws was a major misfortune for Ireland. Short of civil war, no issue in English history has provoked such passion as Corn Law repeal. As a consequence of Peel's decision the country was split in two, and the controversy was conducted with frightful acrimony and party bitterness. The potato failure was eclipsed by the burning domestic issue of Corn Law repeal. The Irish famine slipped into the background.
>
> (*The Great Hunger*, p.50)

Additional similarities exist. Peel changed the laws to allow him to import 'Indian corn' to mitigate the effects of the Famine, because it was exceedingly cheap and, since it did not exist in Ireland, would not compete with any of the current markets. It was largely a band-aid solution, but it initially provided enough of a measure of relief that many English viewed the famine as over before it actually was. Peel's successor chose not to import corn, and the Famine situation worsened. Joyce is also clearly referencing the exploitation of one group of (colonized 'Indians', from whom the corn arrived) for another. In this sense, the tobacco is an appropriate correlate.

34. More immediately harmful to her future health is not her (and his) smoking, but her (and his) prostitution, which Bloom does not discuss, and in which Bloom is once again complicit. If England is responsible for the perpetuation and exploitation of women, colonies and the lower classes, Ireland is responsible for purchasing England's goods and thereby perpetuating England's domination.

35. Bloom's political escalation for failing to tell the truth may be a reference to 'Union Titles'. Woodham-Smith writes, '[A]fter bribery on a scale such as history has seldom witnessed, and a generous distribution of places of profit and titles, "Union titles", the Act of Union became law' (*The Great Hunger*, p.16).

36. As Sir Robert Peel argues even in one of his early letters to Lord Heytesbury dated 15 October 1845, 'There is such a tendency in Ireland to disregard accuracy and to exaggerate that one is unwilling to give hasty credence to Irish statements' (quoted in Kissane, *The Irish Famine*, p.28).

37. Woodham-Smith writes,

> The British Government, however, was unwilling to admit that any epidemic was likely to occur and Mr Labouchere declared in the House of Commons, on January 25, 1847, that though 'some cases' of fever had accompanied hunger, yet at the moment Ireland was free from the fever which follows famine. 'The accounts given to the contrary were, to a very great extent, undoubtedly inaccurate.' Yet in reports from doctors in a wide range of districts, a fever epidemic was stated to have been already raging for several months.
>
> (*The Great Hunger*, pp. 197–8)

38. Chocolate (in the form of a foil-wrapped candy) made from cocoa, a colonial product, was created in England around the same time as the Irish Famine occurred – making it an apt symbol of British decadence contrasted with Irish devastation.

39. Ireland fought the Union, and continued its resistance despite O'Connell's assurances. Woodham-Smith writes,

> It seems, in retrospect, a remarkable determination. Ireland was in the grip of famine in the west and south-west, and deaths from starvation were occurring daily; less than a year before there had been an attempt at armed insurrection, and British journals and spokesmen in both Houses of Parliament never ceased to reproach the Irish for their rebelliousness, ingratitude and 'dogged dissatisfaction with British rule'.
>
> (*The Great Hunger*, p.384)

40. Consider the parallels between this conversation and discussion of the queen's visit to Dublin during the Famine, referenced in 'Wandering Rocks':

> The attitude of the Irish people to the Queen was, on the surface, all admiration; the Repealers were professionally loyal, perhaps, however with tongue in cheek; O'Connell's tributes to the 'darling little Queen' and the fervid protestations of Repealers in the House of Commons and Conciliation Hall must be treated with reserve. Nevertheless, Clarendon could write, in October, 1847, 'Distress, discontent, hatred of English rule, are increasing everywhere', yet add, in the same letter, 'Whatever may be the political feelings or animosities of the Irish, their devotion to the Queen is unquestionable and whenever Her Majesty shall think proper to come to Ireland I am convinced she would be received with enthusiastic loyalty'.
>
> (p.385)

41. I argue that this violence is a reference to the 1798 rebellion. Woodham-Smith writes, 'The rebellion was put down with savagery, the strength of the army in Ireland was increased to a hundred thousand men, and the Union followed. England tightened her hold over Ireland; rebellious action, it was hoped, would henceforth become impossible' (*The Great Hunger*, p.16).

42. In other Celtic legends, it is Fin MacCumhail to whom the power of knowledge through the biting of the thumb is attributed.

43. We recall Ugolino's biting of his fist in frustration as he faces starvation with his sons in Dante's Tower of Famine.

44. Referencing Sidney Godolphin Osborne's writing, Woodham-Smith describes the appearance of famine victims: 'The bones of the frame were covered with something which was skin but had a peculiar appearance, rough and dry like parchment, and hung in folds; eyes had sunk back into the head, the shoulder-

bones were so high that the neck seemed to have sunk into the chest; face and neck were so wasted as to look like a skull; hair was thin and there was an extraordinary pallor such as he had never seen before' (*The Great Hunger*, p.195). Kissane writes, 'The poor famine-stricken people were found by the wayside, emaciated corpses, partly green from eating docks and nettles, and partly blue from the cholera and dysentery' (*The Irish Famine*, p.120).

45. Stephen's killing of his mother is comparable to Christy's killing of his father (who always returns) in Synge's *Playboy of the Western World*. Thus Joyce arguably 'repeats' literary history as well.

46. Stephen shouts, '*Nothung!*' a word that ambivalently points to the absence (nothing) that is the Famine in Irish literature, and the 'needful' or 'Nothung' (Joyce, *Ulysses*, p.583), which is also the Famine in Irish literature.

47. Gibson attributes Freemasonry to the English, but admits that 'How far Freemasonry as a whole can be associated with Anglicization in Ireland is a complicated historical question' (*Joyce's Revenge*, p.190 n.34). Though I believe Gibson is essentially correct in his assertion of the English impact of freemasonry on Ireland, the fact that the scene takes place in a whorehouse, and that freemasonry is non-exclusive in terms of country, but is an exclusively male assembly, suggests that a feminist reading is equally useful here.

48. Kinealy writes:

> A number of newspapers viewed Ireland's failings as stemming from the religion of the majority of the population. The more extreme views, however, tended to be confined to papers and journals with relatively small circulations. In a letter to Lord John Russell, the *Protestant Watchman* explained the reason for Ireland's suffering as: 'Six millions of the people of Ireland are chained to a system that excludes, and is found to exclude, them from the true knowledge of the true God . . . You must endeavour to bring the knowledge of God to every cabin in Ireland. To do this you must use your endeavours to have the word of God taught and preached in every village in Ireland; and when you thus honour God by honouring His word, you may expect redemption in Ireland.' Whilst such articles may not have had the impact and influence of the frequent editorials and letters in *The Times*, they indicate the extent to which the Irish Famine was being debated within the public domain. They also reflect the general consensus that Ireland *had* to change, and that the Famine was the ideal opportunity for this to occur.
>
> (*A Death-Dealing Famine*, p.134)

NOTES to Chapter 9

1. Samuel Beckett, *Malone Dies, Three Novels: Molloy, Malone Dies, The Unnamable*. New York: Grove Press, 1955, 1956, 1958, p.213.
2. Samuel Beckett, 'A piece of monologue', in *Kenyon Review* (Summer 1979), pp.1–4. *Collected Shorter Plays*. Faber & Faber, 1984, p.269.
3. A.M. Sullivan, *New Ireland*. Philadelphia, PA: Lippincott, 1878, p.85.
4. A.J. Leventhal, 'Nobel prizewinner', *Irish Times*, 3 November 1969, p.12.
5. Vivian Mercier, 'The uneventful event', *Irish Times*, 18 February 1956, p.6. This is the famous review in which Mercier describes *Godot* as 'a play in which nothing happens, twice.'

6. Dominic O Riordain, "'Ag Fanacht le Godot" sa Pheacoig', *Irish Times*, 1 March 1972, p.10. 'Until I saw Godot in Irish I did not understand properly how precisely Beckett conveys the spirit of the Gaelic literary tradition. He is a master craftsman of humour, sexual humour, macabre as the Táin and as new as Finnegans Wake.'

7. Hugh Kenner, for example, writes that Beckett 'is not Irish as Irishness is defined today by the Free State', and that Beckett is instead 'willing to be the last Anglo-Irishman' (*A Colder Eye: The Modern Irish Writers*. New York: Knopf, 1983, p.270). Vivian Mercier has commented on the peculiar identity of the Anglo-Irish: 'The typical Anglo-Irish boy . . . learns that he is not quite Irish almost before he can talk; later he learns that he is far from being English either. The pressure on him to become either wholly English or wholly Irish can erase segments of his individuality for good. "Who am I?" is the question that every Anglo-Irishman must answer, even if it takes him a lifetime' ('Beckett and the search for self', *New Republic*, 19 Sept. 1955, p.20). In *Beckett/Beckett*, he writes, 'Samuel Beckett, then, is an Irishman, but to call him an Irish writer suggests some semantic sleight of hand' (*Beckett/Beckett*. Oxford: Oxford University Press, 1977, p.21). Mercier suggests that Beckett was aware of certain Gaelic elements in the oral culture as well as the Literary Revival, but notes also the extreme complexity of his response to both.

8. Cf. W.J. McCormack, *From Burke to Beckett: Ascendancy, Tradition and Bretrayal in Literary History*. Cork: Cork University Press, 1994, p.380. McCormick ties the intense dislocations of Beckett's writing to specific events in Irish history during his childhood.

9. John P. Harrington identifies this historical relevance only in terms of Nagg and Nell as travellers, the sense of being away from home, and the literary allusions in the play to Yeats and Synge (cf. *The Irish Beckett*. Syracuse, NY: Syracuse University Press, 1991, pp.155, 178 and 183).

10. Ronan McDonald, for example, acknowledges that both *Godot* and *Endgame* 'can gesture towards Irish landlordism', but immediately asserts that 'stripped of overt references they become paradigms'. McDonald suggests Beckett's 'method, then, is not an evasion or transcendence of history, but rather lends an amorphous quality to Beckett's work that is indefinite and evocative, rather than abstract and universal' (*Tragedy and Irish Writing: Synge, O'Casey and Beckett*. New York: Palgrave, 2002, p.161).

11. The closest has been Nels C. Pearson's '"Outside of here it's death": co-dependency and the ghosts of decolonization in Beckett's *Endgame*', *English Literary History*, Vol.68, No.1 (Spring 2001), pp.215–39 which argues the need for a sustained treatment of *Endgame* in an Irish context, but which deals chiefly with the way in which language and power structures operate in the play, using these to read *Endgame* in a post-colonial frame. Thus, even when working to correct the omission of Beckett's Irish context, Pearson avoids any mention of Irish history or catastrophe as a possible backdrop. David Lloyd treats absence and the self's lack of authenticity as a reflection of the post-colonial condition, arguing that Beckett's work 'approaches a threshold of another possible language within which a post-colonial subjectivity might begin to find articulation' (Lloyd, 1993, p.56). Decolonization finds its resources in the gaps and absences of Beckett, and his work dismantles the logic of identity that structures and maintains the post-

colonial movement. Cf. David Lloyd, 'Writing in the shit: Beckett, nationalism, and the postcolonial subject', *Anomalous States: Irish Writing and the Post-Colonial Movement*. Durham, NC: Duke University Press, 1993.

12. Cf. Eoin O'Brien's *The Beckett Country: Samuel Beckett's Ireland*. Monkstown, Co. Dublin: Black Cat, 1986, a magnificent book that features the photography of David H. Davison and focuses on the Irish topographical references in Beckett. In Theodor W. Adorno's 'Reconciliation under duress', he argues that 'The primitivism with which [Beckett's] works begin so abruptly represents the final phase of a regression, especially obvious in *Fin de Partie*, in which, as from the far-distant realm of the self-evident, a terrestrial catastrophe is presupposed' (in Ronald Taylor [trans. and ed.] *Aesthetics and Politics: Theodor Adorns, Walter Benjamin, Ernest Blobs, Bertold Brecht, George Lukas*. London, Verso, 1980, p.161).

13. Deane refers to a conversation between Mr and Mrs Rooney in *All That Fall*, in which Gaelic is discussed as a dead language. He reads a passage in *First Love* that discusses Ireland's love of 'history's ancient faeces' as evidence of Beckett's repudiation of Ireland and history. Deane also points out a passage in *Molloy* that refers to Gaelic.

14. McHugh's chapter dealt with the findings of the Irish Folklore Commission in 1945, when they administered a questionnaire all over Ireland requesting Famine stories and lore. The survey yielded nearly 4,000 pages of evidence currently housed at University College Dublin.

15. Cf. Beckett *Endgame*, in Seamus Deane (ed.), *The Field Day Anthology of Irish Writing*, Vol.3. Derry: Field Day Publications, 1991, pp.261, 262, 262, 262, 262, 272, 273, 274, 274, 275 and 276.

16. *It's a bold thing for me to expect a coffin / It's a good thing for me if I get a sheet / And, King of Glory, relieve me / That I may dwell in the churchyard beyond.* (Roger J. McHugh, 'The Famine in Irish Oral Tradition', in R. Dudley Edwards and T. Desmond Williams [eds], *The Great Famine: Studies in Irish History, 1845–1852*. First Published Brown & Nolan, 1956. Reprinted Dublin: Lilliput Press, 1994, p.422).

17. Cf. McHugh, pp.419–27. Hinge-bottom coffins, burial in sacks and sheets and burial in mass graves are recorded in harrowing detail in the folklore.

18. Cf. Luke Gibbons 'Have you no homes to go to?: James Joyce and the politics of paralysis', in Derek Attridge and Majorie Howes (eds), *Semi-Colonial Joyce*. New York and Cambridge: Cambridge University Press, 2000, pp.150–71.

19. The extreme importance of the chair in Beckett raises the question whether he knew of Sigmund Freud's 'Obsessive actions and religious practices' in Peter Gay (ed.), *The Freud Reader*. New York: W.W. Norton & Co., 1989, in which the following passage appears:

> We have noted as a curious and derogatory characteristic of obsessional neurosis that its ceremonials are concerned with the small actions of daily life and are expressed in foolish regulations and restrictions in connection with them. We cannot understand this remarkable feature of the clinical picture until we have realized that the mechanism of psychical *displacement*, which was first discovered by me in the construction of dreams, dominates the mental processes of obsessional neurosis. *It is already clear from the few examples of obsessive actions given above that their symbolism and the detail of their execution are brought about by a displacement from the actual, important thing onto a small one which takes its place – for instance, from a husband on to a chair.* It is this

tendency to displacement which progressively changes the clinical picture
and eventually succeeds in turning what is apparently the most trivial matter
into something of the utmost importance and urgency.

(my emphasis, p.435)

20. Freud discussed repression in terms of a primal repression, in which a fixation is
    established, and repression proper, in which thoughts that become associated with
    the repressed representative are also affected, in which case an after-pressure occurs:

    > We have reason to assume that there is a *primal repression*, a first phase of
    > repression, which consists in the psychical (ideational) representative of the
    > instinct being denied entrance into the conscious. With this a *fixation* is
    > established; the representative in question persists unaltered from then
    > onwards and the instinct remains attached to it. This is due to the properties
    > of unconscious processes of which we shall speak later. The second stage of
    > repression, *repression proper*, affects mental derivatives of the repressed repre-
    > sentative, or such trains of thought as, originating elsewhere, have come into
    > associative connection with it. On account of this association, these ideas
    > experience the same fate as what was primally repressed. Repression proper,
    > therefore, is actually an after-pressure. Moreover, it is a mistake to emphasize
    > only the repulsion which operates from the direction of the conscious upon
    > what is to be repressed; quite as important is the attraction exercised by what
    > was primally repressed upon everything with which it can establish a
    > connection. Probably the trend towards repression would fail in its purpose
    > if these two forces did not co-operate, if there were not something previously
    > repressed ready to receive what is repelled by the conscious.

    (Ibid., 1989, p.570)

21. This language quarrel has come up in the play before. The debate about
    language between Hamm and Clov underlines Hamm's position as master of
    language and Clov's as a newcomer to the language: 'I use the words you taught
    me. If they don't mean anything any more, teach me others. Or let me be silent'
    (Beckett, *Endgame*, p.269). Hamm's mastery also appears in his correction of
    Clov's substitution of 'laying' for 'lying': 'Use your head, can't you? If [the flea]
    was laying we'd be bitched' (ibid., p.267). Clov emphasizes that Hamm has
    taught him the words, and argues that if in light of the catastrophe outside they
    have become meaningless, he should be allowed to remain silent.

22. Cf. Beckett *Endgame*, p.271, 21n.

23. Cf. Mary A. Doll, 'Rites of story: the old man at play', in Katherine H. Burkman
    (ed.), *Myth and Ritual in the Plays of Samuel Beckett*, Rutherford, NJ: Fairleigh Dikerson
    University Press; London and Cranbary, NJ; Associated Universtiy Presses, 1987:
    'Concerning a feudal lord to whom paupers must make petition, the story enables
    Hamm to exercise power over the kingdom of his mind . . . Rather than literalizing
    the situation of his past, Hamm needs to fantasize its terror, returning the moment
    now to the fields of imaginative power then, until power and its opposite terror can
    change, shift, soften, metamorphose, create' (p.77).

NOTES to Chapter 10

1. The book was issued under two similar titles: *The Backward Look: A Survey of Irish
   Literature*, and *A Short History of Irish Literature: A Backward Look*. According to the

WorldCat online database (also known as OCLC FirstSearch), more than a thousand copies of the book are presently available in academic libraries throughout the world.

2. References to poverty and exploitation in Irish history also occur in one of O'Connor's travel books, *Irish Miles*, but they are there less clearly connected to the Famine specifically (see O'Connor, *Irish Miles*. [1940] London: Hogarth, 1988b, pp.127 and 136.

3. See the extensive bibliography of primary works printed at the end of Sheehy (ed.), *Michael/Frank: Studies on Frank O'Connor*. New York: Knopf, 1969, esp. p.181. The date of the article is there incorrectly reported as 10 October 1962. This incorrect date is then repeated in the standard biography, by James Matthews (*Voices: A Life of Frank O'Connor*. New York: Atheneum, 1983, p.436) and in Jim McKeon (*Frank O'Connor: A Life*. Edinburgh and London: Mainstream, 1998, p.188). I am most grateful to Professor Ruth Sherry, O'Connor's indefatigable bibliographer, for informing me of the correct date of publication (10 November 1962) and also for supplying me with a transcript of the article weeks before I was able to attain an actual microfilm copy. For acquiring the latter, I am grateful to the always reliable Carolyn Johnson of the interlibrary department at Auburn University, Montgomery.

4. In the original printing, this sentence ends, apparently incorrectly, with a question mark.

5. This is particularly clear from the many articles he wrote in the 1940s for the *Sunday Independent* under the pseudonym of 'Ben Mayo'. Indeed, in one of the various letters to the editor of the *Irish Times* prompted by O'Connor's review of the Woodham-Smith book, a correspondent named Maura Riordan in fact noted that 'Frank O'Connor, as anyone acquainted with his writings must be aware, would be the last person to subscribe to the idea that "Albion – perfidious Albion" – is always wrong.' Riordan was responding to an angry letter written by D.R. Hall (*Irish Times*, 14 November 1962, p.10), from whom she takes the phrase she quotes. Hall had called O'Connor's review 'a most astonishing effusion' and had termed O'Connor's comparison of the Famine with the holocaust engineered by the Nazis 'arrant nonsense'. Another letter attacking O'Connor (written by Stephen Barcroft) had appeared shortly after the Woodham-Smith review was published, while another implicitly anti-O'Connor letter, by Beatrix Dunalley, appeared the following week, although a letter by Charles Mulloy, strongly endorsing O'Connor's views of a deliberate anti-Irish holocaust, appeared two days later. Implied criticism of O'Connor appeared again in a letter by T. Nisbet. Meanwhile, it is difficult to determine the attitudes of two other letter-writers: Andrew Boyd and John Kerr. By the end of November the controversy seems to have died down, but it made an impact on O'Connor: in *The Backward Look* he observed that, '[h]aving reviewed Miss Woodham-Smith's *The Great Hunger* I realize it [i.e., the Famine] is a subject one cannot discuss without bringing down an old house on one's head' (O'Connor, *The Backward Look: A Survey of Irish Literature*. London: Macmillan, 1967a, p.141).

6. In a notorious and controversial essay on Ireland, first published in 1949, O'Connor had already invoked comparisons with Nazi extermination camps, but in this case he was describing the aftermath of the English re-conquest of the island in the seventeenth century: 'at last there was peace, even if it was only the

peace of Belsen and Buchenwald'; see 'Ireland', in *A Frank O'Connor Reader*, Michael Steinman (ed.), Syracuse, NY: Syracuse University Press, 1994, pp.375–400, esp. p.383. Ironically, although this essay comments at length on Irish history, it never explicitly mentions the Famine. In the scores of articles O'Connor wrote for the *Sunday Independent* in the 1940s (under the pseudonym 'Ben Mayo'), the Famine is rarely mentioned explicitly. An exception occurs in an article titled 'Pouring millions down the drain of artificial idleness', where O'Connor mentions in passing that 'the British authorities insisted that the victims of the great Famine of '48 must be relieved only in such a way that their work could be of no possible use to Ireland, so that these unfortunates were compelled to construct useless roads that led nowhere' (*Sunday Independant*, 2 January 1944, p.10). I have been unable to find any explicit references to the Famine in the nearly 40 articles O'Connor wrote for the *Sunday Independent* in the 1960s (under his own name this time).

7. *An Only Child* first appeared in 1961; *My Father's Son* was first published in 1968. Both titles have been conveniently reprinted in one volume by Pan Books (London, 1988a). All quotations in this essay are from this combined printing.

8. Poverty touched both sides of O'Connor's family; in his notorious essay on 'Ireland', he notes that the 'simplest way of describing the basic poverty [of his homeland, even in 1949] is to record that the old-age pension of one dollar weekly introduced during my own boyhood at once turned people like my [paternal] grandmother, who might otherwise have been destined to die in the workhouse, into independent members of the household who could not only pay for their own modest keep but have a few pence each week for tobacco or snuff. The pension has been doubled, but it still remains an accurate index of living standards.' See O'Connor, *A Frank O'Connor Reader*, p.376.

9. This story was first published in *Dublin Magazine*, Vol.3, No.3 (July 1928), pp.31–8; it never seems to have been reprinted and has attracted very little commentary. For a brief summary of its plot, see Curtis Bowden, *et al.*, 'Selected stories of Frank O'Connor: synopses and quick critiques', in Robert Evans and Richard Harp (eds), *Frank O'Connor: New Perspectives*. West Cornwall, CT: Locust Hill, 1998, pp.297–350 esp. p.302. All the stories mentioned in the present article are summarized, and critical responses to them reviewed, in the article by Bowden *et al.*

10. See Frank O'Connor, *Bones of Contention and other stories* [1936]. Great Neck; NY: Core Collection Books, 1978, pp.1–27. In O'Connor's 1940 novel *Dutch Interior*, a major character does emigrate to America, but poverty seems not to be a prime motivation. Moreover, the character eventually returns to Ireland (ibid., pp.181–5) and, although conceding that Irish youth tend to abandon the country in order to 'get on', he is eager to urge them (apparently sincerely) not to leave, to tell them that 'they'll never be happier' than if they stay home, and that 'all the happiness beyond the seas is bunk. There's no such thing' (ibid., pp.192–3). In addition, his opinions of the Irish living in America are far from complimentary (ibid., pp.224–5).

11. For the text of this tale, plus detailed analysis, see Patricia Angley *et al.*, 'Ways of reading: Frank O'Connor's "Lady Brenda" and the possibilities of criticism', in Robert Evans and Richard Harp (eds), *Frank O'Connor: New Perspectives*. West Cornwall, CT: Locust Hill, 1998, pp.239–61.

12. Perhaps O'Connor felt that writing about such topics ran the risk of seeming exploitative or sentimental. Two comments in his travel book *Irish Miles* (O'Connor,

1988b) imply as much. In one of them, O'Connor recounts an Irishman grimly explaining a particular set of ruins for some apparently foreign travellers:

'You see', he whispered eagerly through his blue lips, preparing a grand history lesson in case we might be English, 'there was a class of people in the old days called landlords'.

'Oh, so they were evictions!' I said, cutting him short. Irish history always sounds to my ears like the hard-luck story that precedes the touch [i.e., solicitation for money].

(Ibid., p.136)

In another passage O'Connor sardonically laments the absence of ghosts in the Irish countryside – ghosts who might appeal to 'sentimental Americans who had returned to the country from which they had sprung' and who 'would have appreciated . . . so much' the opportunity to encounter some lingering spirits (ibid., p.127). His phrasing here, ironically, anticipates the plot of one of his own masterful stories, 'Ghosts', which will be discussed in detail later in this essay.

13. For detailed discussions of the work from multiple points of view, see Kathleen B. Durrer, *et al.*, 'Theories and practice: "Guests of the Nation" and "The Bridal Night" from diverse critical perspectives', in Robert Evans and Richard Harp (eds), *Frank O'Connor: New Perspectives*. West Cornwall, CT: Locust Hill, 1998, pp.219–38.

14. On this issue see, in particular, the comments by Scott Johnson in Evans and Harp (eds), *Frank O'Connor: New Perspectives*, p.229.

15. For another printing of the tale, plus extensive analysis of it from diverse vantage points, see Robert C. Evans (ed.), *Frank O'Connor's 'Ghosts': A Pluralist Approach*. Montgomery, AL: Court Street, 2003.

16. A feminist might ironically note, however, that by this point in the vignette Jer Sullivan's grandmother has disappeared from the picture; the broad social dimension implied by this moment in the story no longer involves explicit reference to the pregnant woman.

17. In his 1949 essay 'Ireland', O'Connor noted that even during the late 1940s most people in the Irish countryside lived 'apart from their neighbors, without electricity, gas, water, plumbing and probably without a school, church, dance hall or social meeting place within miles of them' (1994, p.376).

18. On the pervasiveness of this theme, see the comments by various critics summarized in Bowden, *et al.*, '*Selected Stories of Frank O'Connor*', pp.297–350.

NOTES to Chapter 11

1. Kelleher goes on to challenge this desire to pronounce the Famine 'inexpressible' by suggesting that is more often than not a tactic used to deflect the discomfort caused by over-sympathizing with famine victims.

2. The draft is headed 'Famine' and dated 22 June 1965.

3. In context, this is the vengeful statement of Sarah McGowan, daughter of the Black Prophet, thwarted of her love for Condy Dalton by the heroine Mave Sullivan. The actual lines read: 'This world, father, has nothing good or happy in it for me – now I'll be aiquil to it; if it gives me nothing good, it'll get nothing good out of me' (William Carleton, *The Black Prophet* [1847]. New York and London: Garland, 1979, p.234).

4. These collections are now incorporated into the Department of Folklore of University College Dublin.

5. A variant of this appears in the archive of the Department of Folkore as 'Translation of an Irish caoine, sung by an old woman of Googan Barra, the source of the river Lee and taken by Thomas C. Croker 1814.' It begins: 'Cold and silent is thy repose. Damp falls the dew of Heaven yet the sun shall bing joy and the mists of night shall pass away before his beams. But thy breast shall not vibrate with the pulse of light . . .' IFC1127:128–9. I am most grateful to Anna Bale of the Department of Folkore for supplying this information.

NOTES to Chapter 13

1. See the works by Coogan, Hayden and Kinealy listed in the reference section for this chapter.

2. Christine Kinealy was one of several Irish Famine scholars in the audience when I presented a paper on 'Children's literature of the Irish Famine' at the International Ireland and America Conference at Drew University, Madison, New Jersey in March 2001. Kinealy approached me after my presentation to ask whether the children's authors cited had been influenced by Cecil Woodham-Smith. Encouraged by our conversation, I followed Kinealy's lead and queried these writers about their Famine research. This primary research led to my doctoral dissertation, 'Telling Bridget's tale of hunger: children's literature of the Great Irish Famine', (http://www.il.proquest.cm>) which surveyed and examined this relatively new and significant Irish canon.

3. Bolton, Doyle, Drinkwater, Kositsky, Lally, McKeown, Wilson.

4. Bolton, Doyle, Drinkwater, Heneghan, Lally, McKeown, Morpurgo, Pilling, Wilson.

5. Bunting, Conlon-McKenna, Doyle, Heneghan, Lally, Lyons.

6. Bunting, Conlon-McKenna, Malachy Doyle, Heneghan, Lally, Lyons.

7. Bolton, Bunting, Conlon-McKenna, Drinkwater, Kositsky, Lally, Morpurgo, Pilling.

8. Bolton, Bunting, Doyle, Drinkwater, Heneghan, Kositsky, Lally, Lyons, McKeown, Morpurgo.

9. Kositsky, Lally, McKeown, Morpurgo.

10. Bolton, McKeown, Morpurgo.

11. Branson, *Potato Eaters, Streets of Gold*, Conlon-McKenna, *Under the Hawthorn Tree, Wildflower Girl*, Giff, *Nory Ryan's Song, Maggie's Door*, Lutzeier, *The Coldest Winter, Bound for America*, McCormack, *Mary-Anne's Famine, After the Famine*.

12. Ann Doyle, Litton, Lyons, Murphy.

INDEX